Do Options Exist?

Do Options Exist?

THE REFORM OF PENSION AND HEALTH CARE SYSTEMS IN LATIN AMERICA

Edited by
María Amparo Cruz-Saco
and Carmelo Mesa-Lago

UNIVERSITY OF PITTSBURGH PRESS

Published by the University of Pittsburgh Press, Pittsburgh, Pa. 15261

Manufactured in the United States of America
Printed on acid-free paper
10 9 8 7 6 5 4 3 2 1

A CIP catalog record for this book is available from
the Library of Congress and the British Library.

Contents

Abbreviations Used Throughout This Book

AFAP	Administradora de Fondos de Previsión Social, Uruguay
AFJP	Administradora de Fondos de Jubilaciones y Pensiones, Argentina
AFORE	Administradora de Fondos de Retiro, Mexico
AFP	Administadora de Fondos de Pensiones, Chile and Peru
AD	Alianza Democrática (Social Democrats), Venezuela
AMPO	Aporte Medio Previsional Obligatorio, Argentina
ANSeS	Administración Nacional de la Seguridad Social, Argentina
ATEP	Acidentes de Trabajo y Enfermedades Profesionales, Colombia
BID	Banco Interamericano de Desarrollo, Guatemala (in English, IADB)
BPS	Banco de Previsión Social, Uruguay
CAJANAL	Caja Nacional de Previsión, Colombia
CCSS	Caja Costarricense de Seguro Social
CENITEC	Centro de Investigaciones Tecnológicas y Científicas, El Salvador
CEPAL	Comisión Económica para América Latina y el Caribe (in English, ECLAC)
CIEDESS	Corporación de Investigación, Estudio y Desarrollo de la Seguridad Social, Chile
CIEN	Centro de Investigaciones Económicas Nacionales, Guatemala
COFIDE	Corporación Financiera de Desarrollo S.A., Peru
CONADE	Consejo Nacional de Desarrollo, Ecuador
CONASP	Conselho Consultativo de Administração de Saúde Previdênciaria, Brazil
CONSAR	National Commission for Savings for Retirement, Mexico
COPEI	Partido Socialcristiano COPEI, Venezuela
COPLAMAR	primary health care program for isolated poor peasants (later *Solidaridad*), Mexico

CTM	Confederación de Trabajadores de México, formerly led by Fidel Velázquez
CTS	Compensación Tiempo de Servicios, Peru
CUT	Central Unitaria de Trabajadores, Chile
DIES	Dirección de Investigaciones Económicas y Sociales, El Salvador
EAP	economically active population (in Spanish, PEA)
ECLAC	Economic Commission for Latin America and the Caribbean (in Spanish, CEPAL)
Ecopetrol	Colombian Petroleum Industry
EPS	Empresa Promotora de Salud, Colombia
ESE	Empresa Social del Estado, Colombia
ESS	Empresa Solidaria de Salud, Colombia
FAS	Support for Social Development, Brazil
FEDECAMARAS	major business association, Venezuela
FESCOL	Fundación Friedrich Ebert de Colombia
FFI	fully funded individual [pension system]
FIEL	Fundación de Investigaciones Económicas Latinoamericanas, Argentina
FJPEP	Fondo de Jubilaciones y Pensiones de Empleados Públicos, Venezuela
FONASA	Fondo Nacional de Salud, Chile
FONAVI	Fondo Nacional de Vivienda, Peru
FOSIS	National Fund of Solidarity and Social Investment, Chile
FPP	Public Pension Fund, Colombia
FSG	Fondo de Solidaridad y Garantía, Colombia
FSV	Fondo Social para la Vivienda, El Salvador
FUNDAUNGO	Fundación Guillermo Manuel Ungo, El Salvador
IADB	Inter-American Development Bank (in Spanish, BID)
IESS	Instituto Ecuatoriano de Seguridad Social
IGSS	Instituto Guatemalteco de Seguridad Social
ILO	International Labour Organization (in Spanish, OIT)
IMF	International Monetary Fund
IMSS	Instituto Mexicano del Seguro Social
INAMPS	Instituto Nacional de Acistência Médica da Previdência Social, Brazil
INE	Instituto Nacional de Estadística, Guatemala

Infonavit	Workers' National Housing Fund, Mexico
INP	Instituto de Normalización Previsional, Chile
INPEP	Instituto Nacional de Pensiones de los Empleados Públicos, El Salvador
INSS	Instituto Nacional do Seguro Social, Brazil
INSS	Instituto Nacional de Seguridad Social, Colombia
IPSFA	Instituto de Previsión Social de la Fuerza Armada, El Salvador
IPSS	Instituto Peruano de Seguridad Social
IPSS	Instituciones Proveedoras de Servicios de Salud, Colombia
ISAPRE	Instituto de Salud Previsional (private health maintenance organization)
ISP	Instituto de Salud Pública, Chile
ISR	Impuesto Sobre la Renta, Mexico
ISS	Instituto de Seguridad Social, Colombia
ISSA	International Social Security Association
ISSS	Instituto Salvadoreño del Seguro Social, El Salvador
IVA	*impuesto al valor agregado*
IVM	*invalidez, vejez y muerte* (disability, old age, and death)
IVSS	Instituto Venezolano de Seguros Sociales
MAS	Movimiento de Acción Socialista, Venezuela
MF	Ministerio de Finanazas
MOH	Ministry of Health
MPH	Ministry of Public Health
MS	Ministerio de Salud
MSPAS	Ministerio de Salud Pública y Asistencia Social
MTSS	Ministerio de Trabajo y Seguridad Social
MUNJP	Movimiento Unificado Nacional de Jubilados y Pensionados, Mexico
NAFTA	North American Free Trade Agreement
NGO	nongovernmental organization
OECD	Organization for Economic Cooperation and Development
OIT	Oficina Internacional del Trabajo (in English, ILO)
OMS	Organización Mundial de la Salud (World Health Organization)
ONP	Oficina de Normalización Previsional, Peru

OPP	Oficina de Planeamiento y Presupuesto, Colombia
OPS	Organización Panamericana de la Salud (in English, PAHO)
OPS	Organizaciones Promotoras de Salud
PAHO	Pan American Health Organization (in Spanish, OPS)
PAYG	pay-as-you-go
PECE	Pacto de Estabilidad, Competitividad y Empleo, Mexico
PFC	partially funded collective [pension system]
PNUD	Programa de las Naciones Unidas para el Desarrollo
PRONATASS	Programa Nacional de Asistencia Técnica para la Administración de los Servicios Sociales en la República Argentina
SAFP	Superintendencia de Administradoras Privadas de Fondo de Pensiones, Chile and Peru
SAR	Sistema de Ahorro para el Retiro, Mexico
SERMENA	Servicio Médico Nacional, Chile
SHCP	Secretaría de Hacienda y Crédito Público, Mexico
SIJP	Sistema Integrado de Jubilaciones y Pensiones, Argentina
SIVCM	Seguro de Invalidez, Vejez, Cesantía y Muerte, Mexico
SNCPCH	Sistema Nacional de Controle e Pagamento de Contas Hospitalares, Brazil
SNP	National Social Security System, Argentina
SNP	Sistema Nacional de Pensiones, Peru
SNS	Sistema Nacional de servicios de Salud, Chile
SNSS	National Health Services System, Chile
SOE	state-owned enterprise, Brazil
SPP	Sistema Privado de Pensiones, Peru
SPS	Sistema Privado de Salud, Peru
SSC	Seguro Social Campesino, Ecuador
SSI	Social Security Institutions, Colombia
STPS	Secretaría de Trabajo y Previsión Social, Mexico
SUDS	Unified and Decentralized Health System, Brazil
SUS	Single Health System, Brazil
US-SSA	U.S. Social Security Administration
USEM	Unión Social de Empresarios Mexicanos, Mexico
VAT	value-added tax
WB	World Bank

Do Options Exist?

1 / Introduction

Context and Typology of Reform Models

María Amparo Cruz-Saco Oyague

MOST COUNTRIES IN Latin America and the Caribbean have initiated major efforts toward the institutional reform of their economies. The reform is an outcome of structural adjustment policies that attempt to redirect economic growth along a sustained and stable path—in sharp opposition to the failures of the 1980s. One characteristic of this restructuring is the renewed emphasis on the rules of the market from liberalizing trade and financial transactions, eliminating all types of subsidies and price controls, downsizing the government, a substantial deregulation of economic activities, and the privatization of formerly state-owned enterprises and social security systems.

The goal of the new economic strategy is to establish game rules that will allow a more effective operation of the price mechanism, foster the international competitiveness of economic activities, and fully integrate nations to the so-called global economy. An important expectation is that this strategy will promote a new form of outward orientation of economic growth, which should bring increases in income levels and, ultimately, in living standards of half a billion Latin Americans. At the same time, domestic policy makers and multilateral organizations seek the definite abandoning of import-substitution agendas along with their populist discourses. Despite the global- and market-oriented philosophy, Latin America is expected to need poverty-reduction programs and compensatory policies because of the social costs of these reforms and persistently high poverty levels.

Social security in Latin America has encompassed a broad variety of programs designed to cover workers against the risks of old age, disability, death, common sickness, maternity, occupational hazards, and unemployment. Active programs have included social insurance (for insured workers), public assistance, and public health and other social services (mainly for the population not covered by social insurance). Unemployment programs and family allowances have been very limited in the region. Until the 1990s—and despite years of continuous debate on how to improve and strengthen the social protection provided by a myriad of programs—very little was advanced in terms of reforming a system that was facing severe problems across the board. The only exception to this trend was Chile, which fully privatized its national pension system and restructured its health care programs in 1979–1981.

The knowledge of covering social risks, or social protection in general, is embedded in policies, procedures, and practices used in any given nation to provide social services and thus satisfy basic needs. This knowledge can be conceptualized as technology. At present, the technology that has been used in the region since the inception of social security programs, is being revamped by means of an interinstitutional shifting of the responsibility of service provision—introducing new types of services in the market—and procedural changes affecting the finances, organization, and delivery of the former.

We are witnessing an episode of change in social protection technology that has major socioeconomic and political ramifications. It affects the development of domestic markets and the relative size of the private sector, because this technological change augments both physical (for example, private medical facilities) and financial capital (due to the action of private pension fund managers). It modifies the financial structure of health care and old age coverage by abandoning the traditional redistributive function of governmental agencies and adopting the market-oriented principle of pay for service. It redefines government's participation away from direct provision of services and toward the fulfillment of regulatory and supervisory responsibilities. It therefore reduces the discretionary capacity of governments in redistributing income to guarantee a minimum level of protection to citizens, and this in turn affects citizen's perception of a loss in ownership and in their rights.

An important and growing body of literature analyzes the relevance of pension and health care reforms, the contextualization of these reforms in more ambitious macroeconomic restructuring, and the role of multilaterals. With regard to pension reform, the World Bank (1994) provided the first comprehensive assessment of old age coverage, an organized paradigm for world reform of pensions, and devised a multipillar model that was rapidly absorbed by policy makers and analysts. Iyer (1993) presented the International Labour Organization's (ILO) view on the theoretical debate about pension reform, challenging the World Bank's proposal that the main pillar supporting old age coverage should be privately managed and fully funded. These two approaches are scrutinized in this chapter under the section Pension Reform: What Are the Options? The opposite view to that of the World Bank on pension reform was taken by two key officials of the International Social Security Association (ISSA), Roger Beattie and Warren McGillivray (1995). Estelle James (1996) who led the team that prepared World Bank (1994) wrote a rebuttal to both the ILO (Iyer 1993) and ISSA (Beattie and McGillivray 1995), laying out theoretical and empirical criticisms to the latter. And the debate continues—see Mitchell and Zeldes (1996), for example, and also Feldstein (1997), who analyzes the social security pension reform in the United States.

On health care reform, the World Bank (1993) produced a key report, which opened world debate on issues that had already been addressed, such as institutional fragmentation, inefficiencies in the organization and delivery of health care, equity and quality problems, and proposed solutions. Gerard La Forgia, in the sections on Problems and Proposed Solutions, in chapter 11 of this volume, performs a fine job of guiding the reader to the most representative literature concerning the diverse problematique of the current status of the health sector both in Latin America and elsewhere. In the 1990s, several Latin American countries have implemented structural social security reforms, particularly in health care (Brazil, Chile, Colombia, Costa Rica, Mexico, and recently Peru) and in pensions (Argentina, Bolivia, Chile, Colombia, El Salvador, Mexico, Peru, and Uruguay). Some countries are on the verge of reforming their social security systems, while others are struggling with the politics of defining their reform models. Virtually no country in the region has remained indifferent to the prospect of inevitable reform, and an intense debate on this issue is taking place. In particular, the Latin American pension reform is having a significant influence outside the region, including postsocialist economies in eastern Europe and recently, very notably, in the United States. After more than fifteen years of structural reform in pensions and health care, it is time to discuss the theoretical context in which it is taking place, analyze its main attributes, assess its successes and failures, formulate a framework for comparative analysis, and draw policy recommendations for prospective reformers. That is precisely what we do in this book.

PURPOSE

Our purpose in this book is to bring together the work of specialists on the reform of social security systems in Latin America and to analyze similarities and differences in the reform processes taking place. The national reforms documented in this book show it is possible to find a pattern of regularities that characterizes the reform process. The regularities have to do with the opportunity of a reform and with the social and economic consequences that technological change in the provision of coverage brings about, mainly for health care and old age. The case studies show that reforms are long, painful processes generating negotiation and renegotiation of new policies and procedures to overcome the resistance from organized groups. In the end, reforms are accelerated when political conditions are ripe. An important realization is that structural pension reforms have been "easier" to implement than structural health care reforms, showing that, very probably, institutions, programs, and policies—agents and actors in the health sector—are more complex than in pensions. Assessment of the equity and welfare implications of the reforms are an important research goal of our study. Although it is too soon to evaluate the benefits of the reform, we can say without any reservation that the expansion of coverage to traditionally uncovered citizens is an area in which not much improvement has taken place.

THE PARADIGM OF SOCIAL SECURITY REFORM

Social security reform can be structural or nonstructural depending on whether the foundation of current policies, procedures, and practices for the coverage of health care, pensions, or other programs are modified or not. Reforms can include more than one program, such as in Chile (health care and pensions) or be initially restricted to only one program. It is customary to consider as social security reform any reform processes that change the role of the traditional public social security institute. Thus, if a pension reform is implemented first, for example, in Argentina, Uruguay, or Peru, then the pension reform can be considered a social security reform when actually only one component of the system was changed.

The most important characteristics of structural reforms are the following:

1. *Reforms take place within a context of structural change.* The economic crisis of the 1980s aggravated the crisis of traditional social security systems in some countries and engendered it in others. With few exceptions (Chile and Brazil), the reform of pension and health care programs has been part of a more comprehensive and substantial economic restructuring that began in the early 1990s.

2. *Reforms aim at the separation of the pension and health care programs.* Governments came to the realization that the coverage of various risks (sickness, maternity, old age, disability, survivors) under a public single social security institute is ineffective and inefficient. Thus, the reform separates the coverage of risks under different institutional management.

3. *Reforms introduce new procedures, participants, and products.* The management of both pensions and health care is drastically modified because the private sector begins to play a major role. The social security system is renewed with the participation of private pension fund managers, private health providers, and insurance agencies and with the introduction of new products and services such as individual pension accounts and comprehensive health packages.

4. *Reforms end the public monopoly of social security.* Countries eliminate the public monopoly of pension and health care programs by means of various modalities, ranging from full substitution of the public pension program to the integration (mixed) or competition (parallel) of the private and the public sector in pensions, and from competition of the private and the public sector (selective dual) to collaboration of several providers under different organizational and financial arrangements (selective multiple) in health care.

SETTING UP THE REFORM

The 1980s marked the collapse of several populist projects that ended decades of inward-oriented economic policies. Efforts to industrialize were accompanied by protectionism, inefficiencies, and growing external indebtedness, the latter to compensate for the lack or insufficiency of domestic savings. When, at the beginning of the 1980s, the price of primary commodities collapsed, interest rates skyrocketed, and the external demand for Latin American exports halted because of a worldwide slowdown, countries were unable to service their debts. Soon after Mexico defaulted in August 1982, the debt crisis became almost universal (the exception was Colombia). At first, the crisis was regarded as basically financial and was perceived as short run in nature. But it was not.

Throughout the 1980s countries implemented stabilization programs—mostly under the aegis of the International Monetary Fund (IMF)—that were more or less effective in the temporary improvement of the fiscal and external imbalances and in reducing inflation. Stabilization implied cuts in public expenditures, which led to recessions, at least in the short run. Types of stabilization programs varied from extreme orthodox shock therapy to gradualism, as well as heterodox approaches to suppress galloping inflation, which actually exacerbated price disequilibria. Drastic cuts in government spending, to contain the fiscal imbalance, reduced the provision of social services (education, health care, social security subsidies, transportation, and so on) to extremes that were unforeseen in the past. Most nations registered an increase in unemployment and poverty levels accompanied by the worsening of income distribution. At the end of the decade there was general consensus among international organizations and most countries that structural-adjustment programs were inevitable.

The crisis, therefore, symbolized the end of an economic era based on extensive state intervention and short-run discretionary macroeconomic policies. Years of reliance on government intervention and import-substitution industrialization facilitated the growth and diversification of the industrial sector. This gain, however, had to be weighed against negative side effects such as inefficient enterprises in the productive sector and in services, the stagnation of agriculture, antiexport biases, high labor costs, overstaffed and incompetent public bureaucracies, and the demographic stress originated by fast-growing urbanization and tertiarization of the labor force.

In the 1990s, the restructuring program (tax revamp, financial and banking reforms, cutback and reorganization of government, external opening, privatization of state-owned enterprises, social security reform, and so forth) has meant the dismantling of institutions that were not conducive to the full operation of the market. In some instances, restructuring has also involved the rewriting of national constitutions in order to correct systematic economic mismanagement. Examples of the latter are prohibitions against using expansionary monetary policies to cover fiscal needs or elimination of the state monopoly in the provision of social security such as in the cases of Guatemala, Paraguay, and Peru.

THE SOCIAL SECURITY CRISIS

The adoption and evolution of social security systems in the region took place in three stages (Mesa-Lago 1994). The *pioneers* (Argentina, Brazil, Chile, Cuba, and Uruguay) introduced their systems in the 1920s and 1930s; the *intermediates* (Bolivia, Colombia, Costa Rica, Ecuador, Mexico, Panama, Paraguay, Peru, and Venezuela) in the 1940s and early 1950s; and the *latecomers* (Dominican Republic, El Salvador, Guatemala, Haiti, Honduras, and Nicaragua) from the late 1950s to the 1970s. At the beginning, some countries adopted the general fixed-premium method with full capitalization. With this method, equilibrium is expected to be met indefinitely (or at least for several decades) by means of a fixed premium or contribution—payroll tax—under strict and static assumptions concerning benefits, demographic change, and economic stability.

Political pressures, liberalization of benefits (without proper financing), lack of administrative control of compliance, deficient management, poor investment of the funds, and disequilibria, to cite only the major problems, prompted a shift to partial capitalization, usually with a scaled premium. This method seeks equilibrium for a shorter period of time (one decade) and fixes a premium that would then be revised and scaled up in subsequent periods (although in many cases it was not). The pioneers, with almost universal coverage (62–96 percent) and generous benefits and entitlement conditions, faced severe financial and actuarial imbalances in the 1960s and 1970s. Argentina and Uruguay (as well as some funds in Chile) shifted to pure assessment or pay-as-you-go (PAYG). With this method, current pensions are paid out of current revenues from the social security contributions and the reserve fund is virtually depleted. In the late 1970s in Chile, an average total contribution rate (health care and pensions combined) close to 30 percent (there were more than fifty pension funds in Chile and premia for pensions varied) compounded by other severe problems (financial and actuarial imbalances, fragmentation-stratification, and heterogeneous benefits and entitlement conditions) prompted the radical reform of 1979–1981. The intermediate countries had coverage rates that oscillated between 18 and 50 percent; most of them faced actuarial disequilibria and a few financial imbalances too. The latecomers had very low coverage rates (2–19 percent) and enjoyed the best financial situation.

The economic recession of the 1980s aggravated the magnitude of the social security crisis in the pioneers and accelerated the financial and actuarial imbalance of the other two groups. Real coverage decreased because of high unemployment rates and increasing informalization of the labor force. Rampant evasion, the default of employers and state contributions, negative real capital returns, and lower real wages diminished both social security revenues and the real value of the reserve fund. In the pioneers this situation was further complicated by the demographic transition (the aging of the population) and the subsequent deterioration of dependency ratios (number of contributors per one pensioner). Strong and persistent inflation led to the practice of wage indexing, pension adjustments, and constant increases in the cost of health care (medicines, supplies, equipment, and so on).

In the long run, the real value of pensions fell dramatically. The impoverished middle and working classes and the pensioners, who would have otherwise looked for health care in the private sector or with nontraditional practitioners, turned massively to the public social security system. The shift in demand created congestion of facilities and shortages of medicines and other supplies that further intensified the severity of the crisis. Clearly, the fall in total revenues and the increase in costs aggravated financial and actuarial disequilibria.

Unfortunately, the crisis of social security at this point was so profound, there was little the system could do to compensate for the severe social costs provoked by the economic crisis and structural-adjustment programs geared to solve it. In the 1990s, the economic recovery in most of the region has alleviated some of the most urgent problems (price and exchange rate instability, external and fiscal imbalances, and so on), but it has not helped improve the overall situation of the social security system in countries where the reform is still pending. On the contrary, as this book shows, all basic problems persist, namely, low coverage, financial and actuarial disequilibria, heterogeneous benefits, high administrative costs, and low quality services. In countries with reforms in place, there is the need to assess how the reform is unfolding, the advantages and disadvantages of the new programs, and how emerging problems are being or can be solved. There is consensus about the urgent need to reform the social security systems, but disagreement on the appropriate type of reform.

TECHNOLOGICAL CHANGE

The models of social security that were adopted in Latin America by pioneers, intermediates, and latecomers were inspired very profoundly by the liberal democratic values, attitudes, and institutions that articulated the public philosophy of welfare in industrialized nations, mainly central and western Europe. These are societies with highly skilled and literate populations, and a paternalistic-style provision of all sorts of services. Their philosophy was one of unionism, social services were supposed to comprise the package of citizenship, and distributional conflicts were not allowed to develop. Workers, employers, and governments enjoyed a functional multipurpose relationship that helped create cooperation, order, stability, sense of ownership, and clear negotiating practices between workers and firms. People, technical advancement, labor markets, demographic conditions, spatial aggregation of cities, and standards of living in general, to cite only a few factors, were drastically different than in Latin American nations. Sharp socioeconomic differences notwithstanding, as the integration of Latin American nations to the global capitalist economy grew, in a dependent and subordinated way, local policy makers, politicians, and bureaucracies in Latin America learned that governments had to adapt social security programs to create a welfare culture in their nations.

Enactment of social policies in the region also responded to demands explicitly set forth by organized groups, that is, the armed forces, civil servants, teachers, specific sector labor unions, and so forth. Since the 1920s and 1930s, pioneers, intermediates, and latecomers have established nationwide social security systems. Internalization of social protection in the region was affected by two closely interrelated processes, both external and internal: (1) the transfer of knowledge on how to provide welfare to citizens—or, simply, social protection technology—that was designed in industrialized nations for their own consumption and adapted in Latin America through the support and technical assistance of multilateral organizations such as the ILO and the ISSA; and (2) the country-specific reactions to social requests submitted by organized groups.

Social protection technology is broadly understood as the methods of pursuing programs and activities to cover social risks such as health and old age, for example, that are analyzed in this book, but also of including education, housing, unemployment, and poverty in general. One may use the concept of social protection technology to describe policies, procedures, and current practices that governments enforce with the purpose of covering social risks. First, policies, that are enacted by law—and often expressed as constitutional rights—provide the normative background to the provision of social services. Examples are the right to health care, to a decent pension, to education, and so forth. These policies originate in policy-making discourses that range between public consultation and the use of majority rule in congress, which is to be expected under pluralistic democracies on one end, and governmental decree in authoritarian regimes on the other. The law is not always enforced, or it is enforced without following its letter and spirit, while legal lacunae are often filled arbitrarily.

Policies, procedures, and practice imply very specific models of financial and organizational arrangements and agencies. In the case of the traditional social security in Latin America, the public sector—this includes social security insurance agencies—was the single most important provider of health and old age coverage until the inevitable crisis and subsequent reform of models in the 1990s. The most salient case of this technological change is without any doubt Chile, which innovated the concept of social protection technology by shifting the prominence of the public sector to the private sector and structurally modifying the financial and organizational models that covered health care and pensions. In pensions, Chile revamped the customary knowledge on how to cover old age using exclusively a private pillar with the subordinate but still important role of the state (as discussed in chapters 2, 3, and 10). This technological revolution has allowed Chile to become a global role model in the coverage of old age.

Social protection technologies result in outcomes that vary in both quantitative and qualitative terms. Take the case of health care in Guatemala. The Ministry of Health covers approximately one-third of the population, the Social Security Institute of Guatemala covers 17 percent, and the rest is covered by the private sector. None of these sectors is adequately providing health services to the population because contact of the population with either the private or the public delivery system is very limited and public health facilities are severely underutilized. Evidence from Guatemala shows that the organization and delivery of health care has emphasized a curative rather than a preventive approach, and that the delivery system has expensive hospitals as fundamental anchors to public health. The output of the public health care technology that has been used in Guatemala is pretty slim: the third lowest life expectancy at birth in Latin America (sixty-five years); the leading cause of infant mortality are prenatal causes, diarrhea diseases, and acute respiratory infections, which could be treated at low cost and fairly directly; and the vast presence of vector-transmitted illnesses, tuberculosis, and cholera, which are typical in very poor nations.

Promotion of health care, prevention, and curative procedures are all articulated around (1) the financing of health care; (2) the organization and management of health care consumption; and (3) models of health care provision, public or private (for profit or not). Access to health care is considered a basic human right and, therefore, has to be given the highest priority. Health care has to be produced, regulated, and supervised; the latter usually by means of governmental agencies. Thus, the supply of health care can be envisioned as a production process connecting a vast number of inputs, that is, human resources (physicians, practitioners, nurses, technicians, health managers, and so on), medical facilities, medicines, instruments, and so forth, as well as the immense and heterogeneous lot of regulations, professional organizations, financial programs, public bureaucracies (to cite a few) that participate directly and indirectly in the provision of health care.

The delivery of health services generates an output that can be assessed through improvements in health status (morbidity and mortality rates and other health and demographic indicators), equity and poverty alleviation. In general, improvements in health status can be monitored in terms of attaining welfare goals, partially or fully. In any particular country, the administration and delivery of health care, whether it is publicly or privately delivered, reveals a reservoir of knowledge that encompasses economics, politics, and public health. In other words, a country-specific technology exists that results in the accomplishment of quantitative and qualitative results.

Health sector reforms have the essential intention of implementing technological changes to achieve higher levels of effectiveness, efficiency, and equity. Whether this technological change implies reducing government's participation to a pure regulatory and supervisory role, or privatizing the delivery of curative and preventive health care, or strengthening municipalities in health promotion and prevention needs to be studied on a case-by-case basis. The central point is that health sector reform should modify the way health care is delivered, in order to produce an improvement in equity and welfare.

The critical importance of the technology used by national governments to cover social risks is that it should bring about improvements in human development when assessed on the broad criterion of welfare. However, performance evaluations of social security systems in Latin America before the era of innovation show unambiguously that there were too many problems and failures and that change was irresistible. A key aspect in the transition was the role of government as the most important promoter of technological change. Why?

The answer has to do with the external influence of multilateral organizations such as the IMF, the World Bank (WB), and the Inter-American Development Bank (IADB), which participated in structural adjustment and sector investment loans. These organizations were in the process of articulating their own social protection visions that were in essence market-oriented and government action shifting. Their influence was often too interventionist, in the sense that lending instruments were conditional upon strong recommendation for adoption of market-oriented social protection technologies.

Another important force shaping the type of social protection change is given by the impulses of organized actors pushing for or resisting innovation. The *pushers*, governments included, are the prospective winners from the economic impact of innovation. In this cluster several groups are to be found: the upper-middle class, the rich, the young professionals who oppose redistribution because it knocks down benefits for them; physicians and medical practitioners who can organize for-profit health care organizations; financial investors and the insurance industry interested in constituting private pension fund managers and strengthening the insurance industry; industrialists and entrepreneurs, banks, firms in chemicals, pharmaceuticals, and drugs, mass-media industry, and so forth, that benefit from the technological spillovers. Changing the funding and delivery of health care and pensions to privately managed organizations creates externalities that modernize the capital market and promote preventive health care, which stimulates economic growth in supporting productive activities or services. In contrast, *resistants* or *opponents* are represented by a broad segment of the working class who perceive that they will lose out on benefits; civil servants, the armed forces, and other interest groups that were granted generous benefits in the old traditional social security system; and pensioners who also perceive that their benefits would be cut. In general, because the close past of Latin America is plagued with economic insecurity, people are increasingly worried that they are losing rights.

The interaction of resistance (either active, in the form of street mobilizations and strikes, or passive, in the form of noncompliance with the law) and voluntary acceptance of change generates confrontation and transition.

Technological change in social protection implies an inevitable interference with traditional policies, procedures, and practices; it therefore affects ways of life, values, and trust. Who participates in the policy making that affects the rights of citizens? How will changes in policies, procedures, and practices affect the poor, the disabled, women and children, marginalized groups? In developing countries such as in Latin America, is the goal of government to protect the social coverage that is guaranteed to the people? If coverage is not privately paid, simply because people are too poor to afford it, has government the responsibility of implementing redistributive policies to provide minimum coverage?

HYPOTHESES AND QUESTIONS

Despite the influence of external and internal ideologies, one basic hypothesis in this book is that reforms are actually shaped by various nation-specific conditions. The latter include political and institutional restrictions, the level of socioeconomic development, the success of structural adjustment programs, and the maturity of social security systems. These factors affect the velocity, friction, and type of reform in place (see the conclusion, chapter 17).

Another major hypothesis is that multilaterals such as the IMF, the WB, and the IADB have substituted the roles that once upon a time were played by central and western European nations as producers of welfare technologies. First, because these nations are presently facing their own welfare crisis, in varying degrees, and are addressing their own ways of solving insolvency and unsustainable social security programs they have lost their former dominant situation and can no longer transfer their public philosophies to the rest of the world. Second (with respect to the developing world, and from a purely neoconservative point of view), the Washington Consensus has become the perceived external authority for technical advice. And even if the latter were only half true, since developing nations still need the funding from multilaterals (until they graduate from them as Chile did from the IADB), and because the funding is conditional on the adoption of market-oriented measures, governments find themselves locked into the neoconservative rhetoric of the multilaterals and their social protection paradigms, which clearly means giving serious consideration to the WB's proposal for pension reform and the enlargement of the private sector in the provision of health care, leaving governments to the sole role of promotion and prevention as well as regulatory functions.

In order to best assess the results of social protection technological change we need to ask whether populations are living longer and more healthily. It is difficult to judge the gains of health care reform, because innovations are very recent and still only partial. We have more evidence to evaluate the gains of pension reforms, however. Thus, we shall concentrate on the latter. The following seven questions should guide the reader and provide a focus throughout the chapters. We shall answer them in the concluding chapter.

Question 1. *Has the reform increased compliance, therefore contributions and coverage?* Two underlying weaknesses attributed to traditional social security systems in most countries of the region are their high rate of evasion and their stagnation or very slow expansion of population coverage. In turn, one of the assumptions of the pension reform is that it has a sound incentive mechanism (for example, the insured's ownership of the individual account in pensions) that improves compliance (reduces evasion, payment delays, and underdeclaration of income), thus raising both population coverage and contribution revenue.

Question 2. *Has competition among private pension and health care managers improved efficiency and reduced administrative costs?* Another criticism of the traditional social security system is its inability to operate in an efficient manner. Most social security institutions in Latin America have sizable administration costs that were or are escalating even further. The reform claims that private management is competitive and more efficient than the monopolistic public administration and hence reduces administrative costs.

Question 3. *Have capital markets expanded and national savings increased?* The old social security system, critics say, demanded fiscal subsidies in many countries and was a factor in state budget deficits and low national savings. The increase in contributions, appropriate financial investment, and higher returns supposedly lead to a significant accumulation of the pension fund in the new system and, hence, expands capital markets and national savings that promote economic growth. This process is reinforced when employers' contributions are eliminated, thus reducing labor cost and correcting labor market distortions.

Question 4. *Are pension fund portfolios diverse and safer and investment yields higher?* Investment of the pension fund in the old systems was highly concentrated in high-risk instruments, and real rates of return were either negative or positive but very low. It is assumed that the interaction of competitive private pension fund managers in economies that are expanding, combined with the strict supervision of an autonomous superintendency and institutions that classify instruments by risk, should lead to a safer pension fund, portfolio diversification, and higher real investment yields.

Question 5. *Are real pensions higher?* A typical criticism against traditional systems is that real pensions have declined sharply because of poor management and high inflation, and the elderly cannot afford to make a living with such meager pensions. The reform, supporters claim, will pay better, more adequate pensions to the workers (regardless of sex) because of better compliance, lower administrative costs, and higher capital returns in the new system.

Question 6. *Is the system fairer and more viable, thus improving equity?* The old social security system was unfair, it is argued, because it granted privileges and too generous entitlement conditions to favored groups. Such liberalities in turn contributed to the financial disequilibrium of the system. The reform is expected to eliminate privileges, standardize and tighten entitlement conditions among the insured, and generate a more equitable and sustainable system.

Question 7. *Have governments behaved better, protecting instead of abusing social security?* A major problem confronted by the old social security systems was—and still is—the adverse behavior of the state, which did not pay its contributions as employer and third party, controlled and manipulated the managers of the institutions, stuffed the bureaucracy with unnecessary and incompetent employees, and used their reserves to obtain free or very cheap credit in order to cover fiscal deficit. The state debt either was not reimbursed or was paid with devalued currency and negative real interest rates, which contributed to the depletion of the reserves and the crisis of social security. In order to be successful, the reform requires that the state "behaves properly" (World Bank 1994), that is, honors its obligations with the old and new systems, regulates and supervises them, and finances the costs of the transition.

PENSION REFORM: WHAT ARE THE OPTIONS?

Reformers can be classified into two opposing views and a middle group that combines elements of both. One of the opposing views continues to believe in a public-managed system (although "perfected" through reforms), with a major role for the government, and maintenance of the solidarity principle within the system. The other extreme rejects that idea and endorses private management of pension funds, with a regulatory but subsidiary role for the government, and no endogenous solidarity. In the middle, reformers have argued for the need to keep—but reform—the public system (the first view) but to combine it with supplementary pensions (features of the second view) in a "mixed" system, or to establish two competitive systems that represent each of the extreme views and run "parallel," giving workers the option of selecting freely between the two. The ILO has essentially endorsed the first type of reform, whereas the WB has sponsored the second. Their respective paradigms are summarized below (Mesa-Lago 1996, 1997).

THE WORLD BANK VIEW

According to the WB (1994) view, the old public social security systems are structurally in disequilibria because of severe faults: neglect of the demographic transition, which leads to regressive intragenerational transfers; unsustainable, partially funded, collective methods of financing that, because of incompetent public management, depletes the reserve fund; and lack of incentives to promote compliance and, therefore, reduce evasion and develop the capital market. In this view, the traditional social security principles of universality, solidarity, and equity were, in practice, either not enforced or not viable. This view rejects as nonviable, in the long run, any attempt to reform the old system that does not go to the roots of the problem (a nonstructural reform as the one proposed by the ILO).

The WB paradigm recommends the adoption of a three-pillar model that places the savings, redistributive, and insurance functions under different financing and managerial arrangements: two separate mandatory pillars and a third voluntary pillar. The first mandatory pillar should be publicly managed, tax financed, preferably small relative to the other pillars, and should pay benefits in three different forms: a means-tested program for the poor of all ages; a minimum pension guaranteed to a mandatory savings pillar; or a universal or employment-related flat benefit that coinsures a broader group. The second mandatory pillar should be privately managed and based on a fully funded individual (FFI) method and defined contributions, regulated by the state, and should take two alternative forms: personal saving accounts or occupational plans (nondefined benefits). This pillar should reduce the risks of moral hazard by linking benefits to contributions and years of work and should be an economic accelerator through the indirect link that the boost in the private pension fund would give to financial and labor markets. Deeper and more liquid capital markets should increase the efficiency of using savings, which would promote higher economic growth that, in turn, leads to higher savings. The third pillar supplements the other two, is based also on the FFI method and defined contributions, and provides voluntary occupational or personal saving plans for individuals that desire additional income and insurance in their old age. The first pillar fulfills the redistributive and insurance functions, while the second and third pillars accomplish the savings and insurance functions.

The methodological innovation in the WB model of a multipillar system is the distribution of functions and risks among different pillars instead of concentrating all functions and risks in a single public pillar. There is also a fundamental change in the understanding of the types of incentives that are needed for the sustainability of a pension program. The WB proposal is based, in essence, on the belief that the pension system ought to be a profit-seeking and privately managed activity to increase domestic savings. The role of the government is to subsidize the transition (cover the deficit in the old system), regulate and financially support the private system (taking care of the cost of contributions transferred from the old to the new system), and solve market failures (provide exogenous solidarity through a minimum guaranteed pension in the new system and a welfare pension paid to the noninsured dispossessed).

As an alternative to a single, public first pillar, the WB recommends four combinations of a public system and a savings plan, both mandatory: (1) public system of uniform pension with individual saving plan; (2) public system that guarantees a minimum pension with individual saving plan; (3) public system of uniform pension with enterprise saving plan; and (4) public system of pension conditioned to need with an enterprise saving plan. This recommendation shows that countries should adopt different combinations in each pillar, in the relative proportions of the mandatory pillars, and have diverse rhythms in the implementation of the system. Structural reforms are mostly recommended for countries that are instituting new pension programs and for those countries with old programs in a precarious situation, which, actually, excludes most Latin American countries except the pioneers (only Brazil and Cuba have not introduced a reform yet).

THE INTERNATIONAL LABOR ORGANIZATION VIEW

This paradigm has generated an important debate regarding the role of the private and the public sectors in the coverage of old age risks (Iyer 1993). The WB would like to see a small, first public pillar and a large, second private pillar. In contrast, the ILO would like to see a main first public pillar and a small private one, both second and third. According to this paradigm,

Table 1.1 Comparison of the Three-Pillar Arrangement in the ILO and the World Bank Paradigms

Pillars	*ILO*	*World Bank*
FIRST		
Legal status	Mandatory	
Financial method	Pay-as-you-go (PAYG)	
Contributions	Taxes (fiscal revenue or payroll contribution)	
Benefits	Uniform minimum (based on need)	
Administration	Public (government or social insurance)	
SECOND		
Legal status	Mandatory	Mandatory
Financial method	Partially funded collective (PFC, not exclusive)	Fully funded individual (FFI)
Contributions	Not defined (workers and employers or taxes)	Defined (workers with or without employers)
Benefits	Defined (related to contributions, and optionally with minimum)	Not defined
Administration	Public (social insurance)	Private (publicly regulated)
THIRD		
Legal status	Mandatory	
Financial method	Fully funded individual (FFI)	
Contributions	Defined (individual with or without employer)	
Benefits	Not defined	
Administration	Private	

Source: Mesa-Lago 1996, table 2.

the first pillar should be mandatory, publicly managed, tax-financed, based on PAYG, and should pay a universal subsistence pension under a means-tested program. The second pillar should also be public and managed by the social security institute—but reformed to expand coverage, unify and standardize entitlement conditions and benefits, improve efficiency, and restore equilibrium—and be based on a partially funded collective method with payroll contributions (paid by the insured and the employer), and with defined benefits including a guaranteed minimum pension. The third pillar should be voluntary, privately managed but regulated by the state, FFI (but without completely excluding other methods), with defined contributions paid by the insured or the employer or both and should supplement the other two pillars by providing nondefined supplementary pensions.

An autonomous organization with tripartite representation (workers, employers, and government) should oversee, regulate, and in general coordinate the administration of the three pillars. In contrast to the WB view, the ILO stresses the principles of universality, solidarity, and equity. It emphasizes the role of the public sector and believes in the viability of a nonstructural reform of the old public pillar to overcome the crisis. It regards the state as the main facilitator of the transition, in providing the legal structure for the new scheme and the financial support in case of insolvency, and in providing incentives for the constitution of the third pillar.

Table 1.1 summarizes in a comparative manner the fundamental features of the three-pillar paradigms of the WB and the ILO. It is easily recognized that, in both, the first and third pillars are similar. The fundamental distinction, however, is in the definition of the second pillar.

THE MIDDLE-GROUP VIEW

This view is represented by an important group of countries (half of those that have implemented structural reforms), which follow neither the WB nor the ILO paradigms in their pure forms. Examples are Argentina and Uruguay, which have mixed systems, and Colombia and Peru, which have parallel systems. The WB paradigm so far fits only Chile completely, and Bolivia, El Salvador, and Mexico partially (under the 1995–1996 laws). The former four countries' reforms are closer to the ILO paradigm than the WB one. The extent to which countries have adopted various combinations in the definition of their second pillar is highlighted in table 1.2. This table also

Table 1.2 International Evidence on Elements of the Second Pillar

Financing Method	*Fully Funded Individual (FFI)*		*Partially Funded Collective (PFC)*	*Pay-as-you-go Collective (PAYG)*
Contributions	Defined		Not defined	
Benefits	Not defined		Defined	
Administration	Private	Private, public, mixed		Public
Countries	Chile, Bolivia, and El Salvador; Peru (in the FFI system)	Mexico and Colombia (in the FFI system); Argentina and Uruguay (in the FFI program of the mixed system)	Costa Rica; and Colombia and Peru (in the PFC system)	Argentina and Uruguay (in the public program of the mixed system)

Source: Based on Mesa-Lago 1997.

serves the purpose of illustrating that the simple dichotomy between private and public management of the second pillar is superficial, because FFI systems or programs are not exclusively managed by private corporations, but can be administered by public or mixed institutions such as in Argentina, Colombia, Mexico, and Uruguay.

TYPOLOGY

Table 1.3 (below) presents the typology that is based on the recent history of pension (and health care) reform in Latin America in 1979/80–1997. Based on the type of management (private or public) and considering the pension pillar arrangements, these reforms can be classified as follows:

- Nonstructural reforms change the single public pillar and may include the creation of a third voluntary or mandatory supplementary pillar publicly or privately administered. The reform of the public pillar entails the improvement of the public social security system with more strict entitlement conditions, raising contributions and the overall efficiency, reducing costs, and so on. There are two cases: (1) reformed public (Costa Rica, 1990–1992), and (2) reformed public with mandatory supplementary pensions (Mexico, 1991–1992).
- Structural reforms introduce at least two additional pillars to the system (an FFI with defined contributions or supplementary pensions,

for example) thus establishing a three-pillar arrangement. Experience shows, however, that although all countries have adopted structural pension reforms (with the exceptions of Costa Rica and Mexico, under the 1992 law), only Chile conforms completely to the exact recommendation of the WB. The other countries use three-pillar arrangements, but public administration of one of the pillars continues to play an important role in five of them (see fourth line, administration, in table 1.2).

NONSTRUCTURAL REFORMS

The public reformed pension program in Costa Rica was introduced in the 1980s and early 1990s. The main purpose of the reform was the financial balance of the program administered by the social security institute, Caja Costarricense de Seguro Social (CCSS). The reform included the increase in retirement ages and restrictions for early retirement; higher contribution rates; policies to reduce evasion and delayed payments; rescheduling of overdue contributions owed by the government; and measures to increase the efficiency and reduce administrative costs. All independent pension programs for public servants that enjoyed special privileges are being gradually incorporated into the general system of the CCSS. In 1995–1996, eligibility conditions for teachers in the public sector were drastically limited, and voluntary supplementary pension systems (which are still very small) were regulated. In 1996 a comprehensive reform of the pension program was under study; it included increases in ages of retirement and the creation of a mandatory supplementary program with either public or private administration.

The public pension program in Mexico, as the reformed public pension program in Costa Rica, was initially reformed in 1991. The purpose of the reform was basically the same, the financial improvement of the system. Contribution rates were gradually increased (from 6 percent in 1991 to 8.5 percent in 1996), the management of the reserve fund was strengthened, and real pensions were increased. In 1992 a mandatory supplementary pension program (Sistema de Ahorro para el Retiro, SAR) was created, to which the employer contributes an additional 2 percent and workers can make voluntary contributions (see chapter 8). In 1995 a study by the Mexican Institute of Social Insurance estimated that the public pension program would face an inevitable crisis by the year 2002, which would force the use of the reserve fund, and its complete exhaustion two years later. In December 1995 and April 1996, a structural pension-system reform was approved by congress.

STRUCTURAL REFORMS

These reforms are of three different types: substitutive, mixed, and parallel.

Substitutive

Chile was a pioneer in the full substitution of the single public pillar in 1980–1981. (The politics and the economics of the reform process in its more than sixteen years of experience are analyzed in chapters 2 and 3.) The Chilean model strongly influenced pension reforms in the region and has become a role model elsewhere. The WB's proposal was inspired by this experience, in which the old public system was closed; workers contribute to a mandatory, FFI privately administered program; they can supplement their future pensions with voluntary savings; and the government supervises and guarantees a minimum pension (that is, the insured's individual account, if insufficient, is supplemented by the government who subsidizes the difference to pay the minimum pension). In this model, employers do not contribute. There is a social assistance pension—paid by the government—in the first pillar, which is very small.

The Mexican pension reform (1995–1996, implemented in 1997) creates a pension system based on FFI accounts with defined contributions that is similar to the Chilean reform. In contrast to Chile, however, both workers and employers contribute (government contributes as an employer and guarantees a minimum pension). Another difference is that pension fund managers—denominated AFOREs (administrators of retirement funds)—can be private (including banks), public (including an AFORE managed by the Mexican Institute of Social Insurance), or mixed. AFOREs continue to manage the SAR program. All current insureds must be transferred to AFOREs (nobody can stay in the old system). Other pension programs covering the armed forces, federal employees, and petroleum workers are excluded from the reform. Chapter 4 analyzes the politics of the first pension reform in Mexico and summarizes the key features of the second reform, identifying those that differ from Chile's model.

In December 1996 El Salvador approved its pension reform, but by the end of 1997 the reform was not in operation. It is closer to the Chilean model than the Bolivian or Mexican reforms. An important difference is that the right to stay in the old system or to move to the new one is determined by age. Workers younger than thirty-six must transfer to the new system; workers between the ages of thirty-six and fifty (women) or fifty-five (men) can choose; and workers older than fifty or fifty-five must stay in the old system. The employer's contribution is maintained, and the insured's contribution is significantly raised. Chapter 5 analyzes the public pension system and the reform proposals and summarizes the main features of the substitutive private reform approved in 1996.

The pension reform in Bolivia was approved in 1996 and its regulations in 1997. The reform closed down fifty-one programs that were in financial and actuarial crisis. It has some similarities with Chile (it is based on FFI and private pension fund management) but it possesses unique characteristics. One important feature is that, for the next five years of operation, only two private pension fund administrators will exist, and their markets have been geographically segmented. Both AFPs *(administadoras privadas de fondos de pensiones)* will manage an FFI program and a new innovative "collective capitalization" fund (funded with privatization revenues from the sale of several state-owned enterprises). This novel fund will pay an annual "solidarity bond" for life to all citizens who were aged twenty-one or older on December 31, 1995. The bonus began to be paid on May 5, 1997, but payment was suspended in 1998. The state does not guarantee a minimum pension, nor a minimum investment yield in the AFPs, nor pensions in case of bankruptcy of AFPs or insurance companies, nor the payment of the solidarity bond if the collective capitalization fund is insolvent. Another important aspect of the Bolivian reform is that its law does not exclude the armed forces, but this group may be incorporated with special conditions. (Because of space limitations and its recent implementation, we were unable to include the Bolivian pension reform in this book.)

Mixed Systems

In 1993, Argentina introduced the first mixed system that began its operation in 1994 (this reform is fully analyzed in chapter 6). The insured (current and future) can choose between two alternatives: a public-reformed system (which pays a basic pension and an additional pension estimated as a percentage of the base salary) and the mixed system composed of two integrated programs: the public-reformed and the FFI. The first pays the same basic public pension plus a recognition bond, while the second pays a supplementary pension based on the accumulated individual fund. Thus, the old public single system was substituted by a reformed public system (with stringent eligibility conditions and benefits), which either provides all benefits or is a component program of the mixed system and is publicly administered. If the insured selects the public-reformed systems both his/her contributions and those of the employer go to it. Conversely, if the insured selects the mixed system, the contribution goes to the FFI supplementary component program and the employer's goes to the public-reform component. Self-employed insureds contribute to both components. The FFI component program has some important similarities with the Chilean model, but, as with the Mexican reform, FFI administrators (called AFJPs in Argentina), can be private, public, or mixed. An assistance pension for the noninsured destitute is paid by the state. The armed forces are excluded from the reform and maintain their own separate system, while employees of provinces and municipalities can voluntarily join the national reformed system.

Uruguay adopted in 1995 and implemented in 1996 a pension system that is mixed because it has two mandatory integrated components: a reformed public program, managed by the central social security institution (BPS), which pays a basic pension; and an FFI program, privately or publicly administered, which pays supplementary pensions as in Argentina. (The political controversies and features of this reform are discussed in chapter 7.) In contrast to Argentina, all current insureds in the BPS who are less than forty years old and future entrants in the labor force are mandatorily covered by the new mixed system. Insureds above this age have the choice of either transferring to the mixed system or maintaining the old entitlement conditions. The reformed public system operates only in conjunction with the FFI program within the mixed system. There is no recognition bond because insureds remain in the public system one way or the other, either under the entitlement conditions of the old public system or participating in the public component of the mixed one. Since the public component pays a basic pension there is no minimum pension in the FFI program. As in Argentina, the noninsured destitute is eligible for an assistance pension. FFI administrators (called AFAPs in Uruguay), can either be the BPS, public institutions, or private corporations. Excluded from the reform are the armed forces and four independent, small pension funds.

Parallel Systems

Peru's parallel system was approved in 1992 and began to operate in 1993 (the reform is analyzed in chapter 8). The old public system coexists with an FFI system privately managed (by AFPs, as in Chile), and insureds can choose between one of the two parallel systems. Initially, entitlement conditions and contributions in the public system were not changed; for instance, the insured's contribution was only 3 percent in the public system (employers contributed 6 percent) but it was 14.5 percent in the FFI private system (employers did not contribute). This and other differences (retirement ages, payment of a solidarity contribution, required years of contribution, absence of a minimum pension in the private system) led to stagnant enrollment in the AFPs. In 1995–1997, new legislation was enacted to standardize contribution rates, and most entitlement conditions and transfers to the AFPs resumed. The reform excluded the armed forces, which kept their separate system.

The Colombian pension reform was approved in 1993 and implemented in 1994 (the reform is analyzed in chapter 9). The reform proposal that was initially submitted to congress by the executive followed the Chilean model, but strong public opposition and resistance led to the approval of the parallel model. As in Peru, the insured can choose between the two systems, but the public one was thoroughly reformed initially, and the new FFI system is administered by public or private institutions. Contribution rates in both systems were made equal in 1996 (both employers and workers contribute, the state guarantees a minimum pension). A solidarity fund, to which insureds with relatively higher salaries contribute, supports the expansion of coverage. Because of the increase in contribution rates and the tightening of entitlement conditions, the reformed public system has been financially strengthened, as opposed to the Peruvian public system, which is in considerably worse shape. The reform has excluded the armed forces, congressmen, public teachers, petroleum workers, and numerous provincial and municipal funds.

Chapters 13–16 provide a diagnosis of the situation with social security and discuss the preconditions for the reform in Brazil (pensions), and Ecuador, Guatemala, and Venezuela (the whole system). The first country is in the pioneer group, the second and the fourth are in the intermediate group, and the third is in the latecomer group. This book, therefore, provides a comprehensive survey of virtually all the countries that have implemented pension and health care reforms, and a representative selection of those who are studying them, as well as a selection from the three groups of countries in the region that are in different stages of social security evolution.

HEALTH CARE REFORM: WHAT ARE THE OPTIONS?

In contrast to the Latin American pension reform, the health sector reform is taking much longer and its debate is just beginning. Technological change here will modify financial and organizational arrangements, how resources are allocated, how the financial cost is shared among citizens, and which population groups receive what type of services and how. The direction of the reform and its pace are still unclear. Chapters 10, 11, and 12, which study the reforms in place, show that the search for solutions to the health sector crisis means surmounting several constraints: technical design of the appropriate health care model, paying the cost of the transition, setting up a time path for implementing the reform with its political and administrative implications, and overcoming the resistance of affected interest groups.

The planning, financing, and delivery of health care in most of the region have been administered by three institutions. The social security institute typically provides health care services to insureds and their beneficiaries, often in the low-income bracket. The Ministry of Health provides health care services to the poor and low-income groups, usually uninsured. The private sector provides health care services to the upper-middle and high-income groups. The social security institute and the Ministry of Health jointly cover the vast majority of the population, but the private sector has been expanding in recent years.

The health sector in most of the region is characterized by acute problems, which include excessive concentration and centralization, serious coverage problems and strong inequities, inefficient and deteriorating organization, low quality services, and severe financial restrictions. The allocation of financial resources to the health sector was limited, during the 1980s, because of the tremendous spending restrictions of governments and it has not recovered adequate levels in the 1990s. Reforming the health sector has been an issue in many countries, but reform has been actually implemented in only a few of them. The most important goals of the health sector reform include decentralization of services, universalization of coverage, shift in the institutional emphasis in the provision of health care from the public to the private sector under new organizational and financial arrangements, and greater efficiency and quality.

TYPOLOGY

Six countries have implemented health reforms: Brazil, Chile, Colombia, Costa Rica, Mexico, and Peru. Peru's first reform was enacted in 1991 and aborted because of lack of regulations; a similar fate followed the second reform of 1996; finally a new health reform approved and regulated in 1997 is expected to be implemented in 1998 (see panel B in table 1.3).

Health sector assessments carried out by multilateral and nongovernmental organizations as well as official agencies in the rest of the region are considering reform options. The types of reforms are:

- Nonstructural reforms, which involve a reorganization of the public sector and the collaboration of the Ministry of Health and the social security institute (in some cases involving the private sector in a minor way) to avoid waste and inefficiency. There are two kinds of nonstructural reforms: (1) reformed public with private cooperation (Costa Rica, 1982–current); and (2) multiple public programs for diverse groups of the population as well as minor private schemes, to be coordinated supposedly by the Ministry of Health (Mexico, 1970s–1990s).
- Structural reforms, which imply major changes in the planning, organization, supervision, financing, and delivery of health care and which aim at the sustainability of the reform. Within this category there are two modalities: (1) selective dual (private and public—in Chile, 1981, and Peru, 1997); and (2) selective multiple (many providers—in Brazil, 1988, and Colombia, 1993). In this book we analyze in depth these structural reforms except that of Peru.

NONSTRUCTURAL REFORMS

In Costa Rica, the CCSS and the Ministry of Health have integrated their facilities and coordinate the delivery of services in a very effective way. The Ministry of Health specializes in preventive and primary care for urban and rural marginal groups, while the CCSS administers all hospitals and pro-

Table 1.3 Types of Pension and Health Sector Reforms, ca. 1996

Type of Reform	*Countries and Year of Reform*
Pensions	
Nonstructural reforms	
Reformed public	Costa Rica (1990–92)
Reformed public with mandatory supplementary pensions	Mexico (1991–92)
Structural reforms	
Private substitutive	Chile (1979–81)
	Mexico (1995, but multiplicity of administrators)
	Bolivia (1996)
	El Salvador (1996)
Mixed	Argentina (1993)
	Uruguay (1995)
Parallel or selective	Peru (1992, 1995)
	Colombia (1993)
Health Sector	
Nonstructural reforms	
Reformed public with private cooperation	Costa Rica (1982–)
Multiple providers (public and private)	Mexico (1970s–1990s)
Structural reforms	
Selective dual (private and public)	Chile (1981)
	Peru (1991–aborted 1997)
Selective multiple (many providers)	Brazil (1988)
	Colombia (1991)

Source: Based in part on Mesa-Lago 1994, 1997.

Note: The year of implementation of reform varies. For example, reforms were implemented in Argentina in 1994; Bolivia, 1997; Chile, 1981; Colombia, 1994; El Salvador, 1998; Mexico, 1997; Peru, 1993; and Uruguay, 1995.

vides curative care. The CCSS has reduced costs and increased both efficiency and the quality of service by means of contracting private providers. Further reform, integration, and decentralization of the system were designed in 1992 and were being implemented in 1996–1997.

Mexico's health system is characterized by a high level of segregation between two major providers and minor ones. The Mexican Institute of Social Insurance (Instituto Mexicano del Seguro Social, IMSS) covers the insured and his dependent family with an integral health care program but, in the 1970s, also developed a primary health care program for isolated poor peasants (COPLAMAR, which was split in 1985 with the states, and converted later into Solidaridad). The federal Ministry of Health, the second major provider, as well as ministries in the states and municipalities, have their own programs that cover noninsured who normally are low-income and poor. The armed forces, federal employees, and oil workers, all have their own health care plans. The private sector is subdivided into two subsectors, both small, which basically cover the noninsured: one is profit-making and is geared mostly to the high-income group, while the other is not-for-profit, made up of nongovernmental organizations (NGOs), churches, and other charitable institutions, and protects the poor. This stratified arrangement creates considerable duplication between the main two providers, as well as an unequal allocation of health resources, disproportionate to their respective population coverage and financial burden. In 1992 the ministry was given legal authority to coordinate public providers and develop a sort of national health system, but nothing significant has been done in the 1990s.

STRUCTURAL REFORMS

The Chilean health sector reform (discussed in chapter 10) kept the mandatory affiliation either to the public social security program (direct delivery of medical care or private subcontracting) or to a private health maintenance organization (Instituto de Salud Previsional, ISAPRE). The system is selective-dual because workers can affiliate to the public sector or to the ISAPREs; the contribution rate is set at 7 percent. In the private sector the contribution rate increases if the insured wants a more comprehensive health program from the ISAPRE. Preventive and primary care is delivered at the municipal level. In fifteen years, the private sector has been able to cover close to 30 percent of the population, and despite enormous competition among ISAPREs, six of them cover most of the beneficiaries.

Chapter 11 analyzes the Colombian case, presenting a financial flow model that links sources of finance (households) to health care financial intermediaries (working as contractors and pay providers) and beneficiaries. Before the reform, the Colombian health sector consisted of the three typical components: (1) the Ministry of Health that managed a large network of facilities; (2) the social security institute for private sector workers (Caja Nacional de Previsión, Colombia, CAJANAL), for public employees, and a large number of smaller funds and family allowance schemes that provided health care for specific groups; and (3) the private sector. The Colombian reform mandates the decentralization of health care provision to departments and municipalities; the allocation of resources to fund this process; and the incorporation of the social security system into the overall reform process seeking competition among public and private providers. One interesting feature of the Colombian reform is the organization of corporations representing either the demand or the supply side, which simplifies the allocation of resources and the targeting of subsidies to the very poor.

The Brazilian reform is discussed in chapter 12. The Brazilian health sector is unique in the region. It operates on the basis of public reimbursement of privately provided services to deliver care. Most facilities are privately owned and managed and are concentrated in the South and Southeast. In 1988 Brazil launched a massive institutional, organizational, and financial reform of the public health care sector with the following goals: decentralization of the administration of health care from states to municipalities, consolidation of public delivery and finance, and improvement of equity via universalization of the benefit. The reform has encountered several problems requiring urgent attention: escalation of costs and lack of funding, definition of responsibilities among participants, questions of quality, and regulations.

ORGANIZATION AND ACKNOWLEDGMENTS

This book is organized in the following way. Parts 1 and 2, "Reforms in Place" ("Pensions" and "Health Care"), analyze the pension structural reforms of Chile, Mexico, El Salvador, Argentina, Uruguay, Peru, and Colombia, and the health sector structural reforms of Chile, Colombia, and Brazil. Part 3, "Reforms Under Study," assesses the situation and reform prospects (pensions and health care) in Brazil, Ecuador, Guatemala, and Venezuela. Chapter 17, "Conclusion," analyzes the conditions or factors that affect the type of reform. It summarizes and compares the main characteristics of structural reforms (similarities and differences), reports the findings, answers the seven crucial questions raised in the introduction, and formulates policy recommendations.

We are particularly grateful for the collaboration of Latin American and United States experts at all stages of the project. With only one exception all contributions are original (Bertranou's contribution on the Mexican pension reform was published in Spanish and translated and updated for this book). Grants from the Corporación Financiera de Desarrollo S.A. (COFIDE) and the Superintendencia de Administradoras Privadas de Pensiones del Perú (SAFP) provided financial assistance for the translation of several contributions that were originally written in Spanish. We would like to acknowledge the special support that we received throughout the preparation of the manuscript from Martín Naranjo Landerer, superintendent of the Peruvian Banking and Insurance Activities Supervising Office in Peru, and Enrique Díaz, former deputy superintendent of the SAFP (1993–1998). The Lenore Tingle Howard '42 Chair at Connecticut College and the Center for Latin American Studies at the University of Pittsburgh provided additional financial support for the completion of the book.

References

Beattie, Roger, and Warren McGillivray. 1995. "A Risky Strategy: Reflections on the World Bank Report Averting the Old Age Crisis." *International Social Security Review* 48 (3–4): 5–22.

Feldstein, Martin. 1997. "Is Privatization the Answer?" *Foreign Affairs* 76 (4): 24–38.

Iyer, Subramanian. 1993. "Pension Reform in Developing Countries." *International Labour Review* 132 (2): 187–207.

James, Estelle. 1996. "Providing Better Protection and Promoting Growth: A Defense of Averting Old Age Crisis." *International Social Security Review* 49 (3): 3–17.

Mesa-Lago, Carmelo. 1994. *Changing Social Security in Latin America and the Caribbean: Towards Alleviating the Costs of Economic Reform.* Boulder, Colo.: Lynne Reinner.

———. 1996. "Pension Systems Reform in Latin America: The Position of International Organizations." *CEPAL Review* 60 (December): 73–98.

———. 1997. "Comparative Analysis of Structural Pension Reform in Eight Latin American Countries: Description, Evaluation and Lessons." In *Capitalization: The Bolivian Model of Social and Economic Reform,* edited by Margaret E. Pierce. La Paz: Ministerio de Capitalización.

Mitchell, Olivia, and Stephen P. Zeldes. 1996. "Social Security Privatization: A Structure for Analysis." *American Economic Review* 86.2 (May): 363–67.

World Bank. 1993. World Development Report 1993. *Investing in Health.* New York: Oxford University Press.

———. 1994. *Averting the Old Age Crisis.* New York: Oxford University Press.

one / Reforms in Place: Pensions

2 / Chile

The Politics of Privatization

Silvia Borzutzky

The purpose of this chapter is to analyze the social security reform implemented by the Pinochet regime in the context of the political environment in Chile at the time of the reform and the economic principles guiding the process. The analysis will focus also on the sociopolitical implications of the reform and its impact on the insured, the pension fund managers (*administradoras de fondos de pensiones*, AFPs), and the state. In the second half of the chapter I will explore the democratization process that began in 1989, the economic legacy of the Pinochet regime, and the nature of the socioeconomic policies pursued by the Aylwin administration. Here, the focus will be on the coexistence of the neoliberal economic model with more democratic political institutions.

Central to the analysis throughout the chapter is that social security policies are a crucial policy area both for democratic and for authoritarian regimes and that these policies are an accurate reflection of both the nature of the regime and the economic model. The discussion and analysis of social security policies highlight the nature of the state's activities in a specific policy area and of the relations between state and society. The Chilean case gives us the chance to examine a set of policies that are intimately linked to a given economic model and that have not experienced any significant changes as a result of the process of democratization.

THE 1980 SOCIAL SECURITY REFORM: BACKGROUND AND CONTENT

Although Chile's social security was one of the most comprehensive systems in the region it suffered from serious problems, which included high costs (total expenditures reached a record of 17 percent of GDP in 1971), fragmentation, inequality of benefits, and stratification. The system placed a heavy burden on the economy (the payroll tax was 65 percent) and it required state subsidies that amounted to almost 30 percent of the total state revenues (Mesa-Lago 1994, 129). Each administration had attempted to reform the system in order to reduce its costs and inequities, and each one had failed. Instead, the system had continued its fragmented expansion because of the intricate connections between a highly politicized and fragmented labor movement, a highly competitive political system, and a stagnant economy (Borzutzky 1991).

Just as previous governments had done, the Pinochet regime very early in its administration planned to initiate a reform of the social security system. However, the social security issue was not dealt with until 1979. Its reappearance coincides with the consolidation in power of the Chicago Boys, a group of monetarist economists who were to decide not only the future of Chile's social security system, but also the structure of the entire economy.

The enactment of the Decree Law (D.L.) 2448 in February 1979 was the first step in the reform process. Without any announcement or discussion of any sort, the government enacted this decree, which equalized benefits, eliminated pensions based on years of service, and established a uniform system of pension adjustments. According to the new decree, the general minimum retirement age was sixty-five years for males and sixty for females, and there was a general requirement of at least ten years of contributions. The decree eliminated all the pensions based on years of service, repealed all the existing legislation regarding readjustment of pensions, and established a general, uniform system of readjustability that tied pensions to the consumer price index. With one stroke of the pen, the administration eliminated the *perseguidoras*—special pensions received by top-level public servants in which the value of the pension was linked to the actual value of the salary received by the person if he or she were still performing the job. The financial and political importance of D.L. 2448 cannot be overlooked. There is no doubt this decree addressed the two most critical problems of the social security system (inequities and insufficiency of pensions) while it eliminated its most costly vices (pensions based on years of service and the *perseguidoras*).

From the beginning, the Pinochet administration demonstrated special interest in the area of family allowances because of the cost and socioeconomic impact of this program. Only nineteen days after the coup, on October 1, 1973, the government unified by decree all the family allowances fund, replacing the numerous systems of benefits by one unified family allowances fund (Sistema Unico de Prestaciones Familiares), eliminating the differences that existed in the past between the subsidies received by blue- and white-collar workers. Further modifications took place in 1978, when the administration of the family allowances program was taken away from the pension funds and given to newly created entities such as the Cajas de Compensación de la Asignación Familiar, similar to those proposed during the Frei administration (Borzutzky 1982).

From an administrative perspective, the reforms involved in D.L. 2448 and the reforms to the family allowance system enacted by the Pinochet regime between 1973 and 1978 show a large degree of continuity with the reforms that had previously been proposed by the Frei administration. But what President Frei could not achieve in a democratic context, the authoritarian regime had no trouble accomplishing. The group most affected by the reform—the civil servants, who in the past had proved powerful enough to obstruct any substantial reform to their system—was unable to do anything on this occasion. The civil servants learned (as others had already learned and still others will undoubtedly learn in the future) that the authoritarian government operates with a large degree of autonomy even from the most organized and previously powerful social groups.

If 1978 was the year of the consolidation of power for the neoliberals, 1980 was the year of the great reforms or modernization, which materialized the power this faction had over the state. The reform of the social security system (la Modernización de la Previsión) occupied a central place, and Minister José Piñera was charged with the role of leading the process. Piñera's personal career is similar to that of many of the other Chicago Boys, who have filled the top ranks of the Chilean administration since 1979. Harvard-educated, and a "neoliberal" in his economic beliefs, Piñera was associated with the Cruzat family economic group, one of the two largest. Piñera was also a close associate of Minister Sergio de Castro, the dean of the Chicago Boys and certainly the most influential person in the policy-making arena during the years 1978–1982. The thirty-year-old minister was assigned three specific tasks: to coordinate the labor and the economic sectors of the government; to institutionalize a new system of labor relations, creating a free and depoliticized labor organization; and to reform the social security system (*El Cronista*, December 18, 1978). Before analyzing the impact of the reform, however, it is important to note that the reform covers only the pension system, for all blue- and white-collar workers (either dependent or independent, and in either the private or the public sector, and excepting the military), while it maintains the existing family allowances and the occupational accidents insurance programs.

The 1980 Reform: Content and Impact

The new legislation introduced a number of substantial reforms, which changed the very basis of the financial system, altered the principle of solidarity, and reinforced individualism. The reform involved the elimination of employers' contributions to the social security system, and the transformation of the common fund into individual funds, while its legislation maintained only a 1 percent contribution to the workmen's compensation fund, and a temporary 2.85 percent tax to finance the family allowance and the unemployment insurance programs. The purpose of these reductions was to lower the cost of labor, which, according to neoliberal logic, would in turn reduce the high unemployment rates. Employees' and workers' contributions to the system were also reduced, but only for those workers who transferred their social security funds to the new system (providing a strong incentive to do so). Currently, the employer pays only 0.85 percent to the workmen's compensation fund and 2 percent into the unemployment fund.

The partially funded collective system (PFC, *sistema de reparto*), which had actually become PAYG and had been under attack from the neoliberals since 1974, was replaced by the fully funded individual (FFI) system. For Piñera the PFC had not only failed to achieve its fundamental purpose of social solidarity, it had also generated and encouraged the inequalities, inefficiencies, and insufficiencies that characterized the whole social security system. The problem had to be attacked at its roots, replacing a system based on the collectivist ideology by one based on an ideology that "establishes a clear relationship between the personal effort and the reward," the one "that gives the individual the freedom of choosing and deciding" (Piñera 1980, 2). The elimination of the PFC complemented the elimination of the social security tax and established a system that might be defined as a compulsory private insurance system.

The need to enhance the role of the private sector and the need to improve the administration of the system led Piñera to argue that the management of pension funds should be put in the hands of the private sector. According to Piñera, the action would not only benefit future pensioners but also integrate the social security system into the national economy. It is important to note that, for government economists, one of the major obstacles to Chile's economic development—and one that the market approach had proved unable to resolve—was the low savings rate that resulted from the underdevelopment of the local capital markets. In this context, the social security reform was crucial both for the development of the capital markets and to achieve economic growth.

The transference of the administration of social security funds to the private sector involved the creation of a new type of enterprise: the *administadoras privadas de fondos de pensiones* (AFPs), or pension fund managers, charged exclusively with the administration of the individual funds and the provision of the social security benefits established in the law. The nature and functions of these new private entities are regulated by D.L. 3500, which contains both free market and regulatory principles. The free market principles encouraged the formation of a plurality of AFPs that would compete among themselves, offering the highest interests in the capital accounts, and charging the lowest commissions. The AFP is a lucrative corporation, whose profits result from the commissions they charge for the administration of the funds. Those commissions could be structured as a flat rate, as a percentage of the insured deposit, or as a combination of both. In order to ensure efficiency and the lowest commissions, the insured was free to move from one AFP to another.

The law establishes that each AFP has to maintain two separate funds: a minimum capital fund required to establish an AFP, and a second one formed by the individual deposits. The law also prescribes investment policies and the profitability of the latter fund. In regard to benefits, the legislation establishes that once the basic requirements to obtain a pension have been fulfilled, the pensioner has three options: (1) to buy an immediate life annuity from an insurance company with the funds accumulated in the account; (2) to obtain the pension directly from the AFP—in this case, however, the capital fund has to be large enough to provide for a pension equal to at least 120 percent the value of the minimum state pension; and (3) to combine a temporary annuity paid by the AFP with a deferred life annuity bought from an insurance company (SAFP, no. 174).

Finally, D.L. 3500 created a system of minimum pensions for those affiliated to the new system—to be applied in case of depletion of the individual capital account, or if the rent produced by the fund is smaller than the minimum pension. In order to qualify for this pension the insured must have at least twenty years of contributions. The original value of the pension was about $45 monthly, by 1994 it was about $100. A system of public assistance pensions was created for all noninsureds and those insureds who do not qualify for a minimum pension. The value of these pensions was about $36 a month in 1992 (Mesa-Lago 1994, 121).

The new pension system was fully substitutive of the old one. It was mandatory for new entrants to the labor force (and already insured workers had the option of remaining in the old system). Thus, 2.8 million workers had enrolled in the new system in 1996. Four elements seem to have prompted people to abandon the old social security system: (1) a very expensive and well-orchestrated propaganda campaign; (2) the net increase in income of those that moved to the new system; (3) the desperate situation of the pensioners; and (4) the pressure applied by some employers.

The acceptance of the new system could not be explained only in terms of the skillful propaganda campaign, or the changes in societal values stressed in the publicity. The most important factor has been the net salary increase obtained by those workers that chose to move to the new system. The salary increase ranged from 7.6 percent for those that belonged to the blue-collar workers fund to 17.1 percent for the bank employees. However, perceptions about the AFPs' efficiency have changed since inception. It is reasonable to believe that the desperate situation of the retirees might have also acted as an incentive for people to move to the new system. The combined effects of several years of high inflation, declining real wages, and the system used to compute the pensions had withered away their pensions (Borzutzky 1982).

The social security reform does not eliminate the role of the state, as might be implied by the neoliberal rhetoric. It simply transforms it. Two characteristics of this new role are noteworthy: the compulsory nature of the *nueva previsión* (all new workers are obligated to join the new system, and old workers are forced to remain in it even if they decide to transfer) and the creation of two new bureaucracies to supervise the system.

The establishment of a state-enforced private insurance system is certainly unique, reflecting some of the contradictions that can be exhibited by the application of neoliberal principles with extensive state involvement, especially in the context of authoritarian politics. In order to understand the extent of this contradiction it must be remembered that the government has consistently claimed the new system was designed to enhance the freedom of the Chilean workers. The compulsory aspects of the system reflect both the authoritarian nature of the regime and a paternalistic approach to policy making. From an institutional perspective, the new system involved the creation of two new social security bureaucracies: the Superintendencia de Administradoras de Fondos de Pensiones (SAFP) and the Instituto de Normalización Previsional (INP), charged with supervising the new system and managing the transition from the old to the new. The Superintendencia de Seguridad Social was maintained to control the old system.

Impact of the Reform

As Piñera correctly argued: "The social security reform has been one of the most important steps taken by the present regime. It constitutes a new and original scheme which will contribute decisively to change the economic, social and political culture of all Chileans" (Piñera 1980). The reform stands out as having a profound societal and individual impact, as being significant to Chile's economy and to its politics, and as touching not only the present but also the future of the entire population. Its impact will be analyzed both from an economic perspective, emphasizing questions of equity, capital accumulation, and the role of the state, and from a sociopolitical perspective.

Under the new system the pension received by the insured is a direct result of the deposits made by the individual, plus the interest accrued and less the commissions charged by the AFP. The deposits, in turn, depend on the level of wages; the interest depends on the real rate of capital return. In regard to wages, it is important to note that between 1980 and 1988, because of the nature of the economic policies pursued by the Pinochet regime, the real value of wages grew by only 1.2 percent while the real minimum wage declined by 28.5 percent. During the same period, urban unemployment averaged 15.3 percent per year (ECLAC 1988, 15–18). Clearly, both indicators have a negative impact on the value of the pensions. Despite these indicators, in 1987 the government estimated that the value of a retirement pension paid by the new system was 1.24 times higher than was paid by the old system, while invalidity pensions appeared to be 2.23 times higher (SAFP, no. 174). What also needs highlighting is that, at least in the short run, the reform did not have the expected positive impact on the labor market that the official government economists expected and that was widely used to justify this kind of reform (Borzutzky 1982).

The structure of commissions charged by the AFP also affects the value of the pensions. As it stands now, after several reforms, the AFP usually charges two commissions: a fixed sum, deducted from the old age contribution, and a variable percentage, deducted from the contribution to the disability survivor fund. Until 1987 there was a third commission consisting of a percentage over the balance in the individual account (Mesa-Lago 1994, 122). The fixed commission has a regressive effect on the pensions. Mesa-Lago estimates that in 1987 the commission reduced the deposits of a person in the 10,000 pesos per month bracket by 18 percent, while it reduced the fund of an insured in the 100,000 pesos bracket by 0.9 percent. Mesa-Lago argues also that for the same reason between 1981 and 1987 the investment yield averaged 7.6 percent for the lowest income bracket, compared with 11.34 percent for the 60,000 peso bracket (Mesa-Lago 1994, 123).

Recent changes in the structure of the commissions have reduced their cost. The total combined commission declined from 4.5 to 3.6 percent between 1983 and 1990, whereas the cost for someone with an average salary increased from 8.3 percent in 1981 to 12.3 percent in 1983 and declined to 9 percent in 1991 (Mesa-Lago 1994, 124). In brief, not only does the new system reinforce the economic inequities produced by the labor market but, given the impact of the commissions, it also augments the socioeconomics differences that already exist in the society.

The system also reinforces the differences between male and female pensions, making female pensions considerably lower because women have lower wages, retire at a lower age, and live longer than men. Alberto Arenas de Mesa has estimated that income differentials increase between the labor and the pension market. Women who begin their working life with about 75 percent of the male salary will receive 50 percent of a male salary when they retire and only between 45 and 35 percent of the average male pension after they leave the labor market. Consequently, for women to have a similar pension to that of their male counterparts they should make additional contributions, retire at an older age, and get higher wages (Arenas de Mesa 1994, 24, 25).

Both the monthly minimum pension (about $100) and the public assistance pension ($36) are insufficient to meet even the most basic needs. Moreover, to the extent that about 37 percent of the affiliates to the AFP system are unable to obtain a pension above the minimum pension, one has to conclude that a large proportion of Chile's population will face extreme poverty after retirement (Iglesias and Acuña 1991, 85). It is also clear that women will form a large part of the extreme poor since they will not even qualify for the minimum pension (Arenas de Mesa 1994, 25).

There are several processes that need highlighting with regard to the administrative structure. First, the capital accumulated by the AFPs amounts to about $10 billion, or 34.5 percent of GDP. It is projected that the funds will reach 50 percent of GDP in the year 2000, and 100 percent by the year 2025. The average annual real yield for 1981–1991 was 14 percent, the highest for the region (Mesa-Lago 1994, 124). Despite the large amounts of capital accumulated by the funds, the capital market has not grown as fast as was expected. By 1991 about one-third of the funds was invested in bonds and shares. The lack of growth in the capital markets was probably caused by the numerous regulations on investments contained in the 1980 law (these were liberalized later on).

From the beginning, ownership of the AFP was tied to the "economic groups," the large conglomerates resulting from the privatization policies of 1974–1976. Thus, Provida and Santa María, originally the two largest AFPs, were owned by the two largest groups, the Vial and the Cruzat-Larraín groups, and they captured 63 percent of the insured. Following the 1982 recession two processes unfolded: (1) these groups went bankrupt and their assets were temporarily administered by the state; (2) later, the assets were reprivatized and at least some of them were sold to foreign creditors (the administration has pursued a "debt for equity scheme" according to which foreign creditors are encouraged to transform their credits in Chile into assets). Between 1985 and 1987, foreign multinational corporations began to invest heavily in the AFP given their connection with the economic groups and because of the attractive nature of the investment. By 1987 the four largest AFPs, responsible for administering about 70 percent of the funds, were either totally or partially owned by foreign investors. The two largest AFPs, Provida and Santa María, are controlled by Bankers Trust and Aetna, respectively (Errázuriz 1987, 20).

The effects of the social security reform on the public sector are just as important as those on the private sector. The preeminent theme of the social security reform is that of the subsidiary role that the state should play in this area. The reform carries a budget deficit—the result of transferring the administration and with it the payment of contributions to the private sector—while the state maintains a high level of expenditure because it is responsible for those who remained in the old system. During the first five years, the deficit resulted from the fact that the government receipts were drastically reduced because of the massive transfer of people to the new system. But this reduction in government receipts under the new program was not accompanied by any decrease in social security expenditures because, in order to allow the AFPs to capitalize, the law established that they would not pay old age pensions during the first five years. As a result, during the first five years, the state faced the same social security expenditures, since those workers close to retirement had not moved to the new system.

After the first five years, state expenditures continued, through the financing of the *bono de reconocimiento* (recognition bond) of those beginning to retire in the new system. This bond, which represents the number of years the insured contributed in the old system and which is given by the government to the AFP at the time of individual changes from one system to another, becomes effective at the time of retirement, invalidity, or death. By 1983, the social security deficit reached 7 percent of GDP, and a large part of it resulted from the reform (Arellano 1986, 88, 89). It is estimated that by the year 2000 the government would have paid about two hundred thousand bonds, with an enormous cost for the fiscal coffers (García 1986, 176).

The pattern of transfer to the new system has added a new financial burden. Those affiliated to the civil servants fund, which requires the largest state contribution, have been very reluctant to move to the new system while those affiliated to the self-financed funds (such as white-collar workers and bank employees) have moved in a very large proportion because of the increase in the take-home pay. There is a clear contradiction between this expanding budget deficit and what the government argued as a justification for the total transformation of the system: the large fiscal deficit of the old system.

A study by Iglesias and Acuña established that the deficit amounted to 1.2 percent of GDP in 1981, 3.2 percent in 1982, and 3.9 percent in 1984. In subsequent years it fluctuated between 3.3 and 3.8 percent of GDP. These analysts argue that about 89 percent of the deficit is the result of operational costs, while only 11 percent is the result of the *bono de reconocimiento* (Iglesias and Acuña 1991, 106). These estimates, however, are fairly low compared with those made for instance by Gillion and Bonilla, who argue that the state subsidy for 1990 amounted to 6 percent of GDP (Gillion and Bonilla 1992).

It is not clear how this deficit will be financed. Iglesias and Acuña argue that so far it has been financed with internal savings (Iglesias and Acuña 1991, 109). Others emphasize the use of taxes, public debt, or reduction in consumption. The deficit is expected to increase at least until the year 2000. As Mesa-Lago argues, to secure a sound private pension system the state made a huge financial commitment for the long run (Mesa-Lago 1994, 43).

Finally, one has to look at the administrative system since the authors of the reform claimed that the new system was going to reduce costs dramatically (Piñera 1991). From the very beginning, enrollment in the new system was treated as a commercial product to be sold in the market through highly sophisticated propaganda techniques, and the AFPs have continued this approach in the past twelve years. Consequently, AFP enrollment depends on the actions of their sellers and the publicity expenditures of the AFP. The end result is that there are eight thousand people involved in the AFP administration (about 30 percent are sellers) while there are about thirty-five hundred involved in the administration of the old system. The private scheme now has 10 percent more personnel than the public scheme had prior to the reform (Mesa-Lago 1994, 129).

It is also clear that the administrative costs have not been reduced as a result of the introduction of the market system. Although there are no conclusive findings, the new system appears to be more expensive for the insured than the old one. Whereas costs amounted to 8 percent of contributions in 1980, they increased to 19 percent in 1982, to decline to 14 percent in 1990 (Iglesias and Acuña 1991, 153). Thus, administrative costs appeared higher than in most of the other Latin American countries. In Argentina, Costa Rica, and Panama costs equal 7 percent, in Uruguay and the Dominican Republic they equal about 11 percent (Iglesias and Acuña 1991, 154).

In conclusion, the reform did not have the expected impact either on labor or on expanding the capital markets. The reform, however, increased the liquidity and degree of sophistication of capital markets. It did not reduce the state burden, and it has not produced a reduction of the administrative costs. What the reform has produced is a huge concentration of economic power in the hands of the AFPs.

The Social and Political Impact

The unavoidable question from a social point of view is: To what extent has this reform altered the traditional social security principles? There is little doubt that, at the very least, the reform has substantially transformed the principle of social solidarity, since the new system is based on the notion of individual insurance combined with a social system of minimum and assistance pensions. In other words, providing for old age is an individual responsibility (except in the case of the extremely poor, when it becomes a social one). However, the extremely low value of the assistance pension only reinforces poverty and inequality. As the undersecretary of labor argued, the reform transforms the notion of solidarity both in its role and in its content. From now on, solidarity is not a fundamental notion but a complementary notion and, as such, is not expressed in the entire system but is reserved for those cases in which the principle of individual responsibility cannot be applied (as in the system of minimum pensions and the system of welfare pensions). To a large extent, then, the reform has transformed the social security system into a compulsory private insurance system, in which the state intervenes at two different stages: at the onset, by enforcing enrollment into the new system, and at the final stage, by providing pensions to the lowest income groups.

From a political perspective, the reform has to be analyzed in the context of the other reforms enacted by the government between 1981 and 1982. It is clear that the neoliberal economic model and the authoritarian state converged in their need to disarticulate the entire society and especially those groups perceived as having political power and interfering with the free functioning of the market, such as organized labor and professional associations of white-collar workers and civil servants (Borzutzky 1982). Throughout the last fifty years, there has been a close relationship between the organization of the labor movement, its pattern of interaction with the state, and the evolution of the social security system. After having reformed the role and functions of the state and the nature of the labor movement, the Pinochet regime found it necessary to create a social security system attuned to those reforms. Of course, in an authoritarian context, the reforms came from the state itself, without the participation of the society.

The Plan Laboral, the set of laws that entirely changed Chile's labor legislation, was a crucial component of the process of depolitization and atomization of the society pursued by the regime. With these laws the regime effectively destroyed the old labor movement, limited the right to strike, and deprived the workers of internationally recognized rights. The social security reform was also central to this process. It destroyed large bureaucratic entities such as the pension funds, as well as the groups of workers organized around them, who in the past had played a major role both in the formulation and in the obstruction of public policies. The social security reform during this period (and in the past) reflects the existing political organization and the principles that guide relations between state and society while, at the same time, being a key political mechanism used to shape future political arrangements.

The 1980 reform not only changed the nature of the pension system. It was also an integral part of the process of social and political transformation that was carried out by the Pinochet regime, destroying major sociopolitical organizations, depriving the workers of both political and economic power, and effectively transferring that power to the AFPs and their owners as well as the major banking and publicity concerns involved in the new system. The real measure of the pension industry's political and economic power is its value: controlling the private pension fund of 5 million workers.

DEMOCRATIZATION AND THE SOCIOECONOMIC LEGACY OF THE PINOCHET REGIME

The adoption of neoliberal economic policies—including the social security reform—was an integral part of the authoritarian style of rule of General Pinochet and the neoliberal economic policies that were implemented by the regime (Borzutzky 1982, 1991). A full analysis of the political and economic legacy of the regime certainly falls outside the scope of this chapter. From my standpoint, however, the balance of the sixteen years of military rule shows a mixed record of economic successes and failures and enormous human rights abuses that have been widely verified by international and Chilean organizations. Success, by and large, resulted from a revised application of the model implemented by Hernán Buchi, who became minister of finance in 1985. The new policies, although based on neoliberal principles, called for government intervention in the economy in order to protect and promote specific sectors of the economy, while maintaining a tight fiscal policy and reducing the debt. The central objective of Buchi's program was to emphasize the outward oriented strategy through government investment in the fishing industry and fruit sector. Other aspects of the policy included a new wave of privatizations and the reduction of the external debt through debt-to-equity swap.

The Buchi program certainly had an impact on the performance of the Chilean economy. Between 1986 and 1988 the economy grew at an average of 5.7 percent, and inflation declined to 18.6 percent. The debt that had increased dramatically up to 1982 was reduced to $16 billion, while exports grew at about 5 percent per year between 1986 and 1988. During the same period urban unemployment was reduced to 12 percent (ECLAC 1988).

The policies pursued by Buchi had a positive effect on wages. Real wages grew at an average of 2.7 percent between 1986 and 1988, while the average rate of growth for the 1980–1988 period was only 1.2 percent. In the case of real minimum wages, one sees an improvement in the rate of decline since those wages had declined 28.5 percent between 1980 and 1988. Between 1986 and 1988, the real minimum wages continued to decline at about 3.6 percent per year (ECLAC 1988, 15–18).

The Transition

Chile's transition to democracy was determined largely by the 1980 constitution and the impact of the repressive politics of General Pinochet. The process involved limited negotiations between the regime and the Christian Democrat–led coalition known as the Concertación. At the core of these negotiations was the Concertación commitment to maintaining the neoliberal economic model.

The most striking feature of the transition process is the vast amount of power held by the regime and its ability to determine the nature and extent of the reforms that took place. As Petras et al. argue: "the transition presented a paradox in which greater electoral freedom was accompanied by a shrinking of the acceptable politicoeconomic spectrum of views and policies" (Petras et al. 1994, 83). As a result, the regime managed to determine the nature of the future political and economic system, the power of the armed forces, the power and role of the courts, and the independence of the Central Bank. The basic changes took place with regard to the electoral system and respect for human rights.

Given the success of Buchi's policies, the nature of the transition process, and the ideological orientation of the Aylwin administration, the new government committed itself to maintaining the existing economic model and consolidating the gains derived from the Buchi program in regard to economic growth, low inflation rates, and debt reduction. At the same time, the leaders of the coalition led by the Christian Democratic party recognized the depth of the socioeconomic problems inherited from the Pinochet regime, and they promised to deal with the existing social inequities and the legacy of poverty. According to a study conducted by the Economic Commission for Latin America and the Caribbean (ECLAC), 44.4 percent of the population (5.5 million people) were defined as poor while the extremely poor amounted to 16.8 percent of the population. The extent of the inequities can be illustrated through income distribution data, which indicate that by the mid-1980s the top quintile was receiving 56 percent of the national income against the 3 percent received by the bottom quintile (Hojman 1990, 27). The new strategy would focus on the idea of growth with equity.

The Aylwin Administration: Limited Democratization

According to Finance Minister Alejandro Foxley, the economic program of the new administration rested on three essential foundations: guaranteeing economic stability; achieving a better integration of the Chilean economy into the world economy; and accentuating the process of investment in people, through intense, durable, and systematic action on the part of the state, to open up opportunities for middle-class and poorer Chileans (Petras et al. 1994, 104). In fact, it is important to highlight that the emphasis has been on economic stability and export growth and that the question of social equity has received less attention than the others. In the area of social policy the new administration claims to be pursuing an integral approach to the problem, stressing the idea of "providing tools to overcome poverty" (Raczynski 1994, 18). The priorities are to invest in human capital, support small enterprises, support changes in regard to labor laws and practices, and support organizational activities among the poorest sectors of the society. Welfare assistance is to be used in exceptional situations (18).

The most important accomplishments resulted from the approval of the 1990 tax reform, which increased the tax burden in 2 percent of GDP (Arenas de Mesa et al., forthcoming). The new resources were used to augment social expenditures by 32 percent while the per capita expenditures grew by 24 percent between 1991 and 1994 (ibid.). Central to the new social policies has been the establishment of the National Fund of Solidarity and Social Investment (Fondo Nacional de Solidaridad e Inversión Social, FOSIS), which is geared to finance special programs directed toward the poorest groups in the society (ibid.).

In regard to the labor market the administration sought to pursue what I would call a corporatist policy based on national agreements between the workers represented by the Central Unitaria de Trabajadores (CUT) and the employers under the banner of the Confederation of Employers (Confederación de la Producción y del Comercio). These national agreements produced an increase in the minimum wage and some liberalization of the labor laws. Most important, the 1991 agreement "outlined a shared socioeconomic plan between owners and workers in which they agreed to cast their lot with the success of the open economy and the export-oriented strategy" (Petras et al. 1994, 120).

According to Vergara, the agreements resulted in substantial wage increases for only about 11 percent of the work force (Vergara n.d.). What has been most favorable for the work force has been the substantial reduction in unemployment, which declined from 9.1 to 5.6 percent between 1989 and 1993 (Arenas de Mesa et al. forthcoming). The combined effect of the new social policies, salary increases, and reduction of unemployment had a positive effect on poverty, reducing the number of poor families from 46 to 28 percent between 1987 and 1992, while the percentage of indigent families was reduced from 22.6 to 7 percent (Arenas de Mesa et al. forthcoming).

Although the regime has not focused on social security, any real commitment to improving socioeconomic inequities and formulating a social policy based on solidarity would require at least some modifications to the social security system. Among the most pressing issues is the improvement of the minimum pensions and the welfare pension. This is the only area of the social security system that involves a partial application of the principle of solidarity, and it is highly insufficient and inadequate. Coverage decreased from 76 percent in 1973, to 60 percent in 1980, to 54–57 percent in 1982. Then it increased to about 76–79 percent in 1988. In other words, only by 1988 was the extent of coverage similar to before the reform. However, only 56 percent of the labor force was registered and contributing; another 24 percent was registered and not contributing. Most of the noncontributors were temporary workers and unemployed (Mesa-Lago 1991, 88, 90). Clearly, if one uses the number of contributors as an indicator of effective coverage, there has been a substantial decrease in the coverage. Mesa-Lago reports that, by 1988, 19.5 percent of the labor force was not covered by social security and those not covered included 92 percent of unpaid family workers, 71 percent of the self-employed, 58 percent of the employees of enterprises with less than five workers, 36 percent of the domestic servants, and 16 percent of the salaried workers (88–89). Between 1989 and 1993, the number of active contributors increased from 48.5 to 53.5 percent. Thus, although the total number of people affiliated to the new system increased it is still fairly low. Furthermore, the number of independent workers declined from 2.7 to 2.2 percent. In a democratic environment one might expect demands for more comprehensive coverage and some special provisions for the temporarily unemployed, as well as the incorporation of the independent workers.

There is a large gap between insurable earnings and actual contributions since about one-fourth of the contributors paid on the basis of earnings equal to or lower than the minimum wage (Mesa-Lago 1991, 90). The taxable wages were about 20 percent lower than the actual wages during the 1980s and 13 percent lower in 1993 (Arenas de Mesa et al. forthcoming). To the extent that the level of pension is dependent upon the contributions, one suspects that a large group of pensioners will be able to receive only the minimum pension, which in practice means extreme poverty.

If government is committed to equity, then gender inequalities should also be addressed. The first inequality is that women account for 38 percent of occupied workers without social security; the second is that only 14 percent of women of retirement age are actually retired. This low rate has been linked to the relatively low level of female participation in the work force (Arellano 1989). The system discriminates against women in the calculation of pension benefits since their wages are lower and they live longer (Mesa-Lago 1989; Montecinos 1993). Certainly, gender politics and gender-oriented policies should be an integral part of any democratic agenda. These policies are required both from the standpoint of social equity and to increase the economic power of retired women.

The central issue here is not to list the problems of the existing system but to analyze its applicability in the context of a more democratic environment. Both in Europe and in Latin America the expansion of comprehensive social security systems was closely associated with the expansion of industrialization, the expansion of the political arena, and the incorporation of the masses into politics. The data indicate that the social security systems that evolved out of these processes were supposedly based on principles of solidarity, universality, uniformity, and equity. On the other hand, the Chilean system was developed by an authoritarian regime that had suppressed almost all forms of political expression (although it stressed the principles of individual responsibility) and eliminated the notions of equity and solidarity for all except the very minimum pensions.

The Aylwin administration deepened the neoliberal economic model in the context of a more open political regime. What is the meaning of this approach? From my standpoint, Chile enjoys today full respect of human and political rights, but the nature of the transition was such that the military still holds a great deal of power and has limited the possibilities of reforming the political system (Borzutzky 1993a, 1993b). The electoral laws and other legislation make sure that the Pinochet regime will project its life into the future, and that the political right will keep its veto power, which guarantees the survival of the constitutional and legal edifice built by the authoritarian regime. What we have, then, is a limited democratization, and clearly, in the context of a limited democratization there is no need to address the problems outlined above.

Throughout Latin America we have seen the emergence of protected, or authoritarian, democracies and they have adopted neoliberal programs in one form or another. Privatization is clearly a preferred policy of these regimes given the economic downturn of the 1980s. Privatization of social security is being advocated by national and international experts as a policy that would reduce public spending, increase domestic savings, strengthen the labor market, and provide a more efficient administration among other changes. The policies are appealing to the current political elites because they see a reduction of the state apparatus and corporate taxes. But the Chilean experience shows that the state continues to carry a heavy burden. What is true, indeed, is that corporate taxes have been reduced and very powerful private financial entities are in control of the pension system.

In fact, the state has withdrawn from the administrative and the welfare-oriented tasks. The histories of both Latin America and Europe have taught us a lesson: the decline in living standards and economic conditions would force the state's reinsertion in the process, even in the context of authoritarian democracies, either because the market needs to expand or to avoid larger political problems. The kind of political power that in the past was associated with the administration of the system has not disappeared, it has only moved from the Cajas de Compensación de la Asignación Familiar to the AFP.

If there is a strengthening of democracy, those in power will have to focus on the social issues affecting the country and will have to include some further reforms of the existing system. There is no doubt that the private approach to social security is beneficial for the high- and medium-income groups and that they are going to use their power to keep it. Low-income groups, the self-employed, most of the female labor force, seasonal workers (to cite some) require a system in which the state takes an active role. There is need for a more balanced approach, one that puts into a new perspective the private and the public sectors, an approach that abandons the purely individualist philosophy established by the authoritarian regime. James M. Malloy has argued that the phenomenon of citizenship is determined by public policies (Malloy 1991) and any strengthening of the democratization process in Chile, or any other Latin American country, will produce a new political cycle that will involve an expansion of the notion of citizenship and new demands for policies that fully implement this notion. Chile has not reached that stage yet, and there is neither the political need nor the political will to even discuss the problems of the social security system. As one Christian Democratic senator argued recently: "The assets of the AFPs equal 35 percent of the GDP and that is not conducive neither to a free nor to a democratic economy. . . . But this is not debated. Its discussion has been postponed because of the delicacy of the situation" (*Apsi* 1994, 16).

In a recent study of economic reforms in new democracies Bresser Pereira, Maravall, and Przeworski (1993) argue that state intervention is necessary for growth. The question for them (and for me too) is how to organize state institutions so that they will intervene when appropriate. From their standpoint, Spain provides a good example to those countries seeking social policy reform since the Spanish policies were "perceived as progressing toward social citizenship: a guarantee of reasonably adequate and equal welfare protection for all members of the political community. This experience of social citizenship was distinctly tied in Spain to the consolidation of political democracy" (Bresser Pereira et al. 1993, 205). In a similar vein, von Mettenheim and Malloy write that, "to reverse a potentially vicious cycle of policy failure and democratic neglect, competitive electoral politics must be fully linked to liberal-democratic means of governance. . . . Civilian governments in Latin America must continue to rebuild power capacity into state agencies and democratize state-society relations" (von Mettenheim and Malloy 1998, 3).

The task of deepening democracy is a multidimensional one. It involves the democratization of social, political, and economic institutions; social security is an essential part of all three dimensions and as such needs to be democratized. At the very least, democratizing of social security should include dealing with some of the inequities outlined above and reintroducing into the system the concepts of universality and minimum equity. Chile is in a sound financial position today and it affords a more balanced set of policies than the policies inherited from the authoritarian regime. However, the commitment to the neoliberal model stands in the way. Any redefinition of the role of the state will be interpreted as a threat to the prevailing economic model, and neither the Aylwin nor the Frei administration was interested in threatening the model or those associated with the neoliberal policies.

Note

Throughout this chapter, dollars ($) are U.S. dollars.

References

Apsi. 1994. No. 1468 (January): 16.

Arellano, José Pablo. 1986. "Una mirada crítica a la reforma de 1981." In *Análisis de la previsión en Chile,* ed. Sergio Baeza. Santiago: Centro de Estudios Públicos.

———. 1989. "La seguridad social en Chile en los años 90." *Colección Estudios CIEPLAN,* no. 127 (December).

Arenas de Mesa, Alberto. 1994. "Seguridad social y mercado del trabajo: Inequidades de género en Chile, 1980–1984." University of Pittsburgh. Manuscript.

Arenas de Mesa, Alberto, Carmelo Mesa-Lago, and Verónica Montecinos. Forthcoming. "Chile." In *Market, Socialists and Mixed Economies: Comparative Policy and Performance—Chile, Cuba and Costa Rica,* ed. Mesa-Lago. Baltimore: Johns Hopkins University Press.

Baeza, Sergio, ed. 1986. *Análisis de la previsión en Chile.* Santiago: Centro de Estudios Públicos.

Borzutzky, Silvia. 1982. "Chilean Politics and Social Security Policies." Ph.D. dissertation, University of Pittsburgh.

———. 1986. "Políticas y reformas de la seguridad social." In *La crisis de la seguridad social y la atención a la salud,* ed. Carmelo Mesa-Lago. México: Fondo de Cultura Económica.

———. 1991. "The Chicago Boys, Social Security and Welfare in Chile." *The Radical Right and the Welfare State,* ed. H. Glennerster and J. Midgley. London: Harvester Wheatsheaf.

———. 1993a. "Social Security and Health Policies in Latin America: The Changing Roles of the State and the Private Sector." *Latin American Research Review* 28 (1): 3.

———. 1993b. "Chilean Democracy Before and After Pinochet." Paper prepared for the Conference on Deepening Democracy and Representation in Latin America. Pittsburgh.

Bresser Pereira, L. C., J. M. Maravall, and A. Przeworski. 1993. *Economic Reforms in New Democracies: A Social Democratic Approach.* New York: Cambridge University Press.

Costabal, M. 1981. "Efectos económicos de la reforma previsional." *Gestión* 6: 64.

El Cronista. 1978. December 18.

Economic Commission for Latin America and the Caribbean (ECLAC). 1988. *Magnitud de la pobreza en América Latina en los años ochenta.* Santiago.

Errázuriz, Enrique. 1987. "Capitalización de la deuda externa y desnacionalización de la economía." Documento de Trabajo no. 157. PET. August.

García, Juan A. 1986. "Mercado de renta vitalicia y bono de reconocimiento." In *Análisis de la previsión en Chile,* ed. Sergio Baeza. Santiago: Centro de Estudios Públicos.

Gillion, C., and A. Bonilla. 1992. "Analysis of a National Pension Scheme: The Case of Chile." *International Labour Review* 131: 2.

Hojman, David. 1990. "Chile After Pinochet: Aylwin's Christian Democratic Policies for the 1990s." *Bulletin of Latin American Research,* vol. 1.

Iglesias, A., and R. Acuña. 1991. *Chile: Experiencia con un régimen de capitalizaciones, 1981–1991.* CEPAL/PNUD.

Malloy, James. 1991. "Statecraft, Social Policy and Governance." In *The State and Public Policy,* ed. J. F. Hollifields and B. Guy Peters. Boulder, Colo.: Westview.

Mesa-Lago, Carmelo. 1989. *Ascent to Bankruptcy: Financing Social Security in Latin America.* Pittsburgh: University of Pittsburgh Press.

———. 1991. "Social Security and Economic Adjustment-Restructuring in Latin America and the Caribbean." Study for the International Labour Organization. December.

———. 1994. *Changing Social Security in Latin America and the Caribbean: Towards the Alleviation of Social Costs of Economic Reform.* Boulder, Colo.: Lynne Reiner.

Montecinos, Verónica. 1993. "Economic Reforms and Women in Chile." Unpublished manuscript.

Petras, James, Ignacio Leiva, and Henry Veltmeyer. 1994. *Democracy and Poverty in Chile.* Boulder, Colo.: Westview.

Piñera, José. 1980. "Seminario sobre reforma previsional y plan laboral." Santiago.

———. 1991. *El cascabel al gato: La batalla por la reforma previsional.* Santiago: Zig-Zag.

Raczynski, Dagmar. 1994. "Políticas sociales y programas de combate a la pobreza en Chile: Balance y desafíos." *Colección Estudios Cieplan,* no. 139 (June).

Superintendencia de Administradoras de Fondos de Pensiones (SAFP). Various years. *Boletín Estadístico,* no. 174. Santiago.

Vergara, Pilar. N.d. "Economía de mercado, estado de bienestar y consolidación democrática en Chile." Unpublished manuscript.

Von Mettenheim, Kurt, and James Malloy. 1998. Introduction to *Deepening Democracy in Latin America,* ed. Von Mettenheim and Malloy. Pittsburgh: University of Pittsburgh Press.

3 / The Chilean Pension System

Evaluation, Lessons, and Challenges

Carmelo Mesa-Lago and Alberto Arenas de Mesa

THE CHILEAN REFORM of its pension program at the beginning of the 1980s was the world pioneer in introducing a private pension program to replace completely the traditional public program. This chapter offers a comprehensive evaluation of the reform after fifteen years of privatization. It will analyze the following, among other topics: (1) actual coverage, indices of evasion, and payment delay in the private pension program; (2) entitlement conditions, level of benefits, and their differences by sex; (3) efficacy of competition, decreasing costs both for the insured (commissions) and for the program operation (administration); (4) efficiency of investment and the level of real yields of the pension funds; (5) net impact on the national savings; (6) state costs during the transition from the public to the private pension program. In addition, we also discuss the principal lessons of the Chilean reform for other countries, and the remaining challenges that result from the reform.

THE SITUATION ON THE EVE OF THE REFORM

Chile is a pioneer in the introduction of social insurance in Latin American countries (LAC). At the beginning of the 1970s the Chilean social security system was one of the two most advanced in the Western Hemisphere. It covered all contingencies, reached virtually all the population (combining contributory and noncontributory schemes), and offered generous benefits.

But the system was fragmented, legally complex, and stratified (it comprised one hundred independent pension programs, plus many others covering different contingencies); it lacked effective coordination, allowed unjustified privileges and significant inequalities, constituted a heavy economic burden (the payroll tax was 65 percent, and in 1971 total expenditures reached the historical continental record of 17 percent of GDP), suffered financial and actuarial disequilibria, and required substantial state subsidies (29 percent of total social security revenues). Interest groups blocked the urgently needed reforms of the system, recommended by successive administrations (Mesa-Lago 1978, 1989, 1994; Cheyre Valenzuela 1991; Iglesias and Acuña 1991; Piñera 1991; Santamaría 1992).

A GLOBAL VISION OF THE REFORM

In 1973, the long democratic tradition was interrupted. The new military authoritarian regime destabilized or banned trade unions, professional associations, and political parties. The weakening of the pressure groups and the empowering of the state, combined with social pressure, contributed to the reform of social security. Legislation enacted in 1979 eliminated the most blatant inequalities such as seniority pensions and the *perseguidora* (a high-civil-servant pension that was automatically equaled to the current salary of the former post occupied by the privileged pensioner), and standardized some entitlement conditions. Retirement ages were uniformly set at sixty-five for males and sixty for females, for example.

A gradual process of unification of the old system took place in the 1970s and 1980s. Pension schemes were divided into three groups: (1) blue-collar workers, private white-collar workers, and railroad workers; (2) municipal and race-track workers; (3) merchant-marine workers. Civil servant and banking schemes remained independent, temporarily. The armed forces and police schemes were completely excluded from the reform. An Institute of Social Insurance Standardization (Instituto de Normalización Previsional, INP) was created to manage the unified schemes, develop methods to standardize them, and administer a special fund (financed by the state) to cover the growing deficit. In 1988, seventeen funds were merged in the INP, which by the end of the decade incorporated the remaining civilian pension schemes. The old Superintendency of Social Security continues to supervise the old system, and to collect and publish data on the entire social security system.

A new pension scheme, with uniform entitlement conditions and regulations, was introduced in 1980 and began operation in May 1981. Based on the "social market" ideology, the new scheme has the following characteristics. (1) It assigns to the state a subsidiary role in social security, entrusting the operation of the new scheme to freely competing private Pension Fund Administrative Corporations (AFPs) that are strictly regulated, supervised, and audited by a new Superintendency (SAFP), and with a series of state guarantees. (2) It establishes a compulsory savings pension for old age, plus disability and survivor coverage through separate private insurance companies. (3) It is financed by the insured workers alone; the employers continued paying some contributions for other contingencies until 1988 when the state became the only financier of those programs, except for employment injury, which is still the responsibility of the employers. (4) The insured contributions are credited to an individual account, and all funds are invested by the AFP in different financial instruments; investment returns are proportionally credited to the account of the insured who also is entitled to open a voluntary savings account. (5) At the time of retirement, the insured worker can choose from three old age pension options. There is a debate as to whether the new scheme is truly private. Two International Labour Office (ILO) officials claim that the private-public dichotomy does not accurately reflect the realities of the scheme, as it plays down the important role of the state in providing substantial subsidies and guarantees (Gillion and Bonilla 1992).

Those insured in the old pension scheme were allowed to exercise some of their acquired rights only during a transition period (seniority pensions, for example) but to keep other rights permanently. In addition, they were given a five-year period (which expired in May 1986) to stay in the old scheme or move into the new one. A strong incentive to move was a significant reduction in the insured's payroll contribution in the new system, combined with a publicity campaign criticizing the flaws of the old scheme and exalting the virtues of the new one. By the end of 1982, 1.6 million insured workers (one-half of the labor force and close to 70 percent of all the insured) had moved to the new scheme. Since 1983 all salaried new entrants in the labor force are obligated to join the new scheme. The old scheme is expected to last for between thirty-five and forty years. In the following analysis we refer to the old and new pension schemes, respectively, as public and private (Arellano, 1989; Baeza and Manubens 1988; Ferrara 1989; Mesa-Lago 1989, 1994; Castro Jiménez et al. 1990; Borzutzky 1991; Piñera 1991; Iglesias and Acuña 1991; CIEDESS 1992; Uthoff 1995).

EVOLUTION OF POPULATION COVERAGE

According to the law, all salaried workers—including agricultural workers, domestic servants, and employees of microenterprises—are compulsorily covered in the private scheme, while the self-employed can join voluntarily. Pensioners and their dependent families are eligible for health care. The proportion of the labor force covered by the public scheme steadily increased and peaked at 78 percent in 1973; it declined to about 63 percent in 1980. Combining the two schemes (but excluding the military and the police), coverage continued decreasing to a low of 57 percent in 1982 (in the midst of the economic crisis), then steadily rose thereafter to 79 percent in 1988, 86 percent in 1994, and 95 percent in August of 1995 (the percentage of coverage based on registered insured is considerably higher than that based on contributing insured—see next section, "Evasion and Payment Delays"). The reasons for the decline in coverage were the sharp increase in unemployment, the expansion of the informal sector, and evasion, plus statistical corrections of the registry because of elimination or reduction of double counting of the insured. The upswing in coverage resulted mostly from economic recuperation and a decrease in unemployment during the second half of the 1980s and the first half of the 1990s. At the end of 1995, 60 percent of those in the private scheme were less than thirty-five years of age, while the public scheme had been left mostly with people close to retirement (SAFP 1981–1995; SUSESO 1982–1994; Mesa-Lago 1987, 1988, 1989, 1994; Cheyre Valenzuela 1991; Iglesias and Acuña 1991; Arrau 1992; CIEDESS 1992).

A labor survey conducted in 1988 showed that 19.5 percent of the labor force was not covered by social security, but that percentage varied in different occupational groups: 16 percent among salaried workers, 36 percent among domestic servants, 58 percent among employees of enterprises with less than five workers (but only 8 percent in enterprises with more than fifty workers), 71 percent among self-employed, and 92 percent among unpaid family workers. Most of the noncovered population consists of the self-employed; the majority of those insured are professionals with relatively high income, but the bulk of the informal self-employed are not affiliated. In 1989, only 4.3 percent of self-employed workers paid contributions to the private program, diminishing to 4 percent in 1993. Reasons given for such low coverage are (1) voluntary affiliation (the official explanation for the lack of mandatory coverage is the difficulty to control it), combined with poor information about rights and low foresight of these workers; (2) low and unstable income of this group; (3) high percentage of contribution (however, the self-employed's percentage contribution is equal to that for salaried workers and benefits are the same); and (4) disincentive for affiliation because of available free-public-assistance alternatives, such as pensions, health care, and family subsidies. To become insured, the self-employed must join all social security programs and one-half of the contribution (10 percent) goes to the old age pension scheme. Suggestions to increase protection of this group are: to allow coverage for sickness/maternity (7 percent of the contribution) and disability/survivors (3.5 percent), separate from coverage for old age pension and creation of a special pension program tailored to the self-employed's needs and capacity to pay. So far, the two democratic governments have not tackled this problem. A proposal to incorporate the military and the police into the new system received little attention (SAFP 1981–1995; Mesa-Lago 1987, 1988, 1989, 1990, 1994; Arellano 1989; Marcel and Arenas 1991; SAFP 1994).

EVASION AND PAYMENT DELAYS

The creators of the private scheme thought it would reduce evasion and payment delays and, hence, increase the number of actual contributors. The rationale was that the workers would register and pay their contributions (because these would be safe and grow into a sizable sum), while employers would not have to pay contributions and would lack the incentive to underreport salaries (Piñera 1991; CIEDESS 1992; Santamaría 1992). But this hope has not been realized because of the lack of adequate payment controls, high inflation (especially in the 1980s) that created an incentive for employers to delay the transfer of salary deductions, difficulties in incorporating the self-employed, and cheaper alternatives in public assistance.

The proportion of those registered in the public scheme who pay their contributions steadily increased from 68 to 86 percent in 1980–1987, as they drew closer to retirement age. Conversely, in the private scheme such proportion decreased from a peak of 76 percent in 1983 to 61 or 53 percent in 1991, and 56 or 53 percent in 1995 (based on different calculations, see table 3.1). This behavior, opposite to the economic crisis and subsequent recuperation, might have been caused by: (1) flaws in the SAFP data on affiliation; (2) actual increases in evasion and payment delays—in 1991 obligations of employers who deducted their workers' contributions but did not transfer

Table 3.1 Coverage, Compliance, and Concentration in Chilean Social Security, 1981–1995

	Public Scheme	*Scheme AFPs*	*Total*	*Contributors to AFP as % of Insured in AFP*	*No. of AFPs*	*% of Insured in the 3 Largest AFPS over Total Insured*
1981	—	—	—	—	12	59.0
1982	18	36	54	74	12	57.5
1983	17	38	55	76	12	59.4
1984	15	41	56	71	12	59.4
1985	14	44	58	68	11	59.3
1986	12	46	58	69	12	60.5
1987	12	50	62	70	12	61.6
1988	11	51	63	68	13	63.3
1989	8	51	59	65	13	64.4
1990	8	59	67	71	14	66.2
1991	8	55	63	61	13	67.5
1992	7	56	63	61	19	67.9
1993	6	56	62	59	21	68.0
1994	—	—	—	57	21	67.4
1995	—	—	—	56	16	68.5

Sources: SFP, *Boletín Mensual,* 1981–1995; SAFP, *El sistema chileno de pensiones,* 1994.

them to the scheme amounted to $200 million; (3) temporary workers that enter and leave the labor force; and (4) definitive exit from the labor market. In 1988, 56 percent of the labor force was registered and contributing; 24 percent was registered and not contributing; close to 20 percent was not covered. A good portion of the noncontributors were temporary workers and unemployed, as well as others who had withdrawn from the labor force. Among the noncontributors in 1988, 51 percent had not paid for one year or less, and 49 percent had paid for more than one year; the respective numbers in 1994 were 41 percent and 59 percent. Among the self-employed, the proportion of contributors to those registered was 42 percent in 1989; it decreased to 39 percent in 1993, considerably lower than among salaried workers at 57 percent. If the number used was the number of contributors instead of those registered, the proportion of the labor force covered declined to one-half; in 1990 it was 79 percent (registered) and 56 percent (contributing), and in 1993 the proportions were 90 percent and 53 percent, respectively. (These figures exclude contributors in the public system; adding these, coverage increased to 60 percent in 1993; adding the armed forces, the coverage reached 61 percent.) In addition, in 1994, 15 percent of the contributors paid on the base of earnings equal to or lower than the minimum wage, largely because they were interested in the minimum pension only (SAFP 1981–1995; SUSESO 1982–1994; Iglesias and Acuña 1991; Marcel and Arenas 1991; Arrau 1992; CIEDESS 1992; Mesa-Lago, forthcoming).

Compliance in the private scheme could be improved with the use of a universal single identification for all financial transactions, unification of the collection of contributions, rapid "cleaning" of the registry concerning labor force withdrawals and pensioners, prompt detection of late payers through computerized records, increased reporting by the insured workers on their employers' failure to transfer contributions, and more effective prosecution of delinquent employers. But some of these measures are not easily implemented; for instance, the insured are expected to check regularly the AFPs' quarterly report of their individual accounts *(cartola)* and thus detect if employers are not transferring their contributions. But many do not do this, and others cannot understand the report. A survey conducted by the Association of AFPs in 1994 revealed that 71 percent of those surveyed kept the report without reading it and 48 percent did not understand it. The AFPs can prosecute delinquent employers, but many fail to do so because they fear the employers will encourage their employees to change AFPs. The employer must complete as many monthly forms as social security institutions cover his or her employees, hence, large enterprises complete dozens of forms, but the problem is actually worse for middle-sized enterprises without computer facilities.

A unified fully computerized collection system, with one single form to report, would speed up payments, reduce employer costs, and strengthen control of evasion and payment delays. Both at the beginning and toward the end of the 1980s, there were several projects to accomplish this task, but the SAFP and the largest AFPs opposed the change. Their opposition was based on several factors: fear of a powerful state agency that could use information against the AFPs; loss of the largest AFPs' competitive edge based on a national network of collecting branches; potential that the collecting agency could make computational errors, thus provoking legal disputes on the responsibility for such errors; and the question as to who would pay the collecting agency fee, the AFP, the employer, or the state (SAFP 1981–1995; Mesa-Lago 1987, 1988, 1994; Marcel and Arenas 1991; Arenas de Mesa 1994).

ENTITLEMENT CONDITIONS AND BENEFITS

Entitlement conditions and regulations of pensions are uniform in the private scheme. The old age pension requires a retirement age of sixty-five for males and sixty for females. Early retirement is allowed when the insured individual's accumulated fund can finance a pension higher than 50 percent of his or her average earnings in the last ten years and is at least equal to 110 percent of the minimum pension. The old age pension fund consists of four components: the insured's net contributions, after deducting fixed commissions to the AFP; a state recognition bond (a financial instrument deposited in the insured's account as recognition of the contributions of those who transferred from the public scheme, but which can not be cashed until retirement time); the corresponding investment returns; and the transfer from a potential voluntary savings account.

The insured has three options at the time of retirement. The first option is a life annuity from a private insurance company, calculated on the basis of the insured's sex, age, and number of beneficiaries. The insurance company becomes the owner of the accumulated pension fund (which is transferred from the AFP) and guarantees a fixed monthly pension for the insured and his or her survivors (but there is no right of inheritance of what is left in the fund in the absence of survivors entitled to the pension); the insured's decision for this option is irrevocable. The second option is a programmed pension paid directly by the AFP, calculated annually (hence fluctuating) considering the size and yield of the fund, any changes in life expectancy, and the number of the insured's beneficiaries. The insured retains ownership of the fund (which can be inherited) and can change his decision at any time. The third option is a programmed pension for a number of years and a life annuity later. The AFP must provide all the necessary information (including insurance companies) for the insured to make a selection among the three options. However, reportedly, 90 percent of the insured do not understand the complexities involved and hire an expert who charges a fee ranging from 3 to 5 percent of the total value of the accumulated fund (Gillion and Bonilla 1992). The AFP is never responsible if the insured's decision results in an insufficient length or amount of pension.

Disability and survivor pensions are not paid by the AFP but by the insurance company contracted for that purpose. A total disability pension (for loss of at least two-thirds of work capacity) pays 70 percent of average earnings of the last ten years to those who have not reached the retirement age; a partial disability pension (for loss of at least one-half of work capacity) pays 50 percent of that average. Survivor pensions are paid to widows or disabled widowers, to children below age eighteen (twenty-four if they are students, or regardless of age if they are disabled), and to parents if there are no other beneficiaries.

A minimum pension is guaranteed by the state if the insured's accumulated fund is not sufficient to finance that minimum, provided that the insured has twenty years of contributions (under certain conditions the required years can be reduced to seventeen) and has fulfilled the other requirements for old age or disability retirement. The public scheme is less restrictive in conceding the minimum pension since it only requires 15.3 years of affiliation and 7.7 years of contributions for men, and 9.6 years of affiliation with no requirements for contributions for women. The reduced requirements that women enjoyed in comparison with men were part of a "positive" discrimination that favored women in the public scheme (see the section "Pensions: Differences by Sex"). Insured unemployed and part-time workers are entitled to disability/survivor coverage and the minimum pension for one year after dismissal, if they have accumulated six months of contributions in the previous year. A public assistance pension is paid by the state to three hundred thousand recipients who are either noninsured or insured but not entitled to a minimum pension.

The entire social security system is based on a special monetary currency (*unidad de fomento*, UF), and the value is adjusted daily (using a formula that considers the inflation of the last three months) in order to maintain a constant value. All benefits—including pensions (except minimum pensions, which are fixed at current pesos by the state), individual accounts, and investment returns—are denominated in UF. A comparison of the average level of pensions in the public and private schemes showed that by 1991 the latter was 43 percent above the former in old age pensions ($149 monthly), 100 percent above in disability ($206), and 46 percent above in survivor pensions ($92).

The validity of this calculation in the long term has been questioned for several reasons. (1) In 1991 pensioners in the private scheme were 10 percent of the total number of pensioners, whereas those in the public scheme were 90 percent of the total. (2) Current pensions paid by the private scheme are not necessarily representative of those to be paid in the future, since the accumulated funds and the pensions would largely depend on the value of the recognition bond financed by the state and on the uncertain return on investment. (3) Differences in the amount of pensions can be explained by, among other reasons, divergent contributory wages. In 1987, the average pension for the armed forces (part of the public scheme) was four times higher than the average pension in the private scheme. Although the minimum monthly pension increased from $54 to $103 in 1989–1995, this amount is insufficient to meet basic needs, and it is estimated that close to half of the insured will receive a minimum pension in the future. The public assistance pension is considerably lower ($60 in 1994). Furthermore, the number of such pensions is limited to three hundred thousand and there is a long waiting list. The private scheme does not apply the solidarity principle of social security except for the minimum pension, and the minimum pension is financed by the state out of fiscal revenue outside of the pension scheme (Mesa-Lago 1988, 1994; Arellano 1989; Ferrara 1989; SAFP 1991; Gillion and Bonilla 1992; Mesa-Lago, forthcoming).

The private scheme changed two factors formerly considered in the calculation and amount of pensions and added five new factors. Remunerations and years of contribution are two variables common to both the public and the private pension schemes, though there are greater restrictions in the latter. Both remunerations and years of contribution now depend on 100 percent of the active work life of those insured. The public scheme takes into account only salaries in the last five years, three years, or one year prior to retirement, and the required years of contributions are 71 percent and 64 percent of the active labor life of women and men, respectively. The five new factors are: (1) the rate of return of the pension fund in the financial market; (2) the fixed commission charged by the AFPs; (3) the retirement age; (4) the life expectancy of the insured; and (5) the number of family dependents. The accumulated fund in the individual capitalization accounts depends directly on four factors: the two old (but modified) factors and the first two of the five new factors.

Processing of pensions has been greatly simplified and made much faster in the private scheme. An application form can be mailed or delivered to the AFP, and the individual accounts facilitate the process. Since 1990, a preliminary pension is paid after fifteen days of the application and the pension is readjusted later. In 1988, a program of voluntary savings accounts was introduced; it is handled by the AFPs and total savings increased more than six times in 1989–1994 (Mesa-Lago 1988, 1994; Arellano 1989; Ferrara 1989; Iglesias and Acuña 1991; Margozzini 1991; SAFP 1994).

PENSIONS: DIFFERENCES BY SEX

Pensions should be equal for both sexes in the public scheme, provided that no inequalities exist in the labor market between men and women (that is, both sexes have equal remunerations and years of contributions). In the private scheme, under the same equal conditions, women's pensions should fluctuate between 52 and 76 percent of men's pensions, depending on the age they joined the scheme (Arenas de Mesa 1995). This difference is explained by two factors: the lower retirement age for women, which increases the number of pensioned years to be financed by the accumulated fund, and the longer life expectancy for women, which requires more years of financing by the accumulated fund.

It could be argued that men receive higher pensions compared to women because men are five years older at retirement. The lower age of retirement for women existed already in the public scheme, but it did not discriminate in pension amount by sex because these pensions were equal and the resulting costs were either charged to the insured group or financed by the state. Women's pensions are lower than men's in the private scheme because it eliminated solidarity and redistribution within the scheme, and it takes into account a difference of five years in retirement age plus seven more years for life expectancy against women. Even if a woman retires at sixty-five she would get, on average, only 90 percent of the men's pension. Women's pensions have an even lower average if two other differences exist: (1) lower salaries (26 percent lower in 1989–1994) for women vis-à-vis salaries for men, which results in a smaller accumulated fund in the individual capitalization accounts of women; and (2) fewer years of contribution of women, which also reduces their accumulated fund—in 1989–1994, out of the total insured women, only 44 percent paid contributions vis-à-vis 55 percent of men (Arenas de Mesa 1994; Arenas de Mesa and Montecinos 1996).

It has been stated that the salary replacement rate in the private scheme is about 70 percent of the average real salary in the last ten years of activity of the pensioners. Estimates of future average private pension amounts are based on divergent assumptions (on the annual real interest rate and compliance or payment of contributions), hence, the results (particularly the salary replacement rates) vary considerably depending on whether such assumptions are optimistic or pessimistic. A Chilean research institution—basing its calculations on a 5 percent interest rate and a compliance of contributions from 90 to 93 percent during the active work life of the insured—has calculated salary replacement rates to be 80–86 percent for men, and 52–57 percent for women (CIEDESS 1992). Two ILO officials, basing their calculations on a 3 percent interest rate and a 100 percent contribution compliance, have estimated a 44 percent replacement rate for men (Gillion and Bonilla 1992); such a rate could be reduced to 37 percent, if a 80 percent contribution compliance was used instead. Finally, a study that distinguishes the insured by sex, basing the calculations on a 5 percent interest rate and a 70 percent contribution compliance, has calculated replacement rates for women to be 32–46 percent, and for men 58–83 percent (Arenas de Mesa 1995).

INSURED CONTRIBUTIONS AND COMMISSIONS OF THE AFP

In both the public and the private pension schemes only the insured contribute, but the state finances the deficit of the public scheme and contributes to the private scheme as well (see the section "Net Balance of the General Pension System and State Subsidies"). The employer's contribution for pensions was abolished in 1980 and other employer's contributions (for unemployment compensation and family allowances) were eliminated in 1988 and absorbed by the state—except for employment injury, which is still the employer's responsibility. The insured's percentage contribution for pensions is uniform in the private scheme (although there are still differences in the public scheme): 10 percent for old age plus an additional 2.8–3.7 percent (varying among AFPs), to pay the premium for disability and survivors in a private insurance company (0.85–1.70 percent) and the rest goes as a commission to the AFP (1.95–2.85 percent). There is a voluntary additional contribution of 10 percent to increase the basic old age pension, available for salaried workers but not for the self-employed. The total compulsory contribution to pensions fluctuates between 12.8 and 13.7 percent; the average is 13.2 percent. In addition, the insured pay 7 percent for sickness/maternity, for a mandatory total of 19.8–20.7 percent in the private scheme, compared with 25.6–27.7 percent in the public scheme. The lower contribution in the private scheme was initially justified by its allegedly more efficient administration, but in reality it largely resulted from the 1979 reform, which eliminated costly benefits, increased and standardized retirement ages, and tightened entitlement conditions. And yet, such savings were not passed on to the insured in the public scheme but were offered as an incentive for transferring to the private scheme (Arellano 1989; Mesa-Lago 1989, 1994; SAFP 1995).

The insured must pay to the AFP freely set commissions, usually of two types: a fixed sum (deducted from the 10 percent contribution for old age pension) and a variable percentage (the premium for disability/survivor coverage). In August 1995, 77 percent of the percentage commission was for the AFP and the remaining 23 percent was used to pay the premium; the lack of separation between both components obscured the payment. Because of the large number of insured in the AFPs, insurance companies reduced the disability/survivor premium, and yet the resulting economies of scale were not transferred to the insured but were pocketed by the AFP.

Since 1987, the premium and the percentage commission have been separated and the greater transparency has caused a drop in the commission. The fixed commission has a regressive effect because it is proportionally higher among low-income insured (hence reducing their net contribution for old age and their investment return), while it is proportionally smaller for high-income insured. Thus, in 1987 such commissions represented an 18 percent reduction in the deposit of an insured in the 10,000 pesos per month bracket but only 0.9 percent for an insured in the 100,000 pesos per month bracket. For the same reason, in 1981–1987, the investment yield for the lowest income bracket averaged 7.6 percent compared with 11.3 percent for the 60,000 pesos bracket (Mesa-Lago 1987, 1988, 1994).

Because of such regressivity, the fixed commission was the subject of strong criticism in the 1980s, from both domestic and foreign experts, who suggested different alternatives to substitute it. But the smaller AFPs opposed such change because they have a concentration of lower-income insured and the fixed commission generated most of their revenue. The government also resisted the modification. The more transparent percentage commission and the public criticism of the fixed commission have led to declines in the levels of both commissions. In current pesos, the fixed monthly commission reached a peak of 605 in 1988 and declined to 98 in 1995. The average percentage commission increased from 2.7 percent in 1982 to a maximum of 3.6 percent in 1985, then it dropped to 2.8 percent in 1993; it rose to 3.2 percent in 1995 (supposedly because of rising administrative costs in 1993–1995). As the fixed commission declined, both in absolute level and as a share of the combined commission (from 54 to 6 percent in 1982–1995), its regressive effect also diminished, although it has not been completely eliminated. Despite wide criticism of the fixed commission, it has not been abolished because the

Table 3.2 Commisions, State Subsidy, and Growth of Pension Funds in Chile, 1981–1995

	Fixed Commission (1994 pesos)	*Percentage Commission Average*[a]	*Real Index of Administrative Cost (1989=100)*	*State Subsidy to Social Security (% of GDP)*	*Real Annual Yield of Pension Funds (%)*	*Pension Funds as % of GDP*
1981	—	—	—	6.2	12.5	0.9
1982	90.7	2.7	199.2	8.8	26.8	3.4
1983	123.7	3.6	143.3	8.2	22.7	6.0
1984	92.0	3.6	131.2	8.9	2.8	7.9
1985	166.5	3.6	107.8	8.6	13.4	10.2
1986	186.8	3.4	93.2	8.9	12.0	12.5
1987	198.1	3.4	78.3	8.0	6.4	14.5
1988	605.2	3.5	99.0	7.6	4.7	15.4
1989	414.5	3.3	100.0	5.9	6.6	18.5
1990	286.1	3.3	109.4	7.3	17.6	24.7
1991	235.4	3.2	107.0	7.3	28.6	32.2
1992	147.4	3.2	116.0	6.6	4.0	32.2
1993	87.3	2.8	136.0	6.6	16.7	39.4
1994	91.6	3.2	—	—	17.8	41.2
1995	89.2	3.2	—	—	-4.7	39.1[b]

Sources: Fixed commission, percentage commission, and yield from SFP, *Boletín Mensual,* 1981–1995; state subsidy from Mesa-Lago, forthcoming; fund as percentage of GDP and administrative costs from SAFP, *El Sistema,* 1994, and authors' estimates.

a. December of each year.

b. Authors' estimate based on data for December 1994–November 1995.

seven AFPs (out of a total of sixteen) that charged such a commission at the end of 1995 covered 65 percent of the insured. Finally, differences in the combined commissions charged by the various AFPs have gradually shrunk —allegedly because of increased competition among them (but see the section "Administration: The Role of Competition"; also table 3.2; SAFP 1982; Mesa-Lago 1987, 1988, 1994; Arellano 1989; Bonilla 1991; Cheyre Valenzuela 1991; Marcel and Arenas 1991; Arrau 1992; CIEDESS 1992; Uthoff 1995; Mesa-Lago, forthcoming). Also, the net investment yield (after deducting the administrative commissions) was lower than the interest paid by bank deposits during the first fourteen years of operation of the new system.

INVESTMENT OF PENSION FUNDS

The combined pension funds of all AFPs increased twofold every two or three years in 1981–1995; in the latter year they reached a total of $24 billion, equal to 39 percent of GDP and more than 100 percent of the external debt. It is projected that, under favorable conditions, the combined funds will reach 50 percent of GDP in the year 2000 and 100 percent in 2025. The average real annual investment yield of the pension funds was as follows: 12.5 percent (1981), 26.8 percent (1982), 22.7 percent (1983), 2.8 percent (1984), 13.4 percent (1985), 12.0 percent (1986), 6.4 percent (1987), 4.7 percent (1988), 6.6 percent (1989), 17.6 percent (1990), 28.6 percent (1991), 4.0 percent (1992), 16.7 percent (1993), 17.8 percent (1994), and –4.7 percent (1995). The average annual real yield in 1981–1995 was 12.6 percent, the highest in Latin America and the Caribbean. The yield steadily surpassed (except for 1984 and 1995) the real commercial bank interest for short- and long-term deposits. But many experts claim that such high yields will not be sustained in the future, particularly given the negative performance in 1995 (see table 3.2; CIEDESS 1992; Mesa-Lago 1994; SAFP 1995).

The Central Bank sets the investment caps for financial instruments. In 1983, after the crisis and the state intervention in several banks and companies to avoid a generalized bankruptcy, 97 percent of investments were in debt instruments and 72 percent in public instruments. There was an excessive investment concentration in certain instruments: 44 percent was in public securities and 51 percent in mortgage notes, but only 3 percent was in deposits or bank bonds, 2 percent in corporate bonds (public and private), and nothing in stocks. This situation was very risky, and consequently it was necessary to diversify the portfolio gradually by laws enacted in 1985, 1989, 1990, 1994, and 1995 that broadened the range of instruments. The 1985 law authorized investment in stocks and bonds from private financial institutions; the 1990 law did the same for foreign instruments. The caps in 1995 were as follows: 50 percent in public securities, 35–50 percent in mortgage notes, 30–50 percent in bank deposits of fixed term, 30–45 percent in public and private bonds, 30–37 percent in stocks and 4.5–9 percent in foreign instruments. By November 1995, the portfolio was quite diversified: 40.6 percent in public securities, 16.0 percent in mortgage notes, 9.5 percent in bank deposits, 5.4 percent in corporate bonds, and 28.5 percent in stocks (Mesa-Lago 1991a; Iglesias and Acuña 1991; SAFP 1983; Mesa-Lago, forthcoming).

The creators of the private scheme initially believed it would help significantly to develop the domestic capital market (Piñera 1991). Although the domestic capital has indeed grown, the huge accumulation of pension funds has not met original expectations concerning the capital market. It is argued that the high yields of the 1980s reflected a similar performance in other stock and bond markets throughout the world, recovering from the decline suffered in the second half of the 1970s and the start of the 1980s. The slowdown in Chilean pension fund yields in 1987–1989 thus reflected a similar downward world trend. The very high Chilean yields of 1990–1994 (with the exception of 1992) could then be explained by the high demand for corporate shares and the relatively few that were eligible for AFP investment. (A Commission for Risk Classification—a public enterprise—ranks stocks suitable for AFP investment according to their degree of risk; for debt instruments, the ranking is made by private companies, which is ratified by said commission.) The negative yield of 1995 has been attributed principally to the poor return on stocks in the stock exchange, which was affected at the beginning of the year by the Mexican financial crisis. The effects of this crisis came under control later, but the performance during the rest of the year did not improve, which resulted in the worst yield since the system's inception in 1981. Other concerns voiced by experts are (1) that AFPs can invest jointly or separately in one single enterprise, which influences the value of its shares; (2) that insurance company shareholders in an AFP can also invest in shares; and (3) that the high book value of AFP investment is not necessarily the market value of such instruments, in public securities for example (Mesa-Lago 1988, 1994; Bonilla 1991; Gillion and Bonilla 1992; Uthoff 1995).

An opposite viewpoint is that the pension funds have contributed significantly to increase domestic and foreign confidence in the Santiago stock market and stimulated the growth of insurance companies. In addition, the funds have played a principal role in debt equity swaps, thus reducing the external debt and promoting foreign investment. It is also argued that the Chilean model proves that the existence of a mature domestic capital market is not an essential prerequisite for pension privatization (Cheyre Valenzuela 1991; Iglesias and Acuña 1991; Santamaría 1992).

It is sustained that opportunities for investment broadened dramatically in the 1980s because of the government's privatization program, but now, when such a process is virtually over, there are less opportunities for investment. The public sector cannot continue emission of securities at the same rate, the expansion of corporate stocks and bonds has obvious limitations, and investing in personal or mortgage loans and housing construction is considered too risky. Some believe that the authorization in 1990 to invest in foreign instruments offered an alternative, given the restrictions of the internal capital market. A study by the Center of Public Research argued that if, in 1990–1991, 10 percent had been invested in public bonds of developed countries, the pension fund performance would have increased 0.5 percentage points, or 1.2 points if the investment had been made just in Japanese, United States, or British stock. Although one sector opposes the exportation of domestic savings, the government authorities during 1990–1995 have supported, regulated, and improved pension fund investments in foreign instruments. Even though the investment cap for these instruments was 9 percent in 1995, however, there was actually only 0.3 percent invested in them (Arrau 1991; Marcel and Arenas 1991; Margozzini 1991; Mesa-Lago 1991a; SAFP 1994, 1995).

Consequently, a crucial aspect in the near future will be to offer a sufficiently broad spectrum of investment alternatives for the pension funds. The capital market reform laws of 1994 and 1995 added other investment instruments: (1) new public debt securities previously authorized by the Central Bank; (2) instruments that guard against fluctuations in foreign exchange rates; (3) quotas for investment funds in securitized credits; (4) debt instruments and bonds that can be converted into stock to finance investment projects; and (5) recognition bonds issued by the INP (because of these changes the maximum limit in public instruments increased from 45 to 50 percent). To expedite the incorporation of new financial instruments that pension funds might invest in, the Central Bank was authorized to add new instruments in the future without having to ratify them by law. If the total value of the funds indeed reaches more than 50 percent of the GDP in the year 2000, this could stimulate both higher rates of investment (as long as there are sufficient investment opportunities) and economic growth. On the other hand, if the supply of capital is greater than the demand, the investment yield might decrease or the capital flight increase (SAFP 1995; Mesa-Lago, forthcoming).

Finally, there is the issue of the impact of the private pension funds on national savings and investment. The original argument of the founders of the scheme was that the substitution of the PAYG system by a fully funded pension system would increase capital accumulation (Piñera 1991). A divergent viewpoint was that, in order to have such a positive effect, AFPs' savings had to be greater than the public deficit generated by the reform (Arellano 1989). Recent analyses of the relationship—conducted by experts with divergent views—concur that there is no conclusive evidence that private pensions have generated higher national savings. In 1981–1989, for instance, the increase in national savings occurred thanks to external savings and domestic public savings; and in 1990–1994, such increase was because of private savings outside of the AFPs and public savings (Marcel and Arenas 1991; Arrau 1992; CIEDESS 1992; Gillion and Bonilla 1992; Santamaría 1992; Arenas de Mesa 1994; SAFP 1994; Uthoff 1995; Mesa-Lago, forthcoming).

NET BALANCE OF THE GENERAL PENSION SYSTEM AND STATE SUBSIDIES

The cost of social security in Chile was the highest in Latin America in the second half of the 1980s. Social security expenditures as a percentage of GDP steadily increased in the 1960s; peaked at 17.5 percent in 1971 (a historical record in the Western Hemisphere); declined to 9.3 percent in 1975; steadily rose again to 15.6 percent in 1982 (in the midst of the crisis, because of the rapid fall of GDP while social security expenditures did not subside); decreased to 13.1 percent in 1986; and continued to fall, reaching 11.4 percent in 1993. Two-thirds of total expenditures were from all pension schemes. The active/passive ratio steadily declined, from 10:6 in 1960 to 4:4 in 1970, 2:2 in 1980, 1:9 in 1988, and 1:85 in 1994. The decrease in the share of social security expenditures/GDP in 1983–1994 and the slowdown in the decline of the active/passive ratio in this period were largely the result of the social security reform, particularly the increase in ages of retirement and contribution years. (In addition, GDP grew at a greater rate than social security expenditures.) A reversal of these tendencies, however, will probably occur at the beginning of the next century with the aging of the population and the system (Mesa-Lago 1988, 1989, 1991c, 1994).

The state contributes to the private pension scheme in three ways. The first is the recognition bond, which is estimated from one-half to three-fourths of the accumulated capital of those retiring in the next fifteen years or an average of nine years of their pension, to be paid by the state in a lump sum (instead of being spread throughout the retirement period as in the public scheme). The second is the difference needed to pay the minimum pension for those who lack sufficient funds in the AFP (it is estimated that at the end of the 1990s the annual cost of this program will be $60 million and will increase notably in the first decade of the new century. The third is the state guarantee of the life annuity in case of bankruptcy of the private insurance company.

In addition, the state has to finance the deficit of the public pension scheme (civilian and armed forces), public assistance pensions, unemployment compensation, family allowances, and health care for indigents. Therefore, to secure a sound private pension scheme, the state made a huge financial commitment for the long run, or permanently, in behalf of the entire social security system (Arellano 1989; Bonilla 1991). In 1995, the private scheme had 91 percent of the total active contributors in the entire pension system, but only 16 percent of the total pensioners, which generated a substantial surplus. But the public pension sector (civilian, armed forces, public assistance pensions) had only 9 percent of total active contributors and 84 percent of total pensioners, which caused a major deficit that increased from 2.2 percent of GDP in 1981 to 6.3 percent in 1986 (87 percent of expenditures were subsidized by the state) and 6.6 percent in 1993 (Mesa-Lago 1988, 1991a, 1994; Mesa-Lago, forthcoming).

Unfortunately, there are no consolidated data to estimate the balance of the entire social security system. Experts provide divergent estimates of the state subsidy (as percentage of GDP) to cover the cost of the deficit in various schemes and sectors. CIEDESS (1992) sets the deficit in the old pension scheme as 3.5 percent in 1981 and 3.2 percent in 1991. Gillion and Bonilla (1992) set the state subsidy to the private scheme as 6 percent in 1990. Arrau (1992) sets the deficit related to the overall pension reform (public scheme deficit plus recognition bond) as 1.2 percent in 1981 and 4.8 percent in 1991; when adding armed forces pensions and other state-supported schemes (public assistance pensions, for example), the deficit increases to 4.1 percent in 1981 and 5 percent in 1991. Santamaría (1992) sets the deficit of all the social security system (without specifics) as 7.4 percent in 1984 and 4.1 percent in 1991. The lack of coherence in these figures and the imprecision as to what they exactly cover ratify the vacuum of accurate global data. But it is clear that the state's commitment to the pension scheme has reduced public funds for other programs—such as health care—for the lowest income groups.

The deficit in the public pension sector will last for another thirty years; estimates are that it will peak at the end of the 1990s and slow down thereafter. The deficit from recognition bonds is estimated to be 1 percent of GDP in the next twenty years, reaching a maximum of 1.2 percent of GDP in the year 2005; these figures are double what was estimated in the mid 1980s. It is unclear how the state will finance the pension deficit—with taxes, public debt, reduction in consumption, or a combination of all three.

Financing the deficit with public debt will place the burden on future generations and the young and will benefit the current generation and the old; financing with taxes will place the burden on the current generation. The first alternative has so far been predominant; it has been estimated that if all the deficit is financed with debt, then debt as a percentage of GDP will increase from 25 to 67 percent in thirty years and stabilize at 56 percent later (Marcel and Arenas 1991; Arrau 1992; Arenas de Mesa and Marcel 1993).

There is a vacuum of actuarial studies and even a lack of financial data for the entire public and private pension schemes. The same is true for global simulation exercises based on total contributions, investment returns, state subsidies, and expenditures. These data and studies are badly needed to determine the future equilibrium of the system and assess the state economic capacity to subsidize it.

ADMINISTRATION: THE ROLE OF COMPETITION

The creators of the private pension scheme assumed that its market elements (free entry and exit, competition, free change of AFP by the insured), combined with state supervision and minimum guarantees, would ensure its efficiency and result in expanded population coverage, reduced evasion and payment delays, increased number of AFPs, decreased administrative costs and commissions, and maximized investment yields (Piñera 1991). We have noted that some of these goals have not been met (coverage, compliance), while others have (investment yields, commissions). In this section we analyze whether the system is truly competitive, as well as its effects on administrative efficiency and the role of the state in establishing minimum guarantees.

The number of AFPs was practically stagnant in the first decade of the scheme; there were twelve initially, and fourteen in 1990. Out of these, ten were at the start, one resulted from a merge of two, and three were created in 1985–1990. The legal changes that permitted the creation of AFPs by unions stimulated the creation of ten new ones in 1992–1994; two of these merged and another dissolved, leaving a total of twenty-one AFPs in December 1994. But more mergers and dissolutions occurred in 1995, which caused a reduction from twenty-one to sixteen AFPs. The largest economic conglomerates—which arose in the decade of the 1970s during the privatization process—control nine AFPs (that is, more than half). During the 1982 crisis, two of these conglomerates went bankrupt and their assets were temporarily administered by the state; they were reprivatized later and sold to foreign corporations under the debt-for-equity swap program. Currently, the four largest AFPs are controlled mainly by foreign corporations. There is a high degree of concentration in the AFPs: the largest three combined 60 percent of all insured in 1981; this proportion increased to almost 69 percent in 1995 (see table 3.1; Mesa-Lago 1988, 1989, 1994; CIEDESS 1992; SAFP 1995; Mesa-Lago, forthcoming).

Data on AFPs' operational costs are fragmentary and contradictory. One analyst estimates that in 1982–1986 these costs—per insured, in constant pesos—were halved. Another claims that in 1989 25 percent of total revenue from contributions went to operational costs. In 1981, there were thirty-five hundred employees in the public scheme, which was considered the largest public institution in Chile, but in 1990, the number of employees in the private scheme was eight thousand. In 1994, the private scheme had 10 percent more personnel than the public scheme prior to the reform. About 30 percent of AFPs' personnel is made up by sellers (see below), and the share of publicity expenditures is high; these types of expenditures were not needed in the old pension scheme. Because of the lack of data and divergent proportions of insured and pensioners, it is practically impossible to measure and compare efficiency in the two schemes. We estimate that overall costs of the entire system are almost twice as high as before, because of the two schemes in operation (Marcel and Arenas 1991; Mesa-Lago 1994; SAFP 1994).

During most of the 1980s, the three AFPs with the largest number of insured charged the highest fixed and percentage commissions, yet in 1990–1995 their commissions decreased. One of these AFPs charged the lowest percentage commission; two charged the lowest fixed commissions. In 1981–1995, the average investment yield of those three AFPs was below the overall average yield for the system. Therefore, the selection of AFPs is not made based on their yields; and neither was it made according to the commission charged, at least not in the 1980s, although it was in 1990–1995. Thus, there is uncertainty on whether competition functions properly. What are the reasons, then, that motivate the insured's selection of an AFP?

According to the SAFP, the actual administrative expenditure per insured increased by 38 percent in 1989–1993, because of the greater competition to attract insured when a doubling in the number of AFPs occurred. Although in theory there is no limit on the number of times an insured can change AFPs, in practice it can be done three times a year and at no cost to the insured. In 1990, 17 percent of all contributors shifted AFPs and this proportion grew considerably (to 31 and 40 percent in 1993 and 1994, respectively); 90 percent of these changes were made by sellers (dealers who work on commission), whose number grew from 2,615 to more than 14,000 in 1989–1994. The insured—particularly the elderly and women—usually ignore the differences between AFPs in terms of commissions and yields and, hence, are easy prey for the sellers. The change is not always beneficial for the insured, but it is for the seller. In 1995, new legislation proposed a permanent minimum of one year in an AFP (this project has yet to be discussed in Congress).

Sellers from insurance companies can also harm the insured. Information provided by the AFPs on commissions and yields were poor until the end of the 1980s when the system became more transparent: for example, the percentage commission is now separated from the insurance premium, and real instead of nominal yields are published. In the 1990s, the SAFP regulated the information the AFPs should provide to the insured; the relative figures on yields and commissions were standardized; and the *cartola* was simplified. But a substantial amount of AFPs' costs still go to publicity and very little or none to effectively educate the public on how to make a wise decision based on the real advantages of specific AFPs. In 1987, the Association of AFPs initiated educational campaigns. In summary, the number of AFPs grew (although it decreased in 1995) and the commissions declined (these increased in 1994–1995 but remained lower than at the system's beginning). On the other hand, administrative costs, the concentration of insured, and the number of transfers have increased notably; transfers seem more influenced by the sellers and the propaganda of the larger AFPs than by their investment yields. At least in the first fifteen years of operation of the private pension scheme, the hypothesis that competition would produce positive results becomes questionable in light of the above analysis (Mesa-Lago 1988, 1989, 1994; Iglesias and Acuña 1991; CIEDESS 1992; Mesa-Lago, forthcoming).

The state has established a series of guarantees (particularly after the bankruptcies of 1982) to make the private scheme as sound as possible. These measures largely achieved their goal, but a few of them have raised significant barriers for the entry of new AFPs. The following ten guarantees are the most important. The first is that the SAFP regulates, supervises, and audits the private scheme. The second is that AFPs can neither be involved in business other than pensions nor offer other benefits (except for voluntary savings account services and funeral grants). The third is that the pension fund is separated from the AFP's own assets (in case of bankruptcy the SAFP manages the fund until it is transferred to another AFP). The fourth is that each AFP must have an initial capital, which increases with its number of insured (from 5,000 UF, with less than 5,000 insured, to 20,000 UF, with 10,000 or more insured). To facilitate entry, the initial capital has been reduced and the largest AFPs have been authorized to subcontract to smaller AFPs services such as the collection of contributions, charges to individual accounts, and investment of funds. However, the insured concentration in the largest three AFPs has increased, and the number of AFP decreased by 20 percent in 1995. The fifth is that the AFPs are responsible for a real monthly average yield, in the last twelve months, not less than the lesser of the following two: the average yield of all pension funds minus two percentage points, or 50 percent of the average yield of all funds. The sixth is that all AFPs must establish a "reserve of yield fluctuation" to cover any gap in the required yield. In addition, a second reserve *(encaje)* is required, equal to 1 percent of the value of the pension fund. The seventh is that, if both reserves are insufficient to reach the required minimum yield, the state is obliged to finance the difference. The eighth is that 90 percent of the investment instruments must be deposited in the Central Bank. The ninth is that there are caps fixed to investments in each instrument, and shares are officially classified according to risks. The last is that the AFP must send a quarterly report of the individual account to its affiliates and provide them with other specific information (Bustamante Jeraldo 1991; Marcel and Arenas 1991; Margozzini 1991).

OVERALL EVALUATION: ADVANTAGES AND DISADVANTAGES

The social security reform and the private pension scheme have brought advantages and disadvantages for the three major participants. The insured workers have benefited from lower payroll contributions, freedom of choice among AFPs and retirement plans, the recognition of previous contributions, eligibility for a minimum pension (as long as twenty years of contributions have been paid), a sounder pension program with state guarantees, high real investment yields, and faster and simpler processing of pensions. The disadvantages for the insured are the decline in coverage (based on compliance), the payment of commissions to the AFPs, poor transparency on retirement options (particularly in the insurance market), lack of knowledge on crucial issues and decisions, and the loss of the employer's contribution. The latter has been the employer's gain whose only disadvantage is the considerable paperwork involved in monthly reporting and transferring of their workers' contributions to different social security entities. The state seems to have mostly disadvantages (subsidies to the whole system) and few advantages, most of which are not clearly demonstrated, for example, the potential correction of a negative impact of the employers' payroll tax on employment, the beneficial effect on the capital market (although not as much as originally expected), and the eventual termination of the troublesome public scheme.

Society as a whole has profited with the elimination of unjustified costly privileges (although not all have been terminated) but in the future will have to confront the heavy cost of state obligations. The outcome of the private scheme is extremely sensitive to the investment yield (an increase of 1 percent in investment yield would imply an increment of 20–25 percent in the level of pensions), to the level of compliance, salaries of the insured, and general economic conditions. The state may be required to meet various guarantees at once, and some risks may also occur simultaneously, such as high unemployment and inflation combined with low real investment yield. There is no evidence that the fully funded system has generated higher national savings.

The social security reform and the introduction of the private pension scheme have induced two opposite effects on income distribution, either progressive or regressive. Probable progressive effects are (1) elimination of seniority pensions and *perseguidoras* and standardization in the age of retirement and pension adjustment (which reduced payments to relatively high-income insured); (2) introduction of the minimum pension and expansion of public assistance pensions (which help relatively low-income insured and poor noninsured, respectively, although the levels are quite low, particularly the public assistance); and (3) termination of the employers' contribution, particularly if it stopped the price transfer to noninsured consumers (the effects would be different if the contribution were paid by the employer—a negative impact on employment, or a transfer to workers). Probable regressive (or neutral) effects are (1) a private pension scheme, based on strict correspondence between premiums and benefit with virtual exclusion of solidarity; (2) decline in population coverage and no significant progress in coverage of low-income groups, such as the self-employed and other informal workers; (3) preservation of some inequalities in entitlement conditions and benefits in the public scheme, and particularly in the armed forces schemes; (4) lower pensions for women because of a lower retirement age and longer life expectancy; and (5) the regressive impact of the fixed commission. It has also been argued that the private scheme favors high- and low-income insured (because of proportionally higher investment yields on behalf of the former and minimum pensions in behalf of the latter), while it discriminates against the middle-income and lower-middle-income insured (because of the regressive effect of the fixed commission, and because they will not obtain a minimum pension because of their level of income).

Prior to the 1990 elections, the opposition cautiously accepted the social security reform and the private scheme but was critical of various aspects: the lack of solidarity of the scheme, the absence of participation of the insured in the administration, the poor coverage of important sectors of the population, the low minimum pensions, the regressivity of the fixed commission, the need to have more AFPs, the foreign ownership of AFPs, and the investment of funds in foreign instruments. The two democratic governments since 1990 have promoted the growth of AFPs and have incremented the minimum real pension by 100 percent in the last five years. However, they have not introduced substantive changes to the system, and the majority of problems existing at the end of the 1980s still persist. The democratic governments have concentrated their efforts on tax reform to improve income redistribution, increase resources for social programs, and establish a fund to reduce poverty (Mesa-Lago 1989, 1994; Castro Jiménez et al. 1990; Borzutzky 1991; Gillion and Bonilla 1992; Mesa-Lago, forthcoming).

REMAINING CHALLENGES AND LESSONS FROM THE CHILEAN EXPERIENCE

The private pension scheme faces several remaining challenges. The first is to increase coverage of the noninsured, especially self-employed and low-income workers: only 4 percent of 1.3 million self-employed workers made contributions in 1993. The second is to decrease payment delays: only half of the affiliated workers made contributions in 1991–1995, a period of strong economic growth and low unemployment. The third is to reduce administrative costs: the increase in the number of AFPs in the 1990s brought an expansion in administrative costs per insured; thus, competition among the AFPs for the insured should be regulated to avoid excessive spending of resources. The fourth is to educate the insured concerning requirements, benefits, and the operation of the pension schemes (especially for women): a general consensus exists that the level of understanding of the private program is very low, thus it is necessary to implement education programs, by means of unions and mass communications media, in order to aid the insured in deciding on the pension options at retirement and to decrease the number of transfers among AFPs. The fifth is to improve the pension alternatives: for instance, concerning life annuity, the insurance market has some imperfections such as poor access and lack of transparency in information among selling agents, brokers, and the insured. The sixth is to attenuate the differences in pensions for men and women, a problem that will become more relevant as the scheme matures and the rate of women's participation in the labor market increases (from 20 to 34 percent in 1980–1993).

Why is it that both democratic governments have done very little to tackle these problems and challenges? This important, relevant question deserves further investigation. We have developed some tentative hypotheses in response. First, the Chilean technology was a novel experiment, which now after a decade and a half of close examination is beginning to show clear trends and persistent results. Technical studies, such as the one undertaken here, are sine qua non conditions to understand—and, thereafter, design—viable corrective measures. Social protection should not be exposed to impulsive correction on the part of governments. Second, the more regressive effects are for women, the self-employed, and the poor. These groups have the least political representation, and therefore, their concerns have been traditionally underscored. Third, and supplementing the previous argument, strong interest groups are benefiting from the present state of affairs, namely, AFPs and related businesses (the insurance industry, communications and marketing services, and so on). They tap into the excessive administrative costs that are paid by affiliates. Furthermore, the largest AFPs rent from the high concentration of affiliates, and all of them benefit from the government's guarantee of a minimum yield.

Several lessons can be learned from the Chilean experience. One is that the cost of the transition must be evaluated very carefully. The maintenance of part of the old entitlement, the recognition bonds, and the minimum pension are humane elements of the reform but they are extremely costly; they must be balanced with an accurate assessment of the future burden on society and alternative costs to other public programs for lower-income groups. Another lesson is that the market and private administrators do not necessarily ensure competition, control of evasion and payment delays, and other improvements in efficiency. Huge collective savings have not led to a corresponding expansion of the domestic capital market or to an increase in the rate of national savings. Finally, the exclusion of part of the population (the armed forces) from the reform and the maintenance of its privileged entitlement conditions and benefits can be forced by political reasons but eventually become a salient inequality that must be eradicated. Other Latin American countries (Argentina, Colombia, Peru, and Uruguay) that introduced pension reforms in 1992–1995 have followed models that differ from Chile's, have benefited from Chile's reform lessons, and have eliminated or attenuated many of the problems described in this study (Mesa-Lago 1989, 1994; Castro Jiménez et al. 1990; Marcel and Arenas 1991; Gillion and Bonilla 1992; SAFP 1994; Uthoff 1995; Mesa-Lago, forthcoming).

Note

Throughout this chapter, dollars ($) are U.S. dollars.

References

Arellano, José Pablo. 1989. "La seguridad social en Chile en los años 90." *Colección Estudios CIEPLAN,* no. 27 (December): 63–82.

Arenas de Mesa, Alberto. 1994. "Seguridad social y mercado del trabajo: Inequidades de género en Chile 1980–1994." December. Unpublished manuscript.

———. 1995. "The Gender Effect of the Social Security Reform in Chile: Inequalities and Lesson of Policies." June. Unpublished manuscript.

Arenas de Mesa, Alberto, and Mario Marcel C. 1993. "Proyecciones de gasto previsional 1992–2038: Un modelo de simulación para los bonos de reconocimiento." Documento de Trabajo, Dirección de Presupuestos, Ministerio de Hacienda. Santiago. February.

Arenas de Mesa, Alberto, and Verónica Montecinos. 1996. "The Privatization of Social Security and Women's Welfare: Gender Effects of the Chilean Reform." February. Manuscript.

Arrau, Patricio. 1991. "La reforma previsional chilena y su financiamiento durante la transición." *Colección Estudios CIEPLAN,* no. 32 (June): 5–44.

———. 1992. "El nuevo régimen previsional chileno." In *Regímenes pensionales,* by FESCOL, 37–65. Bogotá.

Baeza, Sergio, and Rodrigo Manubens. 1988. *Sistema privado de pensiones en Chile.* Santiago: Centro de Estudios Públicos.

Bonilla García, Alejandro. 1991. "Informe de Misión Santiago de Chile." Geneva: International Labour Organization. October, 5–12.

Borzutzky, Silvia. 1991. "The Chicago Boys, Social Security and Welfare." In *The Radical Right and the Welfare State: An International Assessment*, ed. Howard Gleenerster and James Midgley, 79–99. Hertfordshire, England: Harvester Wheatsheaf.

Bustamante Jeraldo, Julio. 1991. "El sistema de pensiones en Chile." In *Seminario fondo de pensiones.* Mexico City: Bolsa Mexicana de Valores.

Bustos-Castillo, Raúl. 1993. "Analysis of a National Private Pension Scheme: The Case of Chile, Comments." *International Labour Review* 132 (3): 407–16.

Castro Jiménez, María, et al. 1990. "Los seguros privados en Chile: ¿Evolución o extinción de la seguridad social?" *Seguridad Social*, no. 173 (October–December): 77–125.

Cheyre Valenzuela, Hernán. 1991. *La previsión en Chile ayer y hoy: Impacto de una reforma.* Santiago: Centro de Estudios Públicos.

Corporación de Investigación, Estudio y Desarrollo de la Seguridad Social (CIEDESS). 1992. *12 años de modernización de la seguridad social en Chile: Evaluación crítica y proyecciones.* Santiago: CIEDESS.

Ferrara, Peter J. 1989. "The Privatization of Social Security in Chile." *Journal of Economic Growth* (spring): 18–27.

Fundación Friedrich Ebert de Colombia (FESCOL). 1992. *Regímenes pensionales.* Bogotá: FESCOL.

Gillion, Colin, and Alejandro Bonilla. 1992. "Analysis of a National Private Pension Scheme: The Case of Chile." *International Labour Review* 131 (2): 171–95.

Habitat. 1991. *10 años de historia del sistema de AFP, 1981–1991.* Santiago: Habitat.

Iglesias P., Augusto, and Rodrigo Acuña R. 1991. *Chile: Experiencia con un régimen de capitalización, 1981–1991.* Santiago: CEPAL/PNUD Sistemas de Pensiones en América Latina.

Inter-American Development Bank (IADB). 1980–1995. *Economic and Social Progress in Latin America, 1980 to 1995.* Washington, D.C.

International Labour Organization (ILO). 1992. *Report of the Director General.* Thirteenth Conference of American States Members of the ILO, Caracas, September 30–October 7. Geneva: ILO.

Marcel, Mario, and Alberto Arenas. 1991. "Reformas a la seguridad social en Chile." IADB Series Monografías, no. 5. Washington, D.C.

Margozzini, Francisco. 1991. "El sistema privado de pensiones chileno." Santiago. Unpublished manuscript.

Mesa-Lago, Carmelo. 1978. *Social Security in Latin America: Pressure Groups, Stratification and Inequality.* Pittsburgh: University of Pittsburgh Press.

———. 1987. "Chile SAL III Report on Pension System." Washington, D.C.: World Bank.

———. 1988. "Review of Chile SAL III Conditions: Pension System." Washington, D.C.: World Bank.

———. 1989. *Ascent to Bankruptcy: Financing Social Security in Latin America.* Pittsburgh: University of Pittsburgh Press.

———. 1990. *La seguridad social y el sector informal.* Investigaciones sobre Empleo, no. 32. Santiago: PREALC.

———. 1991a. *Portfolio Performance of Selected Social Security Institutes in Latin America.* World Bank Discussion Papers, no. 139. Washington, D.C.

———. 1991b. *Social Security and Prospects for Equity in Latin America.* World Bank Discussion Papers, no. 140. Washington, D.C.

———. 1991c. "Social Security in Latin America." In *Economic and Social Progress in Latin America, 1980 to 1995,* by IADB, 179–216. Washington, D.C.: IADB.

———. 1994. *Changing Social Security in Latin America: Toward Alleviating the Costs of Economic Reform.* Boulder, Colo., and London: Lynne Rienner.

———. 1996. "The Reform of Social Security Pensions in Latin America: Public, Private, Mixed and Parallel Systems." Unpublished manuscript, University of Pittsburgh.

———, forthcoming. *Market, Socialists, and Mixed Economies: Comparative Policy and Performance—Chile, Cuba, and Costa Rica.* Baltimore: Johns Hopkins University Press.

Piñera, José. 1991. *El cascabel al gato: La batalla por la reforma previsional.* Santiago: Zig-Zag.

Santamaría, Marco. 1992. "Privatizing Social Security: The Chilean Case." *Columbia Journal of World Business* 27 (spring): 38–51.

Superintendencia de Administradoras de Fondos de Pensiones (SAFP). 1981–1995. *Boletín Estadístico Mensual,* nos. 1–130. Santiago.

———. 1994. *El sistema chileno de pensiones.* Santiago: SAFP.

Superintendencia de Seguridad Social (SUSESO). 1982–1994. *Seguridad social: Estadísticas, 1980 to 1993.* Santiago: SUSESO.

———. 1995. *Estadísticas mensuales de seguridad social.* Santiago: SUSESO.

Uthoff, Andras. 1995. *Reformas a los sistemas de pensiones en América Latina y el Caribe.* Santiago: CEPAL.

4 / Mexico

The Politics of the System for Retirement Pensions

Julián F. Bertranou

THE DISLOCATION OF THE pattern of relations between the state, society, and the market, globally prevailing in the most important countries of Latin America between the 1930s and the beginning of the 1980s, slowly convinced governments and the social sectors best positioned after the crisis of the need to reformulate the rules of the game that structure public policies.[1] The reformulation proposals presented by the Latin American leaders were strongly influenced by the neoconservative diagnosis that developed, since the beginning of the 1970s, around the governability crisis of the "Keynesian" states of Europe and North America.

However, it would not be adequate to see in the reformulation of the rules of the game of Latin American public policies only an unproblematic definition of the situation to resolve, or a rational application of optimal means, designed by authorities that previously had defined the specific goals of the public action (for the rational model, see Allison 1971). The criteria of technical optimization in the design of the new rules of the game, of course, took part in the process of reformulation of public policies but did so by interacting with other criteria, values, and issues. Behind public policy making (and especially social policy making) in Latin America, a real "politics" developed, which included various participants, their ideas, interests, and resources, and their strategies of intervention and bargaining. This bargaining was structured by a dynamic process of problematization and definition of proposals for solutions.

My task here is to explain the politics behind the nonstructural pension reform approved in Mexico between 1990 and the beginning of 1992, whose innovative component was the System for Retirement Savings (Sistema de Ahorro para el Retiro, SAR). This is a supplementary pension system, administered by the private financial sector in the form of individual accounts that are open to all the workers of the formal economy. I shall attempt to explore a complex series of situations and interactions that developed prior to this public policy equilibrium: the participants included, the differentiated problematizations, the dynamics of bargaining, the strategies of intervention, and the external influences. I shall analyze only the policy-making process of the SAR, leaving the complex process of implementation for future study.

I shall focus on two main issues. First, behind the formulation of the SAR, a political and dynamic process incorporated various participants differently. The process experienced a gradual problematization process on the part of government, witnessed a changing definition of the game or space of the reform to agree upon, and ended up in a negotiation in the context of other public policy problems. Second, the first government proposal—which contained a more radical reform to the existing rules of the game in the social security system than the one that was finally approved—was modified substantially during this dynamic interactive process. This was because of the trade unions' intervention, which effectively used resources and strategies included in the corporate agreements with the government. Mexican public decision making is characterized by continuous bargaining among three main interest groups (government, business, workers) under a corporate scheme. Thus corporate agreement on public and labor policies constitute fundamental definitions with long-lasting socioeconomic consequences. After a brief analysis of the antecedents of the project, I will explore the different stages of the interaction, and the equilibria—intermediate and final—obtained in its course.

An epilogue, written in collaboration with Carmelo Mesa-Lago, will summarize the principal features of the structural pension reform that was approved and regulated by Congress in 1995–1996, which began implementation in 1997. The purpose of this final section is to inform the reader of the most recent developments in this field in Mexico. Limitations of time and space impede any analysis of the politics behind this second, structural pension reform.

ANTECEDENTS

Among the antecedents of the government's project for the reformulation of the public social security system, three appear the most important and influential: the recent development of the Mexican social security system, the Chilean privatization experience, and the reform-oriented impetus of the private financial sector. The Mexican Social Security Institute (Instituto Mexicano del Seguro Social, IMSS) was created in 1943 for the administration of sickness/maternity, accidents on the job, and pension insurance programs. The IMSS was financed through tripartite contributions (from workers, the state, and employers) for the benefit of all Mexican workers and their families. From the start, the Disability, Old Age, Unemployment, and Death Insurance Program (Seguro de Invalidez, Vejez, Cesantía y Muerte, SIVCM) produced a considerable surplus, given the few number of beneficiaries at the beginning and the great number of contributors. The SIVCM's financial operating method started as one of fixed premium.[2] In 1973 it was transformed into a scaled premium method. (The premium was set for a six-year period, even though in fact it did not change between 1943 and 1990.) After the devastating effects of inflation in the mid-1980s, SIVCM's operation reserves fell in 1987 to 13 percent of that year's pensions program cost. The pensions program began working as a pay-as-you-go (PAYG) or pure assessment method, with a minor contingency reserve (Mesa-Lago 1991b).[3]

Three main elements explain this process. The first is related to the maturity of the system, in particular the growth of beneficiaries at a greater rate than that of the contributors. The pensioner/contributor relation was 20:1 in 1960, 11:1 in 1983, and fell to 7:1 at the end of the 1980s. Even though that relation was still broad, the low level of contribution (6 percent between the employer and the worker before 1990, 7.6 percent afterward) caused obstacles for the autonomous administration of the program, which continues to deteriorate—forecasting for the first decade of the twenty-first century, the incorporation of 500,000 annual benefits, in the midst of a stagnated labor market (Aspe 1992). The second element has to do precisely with this last point. The aging of the population has pressed the system on the side of the number of benefits, but the stagnation of formal employment (with the obligation of contributing) during the last two decades has done so on the side of the revenues. The third element deals with investments made in the past. The important funds accumulated during the first years were used to shore up the imbalance in the sickness/maternity program, mainly through the construction of a hospital infrastructure. A "construction" was chosen for the long-term equilibrium of the SIVCM not through investments with higher yields and on-hand assets but, rather, through the accumulation of fresh funds for the physical construction of the social welfare network (Mesa-Lago 1991a).

The SIVCM's revenue/expenditure relation did not further deteriorate at the end of the 1980s because of the abrupt fall in the value of pensions (almost 60 percent between 1980 and 1988). In 1988, a federal government study shows that 85 percent of the pensions were barely equal to 35 percent of the minimum wage (Eibenschutz 1992). This fall in the level of the pensions generated important protests from the National Unified Movement of Retirees (Movimiento Unificado Nacional de Jubilados y Pensionados, MUNJP), which pressed for reforms to the social insurance act, the Ley del Seguro Social. In 1989, a reform managed to stabilize the minimum pension at a level of 70 percent of the minimum wage. In December 1990, a more integral reform to the Ley del Seguro Social occurred: the minimum value of the pension was established at 80 percent of the minimum wage, while the global contribution to the system was set at 7.6 percent of the salary (2 percent from the worker, 5.6 percent from the employer).

The privatization experience of Chile's public pensions system exerted great influence on the Mexican reform. (See chapter 1 for a summary of the characteristics of the Chilean substitutive-private model, and chapters 2 and 3 for a detailed analysis of this model.) The last section of this chapter will summarize the differences between the Mexican structural reform of 1995–1996 and the Chilean model.

It is worth mentioning, as a last antecedent, the formation and development of the institutions of the private financial sector. After the bank nationalization of 1982, consecutive governments started the gradual opening of opportunities for the consolidation of private institutions. Growth and modernization of the financial market was prompted by several instruments, such as the immediate—though partial—bank reprivatization and the management of the stock market by special stockbrokers *(casas de bolsas)*. Primarily, the stockbrokers were acquiring real dynamism and importance in the financial network, gradually controlling the mobile capital, an economic and political resource of great relevance. The control of this resource and the stockbrokers' ideological affinity with the monetary authorities—the Secretaría de Hacienda y Crédito Público (SHCP) and the Bank of Mexico

(Banxico), both becoming more important in the government structure—made the private financial sector a priority ally of the government, starting in the mid-1980s. The SHCP started a dialogue with government, acquiring a truly proactive capacity with respect to public policy making (Garrido 1991). The Mexican Association of Stockbrokers (Asociación Mexicana de Casas de Bolsa, AMCB) have tried—since 1989, and after the legal permit—to administer directly the pension funds of the private firms and pressed the government to make it obligatory to create those supplementary pension funds on the part of the private firms that would consequently dominate an emerging and very lucrative market. In mid-1990, and through its Commission on Pension Funds, the AMCB prepared a project that was sent to the SHCP, which contained the proposal of privatization of the public pension funds through a mechanism of individual accounts in a private financial system like the one in Chile. The project constituted an important antecedent for the government, at the right moment when the latter was analyzing alternatives for the reformulation of the public pensions system.

THE GOVERNMENT'S PROJECT

The government participants that led the process of problematization in the social security sector were the SHCP and Banxico, with the explicit support (and also control) of the presidency.[4] These participants, as bureaucratic organizations, structured themselves along the years interacting mutually and defining common programmatic standards, even in the context of different presidencies. They succeeded in delineating a common matrix of thought, and in uniting themselves closely with the private financial sectors (both domestic and, in many cases, international). These elements gave the SHCP and Banxico important resources at the moment of the intragovernmental competition over the definition of the policies to pursue, a competition these participants established permanently with the bureaucrats of the Secretariats of Agrarian Reform and of State Enterprises, both strongly related to expansive policies. Beginning with the De la Madrid government, the SHCP and Banxico finally achieved a central position in the network of bureaucratic participants that establishes the government's action lines, intervening in a central way in most of the public policy problems. In the case of SAR, the withdrawal of both the IMSS and the Secretariat of Labor and Social Security (Secretaría de Trabajo y Previsión Social, STPS) from the government problematization process was observed, despite their natural competence. The STPS primarily played the role of presidential operator at the time of the negotiations with the unions.

In the beginning of 1990, and after a first diagnosis of the public pensions system and its impact in the political mobilization of the retired, the Pensions Stabilization Program was created, to be coordinated by both the SHCP and Banxico. In the context of this program, various trips were made to exemplary countries (Chile, Argentina, the United States, and Singapore, among others) with the purposes of studying the different mechanisms of response to the challenges imposed by social security systems and of establishing profound comparisons with the Mexican case. The directors of the program were strongly influenced by the results of the Chilean experience, as much in relation to its ordering of the public pensions system, as to the formation of a local capital market. The Chilean "solution" not only helped consolidate the problem of the IMSS's financial situation but contributed in part to develop the problem of the scarcity of national internal savings.[5]

During 1990, then, the government problematization exhibited two different core ideas: first, the increasing financial problem of the SIVCM and of the IMSS, which had a short-run impact on the low pensions and consequently on the mobilization of the MUNJP and a long-term effect on the future, growing state financing of the public pensions system; and second, the low levels of domestic savings in the country. This second core idea was based on the new governmental considerations concerning the centrality of domestic savings in the process of economic development and the need to raise the rate, in fifteen years, from around 20 percent of the GDP to about 28 percent. Through one public policy (the public pensions system reform), the government attempted to link both problematic points.

At the end of 1990, the government had finished a first sketch of the reformulation of the system. It was not made public and contained very imprecise elements about the reform. But the important point is that the government did present a scheme for changed game rules, different from the existing ones in Mexican social security. The central elements of the proposal were three: (1) the immediate creation of a pensions system that was supplementary to the public one (IMSS) and privately administered (the type of administration was not clear); (2) the gradual incorporation of contributions to the IMSS and to the supplementary system: in five years, half the contribution to the SIVCM would go to the new system, the other half being incorporated in ten years (total transference); and (3) the global contributions to the system would grow until the final privatization (it was not clear what the initial contribution to the system would be, only that it would be paid by the employers).

This first version was informally presented to the IMSS authorities and to the Social Union of Mexican Businessmen (Unión Social de Empresarios Mexicanos, USEM). The high functionaries of the IMSS (the administration council of the IMSS with a three-sided representation—government, labor, and business) and certain mid-level bureaucratic sectors of the IMSS were opposed to the total "privatization" of the public pensions system (specifically, to the separation of the SIVCM from the IMSS, even in a gradual way). There were at least three reasons for their attitude: (1) the defense of the structure of employments probably affected by the measure; (2) certain doubts about the impact of the proposal on the IMSS financial situation; and (3) the existence of a strongly anchored perception in the institution as to who might to be in charge of the administration of social services and under which rules. From an ethic-valorative point of view, IMSS authorities were concerned about the need to preserve the structure of state administration, and to guarantee conditions of solidarity and equity. The businessmen consulted (USEM) expressed their approval of the transference of state responsibilities to the private sector, but they did not hide their fear of seeing the employers' contributions grow (labor costs), especially with regard to the challenges of Mexican integration into the world market. Although the USEM is a relatively marginal institution in the context of business representation, its opinions paralleled the existence in the other institutions (the Chambers), whose participation was to be more relevant at the moment of the crucial negotiations.

During 1990 and 1991, certain new elements would make the government's view more complex. The first intervening element was bank privatization. In the context of government's policy for the liberalization and privatization of state assets, and after repeated pressures on the part of the private financial sector (stockbrokers), the government decided to transfer to private hands the eighteen commercial banks that were allowed to operate in the market. The implementation of this transfer raised important constraints in the money supply and in the banks' levels of deposits. The banks, closely tied to the *casas de bolsa* (in many cases, led by them), pressed SHCP and Banxico for the creation of financial investment instruments that would enable the restructuring of their assets. The government understood the need to create financial mechanisms to stabilize the money supply (including proper regulation for pension funds), which had been requested before by the stockbrokers and now by the banks.

A second intervening element was the struggle that originated among the different financial institutions for the administration of the pension funds that were eventually to be created. The financial participants—*casas de bolsa,* insurance companies, banks—were familiar only with the first government sketch, and (beyond certain discrepancies) they all agreed with the logic of the reform. But it was still not clear which institutions were to be in charge of the funds' administration. The banks argued that they had a broader infrastructure of accounts and agencies across the country. The stockbrokers insisted that they were more flexible to administer financial instruments and to obtain higher rates for the insured. Although the bank reprivatization later bound these two types of institution together, the process of privatization was not sufficiently clear at the outset, and the institutions were quite different.

The third element has to do with the actuarial report of the IMSS, which was presented to the SHCP accompanied by an analysis of the situation of the SIVCM. Until 1990, the register of contingencies of the SIVCM showed a deficit, at a current value of 181 trillion pesos (around US$60 billion).[6] To provide a better financing of the SIVCM within the present scheme, the IMSS recommended actions toward an increase of contributions (both from the employers and from the insured) and a fight against employers' evasion. The SHCP evaluated the figure and delivered an internal document, which emphasized the need not only to raise the levels of contributions but also to change the present rules of the game, including a segment of the private administration.

In mid-1991, the government made the basic scheme of reformulation of the public pensions system even more precise. This was after a complex process of problematization that incorporated four central areas: the first two —the financial problems of the IMSS and domestic savings—have already been mentioned; the third is related to the need to consolidate financially the recently privatized banks, and more generally, the financial system; and the fourth, less important, has to do with the possibility of using genuine sources of state financing. The government presented the proposal in June 1991 to the Labor Congress (Congreso del Trabajo, CT) requesting its approval. The CT coordinates the actions of various different labor confederations such as the CTM, CROM, CROC, and so on that are tied to the corporate agreements.[7] The CT was the most important labor representative at the time of the macropolitical negotiations between government and business; its direction is managed alternatively by the leaders of the principal confederations.

It is worth remarking that in the Mexican political system (contrary to other countries, even of Latin America), the public decision-making process does not include parliament as a clear space of substantive policy definition. Decisions are made outside parliament, among the participants allowed to work in the process (government participants, and others structured under the corporate scheme such as the labor confederations and certain business representatives), and along procedures that limit the possibility of public intervention, to find only formal support in the legislative branch. Despite the relative deterioration of its bargaining power during the 1980s (in comparison with that of business, for example), the labor movement was still an important participant in the definition of the general lines of public action, in the context of the global tripartite agreements that characterize the Mexican decision process.

At the same time, given the characteristics of the project, the labor participation was considered the most self-interested, and also as the biggest obstacle. For this reason, the government privileged labor in the treatment of the proposal, leaving business for another time. The government's project, which was not known publicly, included the following elements: (1) There would be the creation of a complementary system of pensions. (2) The administration would be managed by the banking system, through individual accounts open to all workers. (3) The contribution would be paid entirely by the employers, and it would be established at 2 percent of the salary. (4) The state would establish minimum and maximum values of investments (for the commercial banking sector). (5) The insured would be able to transfer funds to an investment bank or Sociedad de Inversión, assuming individually the risks of lower or higher investment rates. (6) Banxico would control the productive allocation of the funds. The investments would be made, in first stage, in public bonds. It was not yet clear what the program for the investment banks would be. (7) The SIVCM would gradually be incorporated into the new complementary system, separating it from the other insurance programs of the IMSS.

The government decided that the commercial banks would be the receivers of the pension funds but left open the possibility for the insured, that the funds would be administered by investment banks (trying in that way to conform with all the participants of the financial system). At the same time, the government decided to save for itself the right to impose minimum and maximum investment rates for the funds (at least, in the commercial banking sector), and to make it obligatory that these funds be invested, in a first stage, in public bonds. On one hand, the government wanted genuine sources of state financing; on the other hand, it wanted to prove gradually the efficacy of the system, and its real impact on the financial circuit. The government did not want to leave the funds entirely to the free administration of the banks.

INTERACTION WITH THE UNIONS

After the government presented its project to the CT, there began a period of extremely important interactions with labor leaders, a period divided into two main stages. In the first stage, the unions rejected the project, and a precarious public policy equilibrium was established. In the second stage, the government, upsetting this precarious equilibrium, decided to broaden the space of reform, thus originating a new battle with the unions that would end with the final formulation of the SAR. I will treat these points in detail.

The unions' rejection of the project of separation and gradual privatization of the SIVCM was immediate, though not immediately public. It had close antecedents, since the union leaders, facing earlier versions of a possible privatization of the social security system, had already expressed their opposition publicly. This forced then IMSS General Director Emilio Camboa and President Carlos Salinas de Gortari to make pronouncements reaffirming the status quo in order to calm emotions on the eve of federal elections of great importance for the presidential legitimacy.

The labor movement—and especially the CTM, the most important labor confederation, led by Fidel Velázquez—analyzed social security in a manner different from the government's. There are four main elements of its problematization. First, the defense of the welfare network was built over many years thanks to the CTM's protesting action, which tried to assure increasing levels of social service even in a context of salary deterioration.[8] The second element is to resolve the problem of the IMSS, not the domestic savings rate. The instruments of financial ordering of the IMSS do not include privatization, but rather, its administrative rationalization, the increase in the level of the employer's contribution, and the elimination of employers' evasion. The third element is that the problem of pensions is framed by the much broader problem of increasing unemployment. For this issue, the CTM brought back its proposal of creating a national unemployment fund, financed by employer contributions. With this fund, the workers would be protected against all labor contingencies that could end up in temporary or definitive unemployment: actual unemployment, retirement, old age, sickness, and unjustified dismissals. The fourth element is that the structure of social services is a part of the institutional basis of the corporate agreement, so any change in the former is seen as a reduction of the unions' power and resources.

To continue this last point, the corporate agreement in the Mexican political system—although in a gradual weakening process—implies for the government, among other things, a certain political control over the citizens, and popular support for the political system. For business, it implies conditions of capitalist productive accumulation. In the case of labor, it means the extension of social services, union participation in the administration of the services, and the creation of union leadership. The IMSS and, particularly, the system of pensions belong to a much broader structure of social institutions with tripartite administration, such as Fonacot, Infonavit, and ISSSTE.[9] Union participation by the Secretariat of Public Education also figures, especially in favor of the labor movement, as the basic agreements that support Mexican corporatism. The substantial reform of these social service institutions was perceived by the unions as an attempt to change the labor movement's structure of resources derived from the macropolitical corporate agreements.

In this way, the CTM exhibited another vision of the public policy game and, at the same time, the rules that would govern it.[10] For the CTM, the game included a global perspective on the phenomenon of unemployment. The game would be limited and governed by rules that were closer to the existing ones: maintenance of the SIVCM in the IMSS, three-sided administration of the IMSS, and joint administration of the resources, and so on. What the government and the unions discussed at the outset was a vision of the rules of the game that would govern it.

During the months of July and August 1991, most of the interactions between the two central participants—the government and the CTM—took place. The resources used by the participants and the strategies of negotiation were easily apparent. The unions' strong resistance to the gradual transference of the SIVCM to the private financial sector, and the government's later withdrawal of this proposal, showed labor's veto capacity to initiatives that "unstructure" the social service institutes related to the welfare network. This veto capacity is important when the discussion is fundamentally over projects that "affect" the IMSS, given its centrality in the welfare network (service coverage) and in the prevailing corporate agreement. The government, even in the context of important discretional spaces of policy making, needs (among other things) the explicit or tacit support of the participants engaged in the corporate scheme, in order to maintain margins of legitimacy (Salinas needed to reconstruct his legitimacy after his inauguration). This margin of power on the part of the CTM enables it at least to veto initiatives that not only can break the welfare structure it is fighting for but also can undermine the proper institutional basis of the corporate agreement.

The union's rejection thwarted the government's ability to solve the SIVCM's growing financial problem, at least from its own perspective, that is, through the gradual transference of the public pensions system to private administration. Nevertheless, the government insisted on the maintenance of a complementary scheme, only that it would not receive contributions paid to the IMSS. In this way, the government decided to promote the other objectives included in its problematization; fundamentally, the ones referring to the increase of the domestic savings rate, and the consolidation of the financial system. For the CTM, the complementary scheme meant another social service, without even touching the existing structure. It pressed, though, for two changes. Through the first change, the individual funds would be administered by the Banco Obrero, or labor bank. This proposal was not accepted by the government (it meant renouncing another of its goals), which, in exchange, intervened to eliminate the debts acquired by the bank. The second change entailed union intervention in the productive allocation of accumulated funds, but this was also rejected because it meant too great an interference in public policy making. During the process of negotiation, the STPS played an important role in bringing the participants' positions closer.

The public policy equilibrium obtained after the interaction, which later was revealed to be very precarious, consisted of the creation of a complementary pensions system, administered by commercial banks through individual accounts and financed by new employer contributions. The unions obtained the creation of a new service, without any changes to the existing social services structure. They could not impose, though, the project of the Unemployment Fund, which revealed its "defensive" strength (veto) as more important than its "offensive" strength (proposal). The government lost the possibility to tackle structurally the financial problem of the SIVCM, although it managed to create a structure of individual accounts, which would become an instrument that could increase the feasibility of future reform. At the same time, it obtained the creation of an investment system that could eventually raise domestic savings and consolidate the financial system. Nevertheless, the resources aimed at these two goals were relatively scarce (2 percent of wages and salaries).

This last point is the main source of the government's nonconformity with the equilibrium attained, which led the way to the second stage of the already mentioned interactions. At the end of September 1991, the government decided to modify the space of reform, thus broadening the public policy game. It achieved this through the incorporation into the SAR of the employers' contributions to Infonavit. With this move, the SAR would include two subaccounts—retirement insurance and the housing fund—that would then both be administered by the commercial banks. The employers' contribution to Infonavit was 5 percent of salaries, so with the proposal of its incorporation to the SAR, every worker would be the exclusive owner of the accumulation and investment of 7 percent of his monthly salary (5 percent of the housing fund plus 2 percent of the retirement insurance).

The idea of managing the Infonavit funds by private administration arose during the elaboration of the first sketch of the SAR project at the end of 1990. This was strongly anchored on the administration and corruption problems existing in the IMSS. The government used this alternative mainly to maximize the goals that would be attained through the SAR domestic savings (consolidation of the financial system and the banks, state financing), a maximization that would be achieved through an increase in the level of deposits. But it would not be correct to discard from the government's motivations the manifest goal of ordering and clarifying the administration of the housing promotional funds, and the process of allocating these.

The union rejection did not wait. Both the three-sided administration of the IMSS's collective funds and housing construction, and the possibility to allocate closed quotas of loans to worker members of the different confederations (proportionally to the site of their membership) were instruments that formally and informally consolidated, in many ways, the economic power of the unions, and their control capacity over clientele structures of exchange. The governmental initiative dealt a hard blow to the consolidation of these resources, particularly the economic one. The unions presented other solutions: to raise the employer's contribution to 10 percent, to capitalize the

IMSS, to check the housing construction costs, and to make more effective the fight against employer evasion.

The discussion about the inclusion of the Infonavit extended over the next four months, as much in the private sphere of negotiations as in the public discursive one. Meanwhile, the Mexican Republic Employers' Confederation (Coparmex), the highest business representative in the macropolitical agreements with the government and the unions, in October reengaged in an important programmatic and discursive crusade to obtain reforms in the administration of social services, in labor legislation, and in economic policies. These reform proposals were not new since they had been developing gradually during the 1980s in the context of the reorganization of the economic structure.

On one hand, Coparmex searched for reforms in the labor legislation (Ley Federal de Trabajo, LFT), which would allow reductions in the labor cost facing the establishment of NAFTA. On the other hand, Coparmex sought to be politically positioned before the beginning of the negotiations in November 1991 to renew the Stability, Competitiveness, and Employment Pact (Pacto de Estabilidad, Competitividad y Empleo, PECE), the highest example of definition of revenue policy between government, labor, and business and a concrete expression of the corporate political structure (Zapata 1992). Although the exchange between Coparmex and CT ended up in a theatrical session directed by Labor Secretary Arsenio Farell, the skirmish showed other public policy games to impact on the social security game. The other games intervening were labor legislation (reforms to the LFT), NAFTA, and the PECE.

In the context of the PECE, the CTM tried to close the social security reform game in the precariously agreed instance of September, that is, before the government's intention of including the Infonavit. The final contribution to the SAR was set at 2 percent during the PECE negotiations, even though this was not included in the formal and explicit agreements. Business agreed to contribute to the SAR but succeeded in compensating the contribution, directly, through an accepted smaller increase in salaries (only 12 percent) and, indirectly, thanks to the state promise of making the contribution deductible from the Impuesto sobre la Renta (ISR) income tax (35 percent of the capital). The unions thought that negotiations over the reform had concluded, but the government understood the PECE as a definition only of the retirement insurance, so later, the government would insist even more on the incorporation of the Infonavit.

THE RESOLUTION OF THE SAR

The government-union interaction (in its second stage) began after November. It traveled through the channels of the public policy resolution (final decision). This resolution was built during two institutionally precise stages: first (the more important), when the public policy game and the rules that would structure it were defined (which we shall call preparliamentarian); and second, when the discussion was set mainly within the rules of the game previously agreed upon.

The official project of including Infonavit contributions into the SAR was presented to the CT by Finance Secretary Pedro Aspe at the end of November. The banking and individual administration of the contributions were established, so that the total fund reached at least 10 percent of the value of the house. With this amount, the worker could choose to make a down payment to a loan granted by the financial system through the Infonavit, to build or acquire a house. The project kept the unions' intervention in the allocation of residences.

The CT (and particularly the CTM) reacted negatively, because of a different problematization. In the same way as in the retirement insurance, the CTM rejected the inclusion within the social services administration of policies that it believed could damage the principle of collective solidarity among workers. At the same time, it refused to lose influence in a power scheme that had previously assured it spaces of political and economic control over many years. The labor movement decided to consolidate its position by two means: first, through the formulation of a proposal of rationalization of the Infonavit, with a different plan than the one presented by the government;[11] and second, with the rejection of the informal agreements on retirement insurance.

The government answered positively to the union proposals, except to the proposal to increase the employer's contribution. But it insisted not only on changes within the existing scheme of the Infonavit rules of the game, but on a substantial change in these rules through the transference of the contribution administration from the Infonavit to the private financial sector. At the beginning of January 1992, and in the middle of MUNJP mobilizations and sit-ins, the government presented the final SAR project to the CT for approval. The union leaders pointed out various internal contradictions with respect to the presented project. Cuauhtémoc Paleta, CROM general secretary and in turn president of the CT, speaking on behalf of the CT, announced explicitly the support of the proposed measures, as much for the creation of the complementary retirement insurance as for the private administration of the employers' contributions to the Infonavit (see *El Financiero*, January 10, 15, 1992). In turn the CTM, by way of Fidel Velázquez, manifested support only for the creation of the retirement insurance. At the same time, and contradicting other of Paleta's opinions, the CTM leader maintained that the government had not taken union leaders into account in the discussion of the financial reformulation project of the Infonavit (see *La Jornada*, January 15, 1992).

The government used all available resources in its two strategies to obtain the support (even passive) of the CTM, the most important confederation: isolation (by gaining support from certain competitive union leaders such as Cuauhtémoc Paleta) and threats, which took two forms: first, playing with the idea of imprisoning all union leaders that did not fulfill their tax obligations; and second, toying also with the idea of imposing reforms on labor legislation. This last point played a crucial part in the government's domination of the CTM; the union finally approved the Infonavit reform in order to avoid changes in labor legislation (*El Financiero*, January 11, 1992).

January 1992 elapsed in the midst of versions that mentioned the possibility of initiating deep reforms to Article 123 of the Mexican Constitution and to the LFT, versions placated by the CTM support of government projects, particularly the one relating to the Infonavit, were achieved. It was then that Labor Secretary Arsenio Farell publicly announced official intentions of not effecting any reform to the labor legislation. The CTM attempted to introduce two elements in the final lap: the first was that the worker could use 10 percent of the amount in the retirement insurance account in the case of temporary unemployment. The CTM was trying to develop antecedents for the implementation of its unemployment fund proposal. The second (and more important with respect to the rules of the game) was the inclusion of CTM in the fund allocation. The first proposal was accepted; the second was again rejected.

In the middle of this process to resolve the game and its rules, the government decided to call for extraordinary sessions in Congress beginning on February 10, 1992, to discuss (among other important bills) the SAR project, that is, social security, Infonavit, and income tax reforms. Parliamentary action did not present any surprises regarding the movement of the bills. The important PRI majority preserved the bill from substantial modifications from the other parties, especially by the PRD and the PPS, the initiative's main opponents.[12] The PAN proposal of eliminating the 6 percent maximum investment rate for the fund was the only important change, which thus assured the new rules of the game that had been crafted into the Mexican social security with the SAR.[13]

Some skirmishes of relative importance for the government developed with the CTM and its own legislators. Previous to the Congress Commissions' report, the CTM threatened to boycott the approval of the bills if some reforms were not made. These reforms did not represent any major change to the rules previously agreed upon but meant a CTM attempt to position itself in a better way within the accorded general scheme.[14] Beyond the discursive tone of the dispute, it was not a struggle for the game and its rules, but within it. Although the PRI did not need the CTM votes, the government conceded most of the modifications because of the possible political costs derived from a marginalization of the union. On February 24, 1992, the bills were passed, and some days later, retirement insurance was extended to the public employee members of the ISSSTE.

CONCLUSION

In this section, more than a mere summary of the above argument, I intend to extract a set of conclusions from the analysis (referring to the case study), which can then become questions that structure a comparative research agenda. The SAR policy-making study reveals the fundamental role played by ideas in the policy problematization and definition process. Ideas are no more than ways to organize and understand surrounding reality. In a certain sense, they are theories.

Public policies, in parallel fashion, may be understood as working hypotheses. Policy reform proposals do not develop if there is not, as a background, an organized set of ideas that can structure diagnosis of the present situation while considering the construction of a future stage. To the existence of ideas, we can also add the existence of equivalent policy experiences, which can act as empirical proof of the value of those ideas. In the case of SAR, the Chilean privatization experience—from the point of view of the ideas and their verification—exerted an important influence on the form and content of the Mexican government's problematization.

Ideas do not materialize in the same way in every country but depend, in each case, on the existing domestic institutions. The Mexican institutions fundamentally conditioned the formulation of the SAR in two ways.[15] First, the government's initial proposal established from the beginning a gradual, not immediate, transference process of the SIVCM to a private administration and gave the private sector important control over the investment of pension funds. On one hand, the government wanted to control the effects of reform, and on the other it anticipated, in a certain way, the unions' response to an even more radical reform. Second, and more important, at the very moment of the establishment of the final equilibrium: a complementary system was to be administered by the private sector, but without the future transference of the SIVCM, or the present reform of the contributions to the IMSS. The still strong union presence—in the public decision-making system and in the context of the corporate agreement instances—mainly transformed the nature of the SHCP's original project, diminishing the introduction of new rules of the game. The same rules tended to undermine the institutional basis of Mexican corporatism. These institutions, and not the ideas, primarily explain the difference between Mexico and Chile, in the degree of transference to the private sector of the public pensions system.

The space of the public policy game's substantial definition in the SAR case was based on the following elements: the preeminence of the executive over the legislative power, the negotiation with social participants (unions and business chambers, and in the context of corporate agreements), the subordination of the official party to the president, and the quasi-hegemonic system of parties. These elements can be analyzed as intervening institutions in the decision-making process in the SAR case. The importance of these institutions can lead us to ask if they are the only intervening ones in all public decision-making processes, or if it is possible to think, from a different point of view, that the intervening institutions (or their degree of engagement) depend on each public decision area.

The government problematization process was very dynamic, and it incorporated gradually a plurality of motivational axes (from the IMSS financial problem to the consolidation of the private commercial banks). The order of these government preferences changes as negotiations progress with the unions. After the unions' reaction, the motivation of structurally reforming the pensions system descended in the order of preferences; the government searched immediately, with the incorporation of the Infonavit, to maximize the other preference, thus modifying the game of reform. The SAR case reveals also that, in such a process, the problem is not always defined previously nor the solution designed later, but that the same problematic definition itself derives from the availability of solutions. To sum up, any concrete policy-making analysis requires interpretative models that can capture the internal complexity of the problematization processes.

The most important participants in the SAR policy-making process were three: the SHCP and Banxico pairing, the CTM, and the financial sector, in that order. SHCP and Banxico showed they were the most dynamic participants in the state problematization process and in the negotiation with the relevant participants. They diagnosed, searched for solutions in the international context, and structured the government's visions of the definition of the policy game on which to agree. The STPS and the IMSS are situated in a subordinate state role. The CTM showed, in the SAR formulation, its strategy of entrenching in the defense (or "status quo") of the social security institutes, and of the labor legislation. In this way, and tied to the formal and informal practices of the corporate agreement with government, the CTM showed more "defensive" than "offensive" (proactive) power, succeeding in breaking the policy of gradual separation of the SIVCM from the IMSS that was suggested in the first government proposal. The private financial sector played an important role in the government's problematization process, on two levels: the proactive level, related to its technical capacity and to the policy of dialogue with the government; and the bargaining level (pressure to derive resources with the goal of consolidating the banks).

Finally, the negotiation for reform in the public pensions system was situated in a more global context of interactions among the same participants and was composed of different policy games. The positions (and threatened changes in position) of the participants in the other policy games impacted the definition and regulation of the social security pensions game. The analysis of the political dynamics prior to the formulation of public policies needs to integrate different spheres, which are a matter of public decision, with the purpose of capturing with more clarity the strategies of the participants, the relative value of the resources they use, and the policy equilibria achieved.

EPILOGUE

After two years of implementation, it became apparent that the SAR program —combined with other nonstructural reforms of the Mexican pension system introduced in 1990–1992—had not contributed in any significant way to any solution of the pension crisis. In January 1995 the IMSS itself published an actuarial study, which showed that its pension program would endure a financial deficit in the year 2002, and its reserves would disappear in two more years. In October 1995 the two major confederations—of trade unions and businessmen—designed a comprehensive proposal for the reform of the social security system and presented it to President Zedillo. This proposal formed the basis for the pension reform law that was enacted in December 1995 and the regulations that were enacted in April 1996. Initially the system was expected to begin operations at the start of 1997, but because of several difficulties its implementation was postponed until later that year. In this section we summarize the principal features of the Mexican structural reform, particularly those features that differ from the pure substitutive Chilean model that inspired it.

The old age and unemployment/dismissal pension program was taken out of the IMSS and transferred to a new fully funded individual (FFI) system managed by administrators (AFOREs), which also handle the SAR program. The IMSS has kept the administration of the disability and death insurance, as well as other social security programs. All current insured must transfer to the AFOREs (unlike in Chile, the insured in the IMSS do not have the right to choose to stay in this system or move to the new one), and all new entrants in the labor force must join the new system. Thus the IMSS old age and unemployment program is entirely shut down.

The insured in the new system can select the AFORE of his or her choice and may change it once a year (there are no limitations in Chile). As prior to the reform, salaried workers in the private sector (and a few others in the public sector) are mandatorily covered by the new system, while the self-employed has optional coverage. Other social insurance institutions covering the armed forces, federal employees, and petroleum workers are excluded from the reform and retain their own programs.

As in Chile, contributions are defined, but employers' contributions are not eliminated. Both the insured and the employer contributions remain unchanged but the state must increase its contribution to the AFOREs. The total contribution has risen from 10.5 to 12.5 percent—8.5 percent goes to AFORES (which breaks down as 6.5 percent for old age and unemployment/dismissal and 2 percent for SAR) and 4 percent goes to IMSS (for disability and death). Additional voluntary contributions without a cap can be made by the insured to the old age program. The IMSS collects all contributions, retains its own, and transfers the corresponding to the AFOREs and other institutions. AFOREs charge a percentage commission on contributions or the accumulated pension fund.

As in Chile, benefits are not defined. The age of retirement is unchanged (sixty-five years for both sexes) but the years of contribution have been increased from ten to twenty-four. There is no recognition bond as in Chile, but the number of years contributed in the old system are counted to fulfill the twenty-four-year requirement. At the time of retirement the current insured can choose between two pensions: (1) one pension estimated according to the old entitlement conditions (at IMSS) and (2) the sum accumulated in the insured's individual account at the AFORE (such an option does not exist in Chile). If the first option is chosen, the AFORE fund goes to the Treasury. In both cases the insured receives the fund accumulated in the SAR. The insured that decides for the fund at the AFORE can select between a programmed retirement administered by the AFORE or an annuity contracted with an insurance company (similar options as in Chile). There is a minimum pension in the new system as in Chile, submitted to the same conditions of the old age pension, but no assistance pension for the noninsured destitute (such as the assistance pension that is available in Chile).

AFOREs should be administered by corporations of exclusive dedication but, different from Chile, they can be private (including banks), public (including one managed by the IMSS), and mixed. Each AFORE can have various investment companies (SIEFOREs). Insurance companies that administer retirement annuities can also be private, public or "social." According to the law, as much as 100 percent of the pension fund can be invested in public securities during the first year of operation of the system (considerably more than Chile and the highest proportion among all eight countries with a structural pension reform, except Bolivia). After the first year, a maximum of 51 percent of the pension fund can be invested in instruments adjusted to inflation, a unique feature of the Mexican system. The law prohibits investment in foreign instruments (as much as 10 percent can be invested in Chile).

The state has the following responsibilities in the new system. Current pensions and those of insured who in the future decide for the old entitlement conditions are financed out of the IMSS reserves, but when the reserves are depleted (in six or seven years) the state will finance these pensions. The government also guarantees a minimum pension in the new system, equal to one minimum salary in the federal district, annually adjusted to the consumer price index. The state payroll contribution to pensions has been raised from 0.425 to 2.375 percent. CONSAR, a national commission for savings for retirement financed by the state, will regulate and supervise the new system. But the state will neither issue a recognition bond nor guarantee a minimum yield for the AFOREs investment, or pensions in case of bankruptcy of AFOREs or insurance companies (based on Mesa-Lago 1997). It is impossible to evaluate the performance of the new system in Mexico, as it started operation at the time this chapter was finished.

Notes

The author wishes to thank Graciela Bensusan, Anibal Viguera, and Francisco Zapata for helpful comments. Published in Spanish by *Revista Sociologica Mexicana*, 1995; reprinted by permission. Translated by Elizabeth Beaudin.

1. Following Douglass North's (1990) analytical model, by *rules of the game* I mean the set of constraints created by men to limit the conditions of their interactions. In public policies, rules of the game materialize in measures that define, among other things, the actors qualified to intervene, the resources they count on, actions that are permitted or forbidden, and the general conditions of the interaction.

2. The premium is the global percentage upon salaries contributed to finance the insurance.

3. In a PAYG method, current expenditures (benefits) are financed mainly through current revenues (present contributions).

4. By the term *problematization* I mean the process by which a policy issue becomes a decision-making matter for any participant.

5. In a problematization process, the "problem" is not always defined before the "solution." In many cases, the solutions exist previously, and these solutions look for or create public "problems" (see Cohen, March, and Olsen 1972).

6. The register of contingencies reveals an actuarial calculation comparing the amount of assumed future benefits by the IMSS with the revenue to come, all valued in current money. The amount resulting was equal to that of the public external debt.

7. That is, the Confederation of Mexican Workers (Confederación de Trabajadores de México, CTM), the Confederation of Mexican Regional Workers (Confederación Regional Obrera Mexicana, CROM), and the Revolutionary Confederation of Workers and Farmers (Confederación Revolucionaria de Obreros y Campesinos, CROC).

8. The CTM rejects two types of government proposals: first, those that try to extend the IMSS services to rural or "informal" workers that do not contribute (IMSS-Coplamar, for example); and second, those that tend to leave aside persons who should benefit (the SAR, according to the CTM).

9. That is, the Promotion and Security Fund for the Use of Workers (Fondo de Fomento y Garantía para el Consumo de los Trabajadores, Fonacot); the Institute of

the National Fund for Workers' Housing (Instituto del Fondo Nacional de la Vivienda para los Trabajadores, Infonavit); and the Institute of Social Security and Social Services for State Workers (Instituto de Seguridad y Servicios Sociales de los Trabajadores del Estado, ISSSTE).

10. By *game,* I mean the set of strategies and interactions among participants, governed by clearly defined rules, around a public policy issue or space.

11. The elements of the labor proposal included the elimination of personnel, the definition of employer evasion as fraud, and the avoidance of undue municipal extractions, among others.

12. That is, the Revolutionary Institutional Party (Partido Revolucionario Institucional, PRI); the Democratic Revolution Party (Partido de la Revolución Democrática, PRD); and the Popular Socialist Party (Partido Popular Socialista, PPS).

13. Although this essay will not deal primarily with the concrete characteristics of these new social security rules of the game, it is interesting to mention some of the new social security's pillars: a more acute individualization of rights, a direct relation between the contribution and the benefit, a private and individual administration of the funds, an individual and direct relation (with no union intervention) between the worker and the administering institution, a state presence aimed at regulating and not guaranteeing the benefit, and less of a presence of union and employer in the administration of the funds.

14. Among the proposals, I retain the following: the explicit inclusion of CTM in the SAR's technical committee (an institution of legal control) as a member of the three-sided IMSS scheme, and the CTM's intervention as a mediator between the worker and the commercial bank in certain disputes.

15. I refer precisely to the state, the bureaucratic organizations and their characteristics, the public decision-making system, and the corporate agreement.

References

Allison, Graham. 1971. *The Essence of Decision.* Boston: Little, Brown.

Aspe, Pedro. 1992. *Discurso del Secretario de Hacienda ante la Asamblea del Comité Nacional de la CTM (abril 3).*

Cohen, P., J. March, and J. Olsen. 1972. "A Garbage Can Model of Organizational Choice." *Administrative Science Quarterly* 17.1 (March).

Eibenschutz, Catalina. 1992. "¿Modernización o privatización de la seguridad social?" *Uno Más Uno,* January 5.

Garrido, Celso. 1991. "Nuevos circuitos, mercados y actores en el sistema financiero mexicano." *Análisis Económico* 18/19 (UAM-Azcapotzalco).

Mesa-Lago, Carmelo. 1991a. *Portfolio Performance of Selected Social Security Institutes in Latin America.* World Bank Discussion Paper, no. 139. Washington, D.C.

———. 1991b. *Social Security and Prospects for Equity in Latin America.* World Bank Discussion Papers, no. 140. Washington, D.C.

———. 1997. "Comparative Analysis of Structural Pension Reform in Eight Latin

American Countries: Description, Evaluation, and Lessons." In *Capitalization: The Bolivian Model of Social and Economic Reform*, edited by Margaret H. Peirce. La Paz: Ministerio de Capitalización.

North, Douglass. 1990. *Institutions, Institutional Choice, and Economic Performance.* Cambridge, England: Cambridge University Press.

Zapata, Francisco. 1992. "Social Concertation in Mexico." In *Participation in Public Policy Making*, edited by Tiziano Treu. Berlin and New York: Walter de Gruyter.

5 / Social Security Reform in El Salvador

Carmelo Mesa-Lago and Ricardo Córdova Macías

Social security in El Salvador was composed of several programs administered by four agencies: (1) The Salvadoran Social Security Institute (Instituto Salvadoreño del Seguro Social, ISSS) covered salaried workers in the private sector and some self-employed workers for occupational risks, pensions for disability, age, and death (survivors) (Invalidez, Vejez y Muerte, IVM), and health (sickness/maternity). The insurance programs also included a special plan for public employees. (2) The National Institute for Public Employee Pensions (Instituto Nacional de Pensiones de los Empleados Públicos, INPEP) was divided into two components: General Public ("Administrative") and Teaching ("Education"), both of which managed pension programs and loans. Those covered by Administrative received health services from the ISSS; Education had its own health services. Monetary contributions in both were paid by the state. (3) The Armed Forces Pension Institute (Instituto de Previsión Social de la Fuerza Armada, IPSFA) managed programs for pensions, health, and loans. (4) The Ministry of Public Health and Welfare (Ministerio de Salud Pública y Asistencia Social, MSPAS) legally covered the poor and the uninsured.

This chapter analyzes the main characteristics of the principal two social security programs, ISSS and INPEP. There is a brief discussion of the two proposals for reforming the system (substitutive-private and mixed). The chapter then summarizes the essential characteristics of the new pension reform that was approved in December 1996 and raises some questions concerning that reform.

Population Coverage

In 1993 population coverage estimates were as follows: (1) the total population with health coverage was 14.2 percent; (2) the total economically active population (EAP) also having health coverage was 22.2 percent; (3) the EAP having pensions was 22.6 percent. According to these indications, the population covered by social security in El Salvador ranked second lowest (eighteenth) in Latin America; only the Dominican Republic (and probably Haiti) had lower coverage. Assuming that the coverage increased passively at a similar rate, it would take 137 years to incorporate 80 percent of the Salvadoran population (Mesa-Lago, Córdova, and López 1994).

The low coverage of the population and its slow rate of expansion are to a large extent explained by the composition of the labor force. In 1991 almost 41 percent of the employed EAP was informal and this percentage increased to 96 percent for the self-employed. Almost half the EAP is composed of self-employed workers, unpaid family members, temporary salaried workers and employers, who either are legally excluded from protection or receive very low coverage. For example, only 20 percent of the temporary salaried workers and the employers are covered (temporarily self-employed reported not having any coverage), whereas 86 percent of the permanent salaried workers are covered, despite the legal mandate that every salaried worker be covered (Córdova 1993). The traditional Bismarck-type social security covers urban salaried formal workers.

There were also important differences in population coverage among the various economic activities and departments (the country is politically divided into departments). Available data underestimated the EAP in 1991 and consequently overestimated coverage, but the information was useful in that it showed enormous inequities in the level of ISSS coverage. The economic activities of financing, insurance, and real estate were covered by more than 100 percent (because of the underestimation of the EAP), whereas electricity, gas, and water were covered by 67 percent, and manufacturing, mining, and construction fluctuated between 43 and 47 percent. Traditionally, these activities have had the highest coverage. INPEP probably covered 100 percent of all public employees. In contrast, agriculture had only 6.5 percent coverage, and services had 12 percent (these are personal services with high informality). Three activities—manufacturing, finance, and commerce—

concentrated 70 percent of total coverage, whereas agriculture only represented 2.6 percent. The ratio of highest to lowest coverage for economic activities was 15:1 (based on ISSS 1994a).

Notable inequalities also existed in the population coverage of the ISSS by department where the more urban and developed had the highest coverage. For example, coverage in San Salvador was 34.3 percent (almost three times the national average) but was only 0.4 percent in Chalatenango and Morazán, 0.5 percent in Cabañas, and 1.1 percent in Ahuachapán, which had the highest rural populations (64.5–79.6 percent). The ratio of highest to lowest coverage for the departments was 86:1. In one decade, 1983–1993, the degree of concentration of coverage in the metropolitan area increased (based on ISSS 1994a and INPEP 1994).

Financing: Payroll Contributions

The three principal sources of financing were salary contributions paid by insured workers and their employers, state contributions as a third party, and investment returns. The total worker contribution was 4 percent in the ISSS, 7.17 percent in the INPEP-Administrative, 8 percent in INPEP-Education, and 10.5 percent in IPSFA. Differences in contribution rates were explained by pension contributions that fluctuated from 1 percent (ISSS) to 6 percent (INPEP-Education). Pension contributions depended on the maturity of the pension program, the active to passive ratio, and diverse benefits and entitlement conditions. The total employer contribution was 9.5 percent in ISSS, 11.2 percent in INPEP-Administrative, 6 percent in INPEP-Education (this excluded the state contribution to cover the deficit in health), and 11.5 percent in IPSFA. Again, differences resulted from pension contributions' ranging from 2 percent (ISSS) to 6 percent (INPEP-Education). The state should legally contribute, as a third party, to the pension and health programs of the ISSS (INPEP 1990; ISSS 1993b; Crespín 1994; Chavarría 1994).

The total contribution rate fluctuated between 14 percent in the ISSS (this excludes the state contribution to the general health plan) and 22 percent in the IPSFA. A comparison of the total contribution rate among all Latin American countries at the end of the 1980s, considering an average of 12–14 percent in El Salvador, showed that it ranked eighteenth, similar to its ranking in terms of population coverage (Mesa-Lago 1993). Thus, both cost and coverage were low. Nevertheless, this was more accurate for the

ISSS than for the INPEP, and it was less certain in 1994 than in 1989, since the total contribution rate was 3–5 percentage points greater in 1994.

The ISSS financed itself mostly with contributions, which make up 85.4 percent of total revenues (more than two-thirds is paid by the employer). Revenue from investments was small, and the state contribution was null or minuscule. In the INPEP, in contrast, 62 percent of total revenues was derived from contributions and 37 percent from investments. In 1985–1993, the percentage of income generated by contributions grew systematically in the ISSS but decreased in the INPEP, whereas the opposite took place with respect to investment revenues. Part of the reason for these contrasting trends can be found in the number of active contributors (and their employers) in the ISSS, which grew 66 percent from 1980 to 1993, whereas this remained stagnant in the INPEP and, even more, decreased after 1990 because of a major program to reduce the number of public employees (some ten thousand workers were cut). The ISSS was better suited to increase its revenue than the INPEP, since its contribution rate was lower and it had a growing group of active contributors, whereas the number of contributors to INPEP was either stagnant or diminishing.

State and Private Debt

The state had three types of obligations with the ISSS: (1) as employer it contributed to the special health plan that covers public administration employees; (2) as state it contributed 0.5 percent of salaries in the IVM program; and (3) it also contributed a minimum of 5 million colones annually for the general health plan. The first column of table 5.1 shows that the accumulated state debt in 1983–1993 for the three types of obligations grew almost five times (in colones) and reached 318 million colones in 1993. The distribution of the debt among the three functions in 1993 was 28 percent, 54 percent, and 18 percent, respectively; of the three, the deepest in debt was the first, given that public employees by law should receive health care in the ISSS even if the state did not actually defray the cost. In 1983–1993, the accumulated legal state contribution to the general health plan should have been 55 million colones, but it was only 16 million colones; while the state contribution of 0.5 percent should have generated 152 million colones and actually reached 10 million colones; the calculation of the state contribution as employer was more difficult to estimate because the state paid every year, but it paid less than it should have (ISSS 1994a, 1994c).

Table 5.1 Accumulated State and Private Debt with the ISSS in El Salvador, 1983–1993

(in millions of current Salvadoran colones)

	State[a]	Private[b]	Total	Index (1980=100)	Real Debt (in constant colones from 1980)
1983	67.8	42.7	110.5	100.0	110.5
1984	90.7	44.4	135.1	111.8	120.8
1985	106.7	46.4	153.1	136.6	112.1
1986	106.6	49.5	156.1	180.3	86.6
1987	141.0	58.2	199.2	225.6	88.3
1988	169.6	80.2	249.8	270.2	92.4
1989	226.9	99.3	326.2	317.7	102.6
1990	227.9	100.0	327.9	394.6	83.1
1991	252.4	100.0	352.4	451.8	78.0
1992	282.5	96.2	378.7	502.0	75.4
1993	318.2	114.4	432.6	632.1	68.4

Source: Mesa Lago, Córdova, and López 1994.

a. Includes employer contribution to the special health plan, state contribution of 0.5% to the IVM program, and state contribution of 5 million colones annually to the general health plan.

b. To the general health plan and to the IVM.

The accumulated debt of the private employers to the ISSS grew almost three times in 1983–1993 and increased to 114 million colones in 1993: 76 percent went to health and 24 percent to pensions (ISSS 1994c). The total owed to the ISSS in 1993 was 432.6 million colones (74 percent by the state and 26 percent by the private sector), which represented 37 percent of ISSS's total revenues. In real terms, however, because of the high inflation experienced in 1985–1993, the value of the debt diminished by 40 percent (see table 5.1, last column). The state debt as employer to the INPEP was much less than that of the ISSS and reached 3.3 million colones in 1991. However, in 1993 there was also a debt of 45 million colones for default on the fulfillment of payment (by the insured) of the principal and interest from loans. The most serious problem was delay in the reception of contributions because of the old, complicated, and inefficient system having seven thousand cashiers' offices, unique in El Salvador. Finally, some state offices had not registered their employees in the INPEP and avoided payment (Crespín 1994; Chavarría 1994).

Reserves and Investment

The technical reserve was the sum of (1) the difference between current revenues and current expenses in any given year (if the balance was positive, the excess was added to the reserve); (2) the return on investments; and (3) the accumulated reserve from the previous year. The value of the accumulated reserve should equal the value of the investment, but at times there were discrepancies resulting from delays in investing available funds, from yielded income not actually realized, and from short-term investments of current funds not yet actually identified as excesses, which would eventually go to the reserve.

In the ISSS the two reserves amounted to 859 million colones in 1993: the IVM was responsible for 87.5 percent of the total and the occupational risk program in the health plan for 12.5 percent. In the INPEP, two pension reserves in 1992 reported 1,324 million colones: Administrative (82.4 percent of the total) and Education (17.6 percent). The total of the two reserves in 1992 was 2,179 million colones, which represented 4 percent of GDP and 40 percent of current government expenses. These considerable reserves played an important role in the intermediation of funds in the financial sector.

The return on investment also played a crucial role in generating income and in the financial and actuarial balance of both institutions. As a percentage of total income, the return on investment grew significantly in the INPEP, from 23 to 37 percent in 1981–1992. In the ISSS, it increased from 16 to 23 percent in 1981–1985 but dropped systematically thereafter to 11 percent in 1993 (ISSS 1994c; INPEP 1994).

In the ISSS the real return in the two plans (IVM and occupational risk) was negative every year (except three) and averaged –4.3 percent; the real profitability of the professional risk reserves was greater than that of the IVM, especially in 1988–1993 (ISSS 1994c). In the INPEP the real return was negative every year in 1980–1992, and worse than the ISSS, at –6.8 percent annually. These negative rates over such a long period undoubtedly contributed to the decapitalization of real reserves in both institutions: the ISSS reserve was reduced by 65 percent in 1984–1993, and the INPEP reserve by 22 percent in 1984–1992 (based on ISSS 1994c and INPEP 1994). There are multiple causes for such poor performance: (1) the rate of inflation was averaging 18.7 percent in 1980–1993 and 23.4 percent in 1985–1990, in part because of military conflict; (2) the law established rigid conditions for investment (especially in the INPEP); (3) the portfolio's composition showed a concentration in poorly performing instruments (especially in the INPEP); and (4) there were very few alternatives for more profitable investments (Mesa-Lago, Córdova, and López 1994).

The law required that the minimum annual nominal return for invest-

Table 5.2 Cost of Social Security in El Salvador, 1978–1993
(in millions of current Salvadoran colones)

		Government	*Expenses for Social Security*			*% GDP*			*% Government*		
	GDP	*Expenses*	*ISSS*	*INPEP*	*Total*	*ISSS*	*INPEP*	*Total*	*ISSS*	*INPEP*	*Total*
1978	7,692	820	70	7	75	0.9	0.1	1.0	8.5	0.6	9.1
1979	8,607	862	88	8	96	1.0	0.1	1.1	10.2	0.9	11.1
1980	8,916	1,077	113	11	124	1.3	0.1	1.4	10.5	1.0	11.5
1981	8,646	1,233	132	16	148	1.5	0.2	1.7	10.7	1.3	12.0
1982	8,966	1,347	128	26	154	1.4	0.3	1.7	9.5	1.9	11.4
1983	10,151	1,420	132	35	167	1.3	0.3	1.6	9.3	2.5	11.8
1984	11,657	1,797	152	46	198	1.3	0.4	1.7	8.5	2.5	11.0
1985	14,331	1,880	174	60	234	1.2	0.4	1.6	9.2	3.2	12.4
1986	19,763	2,540	196	66	262	1.0	0.3	1.3	7.7	2.6	10.3
1987	23,141	2,674	239	89	328	1.0	0.4	1.4	8.9	3.3	12.2
1988	27,366	2,785	299	125	424	1.1	0.4	1.5	10.7	4.5	15.2
1989	32,230	3,214	380	150	530	1.2	0.4	1.6	11.8	4.7	16.5
1990	41,057	3,685	495	177	672	1.2	0.4	1.6	13.4	4.8	18.2
1991	47,792	4,691	618	217	835	1.3	0.4	1.7	13.3	4.6	17.8
1992	54,853	5,470	792	247	1,039	1.4	0.5	1.9	14.6	4.5	19.0
1993	66,238	5,603	987	n.d.	n.d.	1.5	n.d.	n.d.	17.6	n.d.	n.d.

Source: See table 5.1.

ments should be 5 percent in the ISSS and 7 percent in the INPEP. Legally, then, investments could be made with said rates of nominal performance; however, the average inflation rate in 1980–1993 was 18.7 percent, thus the real return for said rates was −13.7 percent for ISSS and −11.7 percent for INPEP. Furthermore, the law fixed nominal interest rates on mortgages and personal loans for the INPEP (43 percent of the portfolio in 1993) between 7 and 14 percent (both much lower than inflation in 1985–1991) and fixed the percentages of the portfolio that should be invested in specific instruments, for example, 80 percent in mortgages and personal loans whose real average annual return was −8 percent in 1980–1992 (INPEP 1990; ISSS 1993b; Mesa-Lago, Córdova, and López 1994).

Expenditures: Total in Relation to GDP

Table 5.2 presents the estimated total expenses for social security (ISSS and INPEP) in 1978–1993. As a percentage of GDP, expenses increased in 1978–1984 to 1.7 percent, decreased in 1985–1986 to 1.3 percent, and rose again in 1987–1993, possibly exceeding 2 percent. In relation to the government's current expenses, the social security expenses rose (except in

1982–1986) from 9 to 19 percent. The International Labour Office (ILO) underestimated social security expenses in El Salvador as a percentage of GDP, but even so, in 1986 the country ranked fourteenth among eighteen Latin American countries. The four countries with lower percentages were the Dominican Republic, Guatemala, Honduras, and Nicaragua; although Haiti was not included in this comparison, we assume that their expense was also lower than that of El Salvador. Nevertheless, in terms of the general development of social security, El Salvador ranked seventeenth (Mesa-Lago 1994b), which demonstrates an excessive expense. Whereas population coverage was very low (eighteenth place), which reduced the cost, pension benefits were very high because of excessively liberal entitlement conditions.

Expenditures: Benefits

Table 5.3 shows the composition of benefit expenses (health and pensions) by the ISSS and the INPEP in 1970–1992. Note the significant proportion of pension benefits in the INPEP. El Salvador has a relatively high percentage of pension costs compared with the youth of its pension programs (Mesa-Lago 1994b). As the IVM program of the ISSS matures the percentage dedicated to pensions will increase even more, which emphasizes the importance of maintaining and increasing the value of its reserves. In 1978–1992, the number of pensions in ISSS-IVM grew 4.4 times, whereas that of the INPEP increased 11.4 times even though the two INPEP plans were created six and nine years later than the ISSS (the number of pensioners in the INPEP in 1993 probably was 14.5 times the number in 1978).

The great majority of pension payments went to old age or retirement pensions: in the ISSS, 76 percent (then 20 percent to survivors, and 4 percent for disabled and others) and in the INPEP, 80 percent (then 18 percent to survivors, and 2 percent for disabled and others). The proportion of old age pensions in the INPEP was substantially greater in Education (90 percent) than in Administrative (69 percent). This is because in Education it is possible to retire earlier for years of service regardless of age (ISSS 1994c; INPEP 1994).

A comparison of entitlement conditions for pensions between the ISSS and the INPEP demonstrates the generosity of the INPEP, and particularly in INPEP-Education. The retirement age in the ISSS (sixty for women and sixty-five for men) was in 1985 reduced by five years for each (fifty-five/sixty) so that in 1995 it matched the INPEP-Administrative. However, in

Table 5.3 Distribution of Benefit Costs for ISSS and INPEP, by Program, in El Salvador, 1970–1992

(in percentages)

	ISSS			INPEP		
	Health	*Pensions*	*Total*	*Pensions*	*Other*[a]	*Total*
1970	93.3	6.7	100.0	n.d.	n.d	n.d.
1975	89.4	10.6	100.0	99.7[b]	0.3[b]	100.0[b]
1980	86.5	13.5	100.0	99.6	0.4	100.0
1985	75.5	24.5	100.0	95.8	4.2	100.0
1990	65.7	34.3	100.0	93.8	6.2	100.0
1991	76.9	23.1	100.0	93.8	6.2	100.0
1992	68.5	31.5	100.0	97.1	2.9	100.0

Source: Mesa-Lago, Córdova, and López 1994.

a. Allocations to those who do not qualify for a pension and other monetary benefits.

b. 1978.

Education a man could retire at fifty-five, or at any age with thirty years of service. A teacher who began work in the public sector at age twenty could retire at age fifty, with 100 percent of his base salary, and then teach in the private sector. A comparison of ISSS retirement ages with others in the region indicates that four countries with living and social security conditions lower than those of El Salvador required higher ages for retirement: Guatemala required age sixty-five, Honduras ages sixty/sixty-five, Nicaragua and the Dominican Republic required sixty. Entitlement conditions in Education in El Salvador were among the most generous in Latin America (Mesa-Lago 1993).

The laws for the ISSS and the INPEP established a mechanism for revalorization of pensions (annual in the first, and triannual for the second), but no explicit or automatic procedure actually existed, and therefore, revalorization was done on a discretionary basis. Tables 5.4 and 5.5 show estimates of the average nominal annual pension and real pension in ISSS-IVM and INPEP. The average real pension of the INPEP was double that of the ISSS in 1978, but the gap was closing and in 1992 they were almost equal; however, Education pensions in 1992 (1,658 colones) were 74 percent greater than the Administrative pensions (952 colones) and 59 percent greater than ISSS pensions (1,041 colones). The pension in Education grew 78 percent in 1980–1984 and decreased later; in 1992 it was 78 percent of its value in 1980. In Administrative the real pension lost great value, and in 1992 it was only 47 percent of its 1980 value (INPEP 1994). The INPEP pensions were not adjusted for inflation. The minimum monthly ISSS pension is 300 colones, which is notoriously inadequate (Mesa-Lago, Córdova, and López 1994).

Table 5.4 Real Annual Value of Pensions in the ISSS-IVM in El Salvador, 1978–1993

	Annual Total Pensions (thous. of colones)[a]	*No. of Pensions*	*Average Annual Nominal Pension (colones)*	*Index: 1980=100* *Average Nominal Pension*	*Inflation*[b]	*Average Real Pension*	*Average Annual Real Pension (colones)*
1978	5,832	6,176	944	63.0	76.8	82.0	1,229
1979	7,636	7,076	1,079	72.0	91.8	78.4	1,175
1980	12,780	8,532	1,498	100.0	100.0	100.0	1,498
1981	15,698	10,166	1,544	103.1	114.9	89.7	1,344
1982	18,232	10,999	1,658	110.7	128.4	86.2	1,291
1983	24,563	11,268	2,180	145.5	145.2	100.2	1,501
1984	28,332	12,205	2,321	154.9	162.4	95.4	1,429
1985	35,742	12,909	2,769	184.8	198.4	93.1	1,395
1986	43,932	13,849	3,172	211.7	261.4	81.0	1,213
1987	58,211	15,206	3,828	255.5	327.6	78.0	1,168
1988	79,898	16,569	4,822	321.9	392.4	82.0	1,228
1989	107,412	19,074	5,631	375.9	461.4	81.5	1,221
1990	137,198	21,080	6,508	434.4	573.0	75.8	1,135
1991	156,492	23,035	6,794	453.5	655.9	69.1	1,035
1992	189,568	24,972	7,591	506.7	729.0	69.5	1,041
1993	213,448	27,115	7,872	525.5	917.9	57.2	857

Source: Mesa-Lago, Córdova, and López 1994.

a. Pensions for old-age, orphans, widows, disability, and ancestors (in IVM); it excludes pensions for the health plan.

b. Inflation index: 1980 = 100.

Table 5.5 Real Annual Value of Pensions in INPEP, El Salvador, 1978–1992

	Annual Total Pensions (thous. of colones)	*No. of Pensions*	*Average Annual Nominal Pension (colones)*	*Index: 1980=100* *Average Nominal Pension*	*Inflation*[a]	*Average Real Pension*	*Average Annual Real Pension (colones)*
1978	4,175	2,195	1,902	92.8	76.8	120.7	2,476
1979	6,724	3,453	1,947	95.0	91.8	103.4	2,120
1980	10,453	5,099	2,050	100.0	100.0	100.0	2,050
1981	15,033	7,347	2,046	99.8	114.9	86.8	1,780
1982	19,786	9,250	2,139	104.3	128.4	81.3	1,666
1983	30,020	11,255	2,667	130.1	145.2	89.6	1,837
1984	37,737	12,435	3,035	148.0	162.4	91.2	1,869
1985	48,996	13,834	3,542	172.8	198.4	87.1	1,786
1986	56,606	14,815	3,821	186.4	261.8	71.2	1,459
1987	69,195	16,498	4,194	204.6	327.6	62.5	1,280
1988	103,773	19,034	5,452	265.9	392.4	67.8	1,389
1989	125,700	20,418	6,156	300.3	461.4	65.1	1,334
1990	146,467	22,468	6,519	318.0	573 .0	55.5	1,138
1991	181,671	24,851	7,310	356.6	655.9	54.4	1,114
1992	199,163	25,084	7,940	387.3	729.0	53.1	1,089

Source: Mesa-Lago, Córdova, and López 1994.

a. Inflation index: 1980 = 100.

In 1993 the Social Fund for Housing (Fondo Social para la Vivienda, FSV) began an innovative program that established individual pension accounts for the first time in El Salvador. Initially, it was paying 11 percent of annual interest (starting September 1, 1994) and a new system of information for affiliates. By the end of 1995 the FSV had already 341,278 active affiliates (*La Prensa Gráfica*, October 1 and September 27, 1994).

Expenditures: Administration

Table 5.6 shows administrative expenses and employment in 1980–1993. The ISSS administrative expense as a percentage of total expenses grew from 17.5 to 27.2 percent in 1980–1993 (with a drop in 1981–1985), whereas the INPEP expense increased from 7 to 14 percent (with a decrease in 1983–1985). However, it should be noted that the INPEP did not have a health plan, which normally demands a greater percentage of administrative costs. Relative to the other seventeen Latin American countries, the percentage of administrative expense of the ISSS ranked in third place, exceeded only by Peru and Colombia; in the developed countries, the percentage fluctuated between 2 and 4 percent (Mesa-Lago 1993). The INPEP law fixed a cap of 5 percent for administrative expense, but this regulation was violated every year in 1980–1992 since the average administrative expense was double the legal cap. In contrast, the ISSS law did not impose restrictions on administrative expenses (INPEP 1990; ISSS 1993b).

The principal cause of excessive administrative expense was the numerous personnel and their remuneration. In 1980–1992 the number of INPEP employees grew 3.5 times (in 1988 there occurred a jump of 63 percent), and the number of ISSS employees grew 2.3 times. These increases were not justified by any increase in the number of insured, especially in the INPEP. The rate of INPEP employees per thousand insured grew from 1.1 to 3.1 in 1980–1991, whereas the rate in the ISSS increased from 13.3 to 16.2; a slight reduction occurred in both institutions in 1992–1993. The relation of employees to insured in the ISSS ranked the greatest among eleven Latin American countries in 1987 (Mesa-Lago 1993; Mesa-Lago, Córdova, and López 1994).

In 1993 the total cost of salaries in the ISSS was almost equal to total administrative costs (99 percent), since part of the medical benefits were not registered as administrative. Of the total employees that year, 79 percent

Table 5.6 Administrative Expenses and Employment in ISSS and INPEP, El Salvador, 1980–1993

ISSS

	Expenses (in millions of colones)			No. of	No. of	Employees
	Total	Admin.[a]	(%)	Employees (thous.)	Insured (thous.)	× 1,000 Insured
1980	112.8	19.7	17.5	4,063	306.0	13.3
1981	131.7	20.9	15.9	4,449	306.1	14.5
1982	128.3	21.5	16.8	4,509	305.9	14.7
1983	132.5	18.0	13.6	4,793	332.6	14.4
1984	152.3	21.5	14.1	4,858	322.0	15.1
1985	173.6	24.6	14.2	4,780	323.9	14.8
1986	196.5	52.8	26.9	4,836	339.2	14.2
1987	238.9	55.9	23.4	4,749	344.0	13.8
1988	298.6	66.5	22.3	5,005	364.9	13.7
1989	379.9	80.5	21.2	5,768	448.3	12.9
1990	495.1	106.6	21.5	5,781	494.5	11.7
1991	618.2	141.6	22.9	8,679	536.0	16.2
1992	791.7	153.6	19.4	9,194	580.6	15.8
1993	987.6	268.4	27.2	9,594	664.4	14.4

INPEP

	Expenses (in millions of colones)			No. of	No. of	Employees
	Total	Admin.[a]	(%)	Employees (thous.)	Insured (thous.)	× 1,000 Insured
1980	11.3	0.8	7.0	215	196	1.1
1981	16.3	1.2	7.3	232	199	1.2
1982	25.8	3.8	14.8	296	211	1.4
1983	35.0	3.6	10.3	277	212	1.3
1984	45.8	4.8	10.4	290	218	1.3
1985	59.7	5.5	9.3	341	222	1.5
1986	66.3	7.0	10.6	352	234	1.5
1987	89.0	9.7	10.9	379	244	1.6
1988	124.8	14.1	11.3	619	250	2.5
1989	150.0	15.6	10.4	709	274	2.6
1990	177.2	20.7	11.7	813	272	3.0
1991	217.2	23.8	11.0	821	262	3.1
1992	247.1	34.6	14.0	750	277	2.7
1993	n.d.	n.d.	n.d.	n.d.	279	n.d.

Source: Mesa-Lago, Córdova, and López 1994.

a. Administrative costs for both the health and IVM plans.

were working in the medical/hospital area and the remaining in administrative offices (ISSS 1994a). A reason for the high cost of administration in the INPEP is the loan program that absorbs 60 percent of the labor force. The elimination of this program, which causes substantial losses, would entail the elimination of half the personnel. Labor unions in both institutions have lobbied for increased salaries and additional benefits.

Financial and Actuarial Disequilibria

The financial statements of the ISSS in 1981–1992 showed a deficit for the majority of the period in health (1981–1985 and 1992), but a surplus in the IVM plan more than compensated for the deficit in health. In great part this was helped by increases in the maximum taxable salary (in 1986–1989) and in contributions (in 1993). The global surplus, as a percentage of revenue, dropped from 64 to 8 percent during the period. Real reserves of the ISSS fell by 62 percent during the period, mostly because of annual real negative returns (–4.3 percent). The increase in pension expenses as a percentage of the total cost of benefits (despite the fall in the real value of pensions to 57 percent)—because of the process of maturation and flexibilization of entitlement conditions, the growing rise of administration costs, and the problems of evasion, debt, and delay—contributed to the worsening of the financial situation. It was estimated that the IVM plan would require an increase in contributions from 3.5 to 5 percent between 1996 and 2000, and the health plan would need a faster increase on top of an already high contribution of 12.5 percent (Myers 1992; Crespín 1994; ISSS 1994d).

The financial situation of the INPEP was apparently better since Administrative and Education generated a surplus in 1981–1992 (lower in Education than in Administrative). As a percentage of income, this surplus fell from 74 to 34 percent in this period. This is, in part, a result of three and four increases in contributions in the INPEP between 1981 and 1993, by which the legal limits were reached (the ISSS can still increase its contributions). The INPEP reserves were reduced by 22 percent (one-third of the ISSS) but the real annual performance was worse than the ISSS (–6.8 percent). Given prevailing conditions in 1994, it was estimated that Administrative would require a contribution increase from 9 to 12 percent between 1996 and 1998, while Education would need an increase from 12 to 20 percent. Thereafter, it was expected that both plans should continue to increase their contribution rates every four or five years, reaching 40 and 50 percent of respective salaries (Crespín 1994; Servicios 1992).

The financial-actuarial situation of both systems (especially the INPEP), compounded by the other serious problems analyzed here, signify that the reform of social security in El Salvador was urgently needed. The crucial question was, What type of reform was most appropriate? Two reform proposals were developed in El Salvador in 1992–1996. One (prepared by the government) followed the Chilean substitutive private model and the other (elaborated by a private foundation) recommended a mixed model.

THE GOVERNMENT PROPOSAL: SUBSTITUTIVE PRIVATE MODEL

The social security reform—specifically, the pension reform—was on the agenda of the administration of President Alfredo Cristiani, within the framework of state reform. To this end a commission was created, made up of representatives from the Central Bank, the Ministries of Labor, Housing, and Planning, the ISSS, and the private sector, with the goal of preparing a reform proposal. The project started in 1992, with financing from the IADB, and was managed by the consulting firm Socimer International Bank Limited, which concluded its study August of 1992. The study included an analysis and recommendations for pension reform that fell into two stages. In the first stage, partial changes would be introduced that were aimed at modernizing and financially strengthening the social security system and at regulating and consolidating the stock market and the insurance industry (all of which required legal approval). In the second stage, once these reforms had been implemented and were working well, a structural pension reform would replace the old system with a fully funded individual (FFI) system with private management (Socimer 1992). Part of the consultation included an actuarial study by Myers (1992), who concentrated on the health care program of the ISSS.

By mid-1993 the commission had decided to skip the first stage and go directly to the second, the structural pension reform, and commissioned a new study by Socimer, which began in 1994. This study was to review alternative reform models; design the structural reform (which ended in May 1994); and elaborate legal drafts, mechanisms for implementation, and so on. However, the commission did not elaborate or make public the legal drafts, in part perhaps because of the electoral process taking place at the end of 1993 and the beginning of 1994.

In May 1994, the commission presented a reform proposal to then president-elect Armando Calderón Sol (Comisión 1994). In his oath of office as president of the Republic in June 1994, Calderón Sol declared:

> It is of fundamental importance to reform the social security system, which is inefficient and provides little coverage. We must improve the current system that leaves almost 80 percent of the economically active population unprotected. We will promote new alternatives to broaden coverage, stimulating private participation. (*La Prensa Gráfica*, San Salvador, June 4, 1994; translation by the authors)

The commission, government top officials, and the private sector supported a substitutive private model à la Chile. However, critics defended several arguments: (1) The privatization of the social security system did not resolve the crucial problem of low population coverage, which had been highlighted by President Calderón as the fundamental objective of the reform. (2) The number of insured in El Salvador was very small, which posed the question as to whether there would be a sufficient number of insured to support an adequate number of AFPs, thus allowing competition. In Chile, at the end of 1995, there were 4.8 million affiliates in sixteen AFPs, and three of these concentrated 70 percent of the insured; in Argentina, the corresponding figures were 3.5 million, twenty-one AFPs, with 40 percent concentration; in Peru 1.1 million, six AFPs, with 69 percent concentration. In El Salvador, the market was of approximately 435,000 insured (combining the ISSS and the INPEP), which considerably limited the establishment of several competitive AFPs, leading to a duopoly or oligopoly and a greater concentration of insured than in any of the other three. (3) It was not clear how transition costs were going to be paid (Mesa-Lago 1997).

THE PROPOSAL FROM FUNDAUNGO: MIXED MODEL

In 1992–1994, with funds from the Fundación Friedrich Ebert and USAID, the Fundación Guillermo Manuel Ungo (FUNDAUNGO) conducted a study that included a diagnosis of the current social security system and a proposal for its overall reform, including pensions and health care (Mesa-Lago, Córdova, and López 1994). The pension reform proposal recommended a mixed model as the most appropriate for the socioeconomic and social security conditions of El Salvador. The proposal was based on two pillars, both integrated and mandatory.

The first pillar was a reformed public program (unified, standardized, and with tighter entitlement conditions) that was financially viable, with solidarity, based on nondefined contributions and a partially funded collective (PFC) method, which would pay a basic pension. The second pillar would be a program based on defined contributions and the fully funded individual (FFI) method, privately or publicly administered, which would pay supplementary pensions (nondefined benefits). At the time of retirement the insured would collect the two pensions. This proposal was inspired by the Argentinean and

Uruguayan reforms but was modified to respond to Salvadoran conditions and needs.

The first pillar—the public reformed pillar—would unify the two most important pension programs (ISSS-IVM and the INPEP branches) into one unique public program of basic pensions that would be managed by the ISSS or a new autonomous institution. It would standardize benefits, entitlement conditions, and contributions and eliminate privileged benefits (for example, the seniority pension based on years of service regardless of age and the loans program of INPEP). This pillar was expected to gradually expand coverage by incorporating agricultural, self-employed, and temporary workers, with subsidies (since these groups, in general, would have less income than workers who were already covered). Subsidies would be paid by a solidarity mechanism (payroll tax) or by specific state contributions, or a combination of both.

The retirement age in this pillar would increase gradually, over a sixteen-year period, from the current ages of fifty-five for women and sixty for men, to sixty-three for both sexes. A minimum of twenty years of service would be required instead of fifteen. Pensions would be based on real salaries during the last twenty years of work instead of the last three or five years (or the best five years) and would be set at 50 percent of the base salary for a minimum of twenty contributory years, and 1 percent for each additional year (instead of 1.25 percent) in excess of the first twenty years.

The proposal modified entitlement conditions for disability and survivor pensions, regulated the adjustment of pensions to the cost of living, and gave specific measures to reduce evasion and payment delays. This pillar was to be based on nondefined contributions (paid by both employers and insured) and the PFC method (scaled premium) and would perform periodic actuarial evaluations to maintain its equilibrium and determine the contribution for each period. Financial investment of the reserve fund would be liberalized, modernized, and flexibilized and would in general function in a manner similar to the second pillar.

The second pillar was to be operated by multiple administrators (both private and public). It would have a defined contribution and individual accounts, the method would be the FFI, and the retirement age was set also at sixty-three for both sexes. This program had many features that were similar to the one introduced in Uruguay, hence there be no need either for a recognition bond (as the insured would stay in the public-reformed program) or for a minimum pension in the FFI program (because a basic pension would be guaranteed in the public program). Every insured would receive both a basic old age pension paid by the public pillar and a supplementary pension based on the fund accumulated in the individual account of the FFI program.

Because of all of the above reasons, the fiscal costs of the transition in the mixed system would be considerably smaller than in the alternative substitutive system proposed by the government. In conversations with government officials, the FUNDAUNGO team asked that an independent actuary —of international prestige and vast experience in Latin America—evaluate the two proposed models and evaluate the fiscal costs of each. The government accepted this idea and agreed to contract a prominent actuary who worked at the U.S. Social Security Administration; the IADB offered to pay the costs of this consultantship. When the actuary arrived in San Salvador, however, he found that the top government officials in charge of the reform were in Chile; he never received any government help and had to return to the United States without being able to do the evaluation. The government then hired a Chilean consultant firm (CIEDESS), which conducted an actuarial evaluation and indicated that the fiscal costs of the substitutive proposal were lower than those of the mixed model. Several requests by FUNDAUNGO to obtain the calculations supporting those conclusions were not provided by the government or by the CIEDESS consultants (Mesa-Lago 1998).

THE PENSION REFORM OF 1996

Antecedents: The Lack of National Debate

There was never an open national debate on the two alternative reform proposals. The FUNDAUNGO proposal was published, in two editions, and widely disseminated and discussed in meetings and seminars with politicians, leaders of trade unions, employers, and government reformers. But the government proposal was not published or disseminated, and the principal actors and opposition were not consulted. President Calderón Sol enjoyed a wide majority in Congress, which appointed a commission led by his sister to review the official proposal. In December 1996, the Superior Council on Labor (an official agency) requested the technical assistance of the International Labour Office (ILO) to evaluate the proposal, but the ILO expert arrived after the proposal had been approved by Congress (OIT 1997). One of the coauthors of this chapter was invited by the congressional commission to give his opinion, which he delivered on December 18, 1996, noting many flaws in the proposal and exhorting the commission to open a national debate and reach some consensus before passing the law (Mesa-Lago 1996). The same night the commission endorsed the proposal and two days later, with minor changes, it was approved by Congress.

Characteristics of the Reform

The new pension system of El Salvador is similar to the Chilean model (see chapters 1 and 3) but with some important differences: (1) The two old pension systems (ISSS and the two branches of INPEP) are merged and their entitlement conditions and contributions standardized; the armed forces are left out of the reform. (2) The right to stay in the old system or move to the new one is determined by age: insured younger than age thirty-six must move to the new system; those between the ages of thirty-six and fifty or fifty-five can choose to stay in the old reformed system or move to the new one; those aged fifty or fifty-five and more must stay in the old system. (3) Changes from one AFP to another are limited to two annually. (4) The employer contribution is maintained unchanged and the insured contribution is increased enormously (former contributions to the Social Fund for Housing are transferred to the old or the new pension systems). The total contribution in the old system ranged from 3 percent (ISSS) to 9–12 percent (INPEP) and is gradually increased to 14 percent in the old system and 13.5 percent in the new system (10 percent for old age, 3.5 percent for disability/death insurance, plus AFP commissions). (5) Ages of retirement were not increased and are the same in both systems: fifty-five for women and sixty for men (the government proposal raised the ages to sixty for women and sixty-five for men, but Congress rejected this proposal). Twenty-five years of contribution are needed, or thirty years regardless of age. (6) The recognition bond is adjusted to inflation but does not earn interest. (7) The minimum pension also requires twenty-five years of contribution, is calculated based on the average taxable salary, and is limited by the availability of fiscal resources. No assistance pension is paid to the destitute noninsured. (8) The superintendency of pensions is financed by the AFPs (as in Argentina). The state guarantee applies only to the recognition bond and the minimum pension, not to the minimum investment yield and pensions in case of bankruptcy of AFPs or insurance companies (Ministerio de Trabajo 1996; Mesa-Lago 1997).

Problems in the Reform

The pension reform in El Salvador leaves a series of fundamental issues unresolved and has generated additional concerns. It is now even more difficult to extend coverage to the vast majority of the labor force, which is uninsured, because of the 367 percent increase in the contribution of the insured in the private sector. The law states that special provisions will be passed to incorporate certain groups, such as microentrepreneurs and the rural, but does not give any indications as to how that can be done. Retirement ages remain very low, which significantly increases the cost of pensions in the old system and reduces the pensions in the new system. The small insured market of El Salvador would not permit more than two or three AFPs to operate in the long run, which creates a duopoly or oligopoly and prevents any true competition.

Although laws have recently been enacted that regulate the capital market, there were several financial scandals in 1997 that scared investors. The market is just beginning and lacks public confidence. These negative factors make it difficult to achieve a diversified portfolio and alternative financial instruments to invest the pension fund in. The government projects that the real investment yield, even if it materializes, would be 4 percent (one-third of the average yield of Chile's and one-fourth of Argentina's), which would result in lower pensions. As much as 60 percent of investment is allowed in public securities, plus a mandatory minimum of 30 percent in bonds of the Social Fund for Housing. These proportions are considerably higher than was recommended by an expert hired by the government, who assessed that public securities carry high risks and pay low yields in El Salvador. The administrative costs of the new system are estimated as being seven times higher than in the old system. The state guarantees neither a minimum investment yield nor pensions in case of bankruptcy of AFPs and insurance companies. The estimates of the fiscal costs of the reform are plagued by multiple and serious errors, which make their results totally unreliable (Mesa-Lago 1998).

Prospects for Implementation and Reform of the Reform

Implementation of the reform was originally planned to start in mid-1997 but, although the Superintendency has been functioning since the beginning of that year, the first two AFPs are not expected to be authorized to start recruiting affiliates until February 1998. Such delays can be attributed to various factors: several key regulations have not been approved yet, the financial scandals of 1997 probably scared potential organizers of AFPs, and the whole bureaucratic process has been very slow. A serious threat to the reform has been the loss of the congressional majority by the incumbent president in March 1997; the opposition is not very experienced and is fragmented, but there are proposals to abrogate the law, declare it unconstitutional (in toto or in part), amend several articles, and postpone the implementation of the system until a national debate takes place. The absence of public discussion of the government proposal, its quick passage through Congress and the lack of a minimum consensus have brought the probability of either abolition or drastic reform of the pension reform.

References

Chavarría, Mauricio. 1994. "Evolución del sistema de pensiones administrado por el Instituto Nacional de Pensiones de los Empleados Públicos (1983–1992)." *Documentos de Trabajo* (January). San Salvador: FUNDAUNGO.

Comisión de Previsión Social. 1994. "El Salvador: Proyecto de reforma al sistema de pensiones." San Salvador. May.

Córdova Macías, Ricardo. 1993. "La reforma a la seguridad social en El Salvador." *Documentos de Trabajo* (May). San Salvador: FUNDAUNGO.

———. 1994. "Una propuesta de reforma a la seguridad social en El Salvador." In *El Salvador hacia el año 2000: Una plataforma de política económica y social de consenso*, 55–60. San Salvador: CEDEM-CIND.

Crespín, Gustavo. 1994. "Realidad y perspectivas del sistema previsional en El Salvador." In *Sistema de pensiones en América Latina y el Caribe: Diagnóstico y alternativas de reforma*, vol. 3, edited by A. Uthoff and R. Szalachman, 27–87. Santiago: CEPAL.

Dirección de Investigaciones Económicas y Sociales (DIES)–Centro de Investigaciones Tecnológicas y Científicas (CENITEC). 1993. "La crisis del sistema previsional de El Salvador: Situación financiera del ISSS y el INPEP." *Política Económica* 20 (September–October): 1–34.

Instituto Nacional de Pensiones de los Empleados Públicos (INPEP). 1990. *Recopilación de leyes y reglamentos.* San Salvador.

———. 1994. *Estadísticas generales del INPEP.* San Salvador. May.

Instituto Salvadoreño del Seguro Social (ISSS). 1989. *Políticas institucionales para el quinquenio 1990–1994.* San Salvador. December.

———. 1992. *Estadísticas 1991.* San Salvador. April.

———. 1993a. *Estadísticas de salud, 1992.* San Salvador. January–September.

———. 1993b. *Ley y reglamentos del seguro social.* San Salvador.

———. 1993c. "Proyecciones demográficas: Estimación de la demanda de prestaciones y necesidad de recursos del régimen de salud del ISSS, 1992–2000." San Salvador: Unidad de Planificación, Departamento de Actuariado y Estadística. November.

———. 1994a. *Estadísticas, 1993*. San Salvador. April.

———. 1994b. *Estadísticas de salud, 1993*. San Salvador.

———. 1994c. "Estadísticas generales del ISSS." San Salvador. May.

———. 1994d. "Proyecciones actuariales (versión conservadora y versión optimista)." San Salvador: Unidad de Planificación Asesoría Actuarial.

Mesa-Lago, Carmelo. 1993. *Aspectos económico-financieros de la seguridad social en América Latina y el Caribe: Tendencias, problemas y alternativas para el año 2000*. Santiago: CIEDESS, August.

———. 1994a. *La reforma de la seguridad social y las pensiones en América Latina: Importancia y evaluación de las alternativas de privatización*. 2d ed. Quito: INCAE-PRONASEC.

———. 1994b. *Changing Social Security in Latin America: Towards Alleviating the Costs of Economic Reform*. Boulder, Colo.: Lynne Rienner.

———. 1996. "Comentarios al anteproyecto de Ley del Sistema de Ahorro para Pensiones de El Salvador." San Salvador: FESCOL, December 18.

———. 1997. "Comparative Analysis of Structural Pension Reform in Eight Latin American Countries: Description, Evaluation and Lessons." In *Capitalization: The Bolivian Model of Social and Economic Reform*, ed. Margaret H. Peirce. La Paz: Ministerio de Capitalización.

———. 1998. "Evaluación de la reforma de pensiones en El Salvador: Antecedentes, objetivos y perspectivas." San Salvador: Fundación Friedrich Ebert. January.

Mesa-Lago, Carmelo, Ricardo Córdova Macías, and Carlos Mauricio López. 1994. *El Salvador: Diagnóstico y propuesta de reforma de la seguridad social*. San Salvador: FUNDAUNGO. September.

Ministerio de Trabajo y Previsión Social. 1996. *Ley del Sistema de Ahorro para Pensiones*. San Salvador. December 23.

Myers, Robert J. 1992. "Actuarial Report on Social Security Programs in El Salvador." San Salvador. July.

Oficina Internacional del Trabajo (OIT). 1992. *Yearbook of Labour Statistics*. Geneva.

———. 1997. "Memorandum técnico preliminar al Consejo Superior del Trabajo de El Salvador sobre la Ley del Sistema de Ahorro para Pensiones." San José-Ginebra. July.

Servicios Actuariales S.A. de C.V. 1992. "Reporte final del estudio actuarial del INPEP." San Salvador. December.

Socimer. 1992. "Proyecto de reforma a la seguridad social en El Salvador: Estudio sobre la organización, entorno institucional y proposiciones de reforma: Informe final para comentarios." Santiago. August.

6 / The New Argentine Social Security System

A Mixed Model

Ernesto Aldo Isuani and Jorge Antonio San Martino

Social security programs in Argentina were largely motivated by the need to reduce social conflict in the early 1900s. These programs were used by populist governments to attract political support from diverse workers' groups. The best example is provided by the classical populist Juan Domingo Perón, who gave a big push to social security in the 1940s by extending legal coverage to all labor sectors. Since the 1970s, however, the social security system has became unsatisfactory and discredited. A system that was created to prevent and reduce social conflict ended up describing a parabola in time returning to social conflict, this time as its trigger. Without substantial differences, democratic and authoritarian governments have perpetuated a perverse social security model that has failed to honor payment of contractual benefits to pensioners.

The prereform conditions that characterized the pension system (fragmentation, divergent entitlement conditions, evasion, low support rates, low pensions, and financial crisis of the public social security system) made the reform irresistible. Impetus for the reform came from the actual interest groups (pensioners' organizations), which demanded fair treatment and compliance with the law. The public pay-as-you-go (PAYG) pension system was in bankruptcy. The prereform pension system was so expensive that pension payments represented 7 percent of GDP in 1992, and the government could not pay legally defined benefits.

One fundamental characteristic of the pension reform in Argentina is that it is inextricably connected to politics and the full validity of democratic institutions in the definition, negotiation, and concessions that determined the type of pension model adopted. However, despite important political participation of pressure groups in the process of reforming the system at the legislative branch, 12 million Argentineans were uninformed and confused when expected to choose either the public-reformed system or the mixed system in 1994. This chapter summarizes the main problems faced by the old pension system, analyzes the main characteristics of the new one (which is the first in Latin America to introduce a mixed model), and critically assesses the main characteristics of the reform.

PROBLEM SET OF THE FORMER SOCIAL SECURITY SYSTEM IN ARGENTINA

Principal Events in the Evolution of the System

Immigrants in the last decades of the previous century arrived bearing the socialist, anarchist, and unionist ideas that were in vogue in Europe at the time (information for this brief historical account is taken from Isuani 1985 and Feldman, Golbert, and Isuani 1988). These immigrants founded the first workers' unions and were protagonists of a period of high social conflict and activism, which extended into the first decades of this century. To address their labor demands, laws were enacted that regulated Sunday rest, work by women and by children, and the reduction of the working day; and social security was introduced. The first pension fund for civil servants was established in 1904. Another law, in 1915, created a pension fund for railroad workers, in large part the result of frequent and prolonged strikes. During the governments of the Radical Civil Union (1916–1930), coverage reached the majority of public service workers (telephone, gas, electricity, telegraphists, and streetcar conductors, bankers and insurance workers). Toward the end of the 1930s, journalists, graphic artists, workers in the merchant marines and in civil aeronautics were also covered with pension funds.

Coverage was by means of multiple retirement funds, with divergent entitlement conditions and benefits. Thus, since its inception, the system has always been fragmented. Small contributions and a low retirement age caused serious deficits in some of the funds. Coverage increased from 24,000 affiliates in 1904 to 428,000 in 1944. It was, however, a relatively privileged group of salaried workers that was covered, in 1944 only 7 percent of the workforce. Beginning in 1943, and during the period of the Peronist governments that ended in 1955, social security was legally extended to all labor sectors, commercial employees (1944), industrial workers (1946), and rural workers, self-employed, professionals, and management (1954). From 1944 to 1949, coverage quintupled, reaching 2.2 million workers.

In 1954, during the Peronist administration, collective investment was replaced by PAYG. This method meant an implicit pact between the generations, which enabled pensioners, disabled, or beneficiaries to be funded by active workers. Adoption of this method eliminated the balance that was to exist between contribution rates (premia) and a collectively capitalized reserve fund from which benefits were paid. Reasons for the change include: (1) erosion of the reserve fund because of poor financial management and high inflation rates, (2) elevated evasion (in 1961, less than half the affiliates contributed to the system), and (3) generous benefits that eroded the reserve fund because of a combination of reduced retirement ages with high replacement rates. A census of beneficiaries conducted in 1966 indicated that 26 percent of the retirements based on age were held by persons less than fifty years old.

The military government of Juan Carlos Onganía introduced a social security reform in 1967. This reform eliminated the privileges and double coverage that characterized the system. The age of retirement was raised to sixty for men and fifty-five for women with salaried work, and sixty-five for men and sixty-two for women who were self-employed. The position of Secretary of Social Security was created, with the responsibility of carrying out and supervising the National Social Security System (SNP). All diverse existing funds were combined into three: self-employed, state and industrial workers, and commercial and civil workers. Contributions were standardized, and the presence of workers' unions in the funds was eliminated.

The method of calculation of pensions was also modified. The base for calculation of the replacement rate was the average remuneration for the three most favorable years in the last ten years of contributions. Replacement rates were set at 70 percent of this average for retirement and full disability, reaching a maximum 82 percent if additional years of contribution (than legally determined for entitlement) were added. Not even PAYG could create the funds necessary to pay benefits as defined above. Thus, effective pensions were below the levels that were guaranteed by law. The system became illegal, and governments had to find other sources of funds to meet payment of benefits.

The Situation Prior to the Reform of 1993

One of the factors complicating PAYG was population dynamics. Increases in life expectancy and reduction in birth rates accelerated aging. With smaller support rates (the relation of the number of active workers to the number of retirees or pensioners), active workers raised their contributions to maintain the funding of pensioners and beneficiaries. The population older than sixty-five virtually doubled between 1960 and 1980, whereas the overall population grew by 40 percent. Comparing the periods 1975–1980 and 1985–1990, the birth rate decreased from 25 per thousand to 21.4 per thousand. Life expectancy (sixty-five for men and seventy-two for women) in both periods rose to sixty-seven for men and seventy-four for women (*Censo Nacional de Población* 1980, 125, 94; 1991, 15).

Benefits were also growing in a disproportionate way. The percentage of benefits in relation to the population of eligible age to collect these benefits (women older than fifty-five and men older than sixty) experienced a notable growth, going from 12.6 percent in 1950 to 61 percent in 1990 (see table 6.1). Nevertheless, from 1980 on, the rate of growth of coverage began to match the growth in the potentially benefited population, indicating stagnation of coverage.

The economically active population (EAP) was approximately 13 million in 1992; the labor force was slightly higher than 12 million. Not all the

Table 6.1 Coverage in Argentina's Social Security System

	Potentially Benefited Population (thous.)			*National Social Security System*	
	Men Older than 60	*Women Older than 55*	*(A) Subtotal*	*(B) Total Benefits (thous.)*	*Coverage (%)*[a]
1950	613	882	1,495	188	12.59
1955	754	1,082	1,836	473	25.76
1960	912	1,324	2,236	749	33.51
1965	1,069	1,604	2,674	1,086	40.62
1970	1,224	1,899	3,123	1,390	44.52
1975	1,376	2,198	3,575	1,695	47.41
1980	1,521	2,518	4,039	2,342	58.00
1985	1,686	2,842	4,528	2,759	60.93
1990	1,858	3,119	4,977	3,031	60.90

Source: Prepared by the authors based on the 1982 Census of the National Institute of Statistics (Instituto Nacional de Estadísticas), and Feldman, Golbert and Isuani 1988. The data corresponding to 1990 are from the Secretary of the National Social Security System.

a. Coverage (%) is defined as total benefits (B) divided by the subtotal of the potentially benefited population (A) × 100.

working population was obligated to contribute to social security; provincial public workers and the security forces have their own pension systems, for example. The actual number of workers contributing represented a low percentage. The Secretary of the Social Security System estimated that in 1990 approximately 4.9 million workers contributed (Administración Nacional de la Seguridad Social 1992a, 20). This figure showed the existence of a significant evasion of social security obligations. Evasion by the self-employed was the highest. In 1990, out of 2.6 million self-employed, less than 800,000 were effective contributors. Thus, with 4.9 million contributors and almost 3 million benefits in 1990, each benefit was financed by 1.6 workers. Clearly, demographics, the growth of benefits at a rate much greater than that of contributors, and evasion were factors that eroded the financial balance of the system. In view of these problems, contribution rates by employers and employees reached 26 percent of salaries.

Until the end of the 1970s, the system was funded entirely with PAYG. Since the mid-1980s, however, between 20–30 percent of pension payments were funded out of general taxes (Schultess 1990). The annual expenditures of the system in 1992, prior to the reform, reached 10,500 million pesos—or dollars, due to the full convertibility of pesos to U.S. dollars (Administración Nacional de la Seguridad Social 1992b), or approximately 4.6 percent of a GNP estimated at $227,000 million (Instituto Nacional de Estadísticas y Censos 1993, 401). If we add $1,600 million, paid in 1992 to pensioners and beneficiaries in the armed and security forces, and $3,600 million for provincial and municipal pensioners and beneficiaries (*Ambito Financiero* 1992), we come to a total figure of approximately 15,700 million pesos annually, or almost 7 percent of GNP. Despite the additional resources received, the social security system was not in any condition to comply with established laws relating to the benefits it should offer. The relationship between salaries and pensions established by law (replacement rates of 70–82 percent) was for a long time not feasible. In the period 1984–1990, actual replacement rates (the relation of average pension to average salary) was never higher than 55 percent (Instituto Nacional de Previsión Social 1990, 34).

There were also substantial problems of equity in the old system (see table 6.2). Whereas 21 percent of the population in the Capital Federal had social security benefits, only 1.5 percent of the population in Formosa had benefits. The direct association between socioeconomic development and coverage is clearly seen. Capital Federal, Buenos Aires, Córdoba, and Santa Fe—the provinces with greater economic development—had the greater coverage.

Table 6.2 Coverage of the Argentine Social Security System (SNP), by Province

Province	*Benefits (1990)*	*Population (1991)*	*Benefits/ Population (%)*
Cap. Federal	634,158	2,960,976	21.42
Buenos Aires	1,309,583	12,582,321	10.41
Catamarca	10,683	265,571	4.02
Córdoba	246,818	2,764,176	8.93
Corrientes	30,871	795,021	3.88
Chaco	29,721	838,313	3.55
Chubut	14,144	356,587	3.97
Entre Ríos	78,935	1,022,865	7.72
Formosa	6,031	404,367	1.49
Jujuy	15,945	513,992	3.10
La Pampa	19,148	260,034	7.36
La Rioja	9,648	220,729	4.37
Mendoza	90,350	1,414,058	6.39
Misiones	20,919	789,677	2.65
Neuquen	10,267	388,934	2.64
Río Negro	20,571	506,796	4.06
Salta	31,619	866,771	3.65
San Juan	29,671	529,920	5.60
San Luis	15,144	286,334	5.29
Santa Cruz	4,690	159,964	2.93
Santa Fé	308,107	2,797,293	11.01
Sgo. Estero	28,759	672,301	4.28
Tierra Fgo.	833	69,323	1.2
Tucumán	63,165	1,142,247	5.53
Total	3,031,745	32,608,570	9.30

Source: Based on unpublished data from the secretary of the Argentine Social Security System and the National Census of Population, 1991.

Another important inequity was introduced by the regimes of privilege, which were more generous than the regular system (see table 6.3). In February 1992 (excluding the beneficiaries of public administration, which constitute the majority and possess the lowest pensions), these regimes covered only 0.7 percent of the total beneficiaries of the SNP and amounted to 3.5 percent of its total cost. The average monthly benefit in these regimes was $1,040, five times the average of the SNP.

The important gap between legal and actual replacement rates led to judicial disputes that were resolved in court. Most cases were resolved against the government, which was then forced to comply with the law. The accumulation of prosecution against the government caused it, in October 1986, to declare a "state of emergency" in the SNP to suspend execution of the settlements and impede the initiation of new suits. From then on, an intricate process was set up with the purpose of resolving the legal problem, which

Table 6.3 Special Pension Programs in Argentina, February 1992

Law	*Benefited Organization*	*No. of Cases*	*Totals (thous. $)*	*Average Monthly Payment ($)*
16989	President and/or vice-president	18	63	3,477
18464	Judicial branch	2,840	4,621	1,627
20024	Attorney general	10	32	3,163
20572	Legislative branch	1,418	3,610	2,548
20954	Ministers, secretaries, undersecretaries	959	1,714	1,787
21121	National Congress and National Audit Office	3,059	4,729	1,546
21124	Legislative branch (broadening of law 20572)	209	237	1,136
21540	Bishops and archbishops of the armed forces	10	9	859
22430	Catholic curates	131	20	151
22731	Foreign service	420	1,068	2,542
22929	Science and technology	995	1,065	1,071
22955	Public administration	60,796	25,076	412
23682	Extension of law 22955	11,907	6,904	580
23895	Education	1,784	647	363
	Total	84,556	49,794	589

Source: Demarco and Posadas 1992.

included official plans offering diverse forms of compensation to retirees. But these initiatives failed, partly because the pensioners rejected them and partly because of worsening economic conditions (hyperinflationary episodes in 1989–1991).

The Program of Convertibility in 1991—which determined the full conversion of the national currency (pesos) to the dollar, along with privatization of public enterprises and deregulation—was successful in stabilizing the economy and served as the base for a new attempt to resolve the so-called social security debt (the difference between the legal and actual replacement rates). Government consolidated this debt by issuing public debt notes. However, the measure did not resolve the problem of noncompliance with the law, because the law had not been reformed. Thus, the debt continued to grow at a rate estimated at 200 million pesos (or dollars) a month. By August 1992, the social security total debt stood at approximately $13,500 million.

In another desperate move to fund the growing social security debt, federal government agreed with the governments of the provinces that a percentage of the tax revenues distributed to the provinces would be used to bring benefits back up to the levels determined by law. This promise was impossible to keep. In this process, more than 3 million pensioners became well organized and developed key networks with the press and with the opposition. They became so active in their fight for legal and fair treatment that they became an important social force in prompting the resolution of the pension reform by 1993.

THE DEBATE ABOUT THE NEW SYSTEM

In mid-1991, a new Secretary of SNP was designated. Between the end of 1991 and the first months of 1992, the executive branch invited political parties and some social organizations to a public dialogue roundtable (Mesa del Diálogo Público 1992) to consider some fundamental issues, the reform of the SNP included. It was assumed a complete reform that would include a modification to the SNP financing mechanism would be opposed. Therefore, the attempt was to advance the discussion prior to its presentation in Parliament. Public debate about reform options accelerated with the increasing social mobilization of organizations representing pensioners.

A reform proposal was presented in Congress by the executive branch on June 5, 1992 (Cámara de Diputados de la Nación 1992, 1627–70). The plan created a new pension system with two components: a public program (operating with PAYG) and a private program (FFI). The programs would supplement each other and would generate a basic universal benefit for all insured with additional benefit coming from individual capitalization.

The proposal standardized entitlement conditions for dependent workers and self-employed; it increased the age of retirement to sixty-five for men and women; and it made adoption of the new integrated system of pensions (SIJP) mandatory for workers under forty-five, and elective to older workers. Various social and workers' organizations participated in the analysis of the proposal within parliamentary commissions (Isuani and San Martino 1993). Criticisms (to cite the most important) included: lack of trust in the Chilean model of individual capitalization (it was too new); the difficulty in maintaining adequate real returns of the pension fund in the future (because of excessive liquidity in the capital market); the high administrative costs;

rejection of the proposal to not acknowledge previous years of contributions by workers younger than forty-five; and the government's incapacity to supervise private pension fund administrators and the investment of pension funds. Possible modifications to this first version, discussed by various organizations (particularly pensioners' organizations), included the following: (1) unions, foundations, mutual associations, cooperatives, banks, and other organizations both public and private could become pension fund managers; (2) the government could acknowledge previous years of contributions; (3) retirement ages for men and women could be differentiated; (4) benefits for workers older than forty-five who remain in the old SNP could be improved; and (5) the government could warrant profitability of pension funds. After more than eighteen months of heated debate, the new integrated system (or mixed system) was enacted in 1993.

THE INTEGRATED SYSTEM OF RETIREMENT AND PENSIONS (SIJP)

The SIJP was implemented on July 15, 1994. As was the case prior to the reform, the new, mandatory system covers both salaried workers and the self-employed. The old public system—managed by the Ministry of Labor and social security and based on PAYG—was reformed, its entitlement conditions and benefits were tightened, and it continues operating. The insured had a three-month period to select between the public-reformed system and a new mixed system. The mixed system is made up by two mandatory and integrated components: (1) the public-reformed program, which pays a basic pension, and (2) the fully funded individual (FFI) capitalization program, which provides complementary pensions and is administered by AFJPs. The old insured can always move from the public-reformed to the mixed system but not the other way around. New entrants in the labor force have the option to select between the two systems. Thus, both systems operate simultaneously, the public-reformed and the mixed. Excluded from the reform were the armed forces and employees of provinces and municipalities. Employees of provinces and municipalities, however, can sign agreements to join the national system.

As before, the public program operates under PAYG and administers the contributions from employers (16 percent of the base salary), salaried insured (16 percent), and self-employed (27 percent). The administration of this plan is handled entirely by the state, with the general tax director being responsible for the collection of the contributions and the National Administration of Social Security (ANSeS) being in charge of the general functioning of the system and the payment of benefits. In the mixed system: (1) the public-reformed component is financed by the employer contribution (16 percent), plus an equal percentage from the self-employed, and the state subsidy through taxes; and (2) the individual capitalization component (also known as private component) is financed by the insured contribution (11 percent equally for salaried and self-employed). The insured's contribution is divided into the following averages: 7.5 percent for deposit in the individual account for the old age pension; 0.6 percent for the premium to disability/death in an insurance company; and 2.9 percent for the AFJP commission (fixed or percentage on the account balance). Pensioners have the option of programmed retirement with an AFJP or the purchase of a life annuity *(renta vitalica)* with a retirement insurance company. All contributions are deducted by the employer and passed to a central agency, which collects contributions and distributes them to AFJPs and insurance companies.

In both public-reformed and mixed systems, the government pays a Universal Basic Benefit (PBU) to every insured, which fulfills the requirements of age and years of contribution. The ages to receive benefits were increased to sixty-five for men and sixty for women. Thirty years of service with contributions must be accumulated. The PBU is set at 2.5 times the average obligatory social security contribution (in March 1994 it was $63, so the PBU was $157.50). In the case that a worker exceeds thirty years of service with contributions, up to a maximum of forty-five years, the law provides that the PBU would increase by 1 percent for each additional year. Similarly, government recognizes the existing years of contributions to the old system by means of a Compensatory Benefit (PC) that equals 1.5 percent for each year of service with contributions to the old system (with a cap of thirty-five years), calculated by the average of the remuneration of the last ten years worked. Both measures—recognition of previous years of contribution and the PC—increased benefits in the public-reformed system.

So far, in both the single public-reformed and the mixed system, benefits paid by the public-reformed to insured are the same. But workers who chose to remain in the public-reformed system only have additional incentives as explained below. In the single public-reformed system, benefits are defined (entitlement conditions are uniform). The system pays a basic pension, which requires thirty years of contribution and is estimated biannually according to the revenue from contributions and the number of insured. Also it pays an Annual Supplementary Benefit (PAC), an extra paycheck equivalent to one month. An additional benefit calculated as a percentage of the base salary is paid as a reward for those insured who remained in the system. This benefit is called Additional Benefit for Continued Service (PAP) and is equivalent to 0.85 percent for each year of contributions made to the new system, to be calculated in the same way as the PC. An assistance pension is paid by the government to the noninsured destitute. Ages of retirement are gradually being increased from fifty-five to sixty for women and from sixty to sixty-five for men in the year 2001 (Mesa-Lago 1997).

In the private individual capitalization component, each worker capitalizes the personal contribution in one individual account in a unique AFJP, even though the worker may have more than one employer or be self-employed. The norm also permits changing the AFJP—every four months, with a maximum of twice each year. The fund is invested in a diverse portfolio with maximum limits by instrument, and within this by issuer, with all investments authorized by the Central Bank or a risk-assessment firm. The shares are held in the custody of some official entity or stockbroker.

The AFJP can not, under any condition, deny membership. The administrating companies must provide to their affiliates, every four months (at a minimum) and deliver to their residence, a statement containing, among other things, the number of registered shares, the type of activity, the deposit date of the shares, the balance of the account, the profitability of the fund, the price of the commission, the average profit, and the average commission of the system. The system will be controlled by the Superintendent's Office of the AFJPs, an organ of the Ministry of Labor and Social Security, with individual jurisdiction and financial independence, and will be directed by a superintendent appointed by the executive branch. In the case of bankruptcy or dissolution of any AFJP, its members will be transferred to another administrator within ninety days, a lapse during which the fund will be handled by the superintendent who will be able to delegate another AFJP.

The retirement and pension fund is an independent patrimony, separate from the patrimony of the AFJP that administers it, and its assets and rights will be nonsizable and dedicated only to generating benefits established by law, whose property will belong exclusively to the AFJP's affliates. The fund should have a minimum profit, established by the plan at 70 percent of the average profitability of the system or the profitability of the system minus two percentage points, whichever is less. The administrators are responsible that the profit not be less. In such case, the adjustment will occur via the Fluctuation Fund.[1]

The ordinary retirement benefit given by this system will be financed with the balance of the individual investment account of each member. In the case of benefits for disability and death while working, the AFJP will add a supplementary capital that is obtained from the life and disability insurance. With respect to the ordinary retirement benefit and retirement for permanent disability, the initiative establishes that those who meet established requirements can collect the balance of their individual account with the purpose of forming their respective retirement plan according to two modalities: (1) to purchase an annuity from an insurance company,[2] or (2) to start a series of programmed withdrawals with the same AFJP, or a combination of both. If members were to opt for the programmed withdrawals, they would retire (monthly) the quantity of funds (programmed annually) from their individual investment account, maintaining the ownership of the remaining fund.[3] Voluntary social security contributions can be added to the retirement and pension fund (anticipating the approach of retirement or to increase its sum), and the same goes for collected voluntary deposits that third parties can make to the particular account of the member.

The AFJP charges commissions for the task of administration, which shall be equal for all members and which shall be discounted monthly, from the voluntary contributions, from the collected deposits, or from each payment effected via the modality of programmed withdrawals. There is a substantial difference with the Chilean system, which reduces the administration cost of the AFJPs. In Chile, the AFPs charged according to the cost of the receipt of the contributions and pursued evaders. In the Argentine system, this pursuit is assumed by the government, which takes charge of the task and monthly deposit to the AFJPs the applicable contribution, free of charge.

With respect to the disability retirement, the norms are applied equally and uniformly in the two programs, and those persons having a permanent disability originating from any cause that represents a loss of 66 percent of their work capacity are able to draw the retirement. This is established by a medical board according to a standing report and will be called before the Central Medical Commission, by the member, for the AFJP or the life insurance company in charge of the group life and disability policy. The AFJPs must administer and finance jointly, in the corresponding proportion, according to the number of members that solicit disability retirement, the costs that the action of the medical commissions and the Central Medical Commission demand.

A pension as a death benefit also has been established for the widow, widower, common-law wife or husband and unmarried children less than eighteen years of age that have no other social security benefit (the age limitation is not applied if the minor children are considered incapacitated at the time of issuing the benefit). Further, the plan incorporates the benefit of anticipated retirement.[4] Those that opt for this modality, however, will not have rights to the universal basic benefit until they reach the necessary minimum age and years of contribution.

Government guarantees a minimum profit from the invested funds. When the administrator, after exhausting all mechanisms permitted by law, is unable to fulfill the minimum profit, government will maintain it, until such time as all members transfer to a new administrator. Government also guarantees payment at retirement, payment for disability and death benefits, in the case of bankruptcy or insolvency of the retirement insurance company that assumed the responsibility of payment. Finally, government guarantees a minimum income of three and two-thirds of the Aporte Medio Previsional Obligatorio (AMPO). This works for those who—at the moment of collecting the social security benefit and after adding all the components (PBU plus PC plus PAP or investment income)—have an income that is less than the AMPO.

The choice between remaining in the public-reformed PAYG system and the integrated or mixed system was made by each contributor between May 2 and July 1, 1994. If, during this period, workers had not exercised the right to choose, the law established that they will immediately be part of the mixed system, being able to return to the public-reformed program only once, and until July 1, 1996. On the other hand, those who choose the public-reformed program will be able to sign up in the future without time limits for the mixed program, if so desired.[5] In the same way, if workers are not working at this time or are not able to enter the job market, when they do begin work they have thirty days to communicate their choice of pension system to their employer. If they do not, they are inscribed in the integrated or mixed program and their contribution is sent to the AFJP that the majority of employees in their company contribute to. This same disposition was applied to those who did not make a choice between May 2 and July 1, 1994.

CONCLUSIONS

An Assessment of the New Pension System

After a long and winding road, Argentina has a new pension system that has two features of particular interest. First, it is a mixed system, combining a public-reformed PAYG with an FFI system managed by AFJPs. Second, it is a system that emerged from the full validity of democratic institutions. As such, its content is determined by the many negotiations and concessions that took place during its development.

Therefore, it is appropriate to evaluate the new system and its perspectives. The new public-reformed PAYG system is the more rational and tightens up entitlement conditions. An incentive exists to contribute a greater number of years since the benefits given recognize the number of contribution years, demand higher ages for retirement than before, and require (except for the benefit of advanced age)[6] a minimum of thirty years of contribution to receive the benefits. Finally, the new public-reformed PAYG system introduces an element that gives it a redistributive characteristic in a progressive sense: the PBU, being equal for all beneficiaries, represents a larger percentage of salary as the salary decreases.

At the same time, however, the public-reformed PAYG system shows some important limitations (Mesa-Lago 1990). The main one is the sustainability of the system in years to come, given that support rates are decreasing and that relatively generous benefits have to be paid. It seems as if additional support will have to continue coming from general tax revenues as was occurring in the prereform years. A second important concern, related to the previous one, is population dynamic (Eichler 1991). Argentina is a country with an older demographic structure, and a labor force in the process of conversion to greater levels of productivity and with a low grade of absorption of manual labor in the formal sector. This conspires against a PAYG system since the support rate is and will be unfavorable.

Further, given the resources assigned to the PAYG system, the benefits received are expected to be a reduced percentage of an active salary. In other words, the public-reformed PAYG system will not be able to pay a pension that substitutes for a salary. For example, what the system promises to a young person who chooses the public-reformed system (PBU and PAP), who contributes for thirty years in the future, and who possesses an income equivalent to an average salary in the economy ($600) is only 50 percent of the average of the remuneration of his or her last years. The picture is more complicated for workers with higher salaries. For another young person who also contributes thirty years and who earns in his or her last years close to four times the average salary ($2,400), the public system will offer only 30 percent of his or her salary.

The FFI system also presents positive aspects. By linking future non-defined benefits to current defined contributions, a factor of individual effort and responsibility is introduced, which allows workers to escape the adverse population dynamic presented by Argentine society. The private administration of the funds also avoids the chance that (as happened in the past when the collective capitalization systems depended on state administration) its funds are misused because of politics instead of profitability.

On the other hand, the FFI system as it has been formulated presents a series of difficulties. First, it introduces increased risk, because it is more sensitive than the PAYG systems to the unforeseen difficulties that affect a society in the long run. These include international or domestic conflicts and economic problems that can erode the value of accumulated funds. Chile, in the first years of its new social security system, had very elevated real yields. If the same experience had developed in Argentina, however, which suffered acute inflationary processes (including hyperinflationary episodes), surely the system would have found itself in difficulties. Evidently, the investment system implies a strong bet on a future world of stability, peace, and progress.

Second, again as in the Chilean model, a low contribution is combined with a high cost of operation (see Arellano 1989; Iglesias and Acuña 1991). In effect, the contribution to the AFJPs will be 11 percent of the base salary, but only a part of this (7.5 percent) will be capitalized. Commission costs will fluctuate between 3 and 3.5 percent of the salary, or between 27 and 32 percent of the total contribution rate. This implies that the system will be expensive to administer, as a consequence of the contract for life and disability insurance but also because of the high costs that the chosen type of administration presents: buildings, promoters, publicity all come from the beneficiaries' contributions. As a result, it is probable that by capitalizing only 7 or 7.5 percent of salaries, the benefits will be as low as those of the public system, unless the rate of performance is extraordinarily high over prolonged periods. This is, without doubt, a great risk.

The new system of investment introduces the issue of transitional costs. Those who choose the new system stop contributing to the PAYG system so as to contribute to the individual capitalization system. This causes a gap in resources to finance actual retirees, which then entails four alternatives: (1) an additional cost for the society in terms of new taxes to finance the transition; (2) a restriction on spending in other areas if it is decided to shift fiscal resources instead of increasing them; (3) a postponement of the creation of a capital market, if government decides to absorb the funds by means of public bonds and in this way to confront the maintenance of the actual system; or (4) the reduction of the real value of existing benefits.

The Regulatory Capacity of the State

A subject of great relevance is the state's capacity to control the new system administered by the AFJPs. As occurred in Chile, a reform of the social security system that introduces an individual capitalization system administered by the private sector, as in Argentina, requires the design of a methodology for its conduct, regulation, and supervision. A crucial aspect to take into account is that the institution of a regulatory mechanism is not just a mechanical task; rather, it concerns structural characteristics of the society and government in any particular country. The Chilean government, if one compares it to other countries, had shown over the last decades a high level of intervention in various aspects of social life. In other words, the function that the Superintendent's Office of the AFJPs fulfills is inscribed within the state's framework by institutions of great regulatory and fiscal capacity. This has not been a characteristic of the Argentine state institutions, which are more permeated by the prevailing pressures of civil society. The weakness of the Argentine state has permitted routine, unpunished violations of legal norms; it is frequent that, in alarming proportions, the rules of transit are not respected; medications and food in bad condition contaminate, many times aggressively, people, water, and air.

It is not necessary to leave the social security circle to illustrate that public offices are ineffective in regulating and controlling. For example, the National Institute of Social Work (a regulatory organization for social work) did not succeed in correcting the high level of irrationality that characterized medical benefits of the Argentine Social Security system. In effect, government relies on rudimentary information systems, primitive technology, and obsolete procedures. Obviously, with these characteristics government is not in any condition to conduct, regulate, supervise, or authorize. The supervised usually have more power than the supervisor, with the same base of impunity. For this reason, a reform of the social security system that does not comprise, at the center, a reform of the state introduces very serious questions.

Choices of Systems

In 1994 Argentine workers made the choice of joining either the public-reformed system or the mixed system, which integrates the public-reformed and the individual capitalization program managed by the AFJPs. The information available to the Argentinian labor force prior to such an important decision was partial and mediocre. The public debate around the reform process had captured the attention of the press, and the push from several militant pensioners' organizations had been followed by press coverage. However, the common people did not understand the specific details concerning one or other of the systems, or the advantages and disadvantages of joining either one. This may be explained by the dry, technical complexity of social security issues and the enormous economic interests at play. It is worrying, however, that millions of people made a choice without fully understanding what was at stake concerning their retirement, especially when various key factors intervene in the choice.

For example, in the public-reformed system the gender of the worker is not important for the determination of the value of the retirement since this is calculated on the income obtained at the end of the person's career, whereas in the private retirement system, women are at a disadvantage. In effect, since women have a longer life expectancy than men, even when they have accumulated the same amount as men they will have a lower pension. Further, the status of the civil worker does not represent differences in the public system, whereas in the private system it does since spouses and children are eligible to receive benefits. Whereas the calculation of benefits for an unmarried man takes into account only his life expectancy, the calculation of benefits for a married man includes the fact that the benefits do not terminate with his death. His spouse and children under eighteen continue receiving a pension, thus the estimated monthly pension will be lower to account for the presence of survivors.

The public-reformed system is convenient for workers who, starting with a relatively low salary, are able to escalate into higher salary levels by the end of their careers. Since the benefit is calculated on the average salary at the end of an active work life, it may be a good idea to choose this system instead of individual capitalization if chances are high that salary levels will improve at the end of one's career. The public-reformed PAYG system is more convenient for those who have a significant number of years of previous contribution; it is disadvantageous for those beginning their working career. This is so because the Compensatory Benefit (PC), which recognizes past contributions, is almost double the Benefit for Continued Service (PAP), which is applied to future contributions in the public system. Finally, a worker that chooses the public-reformed system will have an annual supplementary salary, while this is not the case in the private system. The person that elects the public-reformed system will be able in the future to transfer to the investment system, but the inverse is only permitted in the first two years that the system functions. This makes the choice more rigid.

Thus, there are many factors affecting the worker's choice. Some factors (gender and years of contribution) are known and easily apparent while others are less predictable, such as how many years of contribution will be made, or what will be the marital status or the age of the spouse at the time of retirement. Finally, there are factors that are impossible to predict, such as what will be the rate of performance of the fund during the working career and retirement of the worker, or what will be the salary level in the later working years.

Uncertainty, then, is an important component when making a decision. In the final analysis, the choice depends upon workers' perceptions of the medium- and long-term future of the economy, the society, and Argentine politics. The public-reformed system may be more adequate for those who prefer security and who accept a low pension (which can be very low, if the public system turns out to be too fragile, financially speaking). The private retirement system may be more appropriate for people who are not afraid of taking risks. In all the above, one unresolved issue is the expansion of coverage to currently uncovered groups. High unemployment rates and evasion may jeopardize universality of coverage. And this is certainly a goal that is pending in Argentina and on which future research should be encouraged.

Notes

Throughout this chapter, dollars ($) are U.S. dollars.

1. The Fluctuation Fund is made monthly, with any profits in excess of 30 percent of the average profit of the system. The fund is measured in shares to cover the difference between the minimum profit guaranteed by the system and the minimum profit of the fund, if this is the lesser, or to increase the profit of the fund in a particu-

lar month, as long as it does not affect more than 10 percent of the fund, and provided that its balance, after the application, is greater than 3 percent of the contribution of the Pension Fund.

2. If members were to opt for life membership, they could contract for the total of the capitalized funds, or contract for a sum no less than 70 percent of the respective retirement base, or for the balance equal to three times the maximum basic universal benefit. In this case, members would be able to draw freely from the balance of their individual account, which could not exceed an equivalent of five hundred times the maximum sum of the basic universal benefit.

3. The base of the calculation is as follows: the annual phased withdrawal is based on the effective balance of the member's account (at the end of the year) and the value of a monthly pension. Thus, actual pensions vary over time. The new legislation establishes a pension for survivors. As with annuities, it is possible to withdraw freely from the funds that exceed the required amount to finance the benefit.

4. This can be used by all members who, even before reaching the established age for accessing the benefit, have a right to a retirement income that is greater or equal to 50 percent of the respective retirement base and at two times the figure of the maximum universal benefit.

5. In the case that a worker chooses the public distribution program and after a time decides to subscribe to the capitalization program, the government will recognize contributions made from July 15, 1994, until the time of transfer.

6. Because of the reform dated March 26, 1994, according to law 24,347, this benefit was instituted for workers of either sex who had reached seventy and who were credited with a minimum of ten years of service with contributions. This gave them access to a benefit equivalent to 70 percent of what would have been awarded to them had they made contributions in the regular manner.

References

Administración Nacional de la Seguridad Social. 1992a. "Previsión social." 2 (5). Buenos Aires.

———. 1992b. "Previsión social." 2 (8). Buenos Aires.

Ambito Financiero. 1992. Buenos Aires. 5 June.

Arellano, José Pablo. 1989. "La seguridad social en Chile en los años 90." *Colección Estudios CIEPLAN* 27 (December).

Asociación de Administradoras de Fondos de Pensiones. 1991. *Análisis del sistema privado de pensiones en Chile*. Santiago de Chile: Congreso Iberoamericano.

Asociación de Bancos Argentinos. 1991. "Propuesta de reforma del sistema previsional argentino." Buenos Aires.

Baeza, Sergio, and Rodrigo Manubens. 1988. *Sistema privado de pensiones en Chile*. Santiago de Chile: Centro de Estudios Públicos.

Cámara de Diputados de la Nación. 1992. "Trámite parlamentario nro. 27." Buenos Aires. 5 June.

Censos nacionales de población. 1980, 1991. Buenos Aires: Instituto Nacional de Estadísticas y Censos.

Demarco, Gustavo, and Laura Posadas. 1992. "Las inequidades en el régimen nacional de previsión social." *Estudios* 15.62 (April–June).

Eichler, Norbert. 1991. "La reforma del régimen pensional ¿Reparto simple o capitalización?: Catálogo de argumentos." In *La reforma del régimen pensional en Colombia.* Bogotá: Fundación Friedrich Ebert de Colombia (FESCOL).

Feldman, Jorge, L. Golbert, and E. A. Isuani. 1988. *Maduración y crisis del sistema previsional argentino.* Biblioteca Política Argentina. Buenos Aires: Centro Editor de América Latina.

Fundación de Investigaciones Económicas Latinoamericanas (FIEL). 1987. *El fracaso del estatismo.* Buenos Aires: Sudamericana/Planeta.

Iglesias, Augusto, and Rodrigo Acuña. 1991. *Chile: Experiencia con un régimen de capitalización, 1981–1991.* Santiago de Chile: CEPAL/PNUD.

Instituto Nacional de Estadísticas y Censos. 1982. *Estimaciones y proyecciones de población, 1950–2025.* Buenos Aires.

———. 1993. *Anuario estadístico de la República Argentina.* Buenos Aires.

Instituto Nacional de Previsión Social. 1990. "El sistema previsional argentino: Desarrollo de un diagnóstico." Buenos Aires. June.

Isuani, Ernesto Aldo. 1985. *Los orígenes conflictivos de la seguridad social argentina.* Biblioteca Política Argentina, no. 129. Buenos Aires: Centro Editor de América Latina.

Isuani, Ernesto Aldo, and Jorge Antonio San Martino. 1993. *La reforma previsional argentina: Opciones y riesgos,* ed. Miño y Dávila. Buenos Aires.

Mesa del Diálogo Público. 1992. *Documento final de la Comisión de Previsión Social.* Buenos Aires. Mimeo.

Mesa-Lago, Carmelo. 1990. "Economic and Financial Aspects of Social Security in Latin America and the Caribbean: Tendencies, Problems, and Alternatives for the Year 2000." Internal discussion paper delivered in Washington, D.C.: World Bank.

———. 1997. "Comparative Analysis of Structural Pension Reform in Eight Latin American Countries: Description, Evaluation and Lessons." In *Capitalization: The Bolivian Model of Social and Economic Reform,* ed. Margaret E. Pierce. La Paz: Ministerio de Capitalización.

Schultess, Walter. 1990. *Sistema nacional de previsión social: Su evolución y situación a fines de la década del ochenta.* Programa Nacional de Asistencia Técnica para la Administración de los Servicios Sociales en la República Argentina (PRONATASS). Buenos Aires: Subsecretaría de Seguridad Social.

7 / The Pension System in Uruguay

A Delayed Reform

Jorge Papadópulos

The Uruguayan social security system is one of the oldest and most developed in Latin America. However, it began declining almost at the same time that it attained its full maturity. Difficulties started more than thirty years ago but full recognition of the situation was only acknowledged very recently. From 1985 to 1995, several attempts to reform the system have failed because of the impossibility of reaching a political consensus. Finally, in September 1995 after ten years of failed reform attempts the new government, which had taken office in March 1995, passed a law that reformed the pensions program, the most expensive and troublesome program. This chapter analyzes the main problems of the pension system, the previous proposals for its reform and the reasons for their failure, the basis of the new social security legislation, and the successful political strategy followed by its supporters.

The first pension law was introduced in Uruguay as early as 1829. It benefited the military that had participated in the independence wars. Others were then gradually incorporated into the system: civil servants (1838), teachers (1896), workers in the modern sector (1919), and rural workers and workers in personal services (1943). A noncontributory pension program for indigents was approved in 1919 (Mesa-Lago 1978, 1985; Papadópulos 1992).

Although the first pension law was approved in 1829, it was not until 1896 (when pensions for teachers were approved) that the pension program became a system organized under the principle of a social insurance system.

Since 1896, the system has followed the principles of social insurance funds administered by the state and by the beneficiaries with contributions from workers, employers, and the state.

During the twentieth century the pension system evolved rather erratically according to initiatives of different governments, political parties, or pressure groups. The output was twofold. First, the consolidation of a highly fragmented administrative structure characterized by inefficiency, clientelism, and privileges created a fragmented and stratified pattern of benefits based on the power of certain social groups rather than on their merit.[1] Second, the result of the "massification of privileges" was the universalization of pension benefits by the mid-1950s. The universalization created citizens rights and the shared perception that, although the benefits could be unsatisfactory and the structure inefficient, the system was basically fair. This perception, as argued below, affected social behavior and attitudes toward the different reforms since 1985.

FEATURES AND DEFICIENCIES OF THE PENSIONS SYSTEM

The Main Features

The Uruguayan social security system includes five programs: family allowances, unemployment, sickness and maternity, employment injury, and pensions. The pension program is the most important one in terms of its cost. In 1988, of the total social security expenditures 81 percent went to pensions, and the remaining 19 percent was allocated to the other four programs (ILO 1992).

Until 1996 (before the reform) three major occupational groups were insured by the Social Insurance Bank (Banco de Previsión Social, BPS). These were civil servants and teachers; workers from the industry and commerce sectors; and rural and domestic workers. The funds were totally controlled by the state. Additionally, there are five other pension programs administered by institutions different from the BPS: workers in the financial sector, university professionals, public notaries, policemen, and the military. Financial and university professionals and notaries are covered by private insurance supervised by the state. Policemen and military funds are under the administrative aegis of the Ministry of Interior and the Ministry of Defense, respectively. Of these pensions, 89 percent were administered by the BPS, and they represented 80 percent of the expenditures of the whole pensions system (Lacurcia 1990).

The pension system had a regular retirement scheme and two other pension programs: (1) survival pensions for widows or children aged under twenty-one of a pensioner or a worker that had paid her or his social security contributions, and (2) a noncontributory pension program for the dispossessed, older than sixty-five. Regarding population coverage, in 1992, the BPS administered almost 700,000 pensions; 115,000 pensioners received more than one pension. Thus, at least 585,000 persons received some kind of pension from the BPS: 350,000 old age pensioners, 170,000 survival pensioners, and 70,000 of the dispossessed. The coverage is around 20 percent on a population of 3 million persons, but, considering that the economically active population (EAP) is around 1,400,000, actual coverage of the EAP is 42 percent (BPS 1993). The legal coverage is around 76 percent (Mesa-Lago 1993).

As for the benefits, the initial retirement pension was a variable percentage (between 60 and 85 percent) of the average income of the last three years of work. The final percentage depended upon a combination of retirement age and years of work (the higher the retirement age and the more years of work, the higher the retirement salary). The retirement age was fifty-five for women and sixty for men who had worked for a period no shorter than thirty years. Since 1987, there were ceilings established as follows: seven minimum salaries when the pension is the result of only one source (a single employment); up to fifteen minimum salaries when the pension results from two or more sources.

The Problems

Because of the universalization of the system, aging of the population, unjustified privileges, clientelism, and inflation that eroded the financial investments in the 1950s, the collective capitalization system became pay-as-you-go (PAYG) and funded by employees, employers, and the state. The state contributed as employer and through cash transfers estimated on a fixed share of the Value Added Tax (VAT). In recent years the state funded the deficit through cash transfers from tax revenues. Employers in the private sector contributed 16 percent from the payroll. As an employer, the state's contribution varied from 19.5 to 24.5 percent depending upon the public sector (central and local government pay more than public enterprises). Employees in both public and private sectors contributed 13 percent.

An early demographic transition and a huge international emigration of the youth led to an aging population; the population over sixty represents 15.8 percent of the total population (UN 1993). These factors plus the growth of informal labor and the growing evasion of the system caused a steady decline in the support rate (ratio of contributors to pensioners). In 1960 there were 3.8 active contributors for each pensioner, whereas in 1983 there were only 1.3 contributors per pensioner.

The indexation system of pensions approved in 1989 (as will be discussed later) produced an explosive growth of expenses. Social security expenditures between 1986 and 1992 rose from 9.6 to 16.1 percent of GDP, becoming the most expensive system in Latin America. This meant a heavier financial burden for both the system and the active population, and eventually, a cut in resources for the elderly and their dependents.

Since 1989 the new BPS administration increased the collection of taxes, although evasion continued high. It was estimated at 32 percent in 1991 according to studies conducted by the BPS (1993). Thus, the deficit of the public PAYG system was growing systematically. Recent figures show that the deficit of the system was 2.8 percent of GDP in 1989, 2 percent in 1990, 2.6 percent in 1991, and 3.1 percent in 1992 (BPS 1994).

Until 1987, Uruguayan pensioners experienced a continuous deterioration of their real pensions. In 1974–1981 the decline of the real pension was 45 percent, representing one of the worst indicators of impoverishment in the Uruguayan population (Mesa-Lago 1992). In 1986, just one year after the new democratic government took office, 64 percent of the old age pensioners, 95.4 percent of the survival pensioners, and all of the disability pensioners each received less than one minimum salary; the minimum monthly wage in 1986 was US$75 (Papadópulos 1992). Additionally, Mesa-Lago indicated that pensioners lacked sickness insurance coverage and that poor pensioners could not afford affiliation in the mutual aid societies and their only access to health was through the Ministry of Public Health (MPH) and a few public institutions and NGOs" (Mesa-Lago 1992). Since the quality of services available at the Ministry of Public Health is low, the access to better health services for the elderly depends upon the nonpension income of the elderly, which normally is nonexistent or very low.

The social security problems that have been discussed so far, the structural adjustment proposals that emerged as a consequence of the failure of former development models, and the conditionalities imposed by the international financial agencies, all created the circumstances for the social security reform.

THE SOCIAL SECURITY DEBATE

The 1970s

The social security crisis has been incorporated into the political agenda of the most relevant political and social actors during the last thirty-five years. This crisis has affected the policy making of the current political actors. It has also led to the building up of new actors and to the articulation of various political coalitions.

The first attempt to overcome the crisis was during the mid-1960s. In 1961 and 1965, Congress approved legislation to adjust real pensions. Under the authoritarian regime (1973–1984), efforts were made to centralize and rationalize the system. Additionally, the regime's macroeconomic policy led to a reduction of the labor costs in order to improve external competitiveness. Thus, the government managed to reduce salaries and social public expenditures. Pensions were reduced both as a means of inflation control and to reduce the public deficit. As Saldain (1987) pointed out, "the pensions' value had become a means to adjust the fiscal deficit." As a consequence, the real value of pensions suffered a loss estimated between 75 and 50 percent between 1955 and 1983 (Fortuna 1984; Papadópulos 1992).

The First Democratic Government, 1985–1989

In 1985, after eleven years of dictatorship, the first democratic government was elected. When President Sanguinetti took office, the system was severely affected by the structural, administrative, and financial problems described above (Mesa-Lago 1985, 1992; Saldain 1993). As a consequence, social security reform was the issue that consumed the most official energy.

Also in 1985, the government signed an agreement with the International Monetary Fund (IMF), which included the reduction of the fiscal deficit by major cuts in pension expenditures. The agreement stated that the reduction in pension expenditures "will allow the government to achieve a budgetary saving of around 0.5 percent of GDP during the first 12 months of the program" (*Búsqueda*, December 9, 1985). The government attempted to achieve this goal by reducing the real value of the higher pensions and manipulating the indexation system. A coalition of leftist parties and pensioners' associations blocked this attempt.

In 1987 the government tried to enact a law that intended to change some of the structural features of the system following guidelines provided by a World Bank mission. The project intended to eliminate Congress participation in the discussion of periodical adjustment and was aimed at raising the retirement age, diminishing the initial retirement salary, eliminating some privileged pensions, increasing workers' contributions, and establishing an indexation system that was perceived by pensioners' associations as prejudicial to their interests. This project was approved, but the government had to make several important concessions to the opposition.

Although the retirement age was not changed, the retirement salary was lowered, and a mechanism that stimulated late retirement was approved. For instance, the retirement salary that was formerly calculated on the basis of the last ten years of work was now to be calculated on the basis of the last three years of work.[2] The VAT was raised and new taxes were created in order to fund the deficit. Some privileged pensions were eliminated.

Finally, a new indexation system was approved. Politicians from both the government and the opposition thought that the new indexation system could provide pensioners with certainty about their future real income. It was also believed that one of the most disturbing issues in the political agenda was to be closed. But this was not the case. Stimulated by the successful result of the indexation battles of the first years of democracy, pensioners' associations emerged as one of the most important political actors of the decade. Leadership for these associations was provided by former labor union leaders. They brought to this new social movement organizational skills as well as images of collective action that were founded on ideas of solidarity learned and internalized in years of unionism. These organizational features allowed pensioners' associations to overcome eventual political differences, making them the most powerful corporatist organization in the country. In a society with a high percentage of persons depending on the pension system, it was easy for these organizations to articulate a powerful lobby that forced political parties to accept pensioners' demands because of fear of electoral consequences.

In 1989, seven months before national elections were held, pensioners' associations—unsatisfied with the indexation established by political parties two years previously—proposed an amendment to the Constitution that was voted on in a referendum. This amendment permitted a new indexation system, by which pensions would be adjusted every four months according to the variation in the national average nominal salary. Thus, any improvement in the general level of productivity or purchasing power capacity would be transferred to pensions.

In the period 1985–1989 pensioners' associations, labor unions, and leftist parties built a political coalition, which backed the reform, whereas other political parties fearing the loss of pensioners' votes either supported the reform or did not take any position on the issue. As a result, 82 percent of the voters approved the amendment, which meant that no government could any longer use pension values as a means of deficit reduction, and the real value of pensions was expected to improve with economic growth. In fact, in the last five years the value of pensions has improved more than public salaries. On the other hand, a structural reform of the system arose as the only way to control the growing deficit.

The Second Democratic Government, 1990–1994

Three reform projects were sent by President Lacalle's government to Congress. None prospered. The first one and the third one were rejected by Congress. The second one, which was eventually approved, was rejected by a popular referendum that took place together with the 1994 national elections.

The first proposal was submitted to Congress in 1992 and established a mixed system—PAYG and a fully funded individual (FFI) capitalization program. The system would remain entirely under public control. With the exception of those persons that needed only two more years for retirement, all the insured would be incorporated into the individual capitalization system. While not eliminated, the executive retained the prerogative of lowering the employer's contribution when the system reached actuarial equilibrium. The retirement age continued the same but the project established incentives for late retirement. This proposed project was the most ambitious attempt at reforming the system. The procedure that followed for the drafting of the law was innovative too.

The Uruguayan technocracy is not independent from the political parties, and in contrast to Chile (Montecinos 1988) its level of coherence is low. The state apparatus is as fragmented as the political party structure, and the logic that drives technical expertise is more political than technical. The relationship between technocrats and policy operators at the level of the social security sector mirrors this reality. Technocrats who operate at the executive branch of the government had designed a market-oriented economic program. However, these *técnicos* working at the social security level responded to different factions of the same political party (or even, to different political parties), thus blocking coherence between the sectoral *técnicos* and the government's economic team.

As a consequence, the technocracy has not been isolated from pressures coming from society. Political inputs coming from civil society have been processed by different fractions of the political parties avoiding technocratic coherence. In order to overcome these problems, in 1991 the president of the BPS initiated the first attempt at building a commission of *técnicos* with social security expertise, taken from different political parties. The project the executive sent to Congress was the result of more than one year of work in the framework of this technical commission.

When the draft was sent to Congress, despite technical agreements, the project was vetoed. The "gray power coalition" had found a way to bring pressure on politicians who feared the political consequences of approving a reform that was disliked by the pensioners' associations. On the other hand, the process of building up a commission of experts with different political identities was an extremely important effort, which enhanced technical coherence on the social security issue. For the first time (the project's failure notwithstanding), party fragmentation was overcome, at least at the technical level, and *técnicos* with different political identities agreed on the basis for the structural reform of the system.

The second proposed project was not conceived as an independent law and was not as deep and comprehensive as the first one. The failure of the first initiative gave grounds for the government to fear that open discussion of a new project could lead to another failure. The executive wanted to isolate the parliamentary debate from the pressures coming from the "gray power coalition." The government attempted to hide the negotiations of the social security reform in the framework of a wider discussion on budgetary matters, instead of following the regular procedure for enacting social security legislation.[3] The multiple issues of the budgetary discussion were supposed to provide an excellent opportunity for negotiation with the opposition.

This strategy was successful, and by the end of 1992 the reform was approved. The project was not as ambitious as the previous one. It had two main features. (1) Instead of calculating the retirement salary on the basis of the worker's last three years of work, the project established as a basis for appraisal the last ten years of work. (2) The basic retirement salary was lowered to 55 percent of the average salary of the last ten years of activity (this had been the last three years in the older system).

The political strategy was successful at the parliamentary level, but its content and the procedures for its approval were censured by the pensioners' associations. The latter opposed the way the retirement salary was calculated. But the most important critic was formal: the Constitution does not allow legislation on social security issues to be decided using the budgetary framework. Thus, similar to 1989, pensioners' associations proposed a referendum in order to derogate the reform. The referendum had to be held in 1994 and coincided with the national elections. As in 1989 politicians fearing the loss of electoral support did not consistently oppose the referendum, and the coalition of pensioners' associations received an 82 percent approval for derogating the reform.

The third proposed project was presented by the executive at the end of 1993. This project proposed a mixed system; sixty-five years as the minimum retirement age for men and women; and a basic retirement salary estimated on the basis of the 65 percent of the average of the last ten years of work. The project established a voluntary private supplementary pension program for those insured who had earned more than a certain minimum. The draft was rejected by Congress.

IMMEDIATE ANTECEDENTS AND MAIN FEATURES OF A SUCCESSFUL REFORM

Beginning in 1994, after the failure of the third reform proposal, the Ministry of Economy and Finance agreed with the Inter-American Development Bank (IADB) on a consultantship. The project was kept secret until it was completed at the end of 1994, and neither the population nor the board of directors of the BPS were informed. The consultantship included experts from Brazil and Uruguay. The final work was a series of reports, which included an analysis of equity in the system, the political viability of five alternative reform models, their impact on macroeconomics, and a final chapter proposing the most viable political as well as financial reform.

The proposed system was a mixed one (Ministerio de Economía y Finanzas 1994). It had three tiers. The first was a program for the dispossessed, supported with general revenues. The second was a PAYG program supported exclusively by employees' contributions, with a ceiling for benefits of four minimum salaries (around US$300). In this program employers' contributions would be transferred to salaries. The third was a fully funded voluntary and supplementary program for workers younger than forty who earn more than four minimum salaries. This complementary system could be managed under private or public administration. The retirement age was set at sixty-five for both men and women. The proposal also established the unification of all existing funds (notaries, professionals, bank employees, policemen, and the military). It proposed the establishment of three separate programs, to be administered by different entities: pensions, health, and social assistance.

This comprehensive reform proposal was released only when the new government from the Colorado Party (the former government's traditional opposition party) took office in March 1995. Soon after the new government was elected in November 1994, but before March 1995, a multiparty commission—appointed by the newly elected government and composed of all political parties that had parliamentary representation—was established with the goal of formulating a reform project for the social security system. All participants, except those belonging to the left (a component of the "gray coalition"), knew the reports from the IADB consultantship.

After a couple of weeks' work the commission released a public announcement in which its members declared that the pension system was going to be transformed into a mixed one. While important differences existed between the IADB's consultantship and the released project (employers' contribution, retirement age, income tiers, obligatory savings, and so on), the core of both proposals—the mixed system—was the same. The Broad Front ("Frente Amplio," a leftist coalition representing 31 percent of the electorate) disagreed with the announcement and left the commission. On the other side, the bipartisan commission working in secret produced a reform proposal that was released to the public only when it was presented in Congress.

The project became a law (16.713/1995) on September 11, 1995, backed by the two Uruguayan traditional parties (Colorado and Blanco) and strongly opposed by the Broad Front, the labor unions, and the pensioners' associations. The new law created a mixed system that combines a public-reformed PAYG program with a mandatory FFI capitalization one. The public-reformed is managed by the central social security institution (BPS) and pays a basic pension. The individual capitalization is managed by pension managers (AFAPs) and pays a supplementary pension. Coverage is mandatory for salaried and self-employed workers. It also maintains (though with some changes) the noncontributory pension program. Individuals will be affiliated with one of the following programs according to their income.

First, the PAYG program covers workers who earn less than 5,000 pesos (5.60 pesos equals 1 $US). The retirement age is sixty years for both men and women, and thirty-five years of contribution are required. The retirement salary is 50 percent of the average of the monthly incomes earned during the last ten years of work. The retirement salary increases 0.5 percent for each additional year of work above the minimum thirty-five. For those retiring aged older than sixty, on the basic retirement salary, 3 percent per extra year of age will be added up to a maximum of 30 percent. The minimum pension is 550 pesos, and the ceiling is 4,250 pesos. Both employees and employers contribute to the BPS. Insured who are older than forty had the option (during a six-month period) to maintain the entitlement conditions of the old system (not reformed) or to move to the mixed system. This measure signified that the old public system stopped operating, because it was mandatory that everybody else and new entrants were covered in the mixed system.

Second, the mixed system is made of the public-reformed PAYG and the mandatory individual capitalization for workers younger than forty and new entrants earning between 5,000 and 15,000 pesos. The retirement requirements are the same as for the PAYG system. For salaries of up to 5,000 pesos, the employee has to contribute to the PAYG system (BPS), and for salaries from 5,000 to 15,000 pesos, the employee has to contribute to a public or private pension fund administrator. The employer has to contribute on the full amount of the payroll to the BPS. The pensioner receives a combined pension from both the PAYG and the capitalization system. The retirement salary from the capitalization system is determined by the cumulative savings and life expectancy of the insured (at the retirement moment). This program and the PAYG system insure disability and death risks.

Public institutions and private companies are allowed to administer new pension funds. The BPS, the Bank of the Republic (Banco de la República), and the Housing Bank (Banco Hipotecario del Uruguay) are state institutions allowed to have AFAPs. The Central Bank authorizes and supervises the operation of the AFAPs, which invest funds in a limited and regulated set of investments. AFAPs earn a profit from a fee charged to contributors; they are not allowed to benefit from their investments. They transfer cumulative individual savings to an insurance company when conditions for retirement (death or disability) are reached. Contributors select an insurance company that is responsible for the monthly payment of the pension.

Third, another type of mixed system is the PAYG, mandatory individual capitalization, and voluntary savings for those workers younger than forty who earn more than 15,000 pesos. The program works as in the second tier, but the employee is free to make savings over the amount of 15,000 pesos in any of the public or private insurance institutions. Fourth, the old age subsidy program is for those workers older than seventy which have contributed to the system for at least fifteen years. These pensions are incompatible with any other pension. Fifth, there is a noncontributory program for indigents older than seventy who are absolutely unable to work. Pensions will be paid through an independent fund administered by the Central Government.

The contribution of the insured was increased by 2 percent (compensated by an equal increase in salary, but only at the start), and that of the employer was reduced by 2 percent. Entitlement conditions have been standardized, and there is no recognition bond because the insured either stayed in the old system or is in the public-reformed component of the mixed system. Nor is there any minimum pension in the individual capitalization component, because the public program pays a basic pension. No superintendency was created, and the central bank exercises regulatory and supervisory functions. The BPS collects contributions and keeps a labor history of each worker (Mesa-Lago 1997).

GOVERNANCE AND THE POLITICS OF EXPERTISE

Social security reform has been a painful issue in Uruguay. All the relevant social and political actors agreed on the need for such a reform. The meaning of this reform, however, was different for those involved in the debate. Reform attempts in the last ten years show that a comprehensive and structural reform was reached only after a broad agreement was achieved on each component of the reform.

In the 1984 and 1989 elections, the most committed reformist parties—Blanco and Colorado—had 75 percent of the votes between them, but they were not able to reform the social security system. When direct democracy was appealed by referendum, the political will of representatives was rejected. When the vote of the Blanco and Colorado parties dropped and the vote of the left increased, a government coalition of the Colorado and Blanco parties consolidated in order to block the left and pass some structural reforms. One of the most important of these reforms was precisely the social security reform. The politics of social security reform in Uruguay in 1985–1995 presented three different but interconnected themes.

First, the lobbying power of pensioners' associations increased systematically during this period. They built a corporatist coalition that successfully blocked any reformist attempt they perceived as dangerous to their interests. Indeed, they were able not only to block the government projects but also to include their own indexation system in the Constitution. Political parties clearly feared that losing the support from the "gray power" could negatively affect their electoral performance. Thus, when debates on pension issues were held too close to elections, political parties did not oppose pensioners' proposals. Second, the only initially successful reform was the one that remained hidden from public debate (and from the "gray power") when it was discussed within the broader secret debate of the public budget in 1992. However, because of its unconstitutional character, the reform was rejected by popular referendum. Third, the most comprehensive and the only effective reform was designed when technical agreement and coherence was achieved. Former projects were able to propose only minor adjustments. The experience gathered in many years of failed attempts helped create a political and intellectual groundwork for more comprehensive reforms.

According to the above-mentioned experience, any structural reform of the system within a democracy requires high levels of technical coherence and expertise, isolation from pressures from civil society, and either negotiation with or defeat of pensioners' associations (Filgueira and Papadópulos 1996). In particular, temporal distance from elections must be taken, in order to allow political parties to express their preferences and build up, eventually, a reformist coalition that can bring a proposal to the legislative branch. The newly elected government in 1995 and its partner, the Blanco party, learned the lessons in governance. Progress made on the content of the reform was accomplished in secrecy, avoiding the incorporation of corporatist interest in the debate until a reform proposal was actually produced (with the support of the IADB). The experience of the 1992 failed reform had created for the first time a team of experts from both parties. The IADB consultantship continued providing technical arguments and expertise, which apparently convinced politicians from the Blanco and the Colorado parties.

The reform was implemented at the beginning of the new administration in March 1996. According to the Constitution it is not possible to convoke a referendum in matters affecting the tax system, which includes the social security system (there are contending constitutional interpretations about this issue), unless a constitutional reform is convoked, which has to await the national elections (1999). The Broad Front, the pensioners' associations, and the labor unions have already agreed on convoking a referendum against the current law. While, apparently, Uruguayans are not eager to engage in the social security debate in the next five years, when the referendum is convoked unpredictable results can occur such as the ones that have plagued the history of social security in the last fifteen years.

Notes

1. Mesa-Lago (1978, 1985) has shown that this pattern was followed by the *pioneer* countries of the region.

2. This way of estimating the retirement salary was rapidly perceived as an incentive for tax evasion. Employees and employers could agree on a false salary, lower than the real one, and raise it three years before the employee retired. Both employees and employers benefited and became partners in this fraudulent maneuver. This is also the regular procedure used by the self-employed and by entrepreneurs.

3. Only the executive power has initiative on pension legislation. Congress can reject, modify, or approve the projects sent by the executive but it can not propose social security reforms.

References

Banco de Previsión Social (BPS). 1993. *La seguridad social en el Uruguay.* Montevideo: BPS.

———. 1994. *Boletín Estadístico.* Año 14, no 47. Montevideo: BPS.

Búsqueda. 1985. December 9, 1985.

Filgueira, Fernando, and Jorge Papadópulos. 1996. "Putting Conservatism to Good Use? Long Crisis and Vetoed Alternatives in Uruguay." In *The New Politics of Inequality in Latin America: Rethinking Participation and Representation,* ed. Douglas Chalmers et al. New York: Oxford University Press.

Fortuna, Juan Carlos. 1984. *Gasto público social en Uruguay.* Montevideo: Informe CIESU-ECIEL.

International Labour Office (ILO). 1992. *The Cost of Social Security: Thirteenth International Inquiry, 1984–1986. Comparative Tables.* Geneva: ILO.

Lacurcia, Hugo. 1990. "El sistema de pensiones en Uruguay." In *Regulación del sistema financiero y reforma del sistema de pensiones: Experiencias de América Latina.* Santiago de Chile: CEPAL/PNUD.

Mesa-Lago, Carmelo. 1978. *Social Security in Latin America: Pressure Groups, Stratification and Inequality.* Pittsburgh: University of Pittsburgh Press.

———. 1985. *El desarrollo de la seguridad social en América Latina.* Santiago: Estudios e Informes de la CEPAL, no. 43.

———. 1992. *Atención de la salud para los pobres en la América Latina y el Caribe.* Washington D.C.: OPS-IAF.

———. 1993. "Changing Social Security in Latin America and the Caribbean: Towards the Alleviation of Social Costs." Pittsburgh: University of Pittsburgh. Mimeo.

———. 1997. "Comparative Analysis of Structural Pension Reform in Eight Latin American Countries: Description, Evaluation and Lessons." Presented to the International Seminar on Pension Reform, Ministerio de Capitalización de Bolivia, and World Bank. University of Miami, May 18.

Ministerio de Economía y Finanzas. 1994. *Viabilidad económico-financiera e impactos macroeconómicos.* Sumario ejecutivo. Montevideo. Manuscript.

Montecinos, Verónica. 1988. "Economics and Power: Chilean Economists in Government, 1958–1985." Ph.D. dissertation, University of Pittsburgh.

Papadópulos, Jorge. 1992. *Seguridad social y política en el Uruguay.* Montevideo: CIESU.

Saldain, Rodolfo. 1987. *El social welfare en el Uruguay.* Montevideo. Manuscript.

———. 1993. "Seguridad social en el Uruguay: Un análisis en proyección y bases de cambio." In *Revista de la Seguridad Social* 1 (1).

United Nations (UN). 1993. *Demographic Yearbook.* New York: UN Publishing Division.

8 / The Pension System Reform in Peru

Economic Rationale Versus Political Will

María Amparo Cruz-Saco Oyague

THE DESIGN AND IMPLEMENTATION of the pension reform in Peru have to be contextualized within the social turbulence of the late 1980s and the neoliberal economic program of President Fujimori in 1990–2000. By the end of Alan García's populist regime, the country reached a turning point in history, struck by political violence, hyperinflation, economic chaos, and insignificant state authority (Crabtree 1992; Graham 1992). When President Fujimori's authoritarian style of governing began to redeem civil society from over a decade of political and economic instability, he could receive only approval from diverse collectives such as impoverished dependent workers, neighborhood and women's organizations, businessmen and professional associations, and so on.

The neoliberal structural reforms that have been implemented since 1990 redefined the nature of the endogenous sources of economic progress. Governmental policies directed at raising investment along with improved productivity in exporting, agroindustrial activities, and services increased the annual average rate of growth to 7 percent in 1993–1997. The implementation of the economic program was achieved within an environment created by attracting foreign investment and reducing state intervention. Peru's foreign investment legislation was one of the most liberal in the world. Economic reforms included the adoption of a flexible exchange rate regime (which has remained stable in the last five years), the liberalization and modernization of the financial system and the capital market, and the enlargement and consolidation of the private sector through changes in property rights and more transparent rules of the game. In 1994–1995 the Peruvian economy, with a yearly growth rate of 10 percent, was the fastest-growing economy in Latin America in a context of increasing price stability, and a solid management of economic policy (ECLAC 1994). In 1996 economic growth fell to less than 3 percent, but in 1997 it resumed again with an estimated growth rate of 4.5 percent.

An important political turning point came in 1997, when President Fujimori's rating hit an all-time low, which polarized the nation mainly because of his obstinate interest in reinterpreting the 1993 Constitution and running for a third time. The 1993 Constitution approves presidential reelections. Fujimori used the argument that his 1995–2000 term (actually his second) was in fact his first constitutional mandate, claiming that the 1993 Constitution had not been drafted when he was elected the first time.

The discussion of the pension reform in Peru was limited to traditional politicians and "public opinion makers"—mainly concentrated in newspapers, television, and radio shows, some selected analysts, and a few workers' organizations. There was no parliamentary discussion of the new pension reform, simply because the Congress was dissolved in President Fujimori's coup on April 5, 1992, the famous "autogolpe."[1] Decree Law (D.L.) 724 of November 1991 established a Private Pension System (SPP) that was to run parallel to the public system, the first parallel model in the region. This legislation was not enforced and a second law was enacted in 1992 after the April 5 coup when constitutional guarantees were suspended. D.L. 25897 created the SPP, which is parallel to the public system, and which initiated operations in June 1993.

The incapacity of civil society to participate in the design of fundamental policies, such as the pension reform, and to respond to government action shows "political desintermediation" (Sagasti and Hernández 1994). The lack of congressional debate resembles the Chilean experience and contrasts very sharply with the reform processes in Argentina, Bolivia, Colombia, Ecuador, Guatemala, Mexico, Paraguay, and Uruguay, where interest groups have either engaged in active confrontation (as in Mexico, Argentina, or Uruguay; see chapters 4, 6, and 7) or are currently completely polarized on the issue (as in Ecuador, Guatemala, and Paraguay). In Colombia, the reform of the public pension system was approved in 1993 and was implemented in April 1994, after two years of intense congressional debate and as part of the structural reforms that began in 1990. In Argentina, the debate over the pension reform took a decade until it was finally implemented in May 1994. Mexico, on the other hand, approved supplementary and voluntary savings accounts in 1992 after an important debate over the type of pension fund reform that should be adopted. In 1995 and 1996, government engaged in an enormous concertation effort and approved the privatization of the pension system that began implementation in 1997. These examples show that reforms under democracy take longer because of the contending forces from pushers and resisters.

Our discussion will now turn to the reform process in Peru. The first section discusses the reasons for the pension reform and its implementation. The second will analyze the main characteristics of the first reform (1993); the third section will do the same for the second reform (1995). The fourth section will review the macroeconomic consequences of the reform. The last section will present conclusions.

ANTECEDENTS OF THE REFORM

Pension reforms in Latin America follow a virtually universal crisis of the conventional public social security systems, because of a combination of problems such as poor population coverage, burdensome and regressive contributions, evasion, inefficient investment policies, inequitable benefits, high health care costs, low-quality health services, heavy administrative expenditures, serious managerial deficiencies, and worsening actuarial and financial imbalances. Until 1993 in Peru one central agency—the Peruvian Social Security Institute (IPSS)—provided both health care and old age, disability, and survivors pensions under a scheme of occupational insurance, with contributions from workers, employers, and the state (separate pension funds existed for civil servants, the armed forces, and fishermen). An important function of the IPSS, which was created in 1974 in order to consolidate various programs, was the administration of the National Public Pension System (SNP). A decade after the creation of the IPSS, it obviously featured the standard problems of all the Latin American public social security systems.

The first fundamental factor explaining the introduction and implementation of the pension reform was precisely the profound crisis of the IPSS and the need for a reform. Most important, the pension fund—managed on a pay-as-you-go (PAYG) basis—was depleted in real terms because of very negative real investment yields, a significant state debt, substantial evasion and payment delays, and extraordinarily high administrative costs (Mesa-Lago 1994). These problems were compounded by low population coverage, extremely low pensions, chaotic administration of services to beneficiaries, and a general lack of professionalism in the management of the pension fund and in the IPSS as a whole.

Although statistical information is poor and incomplete, there is agreement that the total number of active affiliates in the IPSS before the reform was introduced was around 2.5 million, one-third of the labor force estimated at 7.1 million in 1993 (Cuánto 1994, 381) with close to 300,000 pensioners. Such a low coverage is explained by structural factors. At the national level, rural workers comprise one-third of the labor force and they have very little coverage despite isolated attempts to expand it. One-half of the economically active population (EAP)—including both urban and rural workers—consists of the self-employed and nonsalaried family workers, or *informals*. In essence, the salaried labor force in Peru that is subject to direct occupational insurance with the IPSS is only 40 percent of the labor force (Cuánto 1992, 485).

Because of hyperinflation, the real average pension fell 90 percent in 1985–1990. Then, in November 1991 after Fujimori's new stabilization program, the average monthly pension was approximately $70, which was paid to pensioners regardless of years of contribution because the monumental loss of value caused by hyperinflation had generated a uniform distribution of benefits. Despite lagging or partial indexation policies during the late 1980s this type of distribution remained unchanged (Apoyo 1992).

Dissatisfaction with the services of the IPSS prompted several protest campaigns organized by affiliates, pensioners, and the media. Health care services deteriorated rapidly because of increasing costs not accompanied by increasing revenues, overcrowded establishments, lack of personnel, and deficient administration of resources. Complaints intensified by the end of the 1980s because of the extended strikes by health workers in the public sector who demanded higher wages. There was consensus regarding the need for reform in the social security system. The question was, What type of reform should be implemented? Three alternatives existed: (1) reforming the IPSS only, (2) privatizing both the provision for health care and the pension system with fully substitutive models, and (3) adopting a mixed system (both in health care, with a reformed public scheme and private health providers, and in pensions).

A broad segment of the impoverished middle-income and working groups feared that privatization of the social security system would only benefit profit-making health providers and financial interest groups. They still supported the IPSS, despite the agency's deteriorated image, because it seemed to personify the state's commitment to social security and health care. The belief that a benefactor state intrinsically protects citizens was at the basis of the arguments that challenged the management of the IPSS, but the IPSS's mandate was never put into question. This stems from the traditionally populist view of a paternalistic state that is so deeply and culturally engendered in people's ideologies.

On the other side, professionals, upper-middle-income groups, the financial sector, and foreign advisors urged that the social security system had to be fully privatized following the radical Chilean model introduced in 1981. Caught in the middle between these two conflicting views, which reflected an important degree of stratification and class consciousness, President Fujimori sanctioned a mixed pension system, but no action was taken to advance the urgently needed health care reform. The latter was reformed in November 1991 with legislative decree no. 718, which created the Private Health System (SPS) and terminated the IPSS's monopoly in the provision of health care. This legislation was not enforced, and legally, the IPSS continued to be the single provider of health care through the public health insurance program. Numerous unregulated private health insurance institutions and providers existed supplying parallel insurance policies to middle- and upper-level workers. They contracted this coverage at additional cost because contributions for health coverage to the IPSS were mandatory. The 1997 health sector reform gave the option for either maintaining the IPSS coverage or contracting private health insurance and ceased to make health care contributions to IPSS mandatory.

Fujimori's need to legitimate his administration was a second fundamental factor explaining the introduction of a mixed solution to the pension system. History has shown without any doubt, that from the beginning he had a calculated sympathy for the populist view. A civil-authoritarian president, embarked on neoliberal structural reforms, has shown, in the particular case of the pension reform, that in politics there is room for flexibility. In his personalistic style of playing inclusiveness he did not challenge the working classes' prejudices against the SNP, hence, his popular support remained intact.

THE FIRST REFORM, DECREE LAW 25897, 1993

The 1992 pension reform in Peru created a mixed system in which the conventional, public PAYG system of the IPSS coexists with the SPP. Major modifications to the original model were introduced in 1995. The SPP closely replicated the Chilean private pension model. (1) Private pension funds are solely administered by Private Pension Fund Administrators (AFPs) that are strictly regulated and supervised by the Superintendency of AFPs (SAFP). (2) The insured worker alone contributes a fixed portion of his or her salary to a mandatory saving or pension program (under the so-called fixed contribution scheme). (3) The insured's contribution is credited to an individual account, and his or her funds are invested by the AFP. (4) The insured is free to choose among different, competing AFPs. (5) The insured can open a voluntary savings account and the employer can voluntarily contribute. (6) At the time of retirement, the insured chooses from various old age pension options.

The Peruvian SPP and the Chilean private pension system have, however, important differences. (1) The SNP continues to exist and it is administered by a newly created agency, the Institute of Previsional Normalization (ONP). (2) Workers, including new entrants to the labor force, can choose affiliation to the public or the private system; they can not only transfer affiliation from one AFP to another as many times as they want (this option was later limited to one transfer every six months), but until December 1995 they could also affiliate back to the SNP. (3) A maximum of 60,000 new soles (about $27,000 in 1995) was placed on a recognition bond, a limit that does not exist in Chile, and the calculation of the recognition bond is much simpler than in Chile (Mesa-Lago 1994). (4) A minimum pension guaranteed by the government in the SPP did not exist initially but was introduced in 1995 (as of July 1998 it had not been regulated). (5) Finally, in Chile, from the onset the pension reform was part of a comprehensive social security reform that included a national health care reform. In Peru, the newest health sector reform law (1997) was approved five years later so that the pension reform was conceived in isolation.

Decree law no. 25897 left the public system unmodified. Entitlement conditions and contributions in the latter were not changed until 1995. Coverage is mandatory for salaried workers and optional for the self-employed. Excluded from the reform were the armed forces, workers of the fishing industry, and public sector workers who were not included in the old IPSS's

Table 8.1 Three Special Pension Programs Excluded from the Reform in Peru, 1995

Year	*Legislation*	*Scope*	*Benefits*	*Eligibility*	*Financing and Funding*
1965	Supreme Decree 04-65-TR	Fishermen	Health, widow's pension, orphan allowance, etc.	* 55 years of age * Minimum of 15 weekly annual contributions * Registration in the program and with fisher ID	The maximum amount of the retirement pension is equal to 80% of the five-year average salary received during the last five years.
1974	Decree Law 21021	Armed forces and police	Retirement, widow's pension, orphan allowance	* After 15/12.5 years of service for men/women	For 15–20 years of service, the pension would equal 1/30 of the salary corresponding to every year of service. After 30 years of service, the amount will equal that of the salary. For 35 years of service or more, the pension would increase depending on the number of years of service, and remuneration is relative to the remuneration of the total salary of the immediate higher grade. The worker contributes 6% and the employer another 6%.
1974	Decree Law 20530 (under ONP jurisdiction)	Public sector workers not included in the IPSS, regular SNP	Retirement, pension of the suspended official, widow's pension, orphan's allowance, survivor, disability	* 30/25 years of service for men/women	Financed by general revenues. The amount of the pension equals that of the salary of an active worker. The worker contributes 6% and the employer another 6%.

Source: Based on Kane 1995, 14.

pension system (law 19990) and who enjoyed a privileged program that granted retirement pensions that were fully indexed to active salaries. Because of these important exclusions and the marked differences in the financing, entitlement conditions, and benefits of these programs, the Peruvian pension system continues to create important distortions. Table 8.1 presents the main features of the pension programs that were not included in the reform.

This first pension reform gave strong incentives not to transfer to the SPP. The payroll tax for workers and employers in the SNP remained at 3 percent and 6 percent (as opposed to approximately 15.5 percent in the SPP, which included a net pension saving of 10 percent, a solidarity contribution of 1 percent paid to the IPSS, and a combination of administrative costs and life insurance and disability premia plus sales taxes for the remaining 4–4.5 percent). More liberal entitlement conditions existed with regard to retirement age (sixty for males and fifty-five for females, versus sixty-five for both sexes in the SPP), anticipated retirement, and the total period of contribution (from thirteen to fifteen years in the public system as opposed to twenty in the SPP) made the SNP alternative more appealing. Workers who transferred to the SPP received a net salary increment of 13.54 percent to pay for the additional cost of the new pension system. They received a recognition bond for their past contributions to the IPSS, which was based on age, years of contribution, and current salary. They had the ownership of their mandatory savings in their individual account and could make voluntary additional contributions to it. Pensioners from the SPP, however, were not allowed to contribute 4 percent to the IPSS for health insurance as did the pensioners from the SNP.

Five AFPs began to operate in June 1993. Shortly after, three additional AFPs joined the industry with the expectation that a massive transfer of workers from the SNP to the SPP was going to take place. During the first four months of the SPP, affiliation was of the order of a hundred thousand workers a month; it dropped then to eighty thousand, and three months later, it dropped again by half. During June 1994–June 1995, the total number of affiliates in the SPP increased by less than seven thousand workers a month, and the rate of affiliation was further decreasing. Only 13 percent of the labor force and less than half of all the insured were affiliated with the SPP by July 1995. This contrasted dramatically with the Chilean experience where, a year after the reform was introduced, half the labor force and close to 70 percent of all the insured had become affiliated with the new scheme (Mesa-Lago 1994, 116).

Since the implementation of the reform, the AFPs expressed their concerns that the SPP was not going to prosper in a meaningful way unless the strong bias against the SPP was eliminated. In 1994 the drop in the rate of affiliation forced the AFPs to downsize their infrastructure. They cut down the number of promoters from near five thousand to one thousand in the span of one year. They were forced to reduce their advertisement expenses also, to close agencies, and to double their initial capital investments in order to continue operating. In an effort to remain in the industry, four AFPs merged successfully in 1994, and another two in 1996, which reduced the total number of AFPs to five. The industry is made up of four AFPs that are relatively large (Horizonte, Integra, Profuturo–El Roble, and Union) and a small one (Nueva Vida). This industry structure is supposed to remain constant in the medium to long run.

An additional problem faced by the AFPs after their first two years of operation was the noncompliance of employers and employees. Very often, employers deducted contributions and did not transfer them to the AFPs, which is flagrant violation of regulations. Between one-third and one-half of the affiliates, depending upon the AFP in question, did not contribute on a regular basis (Barúa 1994). The economic incentive to evade and incur payment delinquencies was caused by a combination of elements: the lack of adequate control, the relatively high contribution of the worker, and the rapid "informalization" of the labor force. To cope with this problem in 1994 the SAFP put into force severe penalties for noncompliance. An important measure was the authorization of a new regulation allowing immediate judicial payment of delayed contributions. A year later, however, it was reported that the situation had not markedly improved (Díaz 1995).

Strong deceleration in the rate of affiliation troubled AFPs and their superintendency. On top of this, by the extraordinary supreme decree no. 204-PCM/93 civil workers were not allowed to affiliate themselves with the SPP until June 1994 because their salary increases of 13.54 percent had not been budgeted by the Ministry of Finance. This measure was regarded as a lack of commitment on the part of the government to implement the reform. Long delay in authorizing the recognition bonds, which were finally approved at the end of 1994, augmented the lack of confidence that workers perceived on the part of the government to support the SPP. The absence of a minimum pension guarantee in the first reform (1993) suggested that the SPP was a sort of "black hole" that did not provide enough evidence that a decent pension could be achieved twenty or thirty years down the road. And finally, a very important distortion generated by the decree law no. 25897 referred to the differential in unit labor costs, which encouraged employers to dissuade workers from affiliating with the SPP, or worse, persuaded them to agree on informal job contracts (Murillo de Martini 1994 and as explained below).

THE SECOND REFORM, LAW 26504, 1995

In 1995, 1.5 million affiliates contributed to the SNP generating an estimated annual income of $300 million. The ONP paid 330,000 pensions for a total of $382 million (the average monthly 1995 pension was $96). The annual deficit of the SNP was $82 million, which did not include the operational costs of the ONP. In short, the pay-as-you-go SNP had already become bankrupt. The annual rate of growth of pensioners in the SNP was 11 percent, whereas the annual growth rate of active affiliates had stabilized at 3 percent (SAFP 1994). Thus, the gap between total revenues and total expenses was expected to inflate over time.

Next came the issue of the SNP's obligations: to 25,000 requests for pension benefits, to 1.5 million current affiliates, and to the workers who had transferred to the SPP and who were entitled to recognition bonds. When the IPSS transferred the SNP to the ONP it transferred a responsibility only. Because of an extremely inefficient administration, the IPSS lacked a registry and archives of workers that were enrolled in the SNP. Therefore, it is very difficult to estimate the SNP's implicit debt to workers who are contributing either to the SNP or to the SPP. Also, an estimate of recognition bonds, based on the IPSS's registry, for workers who have affiliated with the SPP is impossible to obtain.

Despite these difficulties, Kane (1995) has made some assumptions to estimate the implicit fiscal debt. In his calculations, he considered three types of liabilities: the SNP (liabilities to contributors are the highest), the civil servants fund as per decree law no. 20530, liabilities to current pensioners are the highest) and the SPP (liabilities have two components—recognition bonds and the minimum pension guarantee—still to be regulated). If a 4 percent discount rate is used, the consolidated implicit debt of all three programs is estimated at approximately 50 percent of 1994 GDP. The largest proportion of this debt is attributed to the SNP (33 percent of 1994 GDP), civil servants (10 percent) and the SPP (7 percent). This debt is low compared to countries with pioneer social security systems.

According to the SAFP's statistics, 61 percent of the affiliates (598,000 workers) have declared they are entitled to recognition bonds for the time that they contributed to the SNP. In 1995 only 9,800 workers were sixty-one years and older, which means that in the next four years the governmental subsidy to finance their recognition bonds was relatively low. In 1995 the government approved disbursement of $91 million to pensioners who retired in 1993–1995. Unofficially, it has been estimated that the government's total obligations for recognition bonds is of the order of $3 billion, which will be disbursed over a period of more than twenty years, with payments concentrated around the year 2010.

One of the consequences of the pension reform in Peru was that the time required to process a pension request in the SNP was dramatically increased. Since 1993 more than twenty-five thousand requests accumulated. The ONP estimated that $70 million were required to pay due balances and $3.6 million a month are needed to pay these pensions. Thus, once these benefits are approved, the annual deficit of the ONP to pay pensions alone will jump to $130 million (Arrieta 1995).

The increasing financial demands of the ONP (because of its deteriorating imbalance) and the virtual stagnation of affiliation to the SPP prompted the formulation of measures that attempted to resolve some of the fundamental problems faced by the newly reformed pension system in Peru. The approach taken, supported in Congress by the leading official sector and supported technically by the ONP, was to make both the SNP and the SPP truly competitive by eliminating the cost-bias against the SPP. Most recommendations had been formulated earlier by the SAFP and the AFPs. First, it was proposed that contributions to both systems be unified, and that labor costs be unified too. Second, it was postulated that a minimum pension in the SPP be created to guarantee a decent income to workers who were unable to save enough money in their individual savings accounts because of low wages, low returns, short contribution periods, or combinations of all these. Next, it was also recommended that entitlement conditions and benefits be standardized. Finally, following the Chilean system, the proposal stated that all new entrants to the labor force should affiliate with the SPP only. This recommendation, however, was disregarded because it was interpreted to be unconstitutional not to offer both a national and a private pension alternative to citizens (CCD 1993, article 11).

The first two columns of table 8.2 present contribution rates in the SNP and SPP after the first reform. The main difference in cost is the contribution to pensions in the SPP. Since a health reform had not been enacted, health care contributions to the IPSS remained identical in both systems. Payments to FONAVI were exactly the same.[2] The last row in table 8.2 shows net labor cost, which should be understood as the cost incurred by an employer to generate one net sol of income for the worker. For example, for workers who remain in the SNP, an employer spends 39 cents for each one

Table 8.2 Effects of the Consolidation of Peru's Pension Reform on Unit Labor Costs: An Illustration

	June 1993–July 1995				*Legal Modifications of July 1995*			
	SNP		*SPP*		*SNP*		*SPP*	
	Legal (%)	*Soles*	*Legal (%)*	*Soles*	*Legal (%)*	*Soles*	*Legal (%)*	*Soles*
Worker								
Income[a]		14,000		14,000		14,462		14,000
Contributions								
Pensions	3.0	420	15.0	2,100	11.0	1,591	11.4	1,596
Health	3.0	420	3.0	420	0.0	0	0.0	0
FONAVI[b]	3.0	420	3.0	420	0.0	0	0.0	0
Direct tax[c]						69		
Net income		12,740		11,060		12,802		12,404
Employer								
Income[a]		14,000		14,000		14,462		14,000
Contributions								
Pensions	6.0	840	0.0	0	0.0	0	0.0	0
Health	6.0	840	6.0	840	9.0	1,302	9.0	1,260
FONAVI[b]	6.0	840	6.0	840	9.0	1,302	9.0	1,260
CTS[d]	8.33	1,166	8.33	1,166	8.33	1,205	8.33	1,166
Labor cost		17,686		16,846		18,271		17,686
% Changes in								
Income						3.3[f]		0
Net Income						0.5		11.6
Labor cost						3.3		5.0
Labor cost/ net income		1.388		1.523		1.427		1.426
Net labor cost (%)[e]		38.8		52.3		42.7		42.6

Source: Arrieta 1995; Oficina de Normalización Previsional 1995 and author's calculations.

a. Monthly income is set at 1,000 soles (14 payments in one year, one for national holidays, another for Christmas) for illustration purposes. (1,000 soles = approx. $420, a realistic average income for a semiskilled experienced employee or a low-level civil servant.)

b. FONAVI = national housing fund. The rate was reduced to 5% in 1997.

c. Direct tax is paid when above s/. 14,000.

d. CTS = compensation for years of service, a lump-sum payment upon retirement. Employers deposit one monthly income when workers reach one year of uninterrupted service. Current law allows workers to use up to 50% of CTS at any time after deposit by employer, and the remainder under special circumstances and subject to authorization.

e. Excludes other charges such as SENATI and other related operation taxes.

f. Affiliates of SNP received one wage increment.

net sol the worker takes home. This labor cost is 34 percent higher in establishments with workers who have transferred to the SPP. In the SPP, employers pay 52 cents for each net sol workers take home. The simple exercise, assuming fourteen payments of one thousand soles a year, shows step-by-step how the labor cost is calculated.

The last two columns of table 8.2 present the new contribution rates as approved by law 26504 in July 1995. Workers in the SNP contribute a total of 11 percent (down from 15 percent) to their pension program only (health and FONAVI contributions are eliminated) and receive a salary increment of 3.3 percent. Workers in the SPP contribute 11.4 percent, which includes a net mandatory contribution of 8 percent and a 3.4 percent contribution for commission payments, administration, life insurance, and disability. The solidarity contribution (1 percent) was eliminated. Sales taxes on insurance and administration fees were also eliminated (but income taxes on pension contributions are paid). Employers in both the SNP and the SPP contribute 9 percent each to the health insurance (IPSS) and to FONAVI, and 8.3 percent to the *compensación por tiempo de servicios* (CTS). This new composition of contribution rates raised net labor cost in the SNP from 38 to 43 percent. In the SPP, this indicator went down, from 52 to 43 percent. The new law successfully equalized contribution rates, entitlement conditions, and net labor cost between the SNP and the SPP. Still, however, if the FONAVI tax (9 percent over payrolls) were eliminated, labor cost could fall another 10 percentage points.

Law 26504 allowed pensioners of the SPP to contribute 4 percent to the IPSS for health insurance, thus unifying this benefit across systems. The law announced that, in the future, additional increments would be authorized for voluntary pension contributions in the SNP. It eliminated the worker's contribution for health insurance and FONAVI and raised the employer's contribution to 9 percent for both. It eliminated the salary increase of 13.54 for workers that transferred to the SPP. The retirement age for both systems was set at sixty-five. AFPs were authorized to administer new voluntary savings plans. The approval of changes to the investment portfolio limits of AFPs was made more expedient. More important, the law approved a minimum pension in the SPP. Some temporary measures included the reduction of the worker's contribution during August 1995–December 1996 from 10 to 8 percent in the SPP. Beginning in January 1999, the worker's contribution to the SNP would not be less than 13 percent.

An important deficiency of this law was that it did not attempt to resolve the lack of coverage of approximately two-thirds of the labor force—the self-employed and rural workers. Through more flexible regulations concerning affiliation and contribution rates, the new SPP could provide savings plans for workers currently not covered in the informal sector and in rural areas. After the approval of law no. 26504, some questions remained unanswered. First, if the SNP was facing an imminent financial collapse requiring an annual governmental subsidy of more than $220 million annually (to pay pensions and recognition bonds and without considering the funding of pension funds excluded from the reforms such as the armed forces and fishermen), why was Article 11 of the 1993 Constitution interpreted in a broader way to enable the closing of the SNP to new entrants? Article 11 stipulates: "The state guarantees free access to health care and pensions, through public, private and mixed institutions. It also supervises its effective operation" (CCD 1993; translation by the author). The existence of the ONP and other publicly funded pension programs testified that Article 11 was observed. Second, what are the entitlement conditions for a minimum pension in the SPP, what percentage of the insured will benefit, and how would it be funded? Law 26504 created this benefit but it has not been regulated. Third, the unit labor costs continued relatively high, which provoked an antilabor bias and discouraged private investment. Why was the FONAVI contribution not reduced (it was reduced in 1997 to 5 percent), or even eliminated? Was this another redistribution instrument that funded President Fujimori's incessant mobilization to inaugurate health posts and schools?

MACROECONOMIC EFFECTS OF THE PENSION REFORM

The criteria that should be used to evaluate the macroeconomic impact of any structural reform are country-specific and contain a good amount of unavoidable normative thinking. With such premises in place, it can be postulated that in Peru there are at least three major goals for economic policy making that can be used to appraise the pension fund reform. First, structural reforms should reduce inequities on the understanding that there is a positive association between equity and economic growth (Fajnzylber 1990). Second, in order to build consensus around the direction of economic development and the content of policies, the government and the private sector need to collaborate and find ways for an effective partnership. And finally, the types of policies and collaboration between the government and the private sector should aim at the stability and sustainability of economic growth.

An important limitation of our analysis is that the pension reform in Peru is not old enough. There is general agreement that the shaping of patterns and trends after the implementation of such an important reform can take decades. Another aspect that must be taken into consideration is the introduction of important changes to the reform process in July 1995. These changes were expected to invigorate rates of affiliation and the growth of the pension fund in the SPP.

I begin with an assessment of the equity implications of the pension reform in Peru. In 1995 the SPP had 981,000 affiliates, 35 percent short of the number of affiliates expected by the AFPs in 1993. The second reform raised the number of affiliates to over 1.4 million by the end of 1996. It further increased and stabilized at 1.8 million in 1998. The AFPs had planned they would affiliate 1.5 million workers in the first eighteen months of operations (Barúa 1994) but it took them more than forty-two months to reach this goal. No less than one-third of the total number of affiliates did not contribute on a regular basis because of evasion and the composition of the labor force. The affiliates had the following characteristics: 85 percent were dependent workers, only 30 percent of them were females, 67 percent were younger than thirty-five years. Considering wage levels, 43 percent of the affiliates earned less than $200 a month, and only 3 percent earned over $2,272; 54 percent resided in Lima and Callao. These statistics show that the introduction of the SPP did not change the main features of the demographics of the SNP. The average contributor to both the SNP and the SPP is a young, male, dependent worker who earns an average of $250 a month and lives in Lima or Callao.

In Chile it is argued that the replacement ratio is fairly high, close to 60–70 percent (the replacement ratio is the percentage that results from dividing the pension by the salary at the moment of retirement, times one hundred). In Peru it is still too soon to estimate the replacement ratio or to determine the proportion of pensioners that will be eligible for the minimum pension. The average replacement ratio will be determined by average contribution periods, age of the affiliate, salary, and the financial returns on the pension fund investments in the SPP as the system matures. The only study that exists so far on the real impact of the pension reform in Peru (Seminario and Beltrán 1995, 36–40) suggests that the new system is clearly more regressive—in the sense that, given similar contribution rates and administration costs, pensioners in the lowest quintiles will receive relatively lower pensions. As a corollary, Seminario and Beltrán postulate that the regressive nature of the new SPP could have a positive impact on domestic savings, because the highest quintiles, with higher pensions, have a greater propensity to save. The maximum limit of sixty thousand new soles placed on the recognition bonds and the fact that they do not earn a guaranteed real return, however, serve the purpose of counteracting the regressive nature of the reform, and standardizing pensions among the higher income groups.

Law 26054 equalized payroll taxes and eligibility conditions across systems. At the same time, there has not been any serious attempt to remedy the low coverage of the old age pension system. Also, differences in coverage by age, gender, occupation, and location continue. For example, women earn on average less than men, they live longer, but they obtain lower pensions. The new pension reform in Peru does not address the problems of excessive centralization and concentration of services in Lima and Callao. Therefore, it emphasizes a persistent growth pattern that ignores rural departments where poverty levels are highest (Cruz-Saco 1995). Further, the exclusion of other pension funds from both reforms raises the issue of the lack of horizontal equity. This is a consequence of different contributions and benefits to individuals with approximately the same socioeconomic profile (Kane 1995). In sum, this analysis shows that the pension reform in Peru has not been implemented as part of a comprehensive social security reform that raises equity and coverage and reduces labor costs.

Since the implementation of the reform in 1993, the SAFP and the AFPs have had a mutually beneficial working relationship. In its regulatory and supervisory capacity, the SAFP has shown high professional training and the desire to collaborate with the AFPs in the strengthening of the SPP. Since the introduction of the reform, the SAFP and the AFPs have readily discussed the pitfalls of the process and have made recommendations to correct its major flaws. For two years, however, the efforts of the SAFP and the AFPs were blurred by governmental indifference. The experience of the Peruvian pension reform has shown that the lagging response of the government to economic processes and to the requests formulated by the private sector affects the effectiveness of SPP.

During June 1993 and July 1995, workers had a clear incentive to stay in the SNP even though it was universally known the public system was not viable. The payroll tax structure was such that the allocation of affiliation went in the wrong direction. Workers and employers preferred to contribute less and stay in the SNP. Since there is no economic rationale for this model, I attribute this two-year-long missignaling to President Fujimori's political needs to legitimate himself during the presidential campaign previous to his reelection in April 1995. In essence, his goal was to introduce a private pension fund system in an effort to help modernize the capital market, but to give the worker the alternative of the SNP, which kept the take-home salary higher than in the SPP. As soon as President Fujimori began his second term as president, he was ready to correct the contradictory nature of the reformed pension system. This clearly shows the subordination of the logic of economics to Fujimori's political decisions.

By the end of 1996, the SPP fund stood at $1 billion, just 1.5 percent of GDP, with higher affiliation rates and stronger AFPs. The regulatory changes should result in higher growth rates of the pension fund than in the past few years. It is expected that assets under management will reach $4 billion in the year 2000 (15 percent of GDP and more than 10 percent of total savings). In June 1995, 24 percent of the fund was invested in certificates from the central bank and the government, 36 percent of the fund was invested in time deposits, 26 percent in financial assets, and 13 percent in corporate bonds and shares (SAFP 1995). Seminario and Beltrán argue that the government could have been more supportive of the financial strengthening of AFPs. They recommended that deposit requirement rates for time deposits be reduced, that the government issue long-term instruments, and that it create tax incentives for corporate bonds (Seminario and Beltrán 1995, 30).

The monthly demand for financial instruments was estimated at between $20 and $25 million during 1995 (Díaz 1995). Half of the flow of funds were invested in certificates from the central bank and time deposits at fixed rates. The central bank certificates were used as monetary stabilizers. But they raise the central bank's debt, which may certainly cancel the stabilizing effect that was initially desired. The important demand for time deposits also reveals there was a lack of financial instruments. Essentially, both central bank certificates and time deposits were not as profitable, thus one of the major concerns of the SAFP and the AFPs was that financial institutions and corporations had to participate more actively in the exchange market. Although the AFPs were authorized to invest in foreign denominated instruments (10 percent of the pension fund), they have not exercised this option because of lack of regulation. The average real annual yield of the pension fund investments has been very acceptable: 8 percent since the inception of the SPP (in June 1993) until August 1996. In August 1994–August 1995 it was 6.43 percent, and it increased to 7.8 percent in August 1995–August 1996.

The classification of risk, which enables the participation of new financial instruments such as bonds and shares, substantially raised competition and the transparency of financial market operations. Under close supervision from the SAFP, financial institutions and corporations boosted the very small Peruvian exchange market. The latter was small in 1995 (its daily value was $10 million) but was growing steadily because of the continuous demand for instruments from the AFPs. It was actually considered an "emerging" market. In 1995 AFPs invested only $3 million a month in the Peruvian exchange market (Díaz 1995). As the classification of risk became less costly and firms realized the importance of participating in the exchange market, the AFPs were able to invest greater portions of their resources in the exchange market. Also, as the pension fund increases, the AFPs will become the most important institutional investors in the Peruvian capital market, pushing for the modernization of technologies and the supply of new financial instruments.

According to Díaz (1995), the pension reform has had two fundamental qualitative accomplishments. First, it has caused a major institutional reform in Peru's capital market through the liberalization of procedures and transactions, thus innovating the market and introducing an important source of liquidity. Second, it increased the transparency of financial firms and corporations that participate in the exchange market, which have to publish their audited financial balances and statements and have their stocks and bonds be freely valued and exchanged in the market. During the next five years, the pension fund will be the most important propulsive force of the Peruvian capital market and should support the reduction of intermediation costs and the generation of economies of scale. In contrast to the positive impact of the pension reform in the capital market, its impact on the labor market is less encouraging. The reform has not reduced labor costs and, therefore, the incentive for the "informalization" of labor continues. This element discourages private investment and reduces the prospects of growth of the formal sector.

CONCLUSIONS

In September 1996 the SAFP submitted a law proposal to reform decree law 25897, which means that a third reform of the Peruvian pension system is under consideration. The reform proposal has two major goals: (1) to improve the quality of services to affiliates by means of higher returns, lower commissions, supply of additional products (pension estimation, direct access to affiliate's fund, more expedient procedures for employer's transference of contributions); and (2) to expand coverage (but no specific program is designed) (*El Peruano* 1996). The proposed changes are the following: (1) to increase the portability of individual retirement accounts; (2) to increase the flexibility in administrative commissions charged by AFPs so that they operate more competitively; (3) to regulate new instruments such as subordinated and mortgage bonds, securitization, factoring, specialized investment funds, derivatives and risk coverage operations, and other instruments; (4) to evaluate all investment instruments by risk classificators; (5) to regulate voluntary pension savings; (6) to standardize penalties for noncompliance; (7) to evaluate insurance companies by risk classifiers; (8) to get insurance companies to pay annuities; (9) to eliminate double affiliation to the SNP and SPP; (10) to achieve a systematic revision of contribution rates in accordance with expected rates of replacement. Pending issues not addressed by this reform proposal are several: exempting contributions from direct taxation; government's punctual payment of recognition bonds and due benefits to pensioners in the SNP and the civil servant program; and decisive action in expanding coverage to unprotected groups.

The pension reform in Peru still has a long way to go. This study unfortunately shows that the economic rationale and consistent design of the reform was subordinated to the political agenda of the executive. Gradually, mistakes are being fixed, and so the process goes on, one of trial and error. As expected, government action is always behind, despite technical evidence presented by reformers. Decisions to make payments are based entirely on the priorities set forth by the minister of finance, with pension payments low on the list. Thousands of workers, civil servants included, have already reached the age of retirement. Several years ago, they were covered by the old pension systems, and yet the ONP has not paid their benefits. Government speculates with the minimum pension guarantee in the SPP because, once the pension guarantee is regulated, government fears that affiliation to the SPP will be in the order of millions (these workers will not save enough to meet a decent pension), and how could minimum pensions for millions of *informals* be funded? It seems as if a minimum pension guarantee in the SPP should be combined with a public assistance program and, more important, a device to cover *informals*. Otherwise, the measure is far too regressive. Peruvians have some major creative thinking to do in years to come.

Notes

Throughout this chapter, dollars ($) are U.S. dollars.

1. A Democratic Constituent Congress (CCD) with the mandate of drafting a new political constitution was elected in November 1992. The CCD was subordinate to the executive (Rospigliosi 1994, 46–50). In October 1993 the new constitution was approved in a national referendum. The most important changes were the incorporation of presidential reelection, the legalization of the death penalty, and the institutionalization of military jurisdiction over all trials involving suspects of terrorism (CCD 1993).

2. This program was particularly important for President Fujimori who opposed attempts to eliminate it or reduce the 9 percent payroll tax. FONAVI has funded the building of hundreds of public facilities (schools and health posts) across the country. With great pride President Fujimori has inaugurated every single one of these facilities and used his presence to show his apparent commitment to education and health in the interior of the country. The FONAVI payroll tax was reduced to 5 percent in 1997, still an important payroll tax.

References

Apoyo. 1992. *FORO: El sistema privado de pensiones.* Lima: Grupo Apoyo. Mimeograph.

Arrieta, Alejandro. 1995. Interview with the general director, Office of Previsional Normalization (ONP), Lima. July 3.

Barúa, Ramón. 1994. *Realidades de reformas: El caso de Perú.* Paper presented at the international seminar "El ahorro previsional: Impacto en los mercados de capitales y de la vivienda," organized by the Corporación de Investigación, Estudio y Desarrollo de la Seguridad Social. Santiago. November. Mimeograph.

Congreso Constituyente Democrático (CCD). 1993. *Constitución política del Perú, 1993.* Diario *El Peruano.* Lima.

Crabtree, John. 1992. *Peru under García.* Pittsburgh: University of Pittsburgh Press.

Cruz-Saco, María Amparo. 1995. "Clasificación de departamentos en el Perú por análisis factorial y de acumulación." *APUNTES* (fall). Lima: Centro de Investigaciónes de la Universidad del Pacífico.

Cuánto S.A. 1992. *Perú en números. Anuario estadístico.* Lima: Cuánto S.A.

———. 1994. *Perú en números: Anuario estadístico.* Lima: Cuánto S.A.

Díaz, Enrique. 1995. Interview with the superintendent adjunct, SAFP. Lima. June 21.

Economic Commission for Latin America and the Caribbean (ECLAC). 1994. *Preliminary Overview of the Economy of Latin America and the Caribbean, 1994.* Santiago: ECLAC.

Fajnzylber, Fernando. 1990. *Unavoidable Industrial Restructuring in Latin America.* Durham: Duke University Press.

Graham, Carol. 1992. *Peru's Apra: Parties, Politics, and the Elusive Quest for Democracy.* Boulder, Colo.: Lynne Rienner.

Instituto de Normalización Previsional. 1995. "Statistics on Unit Costs for D.L. 25897 (1993) and Law 26504 (1995)." Lima.

Kane, Cheikh. 1995. *Peru: Reforming the Pension System.* ESP Discussion Paper Series, Human Resources Development and Operations Policy. World Bank. June.

Mesa-Lago, Carmelo. 1994. *Changing Social Security in Latin America: Toward Alleviating the Social Cost of Economic Reform.* Boulder, Colo.: Lynne Rienner.

Murillo de Martini, Pedro. 1994. Interview with the superintendent, SAFP. Lima. June 28.

El Peruano. 1996. "Proyecto de ley de reforma del decreto ley 25897." Separata especial. Special supplement. September 11.

Rospigliosi, Fernando. 1994. "Democracy's Bleak Prospects." In *Peru in Crisis: Dictatorship or Democracy?* ed. Joseph S. Tulchin and Gary Bland. Boulder, Colo.: Lynne Rienner.

Sagasti, Francisco, and Max Hernández. 1994. "The Crisis of Governance." In *Peru in Crisis: Dictatorship or Democracy?* ed. Joseph S. Tulchin and Gary Bland. Boulder, Colo.: Lynne Rienner.

Seminario, Bruno, and Arlette Beltrán. 1995. *Impacto del sistema privado de pensiones en el sector real.* Proyecto AID-SAFP, informe final, May. Mimeograph.

Superintendencia de Administradoras Privadas de Pensiones (SAFP). 1994. *Bases para un diagnóstico de la política previsional en el Perú.* Preliminary version. Lima: SAFP. Mimeograph.

———. 1995. *Boletín informativo mensual no. 04-95.* Lima: SAFP.

9 / The Colombian Social Security Reform

Between Competition and Solidarity

Miguel Eduardo Cárdenas Rivera

BETWEEN 1992 AND 1993, the reform of the social security system was one of several priorities in the political agenda of Colombia. The 1990–1994 administration brought the reform project to light in September 1991, along with the stipulations of the new constitution that was put into effect on July 5 of the same year. After an agitated parliamentary debate, on September 23, 1993, the current social security system was approved by Law 100, which was regulated by fifteen decrees (Ministerio de Trabajo y Seguridad Social 1993). This chapter discusses some fundamental issues related to the 1993 reform. It analyzes the orientation of the reform and reviews the first year of the reform's implementation against the framework of the proposal of the 1994–1998 administration's development plan, called the *Social Leap (El Salto Social)* (Presidencia de la República 1994).

CONTEXTUALIZATION OF THE REFORM

A true social security system has never existed in Colombia, similar to other developing countries. What has been in place is a security system for the official or so-called formal sector of the labor force, while the nonofficial or "informal" sector has remained largely uncovered. Coverage of the formal sector remains stagnant, with minimal rates of increase that parallel the slow growth in demand from the officially salaried labor force.

Social security has been mandatory for salaried employees in the private sector. Their contributions are deducted from the employees' wages and transferred along with the employers' contribution to the Social Security Institute (ISS). Self-employed workers and bureaucracies of high income levels have voluntarily joined private insurance plans for health, retirement, disability, and other risks. In the informal sector a great majority lacks the ability to pay contributions. A minority that lacks coverage, however, could be covered if contributions were less than those in the private sector.

The reform of the incorrectly labeled "social security" (Laws 60 and 100 of 1993) had as an objective the expansion of coverage for the insured population, based on two strategies: (1) the obligation of affiliation for the self-employed with the ability to pay, and (2) the creation of a noncontributory sector that is either partially or totally subsidized for the lower-middle class and the poor. The reform created a new social security system. It did not reproduce completely the Chilean model of privatization but transcended the traditional public model of social security. It acknowledged the proven inefficacy of the ISS to extend coverage to the independent and informal sectors, and the financial impossibility to subsidize the incorporation of the poor. As of December 31, 1994, the insured population (pensions) was approximately 25 percent as can be seen in table 9.1. The total number of active affiliates (to some type of plan) was 5.4 million, which represented 24.4 percent of the demographic group aged between eighteen and sixty-five.

In 1994 pension payments were made for retirement and work-related risks to 650,000 beneficiaries: 350,000 former civil servants affiliated to public funds and 302,000 to pensioners from the private industry affiliated to the ISS for disability, old age, and death (IVM), and job-related injuries and illness (ATEP). The proportion of these totals going to family survivor beneficiaries is unknown. Similarly, the number of pensions given by private corporations that, with legal authorization, have operated their own funds and the number of pensions given by private insurance companies are also unknown. Finally, there is no information on the important number of pensioners from public funds, retired before sixty years of age (without counting the cases of retirement because of job-related risks).

The relation of affiliates to pensioners is 12.6:1 in the ISS; at the government level (public funds) it is only 3.57:1. Given that the population over sixty-five years of age is about 2.2 million and assuming that pensioners are 400,000,[1] the population of the unprotected elderly is 1.8 million and the index of pensioners to population over sixty-five is 18.2 percent. On the other hand, neither the public funds nor the ISS provide information about

Table 9.1 Population of Colombia Covered by Pensions (Contribution Plan), 1994, and Estimates for 1995

	Registrations		Structure of the Plan	
Subsystems	*1994*	*1995 (est.)*	*1994 (%)*	*1995 (%)*
ISS	3,800	3,700[a]	67.3	57.8
Private funds	1,000	1,700	17.6	6.5
State funds	793	950	3.3	14.1
Military funds	250	300		
FPSM	243	300		
CAPRECOM and ECOPETROL	100	100		
Others	200	250		
Insurance companies	100	100	1.8	1.6
Gross total	5,693	6,450	100.0	100.0
Less duplicated registration	343	300	—	—
Net registration	5,350	6,150	—	—

Source: Estimates are based on several institutional reports and Delgado and Cárdenas 1993.

a. This figure does not include some 500,000 affiliates of the subsidized system (farmers, dependent mothers, domestic workers, and other independent workers), who, according to the Development Plan (the Social Leap), should be incorporated over the course of the year.

the number of pensions for survivors that lapse because of the absence of beneficiaries, the death of the spouse, or the children's reaching maturity (eighteen, or twenty-five if enrolled in an educational institution).

Low contribution rates were raised. This measure aimed to give the new private agents of the reform and the ISS sufficient resources for the necessary attention of their affiliates. The new social security system initiated operations on April 1, 1994.

Since January 1, 1995, the total affiliate's and the employer's contributions represent 24.5 percent of the base salary (12 percent for health and 12.5 percent for pensions). Salaried workers pay one-third of the contribution for health coverage (4 percent) and one-fourth of the pension program (3.125 percent), for a total of 7.125 percent. In turn, the employer (private industry or government) pays the remaining two-thirds for health (8 percent) and three-quarters for pensions (9.375 percent), for a total of 17.375 percent. Self-employed pay 100 percent of their contributions. In addition, those covered for retirement whose base salary is greater than four minimum legal wages pay an additional percentage point, which is allocated to the Solidarity Retirement Fund (FSP).

President Samper implemented the social security reform as discussed and approved by the National Congress. The general tenets regarding the "comprehensive social security" were presented in the text describing the development plan, the *Social Leap* (Ministerio de Trabajo y Seguridad Social 1993, 90–100). This development plan omits the function assigned to private agencies in the reform. It only outlines a few programs that refer to the regime of subsidization, which in the case of health ceases to be part of the general insurance regime and becomes a public assistance plan for specific vulnerable groups (children, elderly, and handicapped). Only one paragraph, as discussed below, is dedicated to pensions (Ministerio de Trabajo y Seguridad Social 1993, 98).

Our reading of the *Social Leap* shows a lack of a well-thought policy for the extension of social security coverage. We hypothesized that President Samper's administration has opted for assistencialism, instead of a subsidized plan for health and retirement that forms part of the general insurance regime.

Problems

Regarding the intensity and the direction of the present executive process of social security reform, several doubts arise and are presented in the following observations. First, a majority of countries in the world provide mandatory social security, which covers health, job-related risks, and pensions at retirement from active work. Solidarity permits sharing the benefits with those that are unable to contribute.

In the neoliberal reforms of some countries, including Colombia, there is a difference between the contributory and the subsidized system. The agencies that provide the benefits are fragmented and the health risks are separated from the retirement pensions. The mandatory nature of both risks, however, tends to restructure, in some way, their comprehensiveness in the contributory sectors. In Colombia, however, the coverage of health and old age has been fully separated. Because of asymmetries in the allocation of resources to the noncontributing sector, coverage for health received priority whereas coverage for retirement pensions was relegated to a secondary level of importance. Consequently, in the noncontributory sector there would be great differences in the number of affiliates and beneficiaries. This imbalance could have been corrected by increases in the national budget for the Solidarity Pension Fund (FSP), a solution that was not adopted in the investment plan.

Second, in the investment plan, the allocation of resources for each of the solidarity funds (health and pensions) that are part of the insurance system emphasizes support to the poor and indigent (Ministerio de Trabajo y Seguridad Social 1993, 91, 97–98). This policy has neglected the use of some portion of these funds or other type of resources to benefit other segments of the population. There are several groups that are not necessarily poor, who could have their own plan either partially or totally subsidized. The latter could be done by means of a contribution payment that represents between 25 and 50 percent of the premium or by means of a minimum contribution that gives right to full benefits.

Law 100 considered a semicontributing system for the self-employed lower-middle class. Its omission in the text of the plan, however, could be seen as a strategy to avoid the undesired inclusion of "free riders," or to limit the access of individuals that can afford to pay (but choose not to pay) the minimum contribution for both plans (health and pensions), which has been set at a monthly payment of $29,126 pesos (approximately US$35).[2] While the interest in reducing the incidence of "free riders" is reasonable, it is possible to implement means-tests to both self-employed and the poor to alleviate their incidence. In essence, the goal of extending social security coverage implies that the government provides additional resources to both solidarity funds (health and pensions).

Third, considering that by means of a subsidy in pensions 2 percent of the eligible population (from eighteen to sixty-five years of age) affiliate during the first year of the reform and assuming that this rate of affiliation continues, by the year 2001 coverage in the subsidized regime could reach 14 percent. It is also expected that, by the same year, 40 percent of the population would be covered under the standard contributory regime, while the remaining 46 percent will remain uncovered. A coverage goal of 80 percent by the year 2001 under both the contributory and the subsidized regimes is almost impossible to accomplish given the current rates of affiliation. This is in sharp contrast to the Southern Cone (Argentina, Chile, and Uruguay), and other countries (Costa Rica and Panama), where coverage of the insured population already exceeds 80 percent.

Social Security and Pensions

The two universal methods for the funding of pensions are partial capitalization, which most likely becomes pay-as-you-go (PAYG) at maturity, and full individual capitalization. These two systems coexist in European countries (with the exception of Italy and Spain), in the United States and Canada, and in the rest of the countries of the Organization for Economic Cooperation and Development (OECD). In all of them, affiliation to public social security systems that operate under partial capitalization (or PAYG) is mandatory; and usually, the supplementary affiliation to private funds that operate using full individual capitalization is voluntary and fairly extensive.[3]

Under the new system: (1) affiliates with relatively higher salaries can adopt the European practice of affiliation to both systems, by means of adopting a "supplementary plan," but it is prohibited to simultaneously join the ISS and a private pension fund administrator (AFP) that offers a full capitalization plan; and (2) the government frees itself from the increasing responsibility of subsidization to civil servants, who either paid very low contribution rates to their plans or did not pay at all. Given the lack of resources to pay benefits to civil servants at retirement, the government (central government and state-owned enterprises) always made transfer payments to honor between 90 and 100 percent of the obligations. Similar to the health coverage plan, Law 100 creates a contributory system and a subsidized system in pensions.

Contributory System

The prereform contributory system included four programs: (1) the ISS affiliation, made up of workers in private industry; (2) more than one thousand public funds, with 1.2 million civil servants affiliated; (3) autonomous funds in the private industry, authorized by law, and (4) private insurance companies. Beginning on April 1, 1994, as a further development of Law 100, private AFPs were added to these four programs. Nine months later, AFPs had affiliated almost 1 million workers. The two universal methods to fund pensions—partial (eventually PAYG) and full capitalization—were ignored by almost all affiliates in Colombia.

By law, the ISS did not use partial capitalization, which is the method traditionally employed by public social security systems. The law did not establish a funding model for the ISS, and there was theoretical and technical confusion with the investment method when forming reserve funds and performing actuarial calculations. In practice, however, the ISS used PAYG and defined benefits (the defined benefit is a guarantee by the insurer or pension agency that a benefit based on a prescribed formula will be paid), since an adequate level of reserves never existed because of the lack of a funding method. Law 100 has indeed sanctioned that the ISS will continue to provide defined benefits.

In contrast to ISS, which was able to pay pensions using PAYG, public funds were in financial and actuarial disequilibria because of generalized evasion. Thus, their benefits were paid entirely by government transfers or were paid directly by state-owned enterprises. More recently, the government created the Public Pension Fund (FPP) at the national level to pay ninety-five thousand pensions that were obligations of the National Fund of Social Security (Cajanal).

With the new law, government (as an employer) and civil servants will continue to pay their contributions to the old funds (that were not liquidated), to the ISS, or to AFPs. The law gives workers a choice of affiliation. An important aspect of the law is that the old funds can remain in business if they demonstrate solvency; otherwise they are liquidated.

Civil servants can also choose from two different funding methods: (1) defined benefit, from the ISS or public funds; or (2) individual capitalization that characterizes by law all AFPs. The method of collective capitalization (which requires a significant initial reserve fund) and actuarial projections has not been approved by law. It could be authorized to benefit groups of civil servants that are strongly unionized and that have the ability to exert political pressure.[4]

The National Teachers' Social Security Fund (FPSM) pays monetary benefits to 243,000 teachers (pensions, unemployment, vacations, and health services by means of contracting a national system of service providers). The value of the fund was $634,271 million pesos (approximately US$762 million) in August 1994, an amount similar to the reserves of the ISS. According to Law 91 in 1989 (ratified in 1993 by Article 279 of Law 100), current revenues for the fund originate in contributions from affiliates, government payments, and investment profits (Ministerio de Gobierno 1990).[5] In the future, the FPSM will not pay certain benefits that will be paid by government (Christmas bonuses, services, food, family subsidies, transportation assistance, and vacation bonuses).

We understand that Law 91 should be amended given that (1) the total salary contribution rate of 13 percent is insufficient to fund both the mandatory family health coverage and the pension fund, and (2) Law 91 does not determine the separation of resources allocated to health and pensions. By contrast, Law 100 as implemented by the ISS administers the funding of each of the funds in separate accounts. Another pending issue relates to the entity that should oversee the FPSM, because the banking commissioner (*superintendencia bancaria*) has not been specifically assigned to undertake this role. Finally, it should be noted that the FPSM's returns are used by law to increase the reserve fund, which functions as a general fund to pay different types of benefits in approximately the same way the public funds worked before the introduction of Law 100. With respect to the ratio of Cajanal (three affiliates to one pensioner), it is estimated that FPSM could handle ordinary pension payments for some eighty thousand affiliates or their survivor. Nevertheless, Cajanal continues, by law, to be responsible for complementary pensions, which are not incompatible with the ordinary pensions for the same affiliate.

With the reform, AFPs operate by the method of individual capitalization and defined contributions. Benefits depend on the sum of individual contributions and returns on investments.[6] As shown in table 9.2, during the first three-quarters of 1994, the private system affiliated 1 million workers: 350,000 were affiliated with the ISS; 350,000 with Cajanal and other public funds; 100,000 were with private companies not affiliated with the ISS; approximately 180,000 were self-employed.

In 1994 the private pension fund amounted to some $140,000 million pesos, which is less than 0.3 percent of GDP. In relative terms, the size of the fund was still very small. Private companies managing their own private pension funds should continue payment of pensions directly, but their workers will have to join the ISS or a private fund. Private insurance companies

Table 9.2 Private Pension Funds Affiliates in Colombia, December 31, 1994

Funds	*Affiliates*[a]	*Participation (%)*
Porvenir	358,298	36.13
Colfondos	182,864	19.44
Protección	126,354	12.74
Horizonte	101,218	11.22
Colmena	90,519	9.13
Colpatria	85,915	6.66
Davivir	31,460	3.17
Invertir	14,992	1.51
Total	991,620	100.00

Source: Superintendencia Bancaria, 1994.

a. 85 percent of the affiliates are between 15 and 34 years of age; 81 percent earn less than two minimum legal wages (sml) (US $300); 14 percent between 2 and 4 sml; 4 percent between 4 and 7 sml, and 1 percent between 7 and 10 sml.

should continue the administration of individual capitalization funds; their affiliates, however, should transfer to the ISS or to one AFP. These funds belong to the supplementary coverage.[7]

In addition to the "supplementary" coverage supplied by insurance companies, Law 100 authorized them to AFPs and to fiduciary companies. In 1994, 18,273 individuals signed up for the so-called "voluntary funds" (12,449 to the AFPs and 5,779 to fiduciary companies), making contributions amounting to $76,951 million ($25,478 to the AFPs and $51,473 to the fiduciary groups). All these individuals earn relatively high salaries. While on average in the contributory sector the average contribution per affiliate was $235,000 in 1994, in the supplementary funds administered by fiduciary companies the average contribution per affiliate was $9 million. In one of these companies —Skandia—the average contribution was $10 million per affiliate. In the AFPs the average contribution per affiliate was $2 million (varying from $4,300,000 in Protección to only $144,000 in Davivir).

In December 1994, the contributory sector had 5.3 million affiliates (net registry corrected for duplication). According to our estimates, by December 1995 this number could have increased to 6.2 million (an increase of 15 percent; see table 9.1). In relation to the age group from eighteen to sixty-five years, this increase of 800,000 new affiliates implies a small growth in the estimated coverage, from 29.2 percent in 1994 to 32.9 percent in 1995.

Law 100 does not permit simultaneous affiliation to both the ISS and any AFP. It does, however, authorize voluntary and supplementary coverage with the ISS, any private fund, or any insurance company. Depuration of double affiliation to the ISS and to AFPs has not been done yet. The proliferation of double registration has been attributed to the ISS's delay in cleaning up its registrations, and to the fact that some companies continue remission of contributions to the ISS instead of to AFPs when workers have changed their affiliation. All workers that are covered by insurance companies should belong to either the ISS or an AFP. The rate of double registration has been estimated at 6.4 percent of the total number of affiliates in 1994 and of 4.9 percent in 1995 (see table 9.1).

Contrary to the expectation that affiliation to AFPs would represent workers with relatively high salaries, the actual affiliation by salary structure of the ISS was reproduced. Thus, 81 percent of the total number of affiliates earn less than two minimum salaries (see table 9.2). The participation of the self-employed in the pension plan of the ISS is assumed to be quite low. Only 160,000 self-employed workers have affiliated to the health program of the ISS and their contribution is based on the minimum salary and represents 4 percent of total coverage.

The resources of the contributory sector, consolidated by the concept of contributions for pensions, were $1.26 billion in 1994, and $1.7 billion in 1995. One average contribution has, as a base, 1.7 minimum salaries, which represented in 1994 an income of some $235,000 per affiliate, and in 1995, some $300,000. It is estimated that (1) the ISS collected close to $800,000 million in 1994 and an estimated $1 billion in 1995; (2) the AFPs collected close to $140,000 million in 1994 and an estimated $400,000 million in 1995; (3) the surviving public funds collected approximately $220,000 million in 1994 and an estimated $300,000 million in 1995; and (4) the insurance companies collected some $50,000 million in 1994 and an estimated $70,000 million in 1995.

Finally, the contributory sector manages monthly pension allowances. The government pays 350,000 pensions for retirement and disability. However, the actual number of retired workers and survivors is unknown. The ISS also pays 300,000 pensions for IVM and ATEP. The total payment of pensions in 1995 was estimated at $1.7 billion, distributed as follows: $1.1 billion paid by the government and $650,000 paid by the ISS. In 1995 total payment of pensions represented 2.5 percent of the estimated GDP.

In summary, in 1995, it was estimated that the ISS received $1 billion in revenues from pension contributions, and that it paid fourteen monthly allowances amounting to $650,000 million. In turn, government (administration and state-owned enterprises) has begun a process of regularization,[8] including the partial liberation of future pension payments. But in 1995 it was estimated that government had to pay more than $1 billion in pensions, and higher amounts in future years.

The Subsidized System

In the development plan only one paragraph refers to the subsidized sector. In 1995 funds from the Pension Solidarity Fund (FSP) were supposed to pay benefits to five hundred thousand salaried and self-employed workers and community mothers. These mothers form a target group, which should demonstrate an income lower than one minimum salary and "that it belongs to the lowest socioeconomic strata" (Ministerio de Trabajo y Seguridad Social 1993, 98). Nevertheless, the subsidy will differ according to the residential area (rural in preference), according to the age of beneficiaries (in order to protect the elderly), and according to "greater time that contributions were paid" (Ministerio de Trabajo y Seguridad Social 1993, 98).

In this system (which the government most recently called "solidarity"), there is no freedom of choice. Social criteria and political interests of the worker are emphasized. The ISS administers the program, while company funds for the solidarity or cooperative sector are mentioned in the law, nothing was explained directly in the plan. The ISS compensates the retirement of a portion of its contributing affiliates with a massive incorporation of subsidized affiliates without making distinction between the two legal categories in its publications.

In 1995 the Pension Solidarity Fund (FSP) was estimated to have a total reserve of $80,000 million, contributed in equal parts by (1) the solidarity contributions of the contributing affiliates whose base monthly income is higher than $475,000, and (2) the government, with legal contributions from the national budget. This reserve, representing 488,000 active contributors, can pay—in the ISS or in a fund of the solidarity sector—a minimum legal salary (one percentage point of the contribution rate is allocated to the subsidization system). Under these conditions, any AFP could accept 462,000 affiliates.

To sum up, in 1995, the pension system covered approximately 6.7 million affiliates. These affiliates were distributed as follows: 6.2 million in the contributory system, and 500,000 in the subsidized one. In terms of rates of coverage and considering the demographic group aged between eighteen and sixty-five, the rate was 32.9 percent for contributing affiliates and 2.7 percent for subsidized ones.

BALANCE AND PROSPECTIVE OF THE PENSION REFORM

When a social security system covers basically the middle strata of the population with a relatively high cost for society as a whole, and with pre-established wage contributions (Mesa-Lago 1990, 135–36; Mesa-Lago 1991, 206–7), a change in the social security model that favors the lowest strata of the population at the cost of the intermediate one creates problems of interest and political pressure that must be taken into consideration when designing changes. In the Colombian context, it is irresponsible to wish changes to occur overnight. The restructuring process requires adequate monitoring of social programs and the transformation of fiscal structures.

At the same time, a consensus is needed to define parameters of change, and these include: (1) definition of the strategy, (2) processes to be implemented, (3) capacity of workers that are both benefited and negatively affected by proposed changes. The proposals will receive the pressure to minimize the number of losers and to maximize the number of winners. This is how consensus is reached.

One should not proceed in a mechanical way to adopt structures that might have been used in other countries. To make a social security system work requires a very specific social framework. Bismarckian social security systems use salaried employment as a reference; that is, workers pay a contribution rate on their salaries (payroll taxes) and in return they are entitled to some rights and benefits. In Colombia, another social framework is in place and, therefore, there is a need to design a new model of old age coverage. At the same time, however, radicalization of views have to be avoided. Much pressure is exerted on the government to make radical reforms, but experience recommends taking time to consider the issues cautiously and to make relevant decisions. For example, formal guarantee of minimum returns on privately managed pension funds can only be well-intentioned with little probability of becoming reality, because a law does not stipulate guarantees, and investment returns are totally determined by the market. The reform has to be responsible and possess a "social" focus with technically defined sources of funding.

In 1992–1993 the parliamentary debate in Colombia showed that it is impossible to transcend ideologies. An effort should be made not to lose, from the various ideological postures, a notion of reality and common sense in order to specify that which is viable by means of dialogue. A strong and vigorous social security system that contributes to national development requires an economic structure that guarantees paid, stable, and productive employment. Thus, when speaking of reforming social security, we cannot set aside either the issue of salary policy (since without adequate levels of pay, there is no ability to save) or the issue of labor policy that guarantees stability (because without it there is no trust in the system).

Each country has its own characteristics and it is not possible to copy models. International experiences are important as a point of reference in the national debate about pension reform. Debates demonstrated how industrialized countries, in particular those that do not have too many savings constraints (Germany, Spain, and the United States) tend toward the conservation of PAYG. Germany, for example, has changed from capitalization to PAYG. On the other hand in those systems with savings constraints, in the so-called developing countries, pension reforms are inspired by the goal of strengthening the financial market with a high fiscal cost. As a consequence, the pension system could be more a mechanism of financial savings than one designed for the coverage of social security. In the end, treating the theme of pension reform as an issue of social policy is fundamental, without avoiding the principle that the Colombian Constitution establishes as a norm: solidarity.

As Mesa-Lago has shown, one of the great challenges that democracy faced in the 1990s is the implementation of social security reform in order to reach universality with an economically viable and socially equitable system (Mesa-Lago 1990, 160; Mesa-Lago 1991, 226). This should be accomplished through national consensus, inspired by the responsibility of the leaders and the awareness of civil society. Our purpose in Colombia has been to seek a formula for the pension system that is economically viable and socially just. In this process, we have learned that, although the method of individual capitalization is important, intermediate positions are more reasonable.

The pension reform in Colombia is a unique case because it introduces the method of individual capitalization but it allows freedom of choice. Affiliates can either stay with the reformed public system, or transfer to the private sector. In other words, mandatory contributions cannot support both schemes, and affiliates choose one of them. Thus, two systems that are supplementary in the OECD are competitive in Colombia.

The fact that mandatory payroll contributions are limited to either the publicly managed or private AFPs eliminates the possibility of simultaneous affiliation to both systems, which are complementary in other parts of the world. It actually shows a lack of equity when mandatory contributions that used to fund the traditional social security system are now transferred, partially or entirely, to AFPs in proportions that are presumed to be very elevated and that in a few years could leave social security without affiliates, because of the enticement of expected earned interest in individual savings accounts. As a consequence, the likelihood of intergenerational solidarity is reduced, becoming a mere symbolic element. The cost of management in the AFPs (3.5 of 13.5 percentage points of base salaries) is equivalent to 25.9 percent of total revenues less the cost of insurance for disability and survivors. In contrast, former highly ranked officials of the ISS manifested that the administrative cost of IVM and ATEP is only 2 percent of total revenues (contributions plus returns)—which is understandable if one considers that the greatest administrative cost is typically assigned to the sickness and maternity program (EGM).

Among the good intentions of Law 100, an ingenuous one supposes that the efficacy that should come from competition resolves the multiple problems of traditional institutions administering benefits in the public and private sectors. Government, corporate associations, numerous national and foreign authors have all analyzed the problems of ISS and public funds (see among others Ayala 1993, Gómez Buendía 1993, Poveda Ramos 1993, Arévalo 1993). The agreement was that the most important problems included enormous administrative inefficiency, the public invisibility that protects corruption, confusion in the property of the health and pension programs, and an excessive centralism of the ISS. Law 100 ended the confusion in the property of different programs and the discretion in the allocation of resources (benefits or reserve) of the ISS programs (EGM, IVM, and ATEP). Nevertheless, the law omitted other important measures, such as the restructuring of the ISS into autonomous departmental (or statal) entities and semiautonomous municipalities.

Other measures that should have been taken in the Colombian reform are inspired by Brazilian legislation (Social Security Laws 8.212 and 8.213 of 1991), according to which "irregularities and existing failings" (Article 69 of Law 8.212) imply the revision of the benefit program accompanied by external audits. For example, strict supervision of benefits should include the following: disabled pensioners must report for new additional medical exams; work accident compensation greater than a specific value must be revised; benefits in certain price ranges must be expressly authorized. Similarly, the position of the General Commissioner of Social Security was created for a period of two years without reelection, designed by the National Council of Social Security, with the approval of the National Congress. Furthermore, infractions against social security were made subject to criminal legislation. In summary, delinquency in public social security and in the ISS can be eliminated by various means other than the outlawing of the idea of social security. This could avoid the remedy becoming worse than the disease.

Progress in reducing social inequity and poverty during President Samper's administration has been small.[9] This was an outcome of a social policy that was subject to two different speeds. The first one, concerning the distribution of income, social security, and poverty reduction, was moving at an imperceptible speed, possibly justified by the composition of the social power structure. With the second one, in contrast, social spending in education and the new programs defined in the *Social Leap* plan were moving at high speed, showing Samper's renewed emphasis in education despite the shortness of the overall fiscal budget.

Notes

1. The number of pensions for surviving affiliates younger than sixty-five is estimated at 250,000. This includes an unknown number of retirement pensioners less than sixty years old, as well as the number of those retired for work-related risks who are less than sixty-five years old.

2. The exchange rate in effect here is $832 Colombian pesos to US$1. Unless otherwise specified, amounts mentioned in this chapter will be in ($) Colombian pesos.

3. A description of the practical coexistence of both methods in OECD countries, and the simultaneous insertion of the population in both, can be found in Delgado and Cárdenas 1993, 18–32.

4. For example, teachers who transferred from FPSM to a fiduciary plan with La Previsora; telecommunication workers with the National Industry of Telecommunications Fund (Telecom); Colombian Petroleum Industry (Ecopetrol); Colombian Association of Civil Aviators (ACDAC); Social Security Fund for the Congress of the Republic; and others. La Previsora is a fiduciary entity functioning like a private and state industry, with a mixed economy, that is associated with the Ministry of Housing and under the aegis of the Comptroller General of the Republic (CGR).

5. The funds defined by the law are the following: (1) contributions of 5 percent of the base salary of the affiliates; (2) one-third of the first month's salary earned, and one-third of later increases, as a registration fee; (3) contribution from the nation, 8 percent cleared monthly above the salary factors for personal services of the instructors; (4) 5 percent of each monthly pension, including the additional monthly pensions; (5) five-thousandths of the total paid by the nation for personal services of the instructors; (6) a percentage of IVA that the territorial associations destined for the payment of teacher contributions; (7) a pension tax for the formation of reserves from the economic contributions, which was the initial base of the fund; (8) the profits from the funds' investments and the interest from loans made; and (9) the resources that the fund receives from other concerns (Ministerio de Gobierno 1990, article B).

6. Under the ISS plan or the public funds, with the method of PAYG, the legal limit of a pension is fifteen minimum legal monthly wages and fourteen monthly payments per year (there are exceptions to the law). Under the private individual capitalization plan there are no limits to the pension. However, the contribution base can not exceed twenty minimum legal wages. In some public funds, the benefit has

been up to sixty minimum legal wages. In the social security fund of the Congress of the Republic, based on the special pension system approved by Law 4 of 1992, and decree 1359 of 1993, whereas some ex-congressmen received pensions of up to thirty-eight minimum legal wages, five former employees of Congress in 1994 received between forty and fifty-five minimum legal wages as ordinary monthly payments. For example: Silverio Salcedo received $5,509,061.95; Jairo Bonilla received $4,342,671.59; Estanislao Rozo received $4,342,651.59; Noemi Perilla received $4,239,926.98; and Carmen Gacela Hobaica received $3,996,763.49. The Constitutional Court has requested an investigation of these cases by the Attorney General of the Nation (see sentence T-456, from October 21, 1994; the magistrate in charge is Alejandro Martínez Caballero).

7. The banking commissioner (*Superintendencia Bancaria*) has no information on the number of insured by type of risk or by company, nor does the union association of insurers (Fasecolda).

8. The pension debt of the liquidated Colombian Industry of Ports (Colpuertos) rose to $241,971 million (210 pensioners receive 14 monthly payments per year at $1,800,000 each). In 1995 this represented $25 million per beneficiary. Payment of pensions to workers from the former National Railroad Industry amounted to $75,548 million in 1995.

9. Regarding the traditional administration of social policies in Latin America and Colombia, Cecilia López Montaño and Mauricio Restrepo (1994) stated: "While great reforms are promoted, the sector has been left without management. The traditional institutions find themselves in a legal and administrative limbo and the new funds show the same vices that were attributed to the former ones: very low levels of operation and excess of bureaucracy. Even though in the short term it is difficult for the social indicators to show great changes, increases in poverty within a context of economic growth are seen. The vacuum that an incoherent social policy produces is clear, where a redistributive scheme with little political support subsists, and with new strategies that cannot be financed. Because of the lack of creativity on the part of social scientists, conditions have regressed to a minimalist and residual concept of society dating from the beginning of the century" (15–16).

References

Arévalo, Edgar Iván. 1993. "Una aproximación a la situación financiera del ISS en la década de los ochenta." In *Estructura y crisis de la seguridad social en Colombia 1946–1992,* ed. O. Rodríguez and D. Arévalo, 203–35. Bogotá: CID-UN.

Ayala, Ulpiano. 1993. "Introducción a la seguridad y a los seguros sociales." In *Estructura y crisis de la seguridad social en Colombia 1946–1992,* ed. O. Rodríguez and D. Arévalo, 17–69. Bogotá: CID-UN.

Cárdenas Rivera, Miguel Eduardo. 1992. "Seguridad social y régimen pensional: Balance de argumentos para una reforma." In *Regímenes pensionales,* ed. Carmelo Mesa-Lago, Lothar Witte, et al., 263–86. Bogotá: FESCOL-FAUS-CIID.

Delgado, Oscar, and Miguel Edward Cárdenas. 1993. *Política social en Colombia: Los casos de salud y pensiones.* Programa de Política Social, Documentos de Trabajo. Bogotá, FESCOL.

———. 1995. "Políticas estatales en materia social." In *¿Hacia dónde va el salto social?* Consejaría Presidencial para la Política Social. Bogotá, FESCOL.

Gómez Buendía, Hernando. 1993. "Tres razones para que el ISS no ampare sino a una minoría." *El Tiempo,* p. 5A. August 24.

López Montaño, Cecilia, and Mauricio Restrepo. 1994. *Bases conceptuales para una política social.* Programa de Política Social, Documentos de Trabajo. Bogotá, FESCOL.

Mesa-Lago, Carmelo. 1990. *Aspectos económico-financieros de la seguridad social en América Latina y el Caribe: Tendencias, problemas y alternativas para el año 2000.* Washington, D.C.: World Bank.

———. 1991. "La seguridad social en América Latina." In *Progreso económico y social en América Latina,* 189–227. Washington, D.C.: IADB.

Ministerio de Gobierno. 1990. *Leyes de 1989,* 392–402. Bogotá: Publicaciones del Ministerio de Gobierno.

Ministerio de Trabajo y Seguridad Social. 1993. *Ley de Seguridad Social (Ley 100 de 1993).* Bogotá: Publicaciones SENA.

Poveda Ramos, Gabriel. 1993. *Seguridad social y solidaridad social.* Bogotá: Fundación Konrad Adenauer, Instituto Fiel.

Presidencia de la República. 1994. *El Salto Social: Bases para el plan nacional de desarrollo, 1994–1998.* Bogotá: DNP.

Superintendencia Bancaria. 1994. Estadísticas varias.

two / Reforms in Place: Health Care

10 / Chile

The Effectiveness of the Reform

Brian Cartin

Chile has obtained a level of economic development in the past decade that has amazed specialists and converted this country into a dragon within Latin America. In 1992 GDP grew to US$40 billion (representing a 10.4 percent increase since 1991), while inflation decreased to a record low of 12.7 percent (Banco Central de Chile 1993). This miraculous recovery of a country whose economy suffered a severe crisis during the world recession of the early 1980s is a result of the structural adjustments implemented under the military regime throughout its seventeen-year rule.

These economic policies, which followed a neoconservative framework, have also generated a "social debt" within Chile that has had serious negative repercussions on the Aylwin government's provision of social services to its population. The term *social debt* refers to a decrease in average living standards and an increase in poverty and income inequality. Economic growth under the dictatorship was not paralleled by higher standards of living and greater income equality within Chile (Moran 1989).

The democratic government led by Aylwin (March 1990–March 1994) declared "growth with equity" as one of its major commitments, while maintaining the same development strategy established under the Pinochet regime and responsible for generating the current social debt. The provision of social services, especially health care, and their importance in the development process have moved to the forefront of Chilean politics. The government's answer to the lack of social service provision has been to increase the percentage of its budget devoted to these areas (that is, education, health care, and housing).

Fiscal expenditures within the health care sector increased by more than 40 percent between 1989 and 1993 (ILD 1993; Jiménez de la Jara 1993; MINSAL 1992a, 1993a, c), but such an increment can not compensate for the seventeen years of neglect under the Pinochet regime. This paper will study the dictatorship's health care reform; the inheritance of the social debt by the democratic government; the actions and policies implemented under the Aylwin administration and their impact on alleviating the social debt.

THE CHILEAN HEALTH CARE SYSTEM UNDER THE DICTATORSHIP

The concept of public health care was first adopted by the Chilean government in the 1920s, years before any of the other Latin American governments —or the United States for that matter—adopted such policies. Public health insurance was expanded to the entire population by the end of the 1950s before undergoing a process of restructuring during the dictatorship. The reform was based upon the neoconservative development ideology that was applied to the economy during the 1970s and 1980s. Its structure is delineated in the various law decrees enacted in those years, as well as in the 1980 Constitution (Bertelsen 1989; Novoa 1982). A major characteristic of the system is the complementary roles of the public and private sectors in providing health care.

The Previous Health Care System: SNS and SERMENA

Prior to the dictatorship's reforms, two agencies were responsible for providing health care to the population: the National Health Service (SNS) and the National Medical Service (SERMENA). SNS supplied preventive care to the entire population and curative care to blue-collar workers and indigents (60 percent of the population) free of charge. SERMENA provided curative services to white-collar workers and their families (25 percent) through a voucher-based payment system (Miranda 1990). The remaining 15 percent were either uninsured, or were covered by state-financed medical programs of the armed forces or the police.

The major distinction between SNS and SERMENA, apart from the groups insured, was the type of administration and financing they employed. SNS was a state-run organization and received a major source of its funding from the central government. SERMENA, on the other hand, functioned as an autonomous agency, with the bulk of its funding originating from the sale of vouchers to the insured. Both received employer contributions that usually amounted to 2–3 percent of a worker's declared monthly salary. This cost-sharing method, in conjunction with an overcentralized system, proved detrimental to the coordination and financing of health services.

Toward the beginning of the 1970s, financial and organizational instabilities generated shortages in health care delivery. The cost-sharing model of financing produced a huge deficit: (1) because of employers' defaulting on contributions or underdeclaring employee salaries, and (2) because of overspending by the SNS and SERMENA. Overcentralization of SNS's and SERMENA's administration generated a hierarchical and inflexible structure that was incapable of properly caring for the diverse health needs of the population. High administrative costs reduced the overall level of health care expenditures and imposed limitations on the provision of health services to the population. Under the dictatorship the SNS and SERMENA were eliminated and were replaced by a health care system that emphasizes decentralization, privatization, and limited state subsidization.

Health Politics and the 1980 Constitution

During its seventeen years in power, the Pinochet regime attempted to restore stability to the Chilean economy through a series of neoconservative reforms. The establishment of the 1980 Constitution served to consolidate power within the executive branch, eliminating political opposition to the dictatorship's neoconservative ideology. Two major objectives of the reforms—macroeconomic stability and fiscal solvency—were to be accomplished through privatization, decentralization, and limited state subsidization. All three principles, embedded in the 1980 Constitution, directed the dictatorship's formation of economic and social policies. The health care system was to be redesigned according to these principles, with the basic features outlined in the 1980 Constitution (Bertelsen 1989; Castañeda 1989; Gómez 1988; Novoa 1982).

In the constitution, the most important article related to health is Article 19, Section 9, which established free and equal access to health care, free election between the public and private sectors, and a finance system based on mandatory contributions. The traditional "right to health" was also addressed under this article, but was renamed the "right to health protection." Article 19 contains the only explicit reference made to health throughout the entire constitution.

The 1980 Constitution, unlike its predecessor of 1925, did not establish a national health service. It was created during the 1980s through a series of law decrees that regulated the public and private sectors. Under the new system, the state performs a subsidiary role in providing health services and promotes private sector participation through tax incentives, contracting of private health services, and limited government regulation. Decentralization or municipalization of public health services also occurred throughout the 1980s in order to correct previous overcentralization.

Structure of the Health Care System: Public and Private Sectors

The Ministry of Health oversees the public and private sectors and has an extensive—albeit cumbersome—network of agencies. The public sector covers roughly 80 percent of the population and has five major agencies: National Health Fund (FONASA), National Health Services System (SNSS), Central Supply Agency (CA), Institute of Public Health (ISP), and Superintendency of ISAPREs (hereafter, Superintendency). Each agency performs specific duties defined and supervised by the Ministry of Health. Included within the 80 percent are the private providers that operate in conjunction with FONASA and the state-financed medical programs of the armed forces and the police (Caja de Previsión de la Defensa Nacional, 1993). The private sector is comprised of both for-profit and nonprofit organizations. The two major for-profit institutions are *institutos de salud previsional* (ISAPREs), which are HMOs that cover approximately 20 percent of the population, and FONASA's private providers. Nonprofit organizations include nongovernmental organizations (NGOs) and occupational health insurance funds (mutual aid societies), both of which provide additional health services to certain sectors.

Public Sector

FONASA—created by Law Decree 2763 in August 1979—is responsible for the collection of mandatory contributions (7 percent of an insured's declared monthly salary or earnings) and the distribution of these financial resources to various public agencies, ISAPREs, and other private sector providers. Employer contributions were eliminated under the new system. FONASA serves as direct financier of public health services and offers two options: institutional and free election. The former refers to state-sponsored health care in which the beneficiary might have to make a copayment, depending on his/her income, and receives medical attention from the SNSS. The free election option grants the insured freedom to elect between health services offered by the SNSS or private providers (not ISAPREs) that solicit contracts from the Ministry of Health. ISAPREs are not included within the free election option, as they are independent health care financiers and offer particular insurance packages.

Within each of the two options, FONASA has established four income groups, from A to D, all of which are subsidized to a certain extent by the state. Group A is comprised of indigents who are exempted from paying the 7 percent monthly payroll deduction but only receive attention from the SNSS. The other three groups must pay the 7 percent contribution and can elect between public or private health care providers. In addition to the 7 percent, groups C and D of the free-election option must purchase vouchers from FONASA that are redeemable at private health care clinics. The vouchers are a form of state subsidy, amounting to 75 percent and 50 percent of the costs for groups C and D, respectively. The revenue generated from the sale of vouchers constitutes the principal source to meet the public health sector's operation costs.

The SNSS decentralized the previous public health care system into twenty-six autonomous regional health departments, which operate within a particular location, and the Environmental Health Service, which serves only the Metropolitan Region. Each regional health department supplies both curative and preventive services to its assigned population, while organizing environmental preservation campaigns. All public hospitals, clinics, and health posts are under the direct supervision of the regional health departments and are funded by the central government and municipalities. They currently provide preventive care to the entire population and curative services to 70 percent (MINSAL 1993c).

The CA, the chief purchaser and provider of medical equipment, supplies all public hospitals, clinics, and posts. During national and international emergencies, the CA can be asked by the central government to attend to the needs of those afflicted by such crises.

The ISP is responsible for the health and hygiene of the population. As supervisor of the public sector's laboratories, it controls the quality of medicine, food, and sanitary products utilized within public health facilities. It is the ISP's duty to report to the Ministry of Health on any medical emergencies or epidemics that may arise. The ISP also conducts research and plays an active role in health education.

The Superintendency was created in March 1990 (Law Decree 18,933), under the Aylwin administration. It is responsible for the regulation and supervision of the ISAPREs, a task previously performed by FONASA. The Superintendency serves as an official intermediary in disputes between the ISAPREs and their constituents, works to protect the ISAPREs from market instability, and reports to the president of the republic, through the Ministry of Health, on the overall development of the ISAPREs. Finally, the Superintendency works to rally support within the National Congress for increased government regulation of the ISAPREs.

Private Sector

The ISAPREs were created in November 1981 (Law Decree 3626) to decrease dependence on the public health sector. They are private entities that offer a series of medical insurance and workman's compensation packages in return for the basic 7 percent payroll contribution plus an additional premium of 2–3 percent, depending upon the size of the package. Most ISAPREs are only financial intermediaries, but some own and manage their own infrastructure and medical services.

The number of ISAPREs had grown to thirty-five in September 1992, which roughly cover 20 percent of the population. There are two types of ISAPREs: twenty-one are open and fourteen are closed. The open variety accepts any insured able to pay the costs (premium) associated with membership, whereas the closed type is tied to one or more companies or industries and provides services only to their employees. Approximately 2.5 million insured (92.3 percent of the total) belong to open ISAPREs, and only 212,000 (7.7 percent of the total) to closed ones (Superintendencia 1992, 1993). Because of the nature of the closed ISAPRE, competition occurs only among the open type, which thereby impedes interaction between the two groups.

Private medical providers that pertain to FONASA's free-election system are also within the for-profit group of medical care. These individuals supply health services to the insured within the free-election option but do not receive the insured's 7 percent payroll deduction. Government contracts and

FONASA vouchers provide the majority of revenue, however, these providers also render services to the insured outside of the public sector as well as the noninsured.

A third private provider of health care to the population are the NGOs, whose total reached approximately five or six hundred during the mid-1980s. The emergence of these organizations was a direct result of (1) the decrease in public social programs under the military regime (in order to establish fiscal solvency), and (2) the birth of popular movements and social mobilization attempts among the marginalized groups (CNO 1992; Infante 1989). While the majority of these organizations were founded at the grassroots level (via the Catholic church), both international and domestic support to them has increased over the years.

NGOs perform applied and theoretical functions, including the provision of primary health services and health education, usually for a minimal charge. Both services are extremely critical to the maintenance of preventive care measures, which were emphasized under the dictatorship. The education function involves financing and organizing research and conferences that analyze the sector's situation and provide relief to trouble areas. NGOs offer a channel for the marginalized sectors of society to express their grievances on health care to government and international agencies.

Mutual aid societies constitute a fourth private financier of health care. These nonprofit organizations are financed by employers and satisfy the work-related health needs of employees. The societies only supplement the health care system and do not replace FONASA or the ISAPREs as principal medical providers. Government incentives (that is, tax breaks) are offered to those companies that establish mutual aid societies for their employees.

Pinochet's reform of the Chilean health care system eliminated the problems of overcentralization and inefficiency related to a rigid hierarchical structure. Preventive care programs such as nationwide vaccination programs, government-sponsored milk and food distribution programs (PNAC), and expanding potable water and sewage systems reduced the incidence of "diseases of underdevelopment" (that is, tuberculosis, typhoid, hepatitis, cholera) and infant and general mortality rates (MINSAL 1991a, b). However, the reform reduced public expenditures as a percentage of the total health care bill in 1974–1989 from 61.7 percent to 47.3 percent (Aylwin 1990). Also, decentralization, privatization, and limited state subsidization have transferred the majority of primary health care costs to the municipalities, have inhibited coordination of national health policy, have increased the percentage of operation costs incurred by the SNSS, and have left secondary and tertiary levels of health care ill-equipped to detect and treat the growing number of diseases associated with development (such as cancer and cardiovascular diseases).

THE TRANSITION TO DEMOCRACY AND AYLWIN'S HEALTH POLICIES

Prior to the March 1990 inauguration of President Aylwin, the Christian Democrat Party investigated Chile's social debt crisis and its repercussions on the health care sector in order to establish its modus operandi for the four-year term. The investigation concluded that the public health care sector was short on medical equipment, infrastructure, and personnel (Aylwin 1990; Jiménez de la Jara 1993; MINSAL 1991a). The private sector was also under criticism because of discriminatory policies being practiced by the ISAPREs against the elderly, women of childbearing age, and the terminally ill. These studies, in addition to highlighting the problems, also prescribed remedies to improve the quantity and quality of health care services.

Inheritance of Problems from the Dictatorship

The Aylwin administration inherited several health care problems from the dictatorship. These included an overall decrease in both fiscal expenditures and real investment, as well as reliance on the private sector for the delivery of services. The former led to the deterioration of health care infrastructure and shortages of personnel and equipment within the public health sector; the latter was conducive to the proliferation of discriminatory practices by the ISAPREs.

Deteriorating Expenditures, Personnel, and Infrastructure in the Public Sector

In 1989 only 3.5 percent of total fiscal expenditures were devoted to the public health care sector (as opposed to 7.2 percent in 1974), thus marking the lowest annual percentage of Pinochet's seventeen-year rule. In addition there was a sharp decrease in medical personnel and equipment, and an overall rise in the price of medical care throughout the 1980s. Within the SNSS the number of both doctors and nurses per one thousand inhabitants declined slightly in 1978–1988 from 0.49 to 0.42 and from 0.24 to 0.17, re-

Table 10.1 Public Health Care Sector Employees in Chile, 1992

Occupation	*Total*	*SNSS*	*(%)*	*Municipal*	*(%)*	*Ratio*[a]
Physicians	9,258	7,988	86.3	1,270	13.7	0.7
Dentists	1,874	1,117	59.6	757	40.4	0.14
Nurses	3,573	2,702	75.6	871	24.4	0.27
Midwifes	2,578	1,859	72.1	719	27.9	0.19
Social workers	731	439	60.1	292	39.9	0.06
Nutritionists	835	505	60.5	330	39.5	0.06
Pharmacists	289	277	95.8	12	4.2	0.02
Kinesiologists	336	310	92.3	26	7.7	0.03
Medical technicians	1,114	1,077	96.7	37	3.3	0.08
Other health professionals	1,453	1,398	96.2	55	3.8	0.11
Accountants	281	208	74.0	73	26.0	0.02
Drivers	1,757	1,316	74.9	441	25.1	0.13
Auxiliary nurses	25,752	21,050	81.7	4,702	18.3	1.95
General services	13,239	11,899	89.9	1,340	10.1	1.0
Adminstrative personnel	10,376	8,659	83.5	1,717	16.5	0.78
Others	3,305	2,419	73.2	886	26.8	0.25
Total	76,751	63,223	82.4	13,528	17.6	5.79

Source: Ministerio de Salud 1993c.
a. Per 1,000 inhabitants.

spectively, while the number of auxiliaries per one thousand inhabitants increased more than threefold, from 1.98 to 6.60 (Aylwin 1990). These changes reflect cost-saving measures on the part of the dictatorship to limit the number of high-paid doctors and nurses and replace them with low-paid auxiliary nurses, medical technicians, and midwives (see table 10.1).

The situation was further exacerbated by the decentralization (municipalization) of primary care and the creation of ISAPREs. Municipalization of public health services led to cuts in both salaries and fringe benefits of public health workers at the primary level, forcing the majority of personnel to move either to the secondary and tertiary levels of state-financed health services or to the private sector. ISAPRE enrollment reached 20 percent of the total population in 1993, decreasing the number of recipients of public health care from 100 to 80 percent in 1980–1993. However, those who transferred to the ISAPREs were predominately from groups C and D of FONASA and constituted the majority of the public sector's operation costs. This decrease in public sector revenue, together with a smaller percentage of government financing, led to (1) a decrease in the quantity and quality of health services at all three levels (despite increases in personnel within the latter two); (2) greater monetary strain on municipalities to compensate for the decrease; and (3) an increase in mandatory contributions from 3 to 7 percent of declared monthly salaries over the past decade.

Infrastructure within the public health care sector also suffered under the military regime. As a result of the decrease in government spending and investment, many hospitals and clinics were unable to adapt to modern technological advances. In 1990, 23 percent of Chilean hospitals were built before 1940, and 48 percent were constructed between 1940 and 1970. Despite the aging infrastructure, public expenditures devoted to maintenance and repairs decreased by 0.4 percent in 1981–1989 (Aylwin 1990).

Lack of Government Regulation on the ISAPREs in the Private Sector

Perhaps the greatest problem plaguing the private sector is the lack of government regulation on ISAPREs to protect beneficiaries in disputes against those institutions. ISAPREs are not legally responsible for either financing or providing coverage or medical services to their insured in case of national epidemics as it is the government's obligation to provide treatment to the entire population, insured or not. Another problem is the practice of discrimination by age and sex of beneficiaries. ISAPREs have been reluctant to insure women, especially within childbearing years, and the elderly. Moreover, they do not offer coverage for terminal illnesses such as cancer.

Prior to the establishment of the Superintendency, those insured by the ISAPREs lacked an official channel to express their grievances. Its creation has been a step toward increased government regulation of these institutions. However, legislation to eliminate private sector favoritism has not been forthcoming because of an overcrowded agenda and congressional deadlocks.

Redefinition of the Role of Health in the Development Process and Social Policies

The Aylwin administration concluded in its report on the health care system that the overall shortage of resources within the public health sector was the result of the neoconservative development framework created by the military regime. The administration, however, continued the same development framework but redefined the role of health care in development and established new social policies based on five goals. These are (1) to establish greater equality of opportunity, so as to provide access to basic goods and services to low-income groups; (2) to increase the allocation of fiscal resources to social programs; (3) to increase community participation in the development process; (4) to attain a higher quality of life and standard of living; and (5) to achieve solidarity, or collaboration among all individuals according to their abilities, potential, and resources, in improving health conditions (MINSAL 1991a, 1993c). Health care was expected to play a dual role in the Aylwin administration's strategy for economic growth—with equity as a major component for improving the standards of living and as a prerequisite to attaining higher levels of economic growth. In order to achieve this dual goal and alleviate the social debt, five objectives were set to be reached within the four-year term of the Aylwin administration.

The first and most important objective was to strengthen the public sector's institutional capacity. The decentralization of public health services into twenty-six regional agencies and the municipalization of primary care clinics and rural posts, was a cost-saving measure for the central government (a major goal of the neoconservative strategy), but it severely reduced the power of the Ministry of Health's control over regional and local agencies, thereby complicating national health campaigns (Aedo and Larrañaga 1993; Castañeda 1990; Serrano 1989). Decentralization cum privatization have also resulted in lack of coordination of health care efforts between the public and the private sectors as well as within the public sector. The Aylwin administration attempted to cope with these organizational shortcomings by establishing new agencies and eliminating those considered inefficient.

The most important transformation within the private health sector was the establishment of the Superintendency of ISAPREs. Other agencies and departments—such as the Primary Health Departments (DAP), the National Health Consultation Council (CCNS), the National Private Health Council (CNSP), the Health Programs Division (DIPROG), and the Planning and Budgetary Division (DIPLAP)—were established as instruments for some degree of central control and efficiency within the health care sector. The DAPs, whose purpose is to increase the level of national cooperation within the health sector, has divisions in all twenty-six regional health services of the SNSS and its headquarters in the Ministry of Health. The CCNS was established with the objective of coordinating the actions of workers, professional associations (that is, Chilean doctors and midwives associations), social organizations (such as NGOs), and academic centers. The CNSP was created to advise the Ministry of Health in the analysis of the private sector. DIPROG and DIPLAP replaced the Office of Budget and Planning and the Department of People's Health Programs as coordinators of regional health service activities (Jiménez de la Jara 1993).

A second concern was the effect of the municipalization processes on the provision of primary health services. The Aylwin administration increased both expenditures and investment within this area, while decreasing the costs incurred by the insured. It further committed itself to expanding the number of personnel, while creating third shifts, special primary attention emergency services (SAPU), and special services for infants and children with acute respiratory infections (Salas IRA) in order to improve population access and to address the diverse health needs of the population. Basic laboratories and, in some cases, pharmacies were added to many of the primary health clinics throughout the country (MINSAL 1993b).

The third objective was to resolve the hospital crisis, or the lack of medical equipment and deteriorating infrastructure. State-run hospitals received additional resources to help combat the shortage of medical equipment, personnel, and drugs. The fourth objective was to devise and implement health prevention/protection programs for the entire population, including (1) widespread immunization against diseases, including small pox and diphtheria; (2) educational health, which emphasizes prevention; (3) training of medical personnel in preventive care techniques; (4) health protection for both workers and women; and (5) expansion of potable water and sewage systems. The fifth objective was environmental preservation, especially antismog campaigns within the Metropolitan and other regions. The government called for the establishment of a special interministerial commission to consolidate national efforts in environmental preservation, but it failed to create such an organization.

AN EVALUATION OF THE AYLWIN GOVERNMENT'S EFFORTS

March 1994 marked the end of the first democratic government since the transition. It is important to evaluate the outcome of the Aylwin administration's policies and actions and their impact on health standards. In 1989–1993, fiscal expenditures devoted to the health care sector increased in real terms by roughly 40 percent. Approximately 9.8 percent of the 1993 federal budget was devoted to health care, making it the third highest expenditure after employment programs and social security, and education (ILD 1993; Jiménez de la Jara 1993; MINSAL 1991b, 1992e, 1993c). And yet such a significant rise in spending was insufficient to remedy the numerous inherited problems afflicting the health care system. In order to determine the impact of government policies on the health sector, we will focus on the new health programs and agencies; the provision of services; changes in equipment; infrastructure and personnel; and population coverage; and access to state-financed health services.

The Impact of New Agencies and Programs

One of the major questions regarding the government's initiatives to increase the institutional capacity of the health care sector has been whether the new agencies and programs have been effective in reaching their goals. It may be too early to give a precise answer to this question. One may, however, at least derive a general and tentative conclusion because the majority of those agencies/programs have been functioning since the beginning of the Aylwin administration.

Strengthening of Institutional Capacity

Perhaps the most important health institution created under the Aylwin administration was the Superintendency of ISAPREs. The Superintendency has not only addressed the concerns and complaints of ISAPRE beneficiaries but also pushed for a change, at the National Congress, to impose regulations and restrictions on the ISAPREs and change certain structural aspects of the private health sector. But such efforts have been frustrated by legislative deadlocks and competition among several sectors of Chilean society for limited congressional resources.

Among the other new health care agencies, the DAPs, CNSP, DIPROG, and DIPLAP have improved the Chilean health care sector because of their unique features. Each has successfully filled institutional gaps that existed under the military regime and improved the overall level of coordination within the Ministry of Health, especially at the primary health care level. On the other hand, the CCNS has not achieved its goal. The reason for this failure is not within the agency itself but is, rather, because the groups and associations that the agency is trying to unite are all vying for scarce government resources and congressional favors (increased salaries and benefits).

Expenditures on Personnel, Infrastructure, and Equipment Within the Public Sector

All five agencies discussed above, regardless of their efficiency in reaching their goals, have resulted in a major increase in both personnel and administrative expenditures within the public sector. According to the Ministry

Table 10.2 SNSS Physical Resources in Chile, 1989–1992

Resources	*1989*	*1990*	*1991*	*1992*
Number of hospitals	182	182	180	180
Hospitals per 1 million inhabitants	14	13.8	13.4	13.2
Number of general clinics	322	337	345	376
General clinics per 1 million inhabitants	24.8	25.6	25.8	27.6
Number of rural health posts	982	1,026	1,040	1,080
Number of ambulances	n.a.	592	746	732
Number of scanners	1	2	6	10
Number of beds per 1,000 SNSS insured	3.33	3.34	3.39	3.55

Source: Ministerio de Salud 1993a.

of Health, there are 4,400 new positions created, of which physicians and dentists comprised only 800. Half the remaining new jobs (1,800) were in administration, raising their total number to 10,376 and constituting almost 35 percent of the health sector's total expenditures. The final 1,800 posts went to nurses, midwives, medical technicians, and auxiliaries (MINSAL 1993c). Despite the increase in personnel, the doctors and midwives associations have successfully held nationwide strikes to protest unfair salaries, unfair benefits, and unsafe working conditions. These strikes have resulted in congressional approval of salary increases and improved benefits for both doctors and midwives. Improvements in working conditions, however, especially in the secondary and tertiary levels, have not been forthcoming.

With regard to infrastructure, several clinics and posts have been built, while three hospitals are being enlarged. At the end of 1993 the government planned to have completed 71 clinics, 166 posts, and 3 hospital expansions (Aylwin 1993; MINSAL 1992c, d). In 1990–1992 the number of primary care clinics increased from 337 to 376, which raised their ratio from 25.6 to 27.6 per 1 million people; rural posts increased from 1026 to 1080. The number of hospital beds increased slightly, from 32,515 to 32,584. Conversely, the number of hospitals decreased—from 182 to 180—as a result of deteriorated buildings (MINSAL 1993a) (see table 10.2).

The Ministry of Health has allocated roughly US$12.5 million to improve emergency services, and over US$60 million to acquire new ambulances and technologically advanced medical equipment (MINSAL 1993c). The number of ambulances increased from 592 to 732 in 1990–1992, while the number of scanners rose from 2 to 10 (MINSAL 1993a). Although expenditures on high-tech equipment have steadily risen since 1989, the majority of public hospitals require higher levels of investment to counteract spending cuts during the dictatorship.

Changes in Population Access and Coverage Within the Public Sector

The most accurate indicators of the government's success in the health care sector are the levels of population coverage and access to health services within all three levels of care. At the primary level, the government has continued several of the policies and practices of the military regime, which proved effective in lowering infant and general mortality and morbidity rates through a series of vaccination programs (Jiménez de la Jara 1993; MINSAL 1993c). The creation of the SAPUs, Salas IRA, third shifts, and basic laboratories have been successful in improving population coverage and access to medical services and treatments within the primary care sector. Since the inception of these programs, the primary level of health care has benefited from an increase in the number of consultations and population access to these services. The SAPUs currently number 38, recording 858,536 consultations in 1992 and a total coverage of roughly 3.8 million people. Salas IRAs have provided some 322,343 consultations in over 130 general clinics. Third shifts and basic laboratories are present, respectively, in 83 and 50 general clinics throughout the country and have also increased population access to primary care services (MINSAL 1992b, 1993a) (see table 10.3).

Although the government has for the most part been successful in the primary level, both secondary and tertiary health care are still plagued by shortages and severely deteriorated infrastructures. The hospital crisis has shown only mild signs of abating during the Aylwin years, which is a direct result of the high costs required for upgrading and replacing outdated equipment and infrastructure. The deterioration of both factors during the military regime was unprecedented in Chilean history, resulting in obsolescence of equipment within the state and local health facilities.

These problems have been compounded by a decline in traditional dis-

Table 10.3 Reinforcement Programs of Public Health Care Clinics in Chile, 1990–1992

Type of Program	*1990*	*1991*	*1992*
Primary attention emergency services (SAPUs)	13	23	37
Third shifts (emergency services, evening and night)	28	51	83
Acute respiratory infection services for infants and children (Salas IRA)	26	0	132
Basic laboratories	24	38	57

Source: Ministerio de Salud 1993b.

Table 10.4 Ten Leading Causes of Death in Chile, 1991

	%	*Rate (per 100,000 inhabitants)*
Diseases of the circulatory system	28.5	159.7
Malignant tumors	19.5	109.3
Accidents and poisoning	12.4	69.1
Diseases of the respiratory system	10.9	61.1
Diseases of the digestive system	7.1	39.5
Ill-defined causes	5.8	32.3
Infectious and parasitic diseases	2.8	15.7
Diseases of the endocrine system	2.5	13.7
Diseases of the genito-urinary system	2.3	12.6
Perinatal conditions	2.0	11.4
All other causes	6.2	34.8
Total	100.0	559.3

Source: Ministerio de Salud 1993c.

eases of underdevelopment (tuberculosis, cholera) and a major increase in those predominant in developed societies (cancer, cardiovascular diseases). The four leading causes of mortality in Chile, constituting roughly 70 percent of all deaths (see table 10.4), are diseases of the circulatory system (28.5 percent), malignant tumors (19.5 percent), accidents and poisoning (12.4 percent), and diseases of the respiratory system (10.9 percent) (MINSAL 1993c). Most treatment for these four causes of death occur at the secondary or tertiary levels and require the assistance of technologically advanced equipment, which the public sector lacks and only a small percentage of private providers possess. This statistic also reflects a negative impact on all ISAPRE beneficiaries, who are not insured for terminal illnesses such as cancer and may be unable to afford the high costs associated with treatment of these diseases. Overall, the levels of population coverage have remained constant while access to secondary and tertiary care, especially within the public sector, have decreased because of the unavailability of equipment and infrastructure, and the greater costs that both beneficiaries and the government must incur.

Health Prevention/Protection and Environmental Campaigns

The remainder of the five objectives of the Aylwin administration showed mixed results, recording more successes in health prevention than in environmental programs. The Ministry of Health promoted educational campaigns ranging from AIDS awareness to alcoholism, while encouraging direct participation of the private sector in formulating and administering programs at the community level. Access to potable water decreased in 1990–1992 from 98.5 to 95.2 percent in urban areas, and from 77.0 to 73.3 percent in rural sectors. The percentage of the urban population with a sewage system also declined from 82.9 to 73.3 percent in the same period (MINSAL 1991b, 1993c). Immunization programs against diphtheria, polio, and tetanus have been extremely successful, reaching almost 100 percent of the population by 1991 (MINSAL 1993c).

Environmental campaign results do not match those of health prevention/protection. The principal concern at this time appears to be the amount of air pollution affecting the capital city of Santiago. Government efforts in this area have been scarce, continuing the military regime's highly ineffective practice of vehicle restrictions within the Metropolitan Region, where 35 percent of the Chilean population resides. Congress recently passed a law requiring all imported vehicles be equipped with catalytic converters; this has not had an impact on pollution levels, however. Regulation of businesses and factories has also been insignificant, applying restrictions only when pollution levels reach preemergency or emergency levels.

CONCLUSIONS AND PROSPECTS FOR THE FUTURE

The Aylwin administration increased budgetary allocations to the health sector by approximately 40 percent in 1989–1993, attempting to compensate for the severe cuts under the dictatorship. The government's strategy for strengthening the public sector's institutional capacity was successful, but diverted 35 percent of the rise in expenditures to pay for higher administrative costs. Also, emphasis on greater coordination of national health policy carries with it the risk of overcentralization and government waste. Subsequent governments should concentrate on improving access to and provision of health services within all three levels of care without raising administrative costs or creating an overcentralized and hierarchical structure.

Primary care fared the best under both the dictatorship and the Aylwin administration, quite possibly a result of the lower costs associated with this form of health service. Most preventive care campaigns established by the dictatorship were expanded under the Aylwin government to include a greater percentage of the population. Furthermore, the development of new curative care services at the primary level (that is, third shifts, Salas IRAs, and laboratories) addressed special needs of the population and improved access. Expansion of key public services (such as potable water and sewage) in both urban and rural areas is a must, since access to both have declined since 1989.

Secondary and tertiary levels of health care suffer from shortages that require vast amounts of capital and investment to satisfy the void. Future administrations must increase expenditures devoted to the two higher levels of care without neglecting the primary level or generating a budget deficit. One solution to the hospital crisis would involve borrowing technologically sophisticated equipment and modern facilities from private hospitals, in return for modest payments or tax incentives. Both government and the private sector should consider joint ventures in technologically sophisticated equipment as an answer to decreasing the high costs of secondary and tertiary health care.

Finally, one must not ignore the economic and political constraints that both current and future governments face as a result of the neoconservative ideology and congressional deadlocks. Fiscal solvency led the dictatorship to drastically cut government spending and transfer costs to municipalities. Reversing the social debt while adhering to the spending limitations imposed on the central government will require years of investment in numerous social services. The health system will have to compete with other sectors for scarce government resources. Reforms to the health system may also be halted because of a one-third veto power within the Senate possessed by supporters of the proconservative ideology.

The inability of Congress to reach a consensus has benefited the ISAPREs, who are able to continue discriminatory policies, but at the expense of the insured and the public sector. Over the past four years, the only effective manner for the public sector to attain congressional favors has been to hold nationwide strikes, which interrupt the provision of health services and severely undermine the population's confidence in the health care system. Favoritism of the private sector (a distinctive trait of Pinochet's neoconservative ideology) has increased government costs in health care, forcing the elderly, the terminally ill, women of childbearing age, and the entire population during national epidemics to seek medical attention within the public sector. Private sector protectionism must be minimized and resources previously used to subsidize the ISAPREs' development should be redirected to the public sector.

The congressional elections in December 1993 resulted in an increase of the neoconservative presence in Congress. The new president of Chile, Eduardo Frei, has vowed to eliminate the social debt but will continue adhering to the neoconservative development strategy of the dictatorship. These two factors indicate (1) continued private sector favoritism within Congress; (2) future nationwide strikes among public health care workers because of congressional deadlocks; and (3) slow recovery, at best, of all social services under the Frei administration. Continuance of the neoconservative development strategy should prove beneficial to economic growth, but at the expense of social services provisions.

References

Aedo, Cristián, and Osvaldo Larrañaga. 1993. *Sistemas de entrega de los servicios sociales: Una agenda para la reforma.* Washington, D.C.: Georgetown University–ILADES.

Aylwin, Patricio. 1990. *Mensaje presidencial de la República de Chile.* Valparaíso. May 21.

———. 1993. *Mensaje presidencial de la República de Chile.* Valparaíso. May 21.

Banco Central de Chile. 1993. *Annual Report of the Banco Central de Chile, 1992.* Santiago: Banco Central de Chile.

Bertelsen Repetto, Raúl. 1989. "Chile." In *The Right to Health in the Americas: A Comparative Constitutional Study,* ed. Fuenzalida and Conner, 166–86. Scientific Publication no. 509. Washington, D.C.: PAHO.

Caja de Previsión de la Defensa Nacional. 1993. *Informe de gestión del Fondo de Salud.* Santiago: CAPREDENA.

Castañeda, Tarsicio. 1989. "The Chilean Health System: Organization, Operation, and Financing." In *Health Economics: Latin American Perspectives,* 3–25. Washington, D.C.: PAHO.

———. 1990. *Para combatir la pobreza.* Santiago: Centro de Estudios Públicos.

Coordinadora Nacional de ONG (CNO). 1992. *Las ONG chilenas en los 1990.* Materiales del seminario "ONG y Sociedad Civil en Chile Hoy." Santiago.

Durán, Hernán. 1988. "Los servicios de salud." In *Chile hacia el 2000: desafíos y opciones,* ed. Gonzalo Martner et al. Caracas: Editorial Nueva Sociedad.

Gómez Cova, David. 1988. *Políticas de salud en América Latina: Aspectos institucionales de su formulación, implementación y evaluación.* Washington, D.C.: PAHO.

Infante, Antonio. 1989. "Régimen militar y situación de salud: El rol de las ONG y de la cooperación internacional." In *Una puerta que se abre: Los organismos no gubernamentales en la cooperación al desarrollo,* ed. Rodrigo Egaña Baraona. Santiago: Taller de Cooperación al Desarrollo.

Instituto Libertad y Desarrollo (ILD). 1993. *Política fiscal y presupuesto, 1993.* Santiago: Instituto Libertad y Desarrollo.

Jiménez de la Jara, Jorge. 1993. *Análisis de la evolución: Salud pública, Chile, 1990–1993.* Santiago: MINSAL.

Ministerio de Salud (MINSAL). 1991a. *Sistema de salud chileno: Una agenda para el cambio.* Santiago: MINSAL.

———. 1991b. *Situación y atención de la salud en Chile, 1991.* Santiago: MINSAL.

———. 1992a. *Información estadística de prestaciones otorgadas a beneficiarios de la Ley 18.469 en sus modalidades de libre elección e institucional y sistema de ISAPRE: Chile, 1986–1991.* Santiago: MINSAL.

———. 1992b. *Programa de reducción de listas de espera: Evaluación de cirugía infantil.* Santiago: MINSAL.

———. 1992c. *Racionalización funcional de los servicios de salud: Iquique, San Felipe–Los Andes y Valdivia.* Santiago: MINSAL.

———. 1992d. *Reforma del sector salud: Asistencia técnica y rehabilitación hospitalária.* Santiago: MINSAL.

———. 1992e. *Situación y atención de la salud en Chile, 1992.* Santiago: MINSAL.

———. 1993a. *Principales indicadores biomédicos de recursos y de producción: Sector salud y/o SNSS Chile, 1989–1992.* Santiago: MINSAL.

———. 1993b. *Programas de reforzamiento, 1989–1992.* Santiago: MINSAL.

———. 1993c. *Situación y atención de la salud en Chile, 1993.* Santiago: MINSAL.

Miranda, Ernesto. 1990. "Descentralización y privatización del sistema de salud chileno." *Estudios Públicos,* no. 39 (winter): 5–66.

Moran, Cristian. 1989. "Economic Stabilization and Structural Transformation: Lessons from the Chilean Experience." *World Development* 17 (4): 491–502.

Novoa Fuenzalida, Patricio. 1982. *Nueva legislación sobre salud y previsión social.* Santiago: Editorial Jurídica de Chile.

Serrano, Claudia. 1989. "Política social en salud a nivel local." *Estudios CIEPLAN,* no. 27 (December): 119–48.

Superintendencia de ISAPRE. 1992. *Boletín estadístico del sistema ISAPRE.* Santiago: MINSAL.

———. 1993. *El sector privado en el sistema de salud.* Santiago: MINSAL.

11 / Health Sector Reform

A Financial–Service Flow Model and the Colombian Case

Gerard M. La Forgia

The effects of an economic crisis on public spending in Latin America during the 1980s has forced government authorities to take a closer look at institutional and financial arrangements within the health sector. Deteriorating quality of care, persistent large gaps in population coverage, systematic inefficiencies, and rising out-of-pocket spending have persuaded an increasing number of Latin Americans to question the current configuration of the health system and the state's role therein. The financial crises of social security institutions (SSI), declining budgetary support for health ministries (MS), and escalating private sector prices have precipitated a sense of urgency.

Health care reform presents an opportunity to change how resources are allocated within the health sector; how the financial burden is shared across population groups; and, ultimately, who gets what kind of services. This implies revamping the current institutional configuration of health finance and service delivery. Although it is recognized that meaningful change will not come easily or quickly, a consensus is forming that current institutional arrangements of finance, organization, and provision are seriously flawed and any real improvement will require restructuring the health system. But how much change occurs may depend on breaking through the institutional gridlock that places severe limits on how problems and their solutions are framed. This chapter focuses on proposed responses in Colombia to two aspects of this gridlock: institutional fragmentation and structural deficiencies inherent in government and parastatal health service systems.

As in the case of Colombia, my concern in this chapter is with those Latin

American countries that contain MS and SSI institutions in which each owns and operates separate facility networks, integrating the purchasing and provision roles (examples include most Latin American countries except for Brazil, Argentina, Uruguay, and Chile). In most countries these networks function within a broader health sector that is increasingly dominated by private spending and provision, particularly in urban centers. The emphasis here is on financing and delivery of preventive and curative care provided to individuals. In terms of total spending, these services consume the lion's share of resources. Other important aspects of the health care system, such as public health interventions, training, and regulation, are not directly addressed in this chapter.

The chapter consists of three parts. The first part briefly reviews the main problems affecting countries with large public and parastatal health service systems, usually operating alongside a vigorous private sector. The second part presents an approach to assessing the health sector and developing reform strategies. The approach focuses on mapping the chain of financial flows that directly or indirectly link households to providers and services. It recognizes a role for each subsector (government, social security, and private, for example) but seeks to circumvent narrow institutional-based approaches. The final part of this chapter outlines financial flows and other key elements of reform proposals in Colombia.

The Colombian reform is far-reaching and addresses major inefficiencies and inequities evident in the health sector through the establishment of a new set of financial arrangements among the MS, SSI, and private subsectors. According to a conceptual framework for comparing health care systems, MSs and SSIs can best be classified as "monopolistic integrated" systems (van de Ven, Schut, and Rutten 1994). These institutions are vertically integrated organizations that finance health care, assume the financial risk for their beneficiaries, aim to guarantee universal access, and pay their providers (personnel and facilities, for example) through salaries and budgets.

Reform proposals incorporate measures that, if fully implemented, may radically shift patterns of financing, ownership, and service delivery. This is achieved by separating the finance and provision functions of public institutions, by establishing mechanisms to subsidize the demand for health care, by reorganizing the delivery of health services, and by linking public finance to private provision. An increasing number of countries seek to develop long-range reform strategies that imply rearranging the institutional landscape and corresponding financing arrangements (health care reform is on the policy agenda in Mexico, Peru, El Salvador, Ecuador, Guatemala, Paraguay, and the Dominican Republic). The initiatives proposed in Colombia can inform the policy debate in other countries considering health policy reform.

PROBLEMS

There is increasing evidence of severe deficiencies in many Latin American health systems. In most countries policy makers will agree that persistent coverage gaps, inefficiencies in service organization and provision, deteriorating quality, and severe financial constraints are the main issues facing the health sector. The degree of emphasis placed on each of these elements will vary across countries. These problems are in part attributable to two broad structural features: (1) the segmentation of the public sector into overlapping but rival institutions, each catering to different populations; and (2) the integration of policy, financing, management, and service delivery functions within large, "command-and-control," public bureaucracies, each constituting monopolistic providers that manage the delivery of services to their respective populations.

The institutional fragmentation of the health system has generated negative consequences (Frenk 1992; McGreevey 1990; Ugalde 1985; PAHO 1977; Mesa-Lago 1992; Roemer 1969, 1971; ILO 1986; and Zschock 1983, for example). Little coordination of any kind exists between MS and SSI institutions. Linkages with the private sector are rare. Each institution sets plans, implements programs, and manages service delivery more or less independently. This in turn contributes to stratified access to health care, concentration of resources in large cities, duplication of infrastructure and service provision, and overlapping financial arrangements. Institutional segmentation also inhibits reform. In some countries, persuading SSI and MS authorities to meet to discuss the future of the health sector as a whole can be a difficult task.[1]

Household surveys show that Latin Americans are abandoning public systems in large numbers, seeking health care from private practitioners regardless of affiliation to SSIs, place of residence, or access to public providers. For example, middle-class SSI-insured increasingly seek private care —enrolling in private insurance plans or, more commonly, paying on a fee-for-service basis.[2] Many employers have established work-site clinics to minimize productivity losses because of queues at SSI clinics. The poor bypass low-price or free government clinics, paying out-of-pocket for relatively high-price private care.[3] Inefficiencies in the organization and delivery of care of MS and SSI systems are well documented.[4] Resource allocation tends to favor the provision of hospital-based curative care to residents of large cities while others have little access to services of any kind. More cost-effective services remain underfunded.

Efficiency, equity, and quality problems are in part attributable to the following structural features observed in large "command-and-control" public bureaucracies that own, finance, and operate service delivery systems.[5] (1) Perverse incentive structures mean that systems provide few incentives for efficient utilization of resources or for higher productivity. (2) Overcentralization means that top-down planning, centralized hiring and procurement, collective labor agreements, rigid budgetary mechanisms and bureaucratic procedures, all severely restrict the decision-making authority of lower-level and facility managers. (3) Provider-driven monopolies mean that each public sector institution is the only provider of services for its respective beneficiary populations. These monopolies are often driven by the demands and wants of the staff employed by the systems. (4) The lack of responsiveness to patients means that, since consumers have little voice or choice when they seek care in public systems, the only option for patients dissatisfied with the services is to exit these systems. (5) Weak health-policy-making capacity means that high-level MS and SSI authorities are absorbed in micromanaging day-to-day operations of the delivery system, leaving little time to dedicate to policy making that could influence the future direction of the health sector.

Solving these structural problems requires a serious and broad set of systemwide reforms.[6] Governments face numerous constraints, suggesting the need for precision in defining problems and setting the time path for solving them. For example, implementation can be technically complicated, politically difficult, and administratively time-consuming. Transitional costs are unknown. In addition to resource constraints imposed by broader economic problems, governments must deal with rising costs resulting from the epidemiologic and demographic transition, policies aimed at filling coverage gaps, technological progress, and wage demands by health workers. Moreover, although many SSI and MS systems face decreasing popular support, reform may involve expending considerable political capital to overcome opposition by well-organized health worker unions and professional associations. The search for solutions also may raise difficult questions about the appropriate mission of public institutions in the health sector, generating resistance from bureaucratic elites.

PROPOSED SOLUTIONS

Drawing on the recent proposals and experiences regarding health sector reform in Chile, the United Kingdom, Sweden, New Zealand, Netherlands, and Israel, some observers claim that a new paradigm has emerged, which provides a guide for reforming the health sector (Chernichovsky 1993). In general, recommendations aim to improve efficiency through the reform of health systems dominated by public bureaucracies that integrate the financing and provision functions. The trend is toward initiating market-style solutions in the financing, organization, and provision of health services. These approaches go by various titles: mixed market, internal market, regulated market, and public competition (see Sheaff 1994; Bassett 1993; Saltman 1992; Frenk 1993a; Culyer 1990; Saltman and von Otter 1989; van de Ven 1989; HMSO 1989; Enthoven 1985).

In developing countries as well as the former socialist countries in Europe, the direction of reform has been influenced by the World Bank and other donor agencies. Recent publications have focused on instilling market principles into these systems to control costs, to make systems more responsive to patient interests, to assure quality of care, and to provide incentives to raise productivity and effectiveness of treatment (World Bank 1987, 1993b; Griffin 1992a; Birdsall and James 1990). Other recommended measures seek to improve equity through resource reallocation and defining the services and populations targeted through government finance.

The literature on health sector reform in developing countries is in its infancy, in part because of the dearth of documented experience. Even the European countries from which reform prescriptions are drawn are themselves at an early stage of implementation. Assessments of lessons learned are in short supply. More evidence is needed on how these reforms can be implemented and whether they can meet their objectives of improving quality, efficiency, and equity (Gilson and Mills 1993; Collins, Green, and Hunter 1993; Ensor 1993). Some observers argue that the conditions needed to implement these market-oriented reforms are absent in most developing countries. Others argue that market-oriented policies may raise costs, limit access, and reduce quality for certain services (for a discussion of the risks of market-oriented reforms, see McPake and Ngalande Banda 1994; Broomberg 1994; Dahlgren and Diderichsen 1993). The major strategies emerging from international trends and experience for health sector reform consider the following measures (for a more detailed review see Sheaff 1994; World Bank 1993b; Ensor 1993; Saltman and von Otter 1989; Chernichovsky 1993; Birdsall and James 1992; Frenk 1993b).

1. *Separation of the financing, purchasing, and provision of health services.* From a systemic perspective, this measure aims to break the integrated functions of public institutions and paves the way for initiating more specific measures listed below (that is, competition among multiple providers and greater patient choice of providers). In general, recommendations seek to retain the principal features of public finance but combine them with some form of private or quasi-public provision. Consonant with this measure are calls to eliminate the dual (SSI and MS) delivery systems and to strengthen the policy, oversight, and regulatory role of health ministries.

2. *Patient choice.* Patient choice refers to the ability of patients to select insurers and/or providers. Money (from government or social insurance funds) will follow patients and thus in theory stimulate competition among providers. With the purpose of introducing more market-style incentives, provider revenues will depend on accumulating market share, which in turn will depend on providers' ability to attract and satisfy patients. Implementation will require flexible budgetary procedures combined with appropriate provider payment systems.

3. *Vertical decentralization.* Within the context of proposed market-style approaches, this measure attempts to move beyond deconcentration of internal administrative functions. It involves the transferring of managerial and spending authority to local-level units in part to facilitate the contracting out of services. In effect, decentralized units become purchasers of services from public and private providers who will compete for market share.

4. *Establishment of contractual relations between purchasers and providers.* This measure seeks greater pluralism in service provision through the use of private providers and through the formation of autonomous self-managing enterprises such as hospital trusts overseen by governing boards. It requires effective regulation and the use of provider payment

mechanisms that give incentives for efficient provision of services without compromising quality.

5. *Resource reallocation.* This measure involves shifting government spending to high-payoff, cost-effective interventions and targeting subsidies to low-income and special populations. Essentially, resource reallocation concerns the design and implementation of mechanisms that determine who gets what. It can involve rationing or setting the boundaries of health care coverage financed by government, social insurance, and private sources through the definition of standardized service packages (which in turn facilitate establishing contractual arrangements between payers and providers). Resource reallocation implies setting criteria for measuring performance in both technical and patient terms.

A HEALTH SECTOR FINANCIAL AND SERVICE FLOW MODEL

A fundamental design question in the reform of any health system is, Which elements of the current system should a reform be built on? This section presents a framework for analyzing and reforming health systems, drawing on analysis and instruments used by analysts of the U.S. and European health care systems.[7] It emphasizes financial and service flows, concentrating on how money is channeled through the system in exchange for services. The framework allows policy makers to explore the cost, equity, and efficiency implications of current as well as proposed finance and payment mechanisms. Figure 11.1 schematically depicts the framework, mapping out the linkages among the four principal actors in the health care market (in the vertical boxes): households, payers, providers, and beneficiaries. Actors are connected through three major elements (with horizontal arrows): finance mechanisms, payment systems, and health services. Finance mechanisms link households to payers, provider payment systems link providers to payers, and health services link households to providers.

Households have a dual role in the model, providing the beginning and end points in figure 11.1. Since they are the ultimate payers of health care (not government or employers), the model begins with households as the source of finance. Similarly, the model concludes with households, or more specifically its members, since the latter are the final *beneficiaries* or consumers of health services. However, it is important to note that in some cases

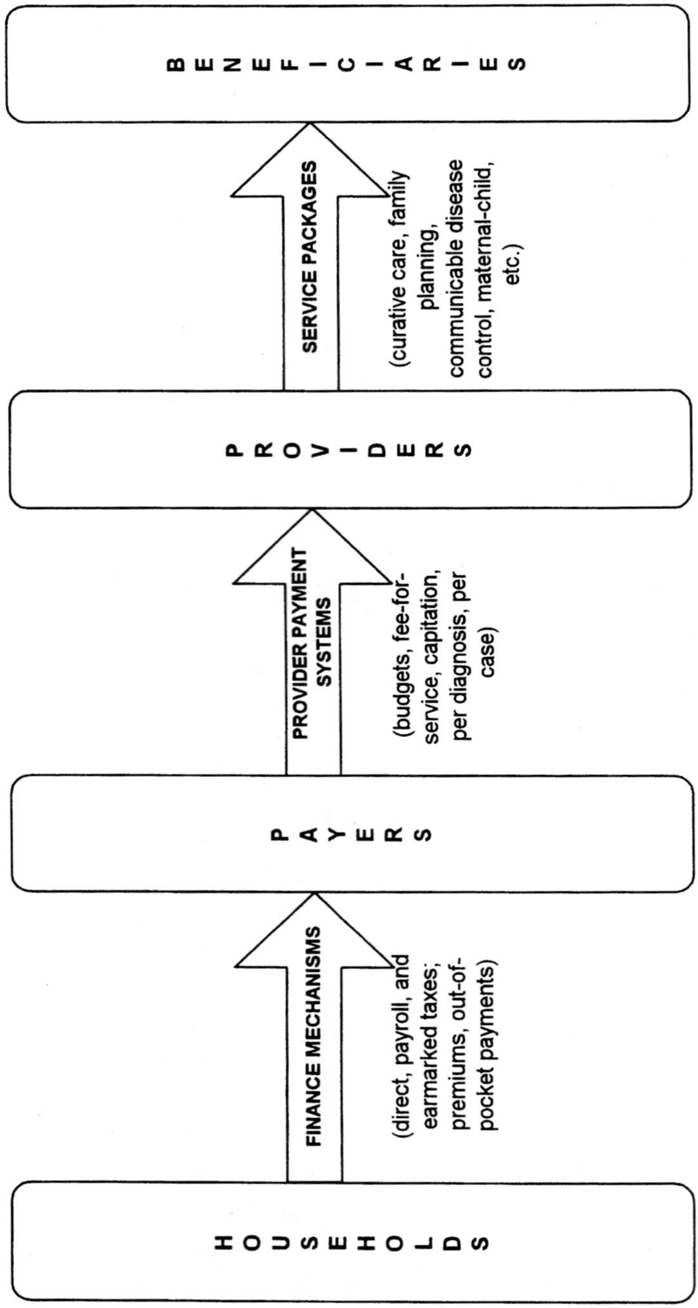

Figure 11.1 Mapping Financial Flows Within the Health Sector

households pay for services but their members are not necessarily the beneficiaries thereof. For example, uninsured populations pay indirectly for social security through higher consumer prices and government tax-financed subsidies, but they are excluded from SSI service systems.

Households pay for care through several *financing mechanisms* including general and payroll taxes, private insurance premiums, and out-of-pocket spending. Institutional *payers* or money movers such as MSs, SSIs, and private insurance companies collect, accumulate, and channel funds to providers for service provision on behalf of households. Payers can use a variety of *payment mechanisms* to pay providers for services rendered to individuals and households, including fee-for-service, salaries, fixed budgets, and capitation payments. In most Latin American countries, households make direct payments to providers for many services. *Providers* can consist of MS and SSI direct delivery networks (consisting of hospitals, ambulatory facilities, and corresponding personnel), private solo practitioners, voluntary and charitable organizations, workplace clinics, and private hospitals. Health care activities are the *services* and programs provided to individuals and households.

From a policy perspective, each of the seven components displayed in figure 11.1 (households, finance mechanisms, payers, provider payment systems, providers, health services, and beneficiaries) contains a set of elements or variables that can be manipulated by government to fashion policy alternatives. For example, government can define one or more standardized packages of services. This package can be directed at targeted beneficiary populations with specified health needs. Government can select the providers who will deliver care as well as determine how (and how much) they will be paid. Institutions that pay providers can be added, modified, or eliminated. Finally, interventions can alter the amount of resources entering the system, how it is financed, and who ultimately bears the burden of health spending.

The crafting of any reform policy involves manipulating elements within each of the components shown in figure 11.1. Each component can be considered a building block for reform or, similarly, a domain for government intervention in the health care system. Policy makers can formulate reform initiatives to introduce different combinations of altered elements within and across the domains. Reform options represent specific patterns of feasible alterations or interventions that address policy goals.

The proposed framework offers other advantages. First, understanding the maze of actors and interactions within a health system can be a bewildering task. The health sector in most Latin American countries possesses a diverse set of participants who interact on multiple levels across subsectoral boundaries. Identifying who they are, how they are financed, what services they produce, and who their beneficiaries are is key to understanding the constraints and opportunities within the total system. Knowledge of the dynamics of the health market, including the formal and informal exchanges within and between public and private subsectors, is deficient. The proposed framework facilitates analysis of the current configuration, which in turn can signal feasible interventions and ultimately give shape to reform strategies.

Second, because of the institutional axis on which conceptualization is often based, it is difficult to uncover the means to realign the health system into a more desirable configuration to meet long-range policy goals. This framework allows for a more inclusive view of the health sector. It stimulates a sectoral perspective on heretofore subsectorally or institutionally defined issues and can facilitate the development of alternative, long-term strategies for reform. Casting off the straitjacket of institutional-based problem and solution definition can give weight to sectorwide strategies and actions aimed at substantive, systematic, and coherent reform.

FINANCIAL AND SERVICE FLOWS IN TYPICAL LATIN AMERICAN HEALTH SECTOR

Figure 11.2 maps the financial and service flows and corresponding transfer mechanisms in a typical country with centralized SSI and MS direct delivery systems, and a private sector. Here the focus is on how money flows among the actors displayed in figure 11.1. Resources can be exchanged between any two actors for the direct provision of individual services (households to providers), for the theoretical guarantee of service coverage (households to payers such as SSIs, MFs and MSs, insurers), and for the direct or indirect provision of institutional services (payers to providers).

Similar to the framework shown before, figure 11.2 starts with households, the ultimate source of financing for any health system. The figure displays three main financial flow channels linking households to services: social security, public, and private. Individuals may use one or more of these channels during a particular illness episode. In addition, they may select channels according to the type and severity of illness, estimated cost, and perceived quality.

The first is the social security channel, in which formal sector workers

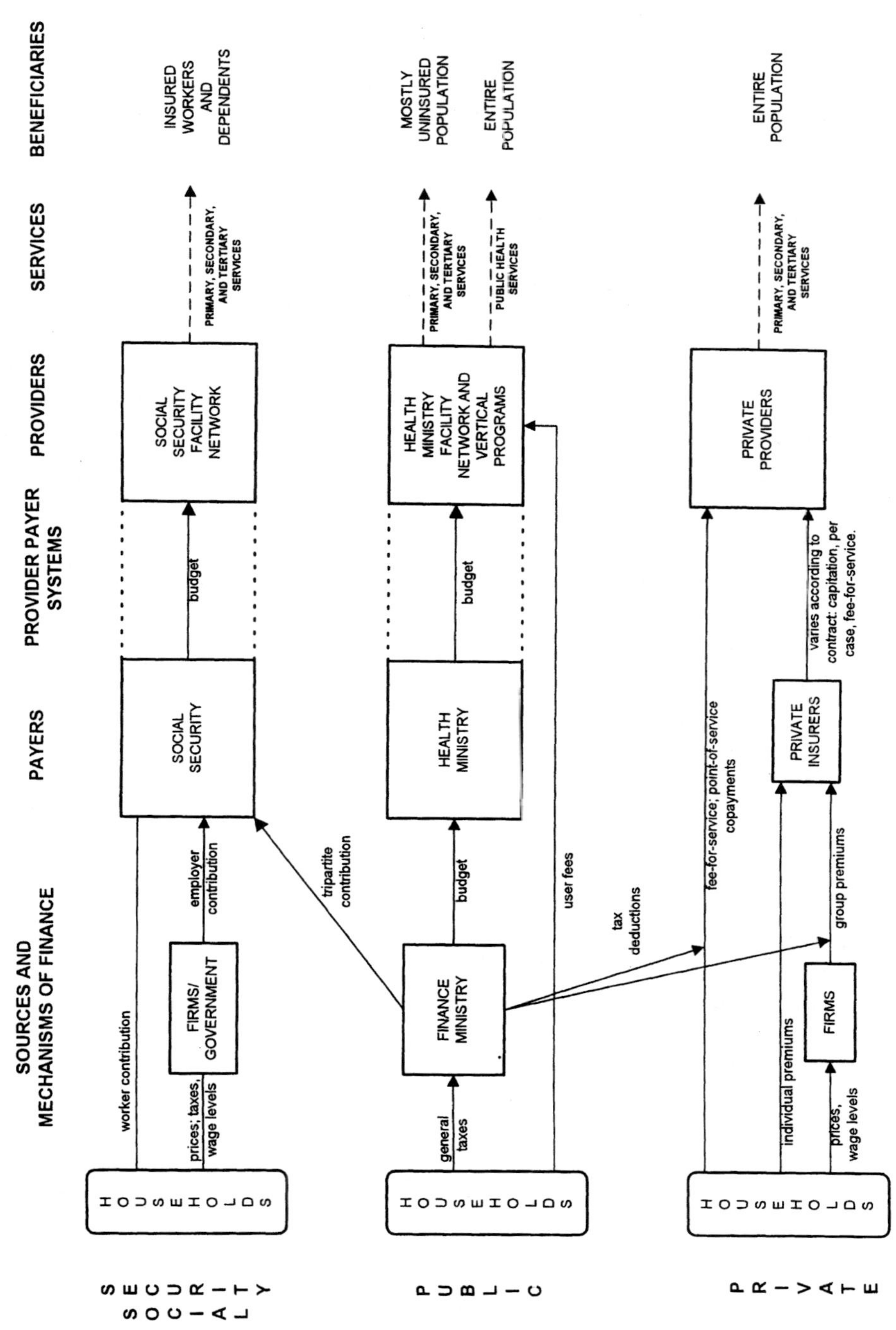

Figure 11.2 Financial Flows in Typical Health Sector with SSI, MS, and Private Subsectors

make mandatory contributions through payroll taxes. The workplace serves as an intermediary tax collection agency for the SSI fund. The SSI fund pumps money, usually through a fixed budget, to its own service delivery network. However, the SSI may contract out services to the private sector, especially in areas where SSI infrastructure is lacking. Some countries have more than one social security system, each catering to specific occupation groups.

The second is the public channel and draws on various tax mechanisms to route money, usually via a finance ministry (MF) onto the MS and its direct delivery system. Invariably, the delivery system is separate from that of the SSI. Again, the network is funded through a fixed budget. In some countries, the government may contribute to the SSI fund as a tripartite partner. Municipalities of some large cities own and operate a facility network, which is financed through local taxes, but may receive a subsidy from the MF or MS. In addition to providing personal medical services, MS operate a number of public health programs.

The third and generally largest channel is the private sector. The main flow of funds consists of direct out-of-pocket payments by households to providers on a fee-for-service basis. In most countries there is a small but growing market for private insurance plans, in which funds are extracted from households through the workplace and channeled to an insurer. In turn, insurers may own and operate a service delivery network, contract services with a group of providers, or allow enrollees to select any provider. An array of provider payment systems can be used to pay physicians and hospitals under these arrangements.

ALTERING HEALTH SECTOR FINANCIAL FLOWS IN COLOMBIA

Prior to the initiation of decentralization in 1990, the Colombian health sector closely approximated the configuration displayed in figure 11.2. It consisted of three major parts. First, in terms of total spending, the government subsector was the smallest actor, representing approximately 21 percent of total health spending in 1980 (Yepes 1990).[8] It contained a centralized MS health service system and a number of semiautonomous institutes. The MS directly managed a large network of facilities. Most decision-making authority was centered in the MS. Regional administrative units had only limited autonomy regarding personnel, financing, and policy making.

Second, representing 32 percent of health spending, the social security subsector consisted of the Social Security Institute (ISS) for private sector employees, CAJANAL for public employees, and a large number of smaller funds that cover health for specific groups and government agencies (for example, police, oil industry, military, banking superintendency, and ministry of communications). Together these SSIs cover about 18 percent of the population, mostly salaried workers. The ISS owns and operates a network of hospitals and ambulatory centers but contracts with MS and private providers in areas where it does not possess facilities. CAJANAL and the smaller funds contract out services to private and MS providers.

Finally, the private medical subsector consists mainly of fee-for-service solo practitioners, but group practices and prepayment plans thrive in the large cities. Although there is a dearth of information on private medicine and insurance in Colombia, the private sector is a major provider of health services, especially in large urban areas. The 1980 National Health Study estimated that the private sector represented 47 percent of total health expenditures.

Health sector reform in Colombia commenced in 1990 with the passage of Law 10, mandating the devolution of management and provision of health and medical services to 32 departments and 1,029 municipalities. Intergovernmental transfers to finance health care—and other social services provided by these entities—are described in the Law 60 (Ley de Competencias y Recursos) of August 1993. The final element of the reform is mandated in the Law 100, the Social Security Reform Law, which passed Congress in December 1993. This law seeks to incorporate the social security system into the overall reform process while establishing formal links between the decentralized entities and the private medical sector. It also seeks to instill competition into the public sector by allowing competition among public, quasi-public, and private providers.

Health reform in Colombia is already partially implemented to the extent that managerial authority has been decentralized to a number of departmental governments and to mainly large urban municipalities (Bogota, Cali, Manizales, and so on) since the passage of Law 10. Implementation of financial transfer mechanisms (to decentralized entities) and the revamping of social security commence in 1995. The reform is expected to take eight years to complete.

The Colombian reform is a complex process involving numerous institutions, funding sources, payers, and finance mechanisms. Because of the existence of regulating decrees (MS 1991a) and a recent evaluation of the implementation process (La Forgia and Homedes 1992; World Bank 1993a), sufficient information is available to delineate vertical and horizontal linkages involved in the decentralization reform. The same cannot be said for the social security reform. A change of government (in 1994) has contributed to delays in the implementation of social security reform and the preparation of regulatory decrees. Therefore, some aspects of the social security law remain ambiguous. This case study will focus on how the Colombians are reorienting financial flows as a means to reconfigure the health system and reorganize service provision.

Decentralization

Decentralization seeks to correct inequities in access and improve the efficiency and quality of services by bringing decision making and financing closer to the beneficiaries. There is a broad consensus in Colombia that the centralized administrative apparatus and direct delivery service system have failed to provide essential coverage to a large number of Colombians at an acceptable level of quality. An estimated one-third of the population lacks access to primary services (MS 1991b). Traditionally, MS resources have been heavily concentrated in hospital services while primary and preventive services were underfinanced. With the exception of a few large cities, the primary care delivery systems are nearly dysfunctional, driving people to seek care at higher-level hospitals or to abandon the public system all together. Approximately half of all persons demanding care at MS facilities are not provided for (MS 1990, 133). Absenteeism and work shirking plague the MS direct delivery system. There is a universal absence of accountability to the public or to MS authorities within the system.

General Features

From an operational standpoint, decentralization will be accomplished in three ways. First, the management of primary-level services will be separated from the administration of all other levels of care. Departmental governments will manage secondary- and tertiary-level hospitals while municipalities are responsible for the organization and provision of primary health care. Second, progressively increasing percentages of the central government's tax revenues will be channeled to municipalities and departments. The additional financing will make coverage extension more feasible. The two major financial mechanisms include the social investment transfer, formally the value added tax (IVA), and the tax allowance or *situado fiscal.* Both transfers use allocation formulas that favor underserved areas.

Third, unlike the former MS/ISS system in which budgetary appropriations were the principal modus operandi of national to subnational financial transfers, decentralization features a kind of block grant (*cesión de recursos*). Departmental and municipal health units have full autonomy regarding the use of these resources, restricted only by the guidelines stipulated in the law. Decentralization law mandates the creation of Local and Sectional Funds, separate accounts within the respective municipal and departmental financial systems, in which *all* income destined for the health sector (from central, departmental, and local sources) is deposited and later disbursed to pay for health services.

From a financial and service flow perspective, decentralization alone does not represent a fundamental reform. Rather, it is a subsectoral reorganization that only indirectly touches other actors. It fails to alter key mechanisms linking payers, providers, and beneficiaries (see figure 11.1) or address key problems facing the public system relating to interinstitutional interaction, incentive structures, accountability, and patient satisfaction. Although the process shifts full administrative authority and financial management from the MS to subnational entities, financial flows remain in the government channel, as displayed in figure 11.2. However, the law does permit a degree of flexibility for departments and municipalities to work with the private sector, allowing the contracting out of the management of municipal health services to a private, nonprofit institute. The Local and Sectional Funds can be used to finance the contracting out of services to private providers. But most decentralized health services managed by municipalities and departments use the funds to finance the direct provision of services through fixed budgets (La Forgia and Homedes 1992). In short, the input-driven, direct delivery system remains intact, though managed at the provincial and municipal levels rather than in Bogota.

Implementation

Decentralization is advancing at a much slower pace than anticipated. Between 1991 and 1993 only one department and fourteen municipalities were officially decentralized (MS 1993). Implementation was hampered by the lack of definition of responsibilities at each level of government (that is, central, departmental, and municipal), by overburdening legal and administrative requirements to achieve certification, and by local politicians' lack of trust in national transfers as a reliable source of funding. Even those departments and municipalities that have decentralized or at least have initiated the process do not appear to have turned their attention to the issues of efficiency, equity, and quality.

Although it may be premature to assess the effect of decentralization on these objectives, some shortcomings have come to the fore. First, although revenue sources are well defined, how funds will be spent is unclear. The lump sum national revenue transfers provided to the subnational entities provides few incentives to improve service delivery. These upfront grants do not correspond to costs and production of services. The central government appears to have little leverage over municipalities' spending of national revenue transfers. Mechanisms to enforce accountability of local authorities in terms of national policy objectives are mostly absent. Further, given the deficient information systems, MS monitoring of spending will be a difficult task.

Second, the above described situation takes on added significance given that most mayors who have initiated the process appear interested in constructing facilities and providing more curative care (La Forgia and Homedes 1992). Seeking to imitate wealthier neighbors, a number of mayors have called for the construction of local hospitals, even in sparsely populated areas. Few have performed health diagnoses to assess the type of system that would best fit the needs of their populations. Moreover, the typical solution for low productivity is to hire additional personnel for the direct delivery systems, which in turn are linked to well-entrenched municipal patronage systems.

Finally, given that the MS has had little success in improving the quality and efficiency of care, it is unlikely that municipal governments can turn the tide within similar (but decentralized) organizational structures and incentive systems. Decentralization only changes the command. For example, although the law calls for full autonomy between the municipal (or departmental) health administrative apparatus and former SSI hospitals, separation appears to be in name only.[9] Facility managers may face considerable difficulty in correcting inefficiencies and raising quality, given the general lack of staff concern for consumer interests, the patronage system, and the heavy representation of local politicians on hospital boards.[10] In short, even though more resources will be available to subnational units, there are few indications that under existing conditions they will be put to better and more efficient use than under MS authority.

Laws 60 and 100 (1993) seek to correct a number of the deficiencies observed in the decentralization process. Law 60 assigns department governments the responsibility of municipal decentralization, ending considerable confusion over who is in charge. The national transfer (*situado fiscal*) will be distributed first to the departments, which in turn will distribute them to municipalities, whereas IVA transfer (*inversión social*) will be assigned directly to the municipalities. Further, the law mandates with greater specificity the proportion of national transfers that will be assigned to the departments and municipalities for health spending,[11] the criteria used to distribute them across subnational entities,[12] and the types of health activities that can be financed with them. By 1995 the criteria for distributing these transfers were not fully operational. Consequently, allocations continued to be based on historical spending patterns, which are negotiated between the subnational entity and the MS.

Although not specified in Law 60, Colombian planners aim to distribute all transfers across departments and municipalities through an average capitation payment, adjusted for levels of poverty, coverage, and basic needs. Similar formula will be used by the departments to capitate the municipalities therein to distribute the *situado fiscal* for the delivery of primary level services. The MS plans to mandate that all national transfers be directed to cover a predetermined basic package of services. The law facilitates the certification process for receiving the national transfer, reducing some requirements while clearly stating others. Nevertheless, it also empowers the MS to remove subnational control over the transfers if funds are misallocated or if subnational entities fall out of compliance with administrative and technical requirements. The law does not give the MS power to withhold transfers. Finally, Law 60 authorizes subnational units to contract out the provision of services to private providers and allows for the creation of mechanisms through which government transfers can be used to finance the demand for health care. With the aim of extending coverage, improving efficiency, and raising quality, these measures are viewed as a means to reform the input-driven, direct delivery systems by substituting demand-driven approaches. These approaches are described in the social security law.

Social Security Reform

Approved by Congress in late 1993, the Social Security Law (LSS) contains two parts. The first relates mainly to economic benefits (pensions, professional risks, survivors' benefits, and so on); the second relates to health. This section focuses on the latter. The overall goals of the legislation are to reduce inequities in finance and coverage evident in the health sector as a whole, extend population coverage to more vulnerable population groups (such as informal sector, self-employed, children), and to make providers more responsive to beneficiaries. Operationally, the reform aims to "unify" the different SSI regimens, transform how these systems finance and provide services, and recast how they interact with the public system and the private sector.

In the long run, social security reform may radically alter the finance and provision of health services in the entire health sector. An important long-term objective is to create competitive but regulated markets of group purchasers and providers. The former will compete for members while the latter will compete to provide health services to individuals and groups enrolled by the group purchasers. Essentially, the reform aims to make consumers, insurers, and providers more sensitive to costs and quality through financial incentives. Some of the incentives are derived through payment mechanisms and others through regulated competition for enrollees and patients.

General Features

The reform contains four central tenets: (1) separation of finance and provision functions of health institutions; (2) substitution of supply-side financing of municipal and departmental direct delivery systems with demand-side subsidies; (3) competition among purchasers (for members) and among providers (for patients) of health services; and (4) definition of a standard benefit package. These characteristics require redirecting financial flows, which in turn involves reconfiguring the institutional landscape.

The social security reform law introduces three new institutional features: a health insurance fund, the Fondo de Solidaridad y Garantía (FSG); public and private group purchasing organizations, *entidades promotoras de salud* (EPS), and provider organizations, *instituciones proveedoras de servicios de salud* (IPSS). These features are grafted on the decentralized health system already underway. Figure 11.3 displays the anticipated institutional fea-

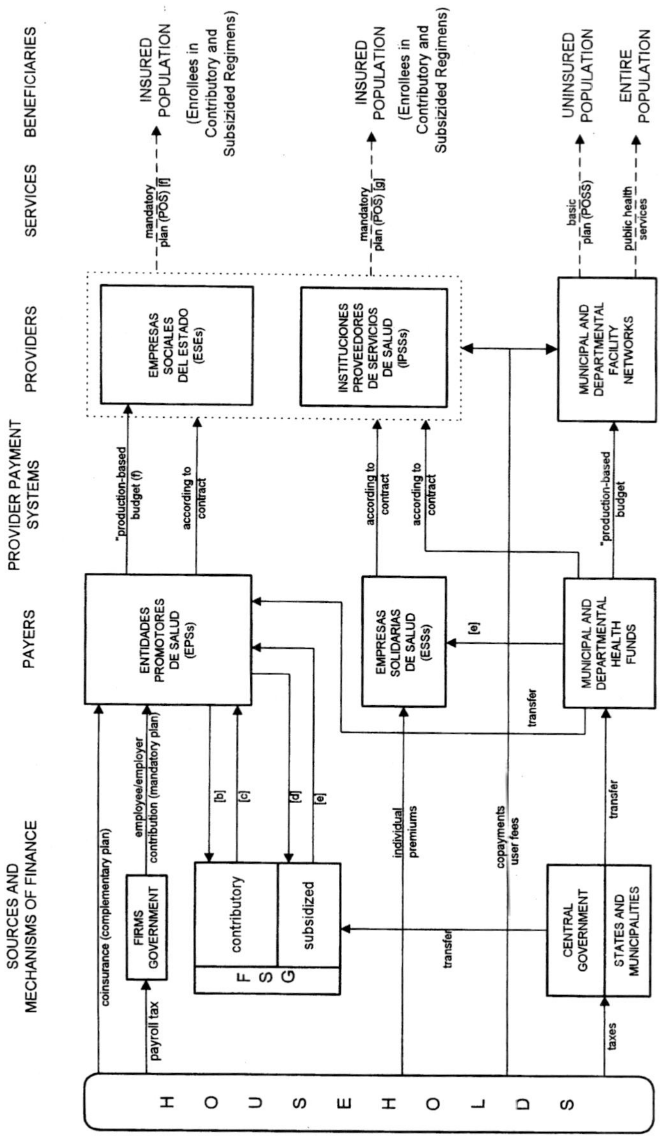

Figure 11.3 Financial Flows Under Decentralization and Social Security Reform in Colombia[a]

[a] Figure shows changes in social security and government health systems. Financial flows and service delivery related to fee-for-service and insurance systems in the private sector remain unaltered.

[b] Contribution less UPC: tax on complementary plans.

[c] UPC less contribution (subsidy).

[d] 1% of salary.

[e] Subsidized UPC.

[f] Refers to ESEs that are owned and operated by EPSs.

[g] Additional services provided to enrollees who purchase a complementary plan.

tures and financial flows of a reformed (and decentralized) health system if the measures stipulated in the law are fully implemented.

Finance Mechanisms, Payers, and Beneficiaries

The law mandates the creation of two regimens: contributory and subsidized. The former financially unifies the heretofore separate SSIs and is financed mainly through payroll taxes. The subsidized regimen, financed in part by tax revenues and by transfers from the contributory regimen, will become the major financial conduit for the gradual incorporation of low-income subpopulations traditionally excluded from SSI coverage into the social insurance system. It is the spirit of the law that over the long run the social security system, through the contributory and subsidized regimens, will enroll all Colombians, guaranteeing coverage for a standard benefit package. The process is expected to take at least ten years.

The contributory regimen consists of channeling payroll contributions to EPSs, which then channel funds to providers. The law sets the obligatory salary contribution at a maximum level of 12 percent for health care, shared by employees and their employers. As envisioned by health planners, EPSs approximate the group purchasing cooperatives proposed under the Clinton health reform proposal in the United States. They are the institutions and organizations through which beneficiaries select benefits and providers. Since beneficiaries are free to direct their contribution to the EPS of their choice, EPSs will compete for enrollment. EPSs will offer a menu of health delivery options, contracting one or more provider networks, group practices, or individual hospitals and physicians in both the public and private sectors. EPSs can be organized by large firms, former SSIs, cooperatives, community organizations, private prepayment plans (HMOs, for example), and parastatals.

Essentially, the principal functions of the EPS are those of any third-party payer. First, EPSs represent a main vehicle within the reform to achieve universal coverage for health services. Second, they are to assume the financial risk (that is, uncertainty of loss or expense beyond expected levels) of their enrollees, though the FSG (discussed below) will assume part of this risk. All EPSs are required to purchase reinsurance to protect against unexpected losses. Third, EPSs are to act in the interests of their members when selecting providers and purchasing health services. But they also are responsible for containing costs and reducing moral hazard (that is, since insurance reduces a person's direct price for medical care it raises the probability that the quantity of care demanded will increase). For example, to achieve these ends the reform encourages EPSs to apply moderate copayments and deductibles to users, utilize efficient provider payment methods (discussed below), and adopt managed care practices.[13] EPSs will be allowed to own and operate delivery networks but these networks must be financially and administratively autonomous.[14] Separation of the finance and delivery functions of public sector health institutions will be achieved through the formation of public firms among MS and social security delivery networks.

The subsidized regimen consists of two mechanisms for financing the demand for health care by nonsalaried workers and low-income groups traditionally excluded from SSIs. The first involves directing public funds through the FSG to EPSs who enroll the poor. In other words, EPSs will receive funds that will partially subsidize the premium (UPC) of low-income enrollees. Enrollees will be required to make an out-of-pocket contribution to be determined through a means test. Government will define who qualifies for a subsidy according to the following criteria: income, education, family size, residence, and access to potable water and sanitation services.

The second feature of the subsidized regimen involves the formation of Empresas Solidarias de Salud (ESSs). ESSs, a type of EPS, are grouping mechanisms to facilitate the enrollment of the self-employed and nonsalaried workers. In effect, they are organized risk pools established through community groups, microenterprise associations, and other organizations that can serve as grouping mechanisms. Social security reform law mandates the MS and subnational entities to establish ESSs as a means to target demand-side subsidies to low-income populations. To facilitate coverage extension through the subsidized regimen, the law authorizes subnational entities to create special accounts within the decentralized local and sectional funds, and to establish agreements and contracts with EPSs. The main sources of finance include national, municipal, and departmental transfers channeled through local and sectional health funds, transfers from the FSG, and individual premium payments (see figure 11.3). LSS specifies several sources of fiscal finance for demand subsidies: (1) 15 percent of "social investment" (IVA) tax revenues earmarked for health, as described in Law 60; (2) 10 percent of the budgetary appropriations (*libre asignación*) destined for infrastructure and equipment; (3) an unspecified proportion of the "national transfer" (*situado fiscal*) and departmental tax revenues directed to secondary and tertiary hospitals; (4) taxes on petroleum exports; (5) earnings from the sale of parastatals; and (6) and a percentage of SSI revenues directed to family assistance programs.

Services

The subsidized and contributory regimens will cover different benefit packages, at least during the early phases of implementation. The subsidized regimen will fund a basic or streamlined package of services, known as the Mandatory Subsidized Health Plan (POSS), which contains less benefits than the Mandatory Health Plan (POS) covered by the contributory regimen. A third package of services, consisting of public health interventions, will be financed by government and provided through the decentralized health systems.

Initially at least, planners estimate that the POSS will cost one-half of POS. Both the POS and POSS will cover the family unit and will vary according to regional epidemiologic profiles. ESSs as well as EPSs that enroll participants of the subsidized regimen will provide the POSS. It is important to note that both the range of benefits and the amount of the subsidy for the poor participating in the subsidized regimen will increase incrementally until the year 2002, when the MS estimates that the subsidy will be sufficient to purchase the more comprehensive POS, and the subsidized regimen will achieve full coverage of low-income populations not participating in the contributory regimen.

Providers

The reform is less defined regarding the interaction between payers and providers. It calls for the formation of provider organizations (IPSSs), which can consist of group practices, organized networks of public facilities, and individual hospitals and individual physicians. (Any EPS that owns an IPSS or vice versa must demonstrate financial and administrative autonomy between these two entities.) IPSSs also can consist of an intermediary organization that contracts individual facilities and physician groups. EPSs and ESSs can contract one or more IPSSs to deliver services to enrollees. In theory, IPSSs will compete for the volume offered by EPSs and ESSs.

Hospitals and provider networks owned and operated by health ministry, social security institutions, and decentralized entities are to be converted into a type of IPSS, known as State Social Enterprises (ESEs). Essentially, ESEs are public firms and represent the mechanism for separating finance and delivery functions of former social security- and government-operated health systems. One or more ESEs can be formed within a predetermined geographic area and can consist of one or more facilities.

ESEs are to operate like private enterprises, receiving property ownership and being overseen by a board of directors. They can contract with EPSs to provide services. In addition, subnational entities can purchase (for example, contract) services directly from ESEs or indirectly through EPSs. However, some passages of the law appear to compromise the ability of the ESEs to become self-managed, autonomous public enterprises as well as the subnational entities' ability to use the contractual relationship to require efficient provider payment methods. For example, a number of members of the boards are political appointees. Workers who staff MS and ISS facilities retain their public employee status. The reform law also allows subnational entities to reimburse ESEs through a "production-based" budgetary mechanism. Although such a measure is certainly an improvement over the current historical budgetary process, this option permits departments and municipalities to bypass any contractual relationship and maintain the direct delivery modus operandi.

Provider Payment Methods

The reform calls for the use of provider payment mechanisms that control utilization and stimulate efficiency, such as capitation, per-case, and all-payer rates.[15] Again the law is vague in this regard, but the spirit of the legislation appears more aligned with a capitation amount for a year's care. Nevertheless, depending on the contract between EPS/ESS and IPSS/ESE, the law encourages other types of provider payment systems such as diagnostic related groups (DRGs) for hospital payments and fee-for-service. Implementation of any method requires accurate and timely information. The law mandates EPSs and IPSSs to develop information systems on costs and utilization.

Other Features

Any system that creates competing purchasing agents or insurers builds selection bias into the choice of agent. Purchasing agents will have an incentive to enroll healthy groups and discriminate against the sick. On the other hand, healthy individuals will have an incentive to refuse participation until they become sick whereas the already sick will seek immediate enrollment. The law contemplates several measures to prevent risk selection by EPSs and adverse selection by individuals. These include community rating, standardized benefits, open enrollment, mandatory participation, and regulations to protect special subpopulations.

The social security system will only recognize the per capita costs (UPC) of the POS.[16] A separate UPC will apply to the POSS. The UPC represents a (capitated) premium payment to EPSs for the provision of this defined package of services. All EPSs within a given market will be required to offer the same set of services, defined by the health plan, to enrollees at the UPC or less. The social security system will only recognize the UPC regardless of an individual's contribution or income. Nevertheless, to discourage discrimination against certain risk groups such as pregnant women, senior citizens, and people with chronic diseases, the UPC will be adjusted according to age, sex, and costs in specific regions. Similarly, the law contemplates the design of a higher cost UPC for individuals residing in impoverished regions or in areas with dispersed populations, and for individuals with chronic diseases. The law also mandates that EPS enrollment contain a minimum proportion of seniors and a more or less equal percentage of women and men between the ages of fifteen and forty-four. Other risk adjustors will be added as information systems improve.

EPSs must accept all applicants, and people can change affiliation during open enrollment periods. Adverse selection on the part of individuals is avoided because participation in the regimen is obligatory for formal sector wage earners and their dependents. Eventually, it is anticipated that all Colombians will participate in the contributory regimen. Exclusions related to preexisting conditions, mandatory waiting periods, and so on are outlawed. But limited waiting periods for unspecified "high-cost" services are permitted. As mentioned, the law authorizes the charging of deductibles and point-of-service copayments to control demand. Enrollees desiring more comprehensive coverage can purchase a complementary plan from their EPS by paying an additional premium out-of-pocket. (As envisioned by the designers of the regimen, copayments, quality, and complementary plan benefits will be the basis for EPS competition.)

Social solidarity is built into the system's financial base through at least three mechanisms, illustrated in figure 11.3. The first is related to the contributory regimen. Each EPS must deposit in the FSG the difference between the total payroll contribution and the UPC, in each case that the former is greater than the latter. These funds are used to subsidize lower-income enrollees of the regimen whose contribution is less than the UPC. The second mechanism involves a subsidy from enrollees of the contributory regimen to their counterparts in the subsidized regimen. One percent of the payroll contribution to the contributory regimen is transferred to a special account within the FSG, to subsidize health care for low-income groups. The third mechanism consists of redistributive taxes and central government transfers, which will be channeled through departments and municipalities to the subsidized account of the FSG, or directly to ESSs.

DISCUSSION

Although a consensus is emerging in many Latin American countries concerning the need for health reform, the debate over what form it should take is just beginning. The direction it takes relates to a vision of the health care system at some future point in time. The content and pace of reform will depend on estimates of how much change is feasible between now and then. But where policy makers first aim their sights can reveal or obscure key issues and, ultimately, facilitate or impede chances for meaningful change. The breadth and depth of any reform relates to policy makers' ability to embrace a sectoral approach to change at an early stage in the process.

This chapter suggests a framework for guiding the first steps toward health care reform in countries characterized by two large public provision systems within a broader private medical sector. The purpose of the framework is to provide guidance to policy makers in analyzing the existing configuration of the health sector, in circumventing narrow institutional perspectives, and in conceptualizing options for reconfiguring the playing field. It directs policy makers to explore feasible interventions in seven components of the health care system: households, beneficiaries, providers, payers, finance mechanisms, provider payment systems, and health activities (see figure 11.1). The combinations of interventions within and across the components become the building blocks for crafting reform policies. Redirecting financial flows lays the groundwork for change elsewhere in the health care system. In other words, any modification in how money is transferred from households to providers (for example, through finance mechanisms, payers, and provider payment systems) can strongly influence other aspects of the systems such as who receives what from whom.

The chapter describes the health reform program in Colombia. The reform envisions a new set of relations between public and private sectors, between health finance and provision, and between heretofore insured and uninsured populations. Through redirecting financial and service flows, it aims to create, eliminate, or modify the payers and providers of health care while altering the finance and provider payment mechanisms that link them. There are a myriad of issues facing the Colombian authorities responsible for implementing the reform. This chapter concludes with a critical analysis of some problem areas.

COVERAGE AND TARGETING

Colombia seeks to break the employer linkage in which formal sector employment is the basis for social insurance coverage. This will be achieved in part through replacing supply-side financing of former SSI and MS health service provision with demand-side arrangements, and through directing public funds to subsidize social insurance premiums (UPC) for low-income groups. Innovative mechanisms have been proposed to group, enroll, and represent individuals traditionally excluded from participation. The EPSs and ESSs will perform this function. Whether these organizations will be able to capture a significant volume of low-income families remains to be seen.

Some observers suggest that full coverage of the population is an unrealistic goal for the reformed social security system, even by the year 2002 (Giedion and Wullner 1995). They predict that less than two-thirds of the insurable population can be covered through the contributory regimen because of the constraints to enrolling independent and salaried informal sector workers. Similarly, even under favorable financial conditions, it is unlikely that the subsidized regimen will reach more than three-quarters of uninsurable, low-income populations. Again, grouping these populations or establishing EPSs and ESSs—especially in rural areas where a significant proportion of the poor reside—may be difficult or exceedingly costly.[17]

Demand-side subsidization is seen as a more appropriate mechanism for targeting low-income groups than supply-side financing of direct delivery systems. Subsidies will follow individuals and families who enroll in the above-mentioned grouping organizations. Selecting who is entitled to a subsidy may be a difficult undertaking given the absence of household-level data. Moreover, tracking enrollment of low-income families in EPSs and ESSs and directing the subsidy to these organizations (through local health funds and the FSG) will require sophisticated and costly management information systems.

Financing

An important issue is whether the government can finance the subsidized regimen as well as the subsidized provision of services by subnational entities. The costs of the reform are difficult to estimate. For example, the conversion of SSIs into EPSs and public providers into ESEs will require considerable investment in administrative, financial, and information systems if these organizations are to compete with the private sector. Transfer of former MS personnel to subnational entities and IPSSs will require liquidating pension and severance pay debts that the MS owes the National Savings Fund on behalf of its employees. However, the source and amount of financing required for implementation are at best unpredictable.

Basing their study on projections of UPC costs, dependency ratios, labor market growth, inflation, GDP growth, and demographic variables, Giedion and Wullner estimated that funding of the contributory regimen will have to increase by 120 percent in real terms (from $2,036 million to $4,509 million) in order to extend (POS) coverage from 38 to 64 percent of the "insurable" population (salaried and formal sector independent workers) between 1995 and 2002. (The Ministry of Health seeks full coverage of this population by 2002.) Similarly, financing of the subsidized regimen and the decentralized health service systems will have to increase by an annual average of 14 percent in real terms from 1994 to 2002 to achieve full coverage of the POS for the uninsured population. (Consonant with reform legislation, the authors assumed that the cost of the UPC [POSS] is one-half of the UPC [POS] for 1994, gradually increasing the former until it equals the latter in 2002.) In comparison, real public financing for health increased by an annual average of 3.9 percent from 1981 to 1990.

Prior to the passage of the social security reform law, the Health Ministry correctly estimated that government health spending as a percentage of GDP would have to double from 1994 to 2001 to meet the financial requirements of implementing social security reforms, including conversion to demand subsidies. The MS anticipates the establishment of a number of fiscal mechanisms to finance part of the cost of the reform. Nevertheless, nearly two-thirds of estimated financing will be contingent on taxes levied on future petroleum exports. If revenues are less than anticipated, delayed, or redirected to other activities, health reform in Colombia will face an uncertain future.

Recent estimates of revenues and expenditures for the new system differ considerably. The MS estimated that an 11 percent payroll tax would cover the costs of the contributory regimen in 1995 with an annual UPC of 141,000 pesos ($167). However, using these figures, the Finance Ministry (MF) estimates that the system will generate a significant deficit. Based on the MF financial analysis, the UPC was lowered to 121,000 pesos and the payroll tax raised to 12 percent of salary. The cost of the benefit plan (POS) also was increased. The lower UPC combined with a higher-cost POS may result in reduced benefits or higher copayments than originally anticipated. In an analysis of MS and MF estimates, Giedion and Wullner (1995) found that the observed variation results from dissimilar assumptions on the number of enrollees, average salary, growth in salaried employment, family size, and fiscal revenues. Both studies did not consider how health sector inflation, employer payroll tax evasion, or copayments would affect the system's financial equilibrium.

Another concern is whether the state will fulfill its financial responsibilities under the proposed arrangements. As suggested above, the government has had a poor track record in paying its legally mandated SSI contributions as an employer. Evasion and underdeclaration of salaries also are serious problems among private sector employers. For example, although the average salary of private sector workers (excluding domestics) was more than twice the minimum wage in 1993, the average salary of enrollees in the ISS was 1.7 minimum wages (Giedion and Wullner 1995). The difference is attributed to the underreporting of wages. The ISS also estimates that employers, on average, shave one or two percentage points from their payroll tax (ISS 1991).

It is hoped the new organizational arrangements will provide incentives to workers to pressure their employers to contribute on a regular basis. According to this perspective, since individuals will select their agent (such as EPS, or ESS), provider, and benefit package, they will have a greater stake in actions and decisions affecting the provision, costs, and quality of care. Nonpayment of a provider or an intermediary agent can result in swift cancellation of coverage. Nevertheless, Law 100 mandates a series of sanctions for evasion and underdeclaration of income.

Client Orientation

Social security reform and decentralization appear to be top-down attempts to revamp the health system. Client and beneficiary participation in the planning and design of these changes appears minimal. Both place considerable decision-making authority in EPSs and subnational health bureaucracies, which in theory should represent the interests of patients and communities. However, mechanisms for making managers accountable to people are either absent or dysfunctional. The ESSs and EPSs are to act as members' agents to select, pay, and monitor health plans and providers. These purchasers may not reflect the interests of the enrollees. For example, EPS managers will have an incentive to seek low-cost providers and may not be responsive to member concerns regarding quality and convenience of provider services. Members have no effective mechanism to voice their concerns, or to ratify or veto management decisions. (Dissatisfied consumers can opt for another EPS, but it is unclear how many options they may have. Employers, unions, cooperatives, trade associations, and so on that organize EPSs may pressure workers to enroll in them.)

Decentralization laws mandate the creation of health committees and facility boards as a requirement for certification. In practice, however, community participation appears to receive little financial or political support in most subnational entities. Mayors and other politicians appear to have little regard for independent community groups and have little intention to pursue greater participation. Moreover, health workers charged with fostering community involvement are not provided the means (transport, per diem, and so on) to visit the communities (La Forgia and Homedes 1992).

The Politics of Benefit Definition

Another problem area concerns the definition of the benefits included in the POS and corresponding UPC. The law aims to define a standard package of benefits in which at least 50 percent of the spending is directed to primary-level care. Planners used cost-effectiveness criteria to set the benefits covered by the POS. Currently, SSI-insured populations are entitled to more benefits (without copayments) than those that will be included in the POS.

Although access to current benefits are rationed *implicitly* through inadequate supply, queues, and so on, the POS will place an *explicit* limit on the benefits covered by the system and purchased through the UPC. Individuals desiring additional coverage can purchase a complementary plan. This will provide an incentive for higher income earners to evade enrollment in the system, thus jeopardizing its financial equilibrium.

However, in an effort to avoid a political confrontation with SSI insured, the law also guarantees current SSI beneficiaries the same open-ended coverage that is offered under the current regimen. This begs the question of how to define a standard package and set its cost (UPC) if the open-ended SSI benefit structure will remain more or less intact. Essentially, then, the POS will result from negotiations with SSI bureaucrats and beneficiaries, and therefore will be less reliant on cost-effectiveness criteria.

Definition of the POSS presents a similar problem for the subsidized regimen. Currently, the uninsured populations are entitled to a full range of services, but access and supply are inadequate. Few individuals may desire enrollment in a plan that provides improved access to and adequate supply of a *more limited* range of services for which copayments will be charged.

Provider Arrangements and Incentives

The reform seeks to reorient how health care delivery is organized and how providers are paid. It calls for the separation of the finance and service provision functions for heretofore direct delivery systems. This measure is viewed as a way to contain costs, improve accountability, and boost client satisfaction. Demand-side financing implies a new set of payment mechanisms, organizational arrangements, and regulations for which few Latin American countries, including Colombia, have prior experience. For example, Colombia has decided to use a capitation approach to cover to-be-determined benchmark benefit packages. However, capitation works best when the entity is a managed care organization such as an HMO. Experience in the Unites States shows that any efficiency gains under capitation may result from highly efficient and well-managed provider networks in an HMO arrangement with limited patient choice. Efficiency gains may be an illusion if payers and providers are able to select low-risk individuals. Whether the mechanisms required for successful prepaid capitation and to avoid risk selection by the EPSs can be established and enforced is unknown.

MS and SSI hospitals and other facilities are to be converted into self-managed entities (ESEs). However, the degree of managerial autonomy remains uncertain. The reform authorizes *but does not mandate* altering the incentive structure that contributes to the inefficiencies and low quality that are evident in public direct delivery systems. For example, it is unlikely that strong economic incentives can be developed if ESE directors are political appointees and salaried workers are protected by rigid civil service rules. If management responds to political criteria, has little control over hiring practices, or has little leverage over medical care organization and production, it is unlikely that quality and efficiency objectives will be achieved.

Social Security Reform and Decentralization

Perhaps the weakest aspects of reform relate to the interaction between social security reform and decentralization of MS health service systems. The decentralization process is oriented toward transferring the direct delivery systems from the MS to municipal and departmental governments. It involves little change in financial flow and service delivery mechanisms and involves a single actor. In contrast, social security reform implies transforming government health care financing from the supply to the demand side, altering the configuration of payers, providers, and beneficiaries, and how these actors are linked. The long-term goal of the subsidized regimen of the reformed social security system is to replace the input-driven public delivery systems with a system consisting of strong demand-side features. In short, the reform appears to be heading in two directions and the potential for conflict is high. How this conflict is resolved will ultimately determine the viability of health reform in Colombia.

Social security reform directs municipal and departmental politicians to establish the organizational and financial mechanisms to subsidize the demand for health care by low-income groups. They are to institute EPSs and ESSs, promote the creation of and contract services to ESEs and IPSSs, define and cost the mandatory service packages, and target households and individuals for inclusion in the subsidized regimen. The reform law mandates that a percentage of national transfers must be directed to demand-side subsidies through social security's subsidized regimen.

Mayors and governors may have few incentives to comply with this mandate in part because Law 60 permits them to maintain the supply-side financing of the former MS direct delivery system together with salaried staff and a fixed budget payment system. To date, many municipal and departmental politicians view decentralization in terms of expanding their resource base for patronage. In most municipalities that have initiated decentralization, the process has resulted in the employment of a relatively large number of personnel. Few mayors and governors may be willing to give up the patronage opportunities derived from operating and expanding direct delivery systems. Others may be reluctant to relinquish control over the provider network because they view themselves as politically accountable for the provision of services.

Under decentralization, lump sum national revenue transfers provided to departments and municipalities do not provide incentives to improve service delivery. How funds will be spent is unclear. Mechanisms to enforce accountability of local authorities are mostly absent. In other words, the transfers are not contingent on costs, production, or other indicators of performance. Similarly, it is unclear how the MS can oblige subnational entities to convert to demand-side financing. The social security reform law gives subnational entities two years to organize the subsidized regimen. Given the general lack of quality information, the slow pace of decentralization, and potential points of conflict between decentralization and social security reform processes, it is likely that implementation will take much longer.

Given political realities and the previously mentioned constraints to enrolling nonsalaried populations, in all likelihood the system may develop into a mixed model consisting of two subsystems. The first is a government-financed direct delivery system managed by decentralized entities. Such a system will most likely be the case for rural areas, in part because insufficient volume and excessive administrative costs will impede the formation of competing EPS and the enrollment of rural populations. The second consists of a social insurance system that uses demand subsidies, contracts service provision with public and private providers, and allows some degree of patient choice of provider. The important question for policy makers, therefore, will be how to make these subsystems complementary.

Addendum

The implementation of Laws 100 and 60 began in earnest in 1995. Colombia has moved swiftly to double the number of people with health insurance, raising coverage from 24 to 47 percent of the population between 1993 and 1996. Enrollment in the contributory regime has increased by nearly 50 percent over this period. Over 5 million (of approximately 15 million) low-income Colombians have enrolled in the subsidized insurance scheme financed through demand-side subsidies.

Thirty EPSs have been formed. In response to the cost control incentives inherent in system design, EPSs are implementing managed care practices to control costs, while enhancing quality. Other have adapted alternative provider payments systems including capitation, discounted reimbursement rates, withholdings, and bonuses. Surveys conducted in 1997 demonstrate that over 80 percent of EPS enrollees are satisfied with their care and nearly three-quarters of the populations covered consider that the health system has improved since the implementation of the social insurance reforms.

The country faces a number of challenges that will require adjustments during the implementation process (Harvard University School of Public Health 1996; and Medici et al. 1997). Other problems suggest the need for modification of certain design features. In only one-third of the departments is financing sufficient to extend the POSS to poor populations while maintaining supply-side financing for secondary and tertiary services (not covered by the POSS). In the remainder, the sum of supply and demand financing is insufficient to extend coverage to low-income populations. Despite increases in the amount of resources dedicated to primary care, many departments are far from fulfilling the legal mandate to allocate 50 percent of the national transfer to primary care services. While spending on hospitals has decreased, administrative costs have doubled because of higher spending by departmental and municipal health secretariats.

Converting funds allocated to facilities (supply-side funding) to demand-side financing has proven problematic. Little or no funds directed to the supply-side have been converted to demand-side financing. Only new revenues entering the system are used to finance demand-side subsidies. In an undetermined number of areas a competitive market of insurance administrators (EPSs) and providers (IPSSs) has yet to take shape. This results in part from a tendency of some departments and municipalities to intervene at various market junctures, restricting market entry and controlling enrollment. Another concern is the practice of EPSs to integrate the POS with complementary plans, thereby undermining competition for a homogeneous service plan. Because of high administrative costs and risks of adverse selection, few EPSs are enrolling independent workers. Further, independent workers have weak incentives to enroll because they must pay the full 12 percent wage tax. There is evidence that wealthier independents are underreporting income and purchasing complementary plans, and thereby paying less for coverage than would otherwise be the case by paying the wage tax.

By late 1996, only half of MS hospitals have been officially recognized as public firms (ESE) and fewer operate autonomously. In fact, most hospitals continue to perform within a supply-side framework and few have entered into contractual relations with private EPSs. In general, hospital boards—consisting of civil servants, politicians, and labor union representatives—have done little to reduce patronage in human resource management. In some cases, board members' political agendas have taken precedence over management and organizational strategies aimed at improving efficiency and equity.

Notes

The author is grateful to María Luisa Escobar and Charles C. Griffin for comments made on a previous draft. The findings, interpretations, and conclusions expressed in this article are those of the author and do not necessarily represent the views and policies of the Inter-American Development Bank. Throughout this chapter, dollars ($) are U.S. dollars.

1. During the last three decades it has been standard practice for Latin American policy makers, international experts, and donor agencies to call for reorienting the overlapping finance and provision arrangements between centralized SSI and MS public provider systems. Available evidence suggests that reality has fallen far short of the rhetoric (Castellaños 1986; PAHO 1977; Ugalde 1985). Even attempts at relatively simple coordination, such as the sharing of expensive but underutilized high-tech equipment, have had either short-lived or limited success.

2. Nearly one-third of SSI insured in Mexico, 80 percent in the Dominican Republic, and 28 percent in El Salvador irregularly use or have abandoned their respective SSI delivery systems. See Fundación Mexicana para la Salud 1994 (Mexico); Bitrán 1990 (Dominican Republic).

3. Between 1987 and 1994, use of the MS in Mexico by the very poor (earning less than one minimum salary) decreased from 23 to 18 percent, while utilization of private providers increased from 41 to 48 percent. In El Salvador and Guatemala, respectively, 30 and 50 percent of people in the bottom two income quintiles demand consultations from private providers. See Fundación Mexicana de Salud 1994 (Mexico); Instituto Nacional de Estadística 1989 (Guatemala).

4. See World Bank 1987, 1993b; Fundación Mexicana para la Salud 1994; Trejos et al. 1994; Barnum and Kutzin 1993; ANSAL 1994; Homedes 1994; Birdsall and James 1990; Mesa-Lago 1989, 1992; Ruelas Barajas et al. 1990a, 1990b, 1990c, 1990d; Ugalde 1985.

5. These items are drawn from the published accounts listed in note 4, country

sector analyses prepared by the World Bank and the Inter-American Development Bank, and the author's experience in Mexico, Ecuador, Dominican Republic, El Salvador, Guatemala, Colombia, and Panama.

6. Bovbjerg and Griffin (1993) review lessons learned from the development of health insurance and the health care system in the United States that may apply to developing countries. Attempts at reforming the patchwork U.S. system have failed, in part, because of the array of complex interactions (among consumers, payers, and providers) and corresponding entrenched interests that have emerged, especially since the 1940s. As the system became more fragmented, policy responses aimed at efficiency and equity problems have become more difficult to implement. The authors recommend that the best way to address these issues is through systemwide reform rather than incremental change.

7. See, for example, Reinhardt 1993, 1989; Starr 1992; Enthoven 1988; Graf Schulenberg 1983; Evans 1981. See Griffin 1992b for a strategic planning framework for health financing in Kenya. More comprehensive frameworks have been proposed by Frenk (1993a, 1993b), Culyer (1991), and Glaser (1991).

8. Data is based on a household survey. According to government national accounts registers, total spending on health was $1,419 million in 1990 (MS 1991c, 60). But these figures underestimate private spending.

9. Law 10 mandates that facilities, especially hospitals, receive legal personality, property ownership (*patrimonio propio*), and administrative autonomy. These facilities are to be directed by a board of directors composed of representatives of government, employees, and the community at large (usually appointed by the mayor or governor). Although a number of hospitals have been "decentralized," these facilities are financed mainly by local government through a fixed budget. As was the case under the former SSI system, the budget responds to the availability of funds, the deficit generated during the previous year, and political and professional pressure. (Production and costs do not enter into the equation.)

10. According to Law 10, the board of directors have a tripartite makeup: politicians, medical professionals, and community members. In practice, community representatives are appointed by the mayor or governor.

11. Law 60 stipulates that the "social investment" (*inversión social*) transfer, directed only to municipalities, will begin at 15 percent of the central government's current income in 1994 and increase by 1 percent annually until it reaches 22 percent in 2001. One-fourth of this transfer is to be spent on health and another 20 percent on water supply and sanitation. The "national transfer" (*situado fiscal*), transferred to and managed by the departments, is the principal mechanism of central funding for health and nonuniversity education. It will increase from 23 percent of current revenues in 1994 to 24.5 percent in 1996. At least 20 percent of the subsidy is mandated for health. Of this amount, half is to be transferred to municipalities (for primary care) once these assume decentralized management. Most of the remainder is used by the departments to finance secondary and tertiary care. Departments and municipalities should dedicate no less than 5 percent of the *situado fiscal* for health to preventive and promotional activities.

12. Criteria to determine the distribution of the social investment transfer include population size, population with unsatisfied needs, level of poverty, fiscal effort, administrative efficiency, and quality of life. Similarly, the criteria for distribution of the *situado fiscal* across departments include most of the above, plus population density, per capita income, utilization, and potential population coverage. Many items will be defined operationally, in regulations currently under preparation. Whatever the final formula, the objective is to redistribute resources from wealthier municipalities and departments to poorer ones. More recently, planners have focused on only two criteria: population with unsatisfied needs and disease burden.

13. The term *managed care* refers to health care systems that manage the delivery and utilization of services, to control costs and maintain an acceptable level of quality. Mechanisms of managed care can involve the establishment of organizational arrangements (HMOs), payment and compensation systems, utilization review measures, physician performance evaluations, use of gatekeepers, and quality assurance programs.

14. EPSs replace the various social insurance institutions active in Colombia. Originally, the design for the EPSs called for the proprietary separation of finance and provision functions. However, this feature was altered because of pressure from the Colombian ISS, which sought to retain its direct delivery system. SSIs that do not convert to one or more EPSs will be liquidated.

15. How providers are paid can affect the efficiency and equity of service delivery. Any payment system ultimately structures patients' incentives to demand care, as well as providers' incentives to supply care. Depending on the country, governments and other payers use one or more methods to pay hospitals and physicians: discounted charges, cost reimbursement, per diem (cost per day), cost per procedure/diagnosis, cost per case, capitation, payments based on relative value scales, and standardized fee schedules. Some of the above mechanisms enhance efficiency (and quality) better than others. For example, capitation, per procedure/diagnosis, and relative payments for specific services seem to have relatively greater impact on efficiency. Each mechanism has advantages and disadvantages. Some methods have greater data needs than others.

16. The POS consists of interventions related to five hundred diseases. The interventions were ranked according to cost-effectiveness criteria, determined by international standards and panels of Colombian physicians. Average costs were obtained through an in-depth cost study of a large sample of facilities. The estimated per capita cost of the POS in 1994 was $120. It is important to note, however, that long-term care and treatments involving large expenses will be financed through a special fund. An undetermined proportion of the UPC will be transferred to this fund. A catastrophic fund, a subaccount within the FSG, will assume risk for large expenses, including the treatment of victims of transit accidents, natural disasters, and terrorist attacks. This fund draws on separate financing mechanisms.

17. Giedion and Wullner (1995) maintain that approximately two-thirds of estimated spending in social security's subsidized regimen and decentralized entities will be directed to demand-side subsidies by the year 2002. The remainder will sup-

port decentralized direct delivery systems, which will cover populations not enrolled in the subsidized regimen.

References

Akin, John S., David K. Guilkey, Charles C. Griffin, and Barry M. Popkin. 1985. *The Demand for Primary Health Services in the Third World.* Totowa, N.J.: Rowman and Allanheld.

ANSAL. 1994. "Análisis del sector salud de El Salvador." USAID-funded project. San Salvador.

Arnold, Richard J., Robert F. Rich, and William B. White. 1993. *Competitive Approaches to Health Care Reform.* Washington D.C.: The Urban Institute Press.

Barnum, Howard, and Joseph Kutzin. 1993. *Public Hospitals in Developing Countries: Resource Use, Cost, Financing.* Baltimore: Johns Hopkins University Press.

Bassett, M. 1993. *Ensuring Health: A Case for Moving from Managed Competition to a Regulated Market in Health-care in the U.K.* London: European Policy Forum.

Berman, Peter. 1993. "Health Sector Reform in Developing Countries: Framing the Issues." Paper presented at the Conference on Health Sector Reform in Developing Countries: Issues for the 1990s. Durham, N.H. September 10–13.

Birdsall, Nancy. 1989. "Thoughts on Good Health and Good Government." *Daedalus* 18.1 (winter): 89–123.

Birdsall, Nancy, and Estelle James. 1990. "Efficiency and Equity in Social Spending: How and Why Governments Misbehave." World Bank Working Paper Series No. 294 (May).

———. 1992. "Health, Government, and the Poor." Policy Research Working Papers, No. 938, Country Economics Department. Washington, D.C.: World Bank.

Bitrán, Ricardo. 1990. "Estudio de demanda por servicios de salud en El Salvador." USAID-funded REACH Project. Arlington, Va.

Bovbjerg, Randall, and Charles C. Griffin. 1993. "The Evolution of U.S. Health Coverage and Its Problems: Key Patterns Were Set by the 1970s." In *Extending Coverage and Benefits of Social Financing Systems in Developing Countries: A Review of Concepts and Experience*, ed. Gerard M. La Forgia and Charles C. Griffin. Research Report, Health Financing and Sustainability Project, Abt Associates, Bethesda, Md.

Broomberg, Jonathan. 1994. "Managing the Health Care Market in Developing Countries: Prospects and Problems." *Health Policy and Planning* 9 (3): 237–51. Oxford University Press.

Castellaños, Jorge. 1986. "Coordinación entre las entidades del sector público que prestan servicios de atención de salud." In *Primary Health Care and Health Services in Latin American Social Security*, PAHO-ILO-CPISS. Geneva: ILO.

Chernichovsky, Dov. 1993. "Health System Reforms in Industrialized Democracies: An Emerging Paradigm." Human Resources Unit Country Department II, World Bank. May.

Collins, Charles D., Andrew T. Green, and David J. Hunter. 1994. "International

Transfers of National Health Service Reforms: Problems and Issues." *The Lancet* 344 (July 23).

Culyer, A. J. 1990. *The Internal Market: An Acceptable Means to a Desirable End.* Discussion Paper No. 67, Centre for Health Economics, University of York. June.

———. 1991. "Introduction." In *The Economics of Health,* ed. A. J. Culyer. Aldershot, England: Edward Elgar.

Dahlgren, Goran, and Finn Diderichsen. 1993. "Health Care Reform in Sweden: Some Reflections on the Economical and Political Problems It May Solve and Create." Paper presented at the Conference on Health Sector Reform in Developing Countries: Issues for the 1990s. Durham, N.H. September 10–13.

Ensor, Tim. 1993. "Health System Reform in Former Socialist Countries of Europe." *International Journal of Health Planning and Management* 8: 169–87.

Enthoven, Alain C. 1985. *Reflections on the Management of the National Health Service.* London: Nuffield Provincial Hospitals' Trust.

———. 1988. *Theory and Practice of Managed Competition in Health Care Finance.* Amsterdam: North-Holland/American Elsevier.

Evans, R. G. 1981. "Incomplete Vertical Integration: The Distinctive Structure of the Health-Care Industry." In *Health, Economics, and Health Economics,* ed. J. van der Gaag and M. Perlman. Amsterdam: North-Holland.

Frenk, Julio. 1992 "Integración de la prestación de los servicios de salud." *Salud Pública México* 34 (supplement): 85–104.

———. 1993a. "Dimensions of Health System Reform." Paper presented at the Conference on Health Sector Reform in Developing Countries: Issues for the 1990s. Durham, N.H. September 10–13.

———. 1993b. "The Public/Private Mix and Human Resources for Health." *Health Policy and Planning* 8 (4): 315–26. Oxford University Press.

Fundación Eugenio Espejo. 1986. "Oferta y demanda de salud." Quito. Unpublished paper.

Fundación Mexicana para la Salud. 1994. *Economía y salud: Propuestas para el avance del sistema de salud en México, informe final.* Mexico City.

Giedion, Ursula, and Andrea Wullner. 1995. "La unidad de pago por capitación y el equilibrio financiero del sistema de salud." Bogotá: Fundación para la Educación Superior y el Desarrollo. February. Mimeo.

Gilson, Lucy, and Anne Mills. 1993. "Health Sector Reforms in Lower Income Countries: Lessons of the Last Ten Years." Paper presented at the Conference on Health Sector Reform in Developing Countries: Issues for the 1990s. Durham, N.H. September 10–13.

Glaser, William. 1991. *Health Insurance in Practice.* San Francisco: Jossey-Bass.

González Block, Miguel Angel, Beatriz Zurita, Julio Frenk, Francisco Franco, Armando Arredondo, Mónica Queisser, and Ricardo Ramírez. 1994. "Demanda y oferta de servicios: Obstáculos a la mejoría del sistema de salud en México." Documentos para el análisis y la convergencia 6. Mexico, D.F.: Fundación Mexicana para la Salud.

Graf Schulenberg, J.-Mathias. 1983. "Report from Germany: Current Conditions and Controversies in the Health Care System." *Journal of Health Politics, Policy, and Law* 8.2 (summer): 320–51.

Griffin, Charles C. 1992a. *Health Care in Asia: A Comparative Study of Cost and Financing.* Washington, D.C.: World Bank.

———. 1992b. "Strategic Planning for Financing Health Care in Kenya." Washington, D.C.: The Urban Institute. October. Mimeo.

Grindle, Merilee S., and John W. Thomas. 1991. *Public Choices and Policy Change: The Political Economy of Reform in Developing Countries.* Baltimore: Johns Hopkins University Press.

Harvard University School of Public Health. 1996. Report on Colombia Health Reform and Proposed Master Implementation Plan. Report produced by the Colombia Health Care Reform Project Team. Cambridge, Mass.

Her Majesty's Stationery Office (HMSO). 1989. *Working for Patients.* London: HMSO.

Homedes, Nuria. 1994. "Social Security: Ministry of Health Integration in Costa Rica." In *Extending Coverage and Benefits of Social Financing Systems in Developing Countries: A Review of Concepts and Experience,* ed. Gerard M. La Forgia and Charles C. Griffin. Research Report, Health Financing and Sustainability Project, Abt Associates. Bethesda, Md.

Instituto de Seguridad Social (ISS). 1991. *Memorias.* Bogotá: ISS.

Instituto Nacional de Empleo. 1992. *Encuesta permanente de hogares: Modelo de salud, nacional 1990.* Quito: Ministerio de Trabajo y Recursos Humanos.

Instituto Nacional de Estadística. 1989. *Encuesta nacional sociodemográfica, 1989.* Guatemala: INE.

International Labour Office (ILO). 1986. *Primary Health Care and Health Strategies in Latin American Social Security.* Geneva: ILO.

Jiménez de la Jara, Jorge, ed. 1993. *Sistema de salud en transición a la democracia.* Santiago de Chile: Ministerio de Salud.

La Forgia, Gerard M., and Mercy Balarezo. 1994. "Cost Recovery in Public Sector Hospitals in Ecuador." Health Financing and Sustainability Project. Bethesda, Md.

La Forgia, Gerard M., and Nuria Homedes. 1992. "Decentralizing Health Services in Colombia: A Review of Progress and Problems." Consultant's report to the World Bank, Washington, D.C.

Levine, Ruth, and Gerard La Forgia. 1991. "Resource Allocation in the Public Health Sector in Belize." Health Financing and Sustainability Project. Bethesda, Md.

McGreevey, William. 1990. *Social Security in Latin America: Issues and Options for the World Bank.* World Bank Discussion Papers, No. 110. Washington, D.C.: World Bank.

McPake, Barbara, and Elías E. Ngalande Banda. 1994. "Contracting Out of Health Services in Developing Countries." *Health Policy and Planning* 9 (1): 25–30.

Medici, Andres Cesar, Juan Luis Londono, Oswaldo Coelbo, and Helen Saxenian. 1997. "Managed Care and Managed Competition in Latin America and the

Caribbean." In *Innovation in Health Care Financing*, ed. George J. Schieber. Washington, D.C.: World Bank.

Mesa-Lago, Carmelo. 1989. *Financiamiento de la atención a la salud en América Latina y el Caribe, con focalización en el seguro social.* Estudios de Seminarios del IDE, No. 42. Washington, D.C.: World Bank.

———. 1992. *Health Care for the Poor in Latin America and the Caribbean.* Publication No. 539. Washington, D.C.: PAHO.

Ministerio de Salud (MS). 1990. *Reorganización del sistema nacional de salud: Una respuesta al cambio social.* Bogotá: MS.

———. 1991a. *Reorganización del sistema nacional de salud: Reglamentación Ley 10 de 1990.* Bogotá: MS.

———. 1991b. *La revolución de la salud: Memoria, 1990–1991.* Bogotá: MS.

———. 1991c. *Análisis financiero del sector salud.* Bogotá: MS.

———. 1993. "Descentralización del sistema de salud y la ley de competencia y recursos." Bogotá. Mimeo.

Ministerio de Trabajo y Seguridad Social (MTSS). 1993. *Ley de seguridad social: Ley 100 de 1993.* Bogotá: MTSS.

Oficina de Planeamiento y Presupuesto (OPP). 1988. *El mercado de trabajo médico en el Uruguay.* Montevideo: OPP.

Pan American Health Organization (PAHO). 1977. "Coordination of Social Security and Public Health Institutions." Technical discussion. Washington, D.C. Mimeo.

Reich, Michael R. 1993. "The Politics of Health Sector Reform in Developing Countries: Three Cases of Pharmaceutical Policy." Paper presented at the Conference on Health Sector Reform in Developing Countries: Issues for the 1990s. Durham, N.H. September 10–13.

Reinhardt, Uwe. E. 1989. "The U.S. Health Care Financing and Delivery System: Its Experience and Lessons for Other Nations." Paper presented at the International Symposium on Health Care Systems. Taipei, Taiwan. December 18–19.

———. 1993. "Reorganizing the Financial Flows in American Health Care." *Health Affairs* 12. Supplement.

Roemer, Milton J. 1969. *The Organization of Medical Care Under Social Security.* Geneva: International Labour Office.

———. 1971. "Social Security for Medical Care: Is It Justified in Developing Countries?" *International Journal of Health Services* 1 (4): 354–61.

Ruedas, Enrique y Julio Querol. 1994. "Calidad y eficiencia en las organizaciones de atención a la salud." Documentos para el Análisis y la Convergencia No. 8. México, D.F.: Fundación Mexicana para la Salud.

Ruelas Barajas, Enrique, et al. 1990a. (With Lilia Durán, Mariana García Rojas, María de Lourdes Campero, and Antonio Hurtado Beléndez.) "Análisis de problemas de los médicos directivos en diferentes organizaciones hospitalarias: I. Una metodología para la búsqueda e identificación de problemas." *Journal of Health Administration Education* 8.2.

———. 1990b. (With María de Lourdes Campero Cuenca and Mariana García Rojas Alarcón.) "Análisis de problemas de los médicos directivos en diferentes organizaciones hospitalarias: II. Formación académica y trayectoria laboral de los médicos directivos en México." *Journal of Health Administration Education* 8.3.

———. 1990c. (With María de Lourdes Campero Cuenca and Mariana García Rojas Alarcón.) "Análisis de problemas de los médicos directivos en diferentes organizaciones hospitalarias: III. Caracterización cuantitativa de los problemas percibidos por los médicos directivos en México." *Journal of Health Administration Education* 8.4.

———. 1990d. (With Lilia Durán, Julio Querol, María de Lourdes Campero Cuenca, Mariana García Rojas Alarcón, and Antonio Hurtado Beléndez). "Análisis de problemas de los médicos directivos en diferentes organizaciones hospitalarias: IV. Caracterización cualitativa de los problemas percibidos por los médicos directivos en México e implicaciones educacionales." *Journal of Health Administration Education* 9.1.

Saltman, Richard B. 1992. *Planned Markets and Public Competition.* England: St. Edmundsbury Press.

Saltman, Richard B., and Casten von Otter. 1989. "Public Competition Versus Mixed Markets: An Analytic Comparison." *Health Policy* 11: 43–55.

Sheaff, Rod. 1994. "What Kind of Health Care 'Internal Market'? A Cross-Europe View of the Options." *International Journal of Health Planning and Management* 9: 5–24.

Starr, Paul. 1992. *The Logic of Health Care Reform.* Knoxville, Tenn.: Whittle.

Trejos, Juan Diego, Leonardo Garnier, Guillermo Monge, and Roberto Hidalgo. 1994. "Enhancing Social Services in Costa Rica." In *Social Service Delivery Systems: An Agenda for Reform,* ed. Christian Aedo and Osvaldo Larrañaga, 51–90. Washington, D.C.: IADB.

Ugalde, Antonio. 1979. "The Role of the Medical Profession in Public Health Policy Making: The Case of Colombia." *Social Science and Medicine* 13C: 109–19.

———. 1980. "Physicians Control of the Health Sector: Professional Values and Economic Interests." *Social Science and Medicine* 14A: 435–44.

———. 1985. "The Integration of Health Care Programs into a National Health Service." In *The Crisis of Social Security and Health Care,* ed. Carmelo Mesa-Lago. Pittsburgh: Center for Latin American Studies, University of Pittsburgh.

van de Ven, Wynand. 1989. *A Future for Competitive Health Care in the Netherlands.* NHS Occasional Paper No. 9, Centre for Health Economics, University of York. England.

van de Ven, Wynand, Frederik T. Schut, and Frans F. H. Rutten. 1994. "Forming and Reforming the Market for Third-Party Purchasers of Health Care." *Social Science and Medicine* 39 (10): 1405–12.

Vanormelingen, Keenraad, and Véronique Goblet. 1990. "Actitudes frente a la enfermedad: Utilización de los servicios de salud en el Cañar." Quito. Unpublished paper.

Vargas González, Jorge, and Alfredo Sarmiento Gómez. 1997. "Descentralización de los servicios de educación y salud en Colombia." Bogotá. Unpublished paper.

World Bank. 1987. *Financing Health Services in Developing Countries: An Agenda for Reform.* Washington, D.C.: World Bank.

———. 1993a. *Colombia: Toward Increases in Efficiency and Equity in the Health Sector. Can Decentralization Help?* Country Department 3, Human Resources Operations Division. Washington, D.C.: World Bank.

———. 1993b. *World Development Report, 1993: Investing in Health.* Washington, D.C.: World Bank.

Yepes, Francisco J. 1990. *La salud en Colombia.* Vol. 2. Bogotá: Ministerio de Salud, Departamental Nacional de Planeación.

Zschock, Dieter. 1983. "Review of Medical Care Under Social Security in Latin America." Stony Brook. Unpublished monogragh prepared under USAID contract PDSC-I406-I-1125.

12 / Health Care Reform in Brazil

Phasing Change

Maureen Lewis and André Medici

Reform is the major focus in health throughout Latin America in the 1990s. Following closely on the heels of the OECD countries and innovators in Latin America (notably Brazil and Chile), the countries of the region are seriously examining their health systems and seeking fundamental change. Argentina, Colombia, Dominican Republic, Ecuador, Mexico, Nicaragua, Peru, Uruguay, and Panama are all in the process of health reform.

Rising costs, quality lapses, dissatisfied constituents, gross inefficiency, and political pressures are making scrutiny of how health care is organized, delivered, and financed of paramount economic and political concern. In Europe efforts to trim costs and improve efficiency have led to separation of financing and delivery, incentives to improve provider productivity, and greater reliance on competitive forces (Hurst 1991). The irony is that in some countries (such as Canada) government is taking a stronger role, whereas in others (such as the United Kingdom) competition is being introduced into a largely public model of care, and in still others (such as Holland) government is reducing its involvement. This convergence toward an intermediate position reflects a movement toward greater government intervention to ensure coverage, particularly to the poor, and to stimulate efficiency and control costs, and this convergence is strengthening. What varies is the nature of the role of government.

While many of the objectives—adequate coverage, improved efficiency, better delivery—are the same, the pattern of change in Latin America varies between countries, because of where the countries are starting from, their epidemiological circumstances, the specific obstacles they face, and the different societies' priorities in health care. The majority of Latin American countries have embraced a British-type arrangement where government finances and delivers care through a network of public facilities. Lack of information on performance and costs has led to a virtual absence of accountability; oversight is minimal, where it exists at all. Brazil and the Southern Cone countries have dramatically different systems; the latter rely on a modified health maintenance organization (HMO) model.

Brazil is something of an outlier in Latin America. Its health system is much more similar to the U.S. system than to the systems in the rest of Latin America, although it includes many elements of other regional systems. The country, however, is facing the same challenges as the rest of Latin America, and for that matter the rest of the world, including the OECD countries. Some of the key objectives of the Brazilian government—decentralization, raising coverage, improving quality, controlling expenditures—mirror those of the rest of the region. In some cases, as in decentralization, Brazil has been at the forefront; in others, such as cost containment, quality, and regulation, Brazil has paid little attention, a pattern familiar throughout the region.

This chapter reviews the experience of Brazil, a country that designed and implemented a massive reform in the 1980s and is still implementing some of those changes. The health care system is ready for the second wave of reform to adjust for political and economic shifts of the recent past, address the plethora of new issues that have arisen, and accommodate the unforeseen side effects that emerged from the changes of the last decade. This experience provides an opportunity to understand both the political imperatives of health care reform and the economic forces that underlie efforts to reform health care. Moreover, this experience is of relevance to other countries and regions in its testing of unique financing arrangements that have applicability elsewhere.

Brazil, a country of 8.6 million square kilometers and almost 150 million people, is the largest in South America in size and population, and borders ten other countries on the continent. Divided into five regions, about 75 percent of the population is urban, with over 40 percent of all residents concentrated in the southeast region (PNAD 1981, 1990). Per capita income in 1995 was $3,620 but regional disparities are pronounced, with wealth and income concentrated in the southeastern part of the country.

Health problems in Brazil encompass both the diseases of infants and children (such as diarrhea) and the chronic and degenerative diseases of an aging population (World Bank 1989). As the country passes through the epidemiological transition from the disease patterns of developing to those of industrialized countries, both sets of health problems are prominent. An infant mortality rate of 58 per 1,000 live births suggests the need to reach high-risk pregnant women. However, recent evidence also points to the growing need to prevent and treat diseases of adults, particularly communicative diseases such as TB and AIDS. This pattern has serious implications for resource allocation decisions and costs.

THE IMPETUS FOR HEALTH REFORM

In the early 1980s Brazil launched a comprehensive institutional, organizational, and financial reform of the public health care sector that was meant to shift the responsibility for health care provision from the center to the periphery, consolidate public service provision and finance, and improve the equity of access to health services. Simultaneously, Brazil launched a nationwide financing experiment that paralleled the more comprehensive and visible changes.

The reform, known as the Reforma Sanitária, was a response to the inequity in health care access, the overlapping and competing systems of publicly financed care, and the centralized nature of provision and financing. At the federal level, access was divided into two federal programs: the Ministry of Social Security (Instituto Nacional de Asistência Médica da Previdência Social, INAMPS) and the Ministry of Health (MOH). Traditionally INAMPS, financed by wage and employer taxes and supplemented by transfers from general revenues, extended services only to formal sector wage earners. In contrast, the MOH provided ambulatory and preventive services (such as malaria control in the northern part of the country). In addition, states and large municipalities delivered some services to their populations drawing on their own revenue base, but coverage was uneven and the services provided selective. Various segments of society pressed for change in the perceived elitism of that system.

Under the military government, between 1964 and the mid-1980s, health service financing and delivery were centralized, which translated into the federal government's managing the financial and clinical requirements of roughly 76 percent of all inpatients and 38 percent of ambulatory visits, across a huge and diverse country. The method of financing encompassed both direct payment of INAMPS-provided care and cost reimbursement to private physicians and hospitals for services extended to INAMPS patients (see below for a discussion of the latter). Both payment mechanisms are difficult under a centralized system.

Eroding of the public health system served to reinforce criticism. A recession that began in 1979 affected the level of expenditures, which in turn led to reduced care or lower-quality services because of reduced expenditures. At the same time, there were vocal criticisms of mismanagement and fraud in the social security systems. During this period of criticism in the 1970s and subsequent restructuring in the 1980s, other factors both within and outside the sector affected the patterns of finance and delivery. Physical expansion of the public health care service network was significant during the decade of the 1980s and the patterns of service were altered. Growth in the private sector, already a major provider of health care, was even greater, with particularly important changes in the range and type of private financing (Lewis and Medici 1995; World Bank 1994). More generally, high inflation (accumulated inflation between January 1980 and December 1991 reached 4,337 million percent, for example), macroeconomic policies, and wage and price controls played havoc with public budgets and private investors. At the same time, the public discovered the rights and privileges of democracy and began to define its priorities and concerns in health care.

REFORM AND DECENTRALIZATION

The immediate impetus for the Reforma Sanitária was the recession of 1982. Between 1980 and 1983 federal health expenditures declined by 20 percent, and INAMPS spending by even more (Vianna et al. 1991). The problems confronting the sector, its fragmentation across the Ministries of Social Security, Health, and Education (where university hospitals are overseen and financed), and the pressure to decentralize culminated in the establishment of a high-level commission in 1980, the Conselho Consultativo de Administração de Saúde Previdênciaria (CONASP). This commission consisted of representatives of seven federal ministries, and included the participation of unions, firms, and the medical profession. The representatives were charged with the task of reducing costs in the short term. In the long term, they were to create a unified health system with an emphasis on primary care, greater reliance on underutilized public health facilities, cost controls, and simplification and cost reductions in the payment of contracted services.

The commission recommended a three-phased approach to change, and the Reforma Sanitária's three phases—the Integrated Health Activities Program (AIS), the Unified and Decentralized Health System (SUDS), and the Single Health System (SUS), the latter of which has not yet been fully implemented—were guided by the parameters set out by the recommendations of the commission. The initiatives encompassed a systematic divestment of responsibility and authority for health care to the local level, merged social security and public health services, and guaranteed unrestricted access by all citizens to publicly provided or financed care.

The first phase, AIS, went into effect in 1984 and is credited by some (Piola and Vianna 1991) with improving coordination in the sector and stimulating both decentralization and efficiency through budgetary tightening, greater use of underutilized INAMPS facilities, and some shift of services from inpatient to outpatient care. The next phase of reform, SUDS, in 1987–1988 began the transfer of INAMPS staff and facilities to the control of state health secretariats. Each state was expected to constitute a single "system" rather than a part of a nationwide network. The step would effectively eliminate the distinction between the two federal ministries, universalize access to what had been the social security health system and convert INAMPS to Instituto Nacional de Segurança Social (INSS), a purely financing or insurance agency responsible for transferring resources to lower levels of government and to private providers, but no longer directly providing medical care. INAMPS's regional offices were abolished, and their functions transferred to state health secretariats. Besides changing the relative power of different agencies, this proposal required much larger financial transfers to states and large municipalities to accompany the transfer of physical capacity; and it required confronting the problem of greatly differing pay scales for staff of INAMPS, the MOH, and the state secretariats. It also implied substantial change to a system that had not yet completely absorbed the changes implicit in the AIS.

The ultimate phase, SUS, was meant to transfer public responsibility for health care to the municipal level. However, because it was understood that municipalities were not always ready to take on greater responsibility, SUS involved the transfer of INAMPS hospitals to state governments, and of state health centers and local hospitals down to the municipalities. Similarly, the authority to contract with private providers—the bulk of INAMPS's providers of care—was passed to state government, with the intent of eventually handing it over to those municipalities able to administer them (Couttolenc 1991). This meant that control over the health system continued divided rather than "unified" during what might be a very long transition period, and that the speed of the reform would vary across states, and even within states. While these might be considered practical responses to the immense difficulty of actually decentralizing the Brazilian health system, they also led to confusion over roles and powers and to frustration with the reform—conditions that affected the next phase of change.

The Brazilian Constitution of 1988 overtook and ratified shifts that had been occurring over the preceding two decades, and it opened the way to further change. The constitution also left some questions unresolved and failed to address other problems where political consensus was blocked by interest groups. The translation of the constitutional principles into legislation (Lei Orgánica de Saúde) is the final major reform under SUS. Both the title and the content of this final phase can be seen as the consolidation of efforts begun during AIS and SUDS.

The principal change in 1988 from previous constitutions is the declaration of a right to "universal and equal access to [health] actions and services," independent of one's income or occupation and of the level of service in question. Public funds for health care are, in principle, to be used without discrimination across citizens. In practice this meant that the services provided by INAMPS, the MOH, states, and municipalities are open equally to all. In effect the constitution confirmed the evolution of the Reforma Sanitária.

The 1988 Constitution also ratified the integration of INAMPS and MOH, and specified that all public health services are to be provided by the municipalities, "with the technical and financial assistance of the [federal government] and the states." Despite this, the constitution is vague about the exact responsibilities of federal, state, and municipal government for health care—but highly specific about the distribution of federal funds among the three levels of government. (In order to ensure that constitutional provisions were carried out, considerable detail was provided, particularly regarding items that could be measured.) The share to be retained by the federal government is to decline from just over half in the late 1970s to 36.5 percent by the end of 1993. The share going to the states is to rise slightly, and that going to the municipalities will increase by more than half, from 14 to 22 percent. The implications and value of specified revenue-sharing levels is unclear. Overall, Brazil spends about 4.8 percent of GNP on health care, with two-thirds of that coming from public funds (World Bank 1994).

On one hand, the 1988 Constitution clearly establishes a basis for a truly decentralized system. On the other hand, the vagaries of responsibilities associated with these transfers leaves the system open to abuse and chaos. It is not clear what entity or level of government has ultimate authority to control the system or its costs. All levels of government continue to be involved in financing and delivering care. Moreover, does the assistance of other levels of government also imply that municipalities have access to additional resources of the state and federal governments? The constitution does not make clear which functions, if any, the federal level should continue to exercise because of economies of scale, particular competence or externalities, or what should be the responsibilities of states.

The implications of the Reforma Sanitária are mixed. It achieved its objectives of "universal access," a decentralized health system, and a sharper division between financing and provision of health services. The original intent, however, to bring about integration at the local level was an elusive goal. The waves of reform also had the positive effect of creating an atmosphere of reform in which experimentation was fostered, and simple, valuable improvement in service could be offered (Couttolenc 1991). These were unevenly distributed, but the reform stimulated innovation and passed authority to bodies who could and would act if they faced the proper incentives. But at the same time, it introduced confusion in roles and responsibilities, exposed inherent weaknesses in the system, and overlooked some important issues. It is too early to offer definitive assessments of the reforms, but some preliminary effects are already obvious and will have profound implications if not addressed (World Bank 1994).

First, while the concept of municipalization was meant to decentralize health services to a level more in touch with the population, the arrangement in Brazil poses problems. Several other institutions—federal and state—continue to function independently of municipalities. Most of the 5,500 municipalities have been given more authority than they can handle. The large municipalities (over 1 million population) have benefited greatly because of economies of scale and stronger, more accountable management. Smaller municipalities (between 5,000 and 30,000 population) have neither the managerial expertise nor the resources to manage and deliver services efficiently and effectively.

Indeed, in the first four years of municipalization, there has been an explosion in public construction of clinics, especially in smaller municipalities, most of which have never been completed because of insufficient funds (Medici 1990). The notion, implicit in municipalization, is that closer accountability will improve decision making, expenditures, and outcomes. Given the incentives facing mayors they are just as likely to spend on visible, costly construction projects such as hospitals and clinics, leaving operating cost problems to future elected officials. This is not an unexpected outcome given political imperatives.

A second and related issue is that of state roles. The states are potentially the most important actors in the system. Health care delivery should be integrated within states, and tertiary care and some secondary care, as well as planning functions, are most efficiently accomplished at the state rather than the municipal level. SUDS initiated this process, but SUS made municipalities dependent on the federal rather than the state government for funds. State roles are undefined, although, given the size of Brazil, they are probably the most logical bodies to oversee health care. States can mitigate the political desires of mayors and provide an integrated approach to public health spending.

While the success of increased access by all levels of society has met equity goals, it also has raised costs considerably and fueled expectations. Both have placed serious pressures on the government, and the policy debate has become one of complaints regarding inadequate resources and the underfunding of services. The objectives and priorities of the commission were met, but the question of resources was not considered, and these practical issues have impeded the rational implementation of the policy. The full effects are not yet obvious, but the frustration of providers and patients has taken a toll and undermined the credibility of the government. Finally, the rapidity of the changes also caused problems, since consolidation of shifts could not be achieved before the next phase was legislated and changes began.

FINANCIAL REFORM

While institutional reforms were the major focus of the Reforma Sanitária, Brazil's financing and delivery system was simultaneously overhauled and redirected. Some of the perversity of decentralization under SUDS and SUS can be attributed to the need to accommodate Brazil's financing system.

The second prong of health reform was the restructuring of INAMPS's financing system. Beginning in 1976 INAMPS initiated a payment system for its private providers, the National System for the Control and Payment of Hospital Billings or Sistema Nacional de Controle e Pagamento de Contas Hospitalares (SNCPCH), that reimbursed contracted private providers under fee-for-service arrangements. That is, the provider set the price and INAMPS agreed and reimbursed at that level. The Guide for Hospitalization (Guia de Internação Hospitalar, GIH) and the Physician Fee Schedule determined and managed hospital and physician payments, respectively. Billings and oversight were provided by the parastatal DATAPREV under the auspices of INAMPS.

With the growth in private contracts, and limited controls on how much care was consumed (volume of services) or at what price, INAMPS's costs soared. Despite the data quality and account auditing improvements brought by GIH, problems with managing the paperwork of billings, uncontrolled expenditures, inability to predict expenditures at the federal and hospital levels, and widespread accusations and documentation of fraud led INAMPS to consider alternative organizational and payment structures (Gentile de Mello 1983). Under the guidance of a national commission of experts drawn from the public and private sectors, including representatives from all medical advocacy groups, alternative options were explored. The commission established key parameters for a new system, stressing priority for (1) allowing patient access to services of their choice; (2) defining standards for hospital participation in the system; (3) defining mechanisms to readjust payments to providers; (4) determining criteria for hospital admittance; (5) separating hospital and physician payments; (6) facilitating financial control and oversight; and, (7) linking payments with hospital performance. In doing this, Brazil became one of the few countries that pragmatically set out its priorities and requirements for health care.

The resulting system was on the cutting edge, adopting practices that had been introduced only in the United States by the early 1980s and that have now been embraced in many forms in much of Europe. Brazil's prospective payment system (PPS) is very similar to the Diagnosis Related Group (DRG) arrangement under the U.S. Medicare program, the social insurance system for the elderly, whereby providers are paid a fixed amount according to diagnosis, using average costs and WHO's International Classification of Disease (ICD-9) Codes to set payment levels. (A recent study [Silver, Travassos, and Maria 1992] has concluded that Brazilian [AIH] procedures and those of the United States [DRGs] under Medicare are virtually equivalent.) Thus every appendectomy is reimbursed the same amount regardless of patient severity, hospital costs, or the diagnostic tests provided.

Adjustments for services provided at high-tech hospitals, an element of the U.S. program as well, was and has remained a feature of the program (Levcovitz 1992).

Tested for two years in Curitiba, the state capital of Parana, the payment system was established nationwide at the end of 1983. The system was based on reimbursement for clinical and surgical procedures authorized by INAMPS medical auditors prior to admittance, known as the authorization for hospitalization (*autorização de internação hospitalar,* AIH) under social security's system of medical-hospital assistance (*sistema de assistência médico-hospitalar da previdência social*). Reimbursement levels were set according to the average billings under GIH for each procedure or diagnosis. While the initial participants consisted of *convenios* (unbinding agreements) with some public foundations and nonprofit hospitals and contracts with for-profit hospitals, by 1991 the entire hospital network, public and private, that was financed by the federal government was paid on a reimbursement basis.

To supplement the inpatient financing, the federal government launched a prospective outpatient payment system in 1990, a system no other country has. With little or no preparation, the Coverage for Ambulatory Care (*unidade de cobertura ambulatorial,* UCA) was launched to include emergency and outpatient care under a separate prospective payment system. Part of the rationale for UCA was to blunt the incentives for hospitalization and to reimburse hospitals for outpatient as well as inpatient care (Czapski 1993). Unlike the hospital reimbursement system, UCA's reimbursement levels do not reflect costs or existing prices for outpatient services, as when UCA went into effect these were not available (they still are not). As an alternative, a per capita transfer was designated for the states and municipalities—based, theoretically, on population size, supply capacity, performance, case mix (profile of patients' illnesses and their severity), and historical expenditures. In practice, population and historical expenditures serve as the basis for transfer amounts. Because of excess demand in large urban centers and excess supply in less densely populated states, tertiary care centers receive higher per capita transfers than other states because of their greater capacity and more sophisticated services.

The hospital reimbursement system, AIH, has only one built-in method to control the number of patients: a ceiling on the total number of patients to be financed, controlled by numbering patient forms. Hence, who has control over the distribution of the AIH forms determines the earning of participating facilities. While all participating hospitals must be registered and approved, the list of such hospitals is extensive, and the distribution of AIH is at the discretion of the responsible government level.

The advent of AIS, SUDS, and SUS has had little impact on the operation of the payment system. Under SUDS the federal government transferred AIH operating budgets to some state secretariats of health who then allocated the authorizations to hospitals, controlled and evaluated participating hospitals, and submitted complete patient forms to DATAPREV for payment. Under SUS some of these same functions have been allocated to municipalities, although states still have some role in assisting smaller municipalities and operating their own hospitals. Payments, however, were and continue at the federal level. The process for payments under AIH is shown in figure 12.1.

Prospective payment (per case) is first and foremost meant as a method of cost control and data generation, and that was the intent of its Brazilian creators. Its strengths are its ability to anticipate and control the magnitude of expenditures, the potential for using incentives to enhance hospital productivity, reduce the incidence of unnecessary diagnostic exams, lower lengths of (hospital) stays, and achieve other efficiency gains, and adequate data on each patient for monitoring the system.

The drawbacks of DRGs have become apparent in Brazil. Under prospective payment, hospitals are reluctant to treat severely ill patients; they discharge patients too early and reduce the use of needed technologies, all of which lower costs since the diagnosis-specific payment remains the same regardless of provider's costs (Veras 1989). Price differentials across states and the limited accommodation of case severity cause difficulties for providers. As will be discussed below, however, the management of the system at the federal level has been abysmal and has undermined the effectiveness of prospective payment.

The growth in health demand, fueled by the promise of free access, has placed pressure on the federal budget, and the volume of services has grown rapidly in both the inpatient and outpatient programs. Figure 12.2 shows the trends in the number of patient discharges (AIHs) from the beginning of 1987 to the end of 1991 as well as the growth in inpatient expenditures. By the end of 1991 SUS was admitting over 1.2 million patients per month with an average length of stay of 6.4 days, a level that has remained stable over the past decade. Length of stay is also very low as compared to other developing and developed countries (except for the United States). Hospital use between 1987 and 1991 increased by 53 percent while population grew by less than 2 percent a year. Some of the growth is because of the opening of

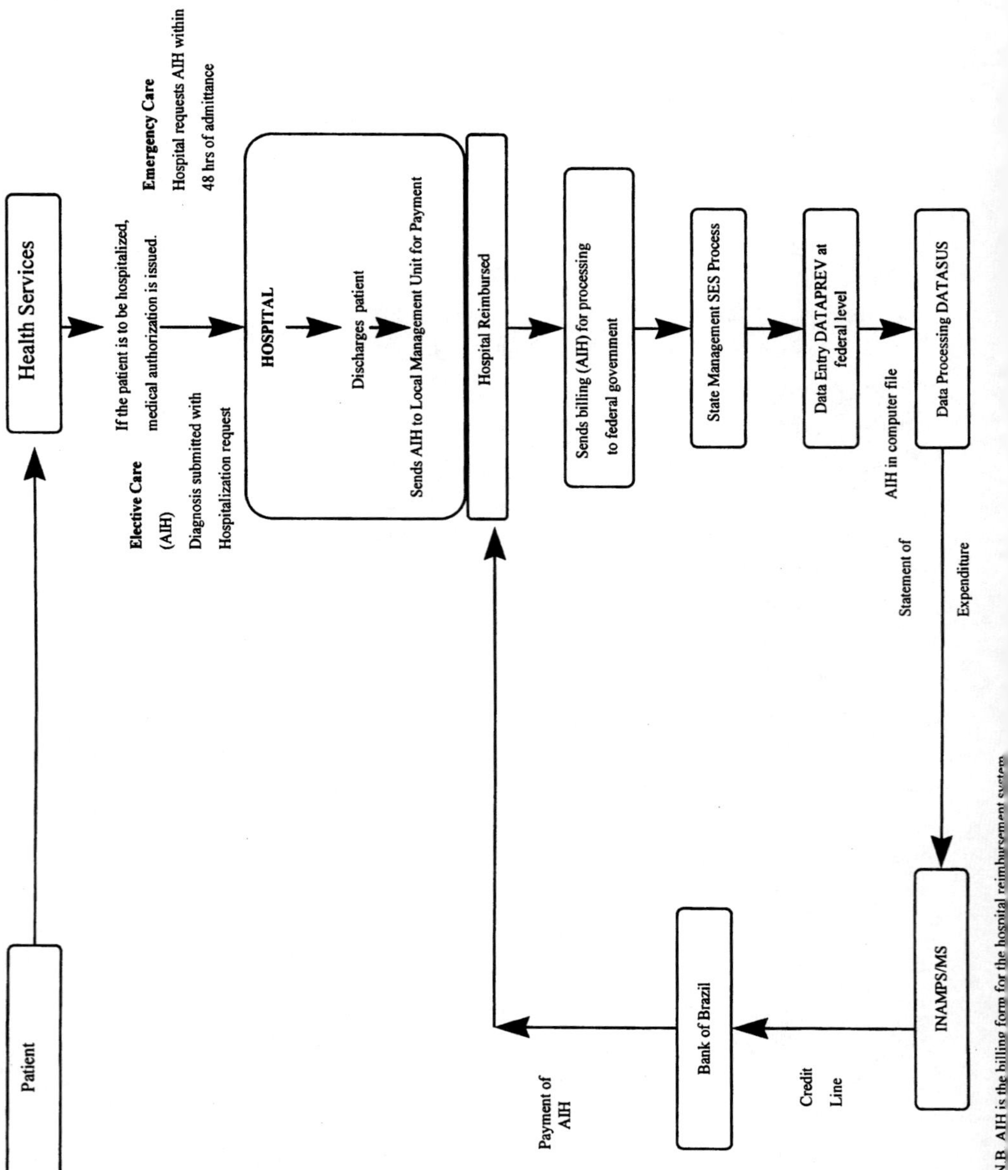

Figure 12.1 Schematic of AIH Process

Source: Lefcovitz 1992.

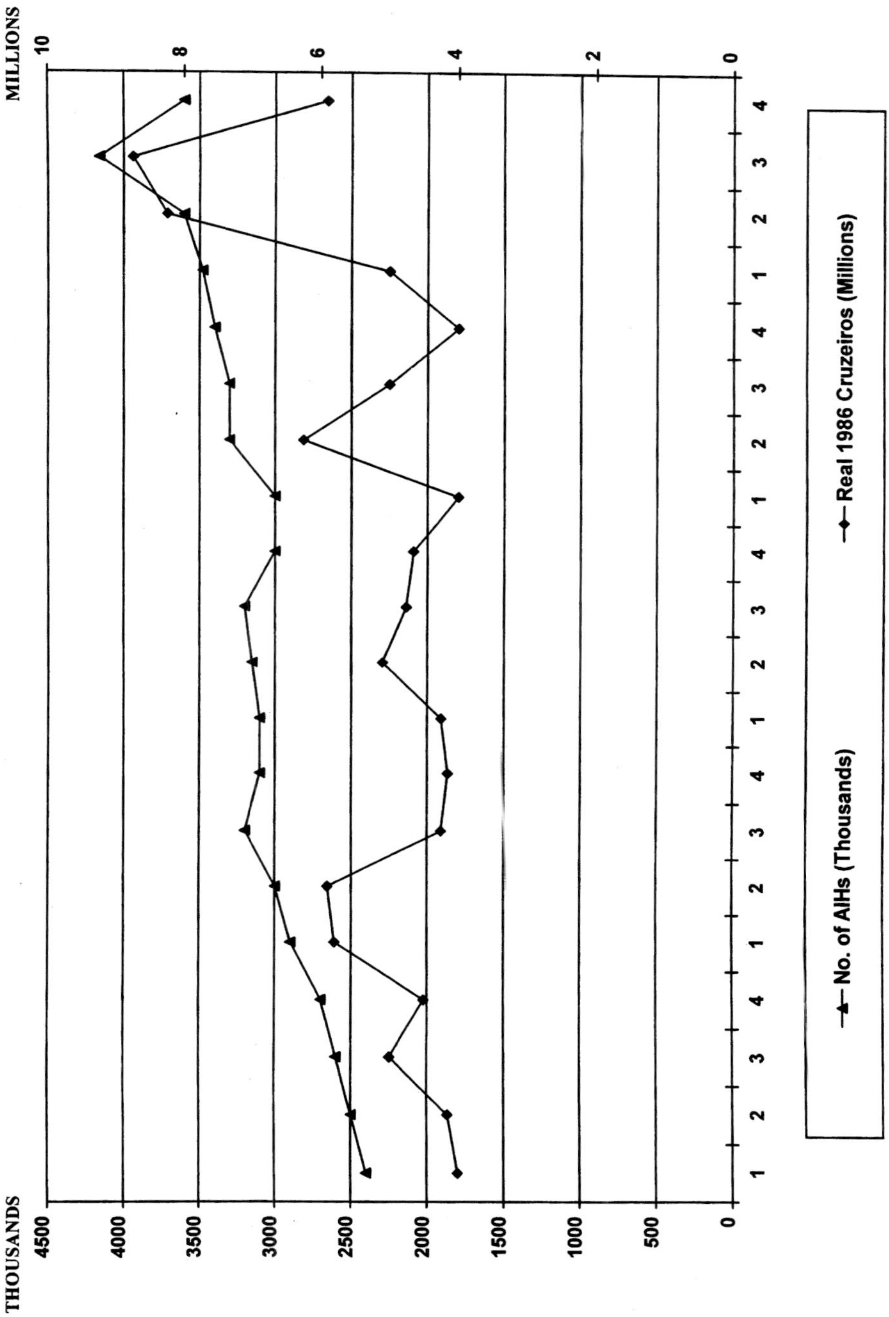

Figure 12.2 Trends in AIH Expenditures and Number of Patient Discharges by Quarter, 1987–1991

the system to all citizens, the rest is attributed to fraud in "ghost" billings, and rising sophistication of urban residents who want hospital care.

The growth in real AIH expenditures in figure 12.2 indicates little growth in expenditure until the beginning of 1990 and then erratic increases. The average cost of an AIH (a patient discharge) grew from $138 in the first quarter of 1987 to $295 in the third quarter of 1991 (using constant dollars). Thus not only are the number of AIHs increasing, but the average and total expenditures are as well, but not commensurately.

Data on UCA is less readily available, and as a new program its data are incomplete. Expenditures and billings (numbers of consultations not available) for January 1991, 1992, and 1993 indicate expenditures of $145,618 in 1991, a 19 percent decline in 1992, and a 70 percent increase in 1993 to $200,239. More recent trends are clearly upward (Czapski 1993).

The expected rise in patient demand was not budgeted. Combined with the organizational confusion caused by the 1988 Constitution, the financial pressures led to serious problems of underpayment of providers, quality reductions because of inadequate reimbursements, no oversight of system performance, and virtually no accountability for clinical performance. While some of these apply regardless of the financing system, prospective payment with its rich data base permits auditing and oversight; although these were collected, collated, and stored but never used to evaluate the system or ensure its proper operation. Oversight, however, was never truly decentralized. Therefore, a national payment system was managed by the federal government, which made the waves of decentralization either meaningless or a contest between levels of government. PPS may have positive effects on the health care system but effective public management and evaluation are essential. These were not brought to bear in Brazil.

CHARACTERISTICS OF DELIVERY AND FINANCE, LEGACY OF REFORM

The two sets of reform have shaped the delivery of care and have had a profound effect on expenditure levels of the federal, state, and municipal governments. This section describes the composition of delivery in Brazil and then analyzes expenditure patterns between 1980 and the early 1990s within the context of the reforms discussed above, and the problems they engender.

It then turns to some specific financial-reform issues that demonstrate emerging difficulties.

Unlike most of Latin America, Brazil's health care system is largely private, a legacy of both a vibrant private sector and pragmatic decision making on the part of the government, which believed it had neither the capacity nor the flexibility to meet rapidly changing needs through public construction. Indeed growth in demand for services in the 1980s was met largely through subsidized grants to private investors who built hospitals throughout Brazil. The availability of public funds to finance care provided a strong incentive to the private sector, both for-profit and nonprofit, to invest in the sector.

Table 12.1 summarizes the trends, levels, and proportion of public and private health facilities offering outpatient and hospital services. The private sector has systematically dominated inpatient supply, although the public sector has built much of the ambulatory care infrastructure. Nonetheless, in 1987 INAMPS financed 64 percent of all hospital stays, less than 20 percent of which were in public hospitals; INAMPS also paid for over 70 percent of outpatient care, with almost half provided in public facilities. The private role in provision is clear from these statistics, but what is equally evident is that the government is the major payer of services, especially for hospital care, the most costly element of health care (World Bank 1994).

The revenue base for publicly financed health care comes from a number of different sources. The federal, state, and municipal governments all have independent taxing and spending authority. Federal government revenues far exceed those of the other two levels of government, and decentralization

Table 12.1 Distribution of Public and Private Health Care Facilities in Brazil, 1978–1990

	1978		*1980*		*1988*		*1990*	
	No.	*%*	*No.*	*%*	*No.*	*%*	*No.*	*%*
Facilities with beds								
Public	1,072	19	1,217	20	1,823	26	2,034	28
Private	4,636	81	4,893	80	5,300	74	5,246	72
Total	5,708	100	6,110	100	7,123	100	7,280	100
Facilities without beds								
Public	6,767	70	8,828	71	19,649	74	21,587	77
Private	2,870	30	3,551	29	6,860	26	6,597	23
Total	9,637	100	12,379	100	26,509	100	28,184	100

Source: IBGE/AMS, from Iunes 1991.

Table 12.2 Sources of Federal Revenues for Health Care in Brazil, 1980–1990

	Total (in billions of 1992 US$)	*General Revenues (%)*	*FINSOCIAL*[a] *(%)*	*FPAS*[b] *(%)*	*FAS*[c] *(%)*	*Other (%)*
1980	7.36	—	—	85.3	1.5	—
1981	6.85	12.9	—	83.9	1.3	0.3
1982	7.15	14.5	—	82.4	1.5	0.3
1983	5.72	15.8	—	79.5	1.2	0.3
1984	5.96	16.6	1.9	82.2	0.7	0.8
1985	6.86	14.8	2.2	78.4	0.7	0.1
1986	7.34[d]	18.4	2.5	76.8	1.0	—
1987	10.62	22.2	—	80.2	0.5	—
1988	10.03	19.3	—	79.5	0.6	—
1989	11.32	19.9	—	72.2	0.2	—
1990	9.45	21.1	—	78.9	—	—

Source: IPEA/CSP, from Medici 1994.

a. FINSOCIAL = the social fund raised through a special wage tax.
b. FPAS = the Social Security Fund.
c. FAS = the Fund for Support of Social Developments, abolished in 1990.
d. FINSOCIAL was incorporated into general revenues in 1986.

expanded modest revenue sharing by the federal government. Indeed each of the phases of the Reforma Sanitária entailed shifts in revenue-sharing levels and recipients, and commensurate shifts in state and municipal expenditures. Table 12.2 shows federal sources of revenue for 1980–1990 (although total revenues are available for subsequent years, breakdowns of source are not available).

Over time general revenues have replaced special earmarked revenues for social programs, such as Support for Social Development (FAS) and the social fund raised through a special wage tax (FINSOCIAL). Moreover, in 1993 the Ministry of Social Security suspended payments to the MOH, because new legislation indexing pensions claimed the surplus funds from social security taxes and the MOH could not afford to subsidize health care. After a month without resources, the federal treasury resumed transfers, but this time from general revenues. Thus, although historically the MOH had no legal claim on social security revenues but received about 25 percent, it was abruptly weaned and remains so. The resulting difficulty is the uncertainty of transfer levels and the constant lobbying entailed in maintaining allocations to keep the system solvent.

In 1980–1992 the expenditures of federal, state, and municipal governments were quite volatile, especially for the federal government where big increases between 1987 and 1989 reflected public pressure and imminent elections. Total spending, however, varied far less, indicating the importance

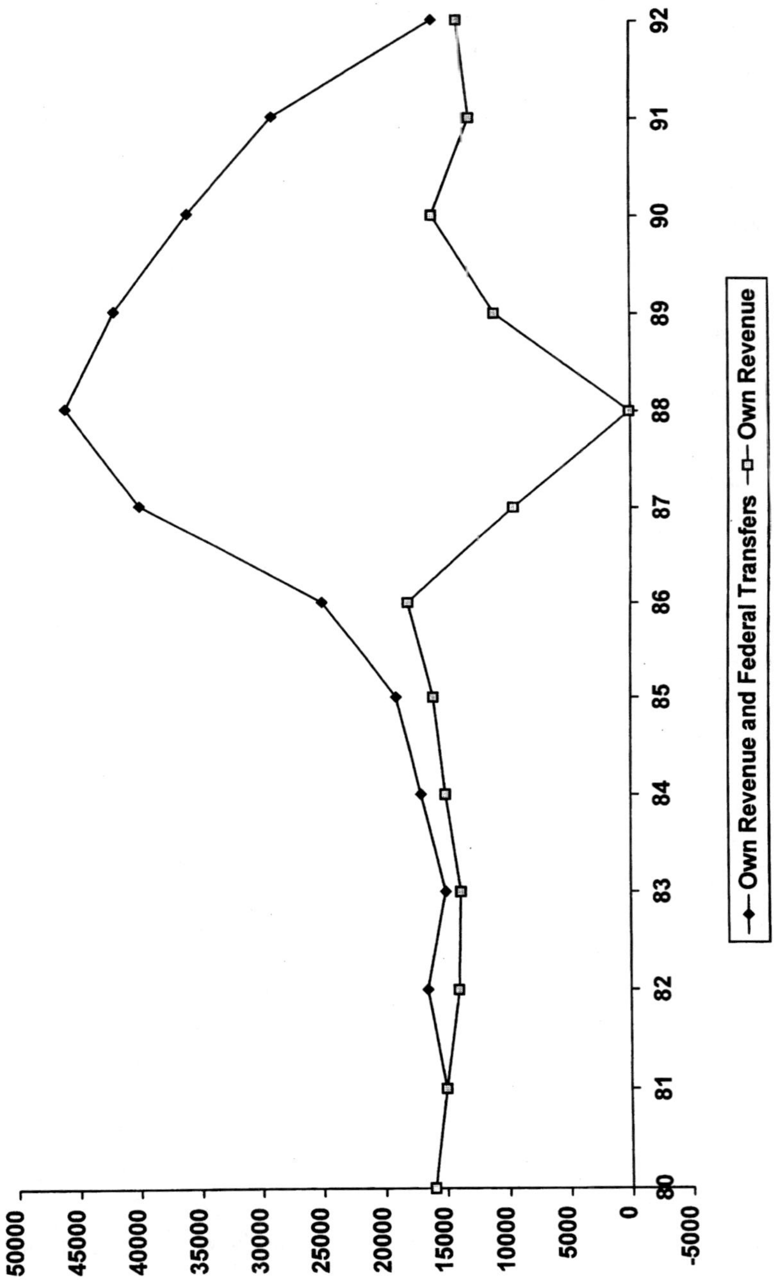

Figure 12.3 Trends in State Health Spending, 1980–1992 (in 1992 US$ millions)

of other levels of government. (Private spending is independent of public expenditures and has been on an upward trajectory for the past decade. See Lewis and Medici 1995 and World Bank 1994 for discussion of trends in private spending and insurance coverage.) Overall and federal spending per capita, was also fairly erratic. These patterns suggest the randomness of budgeting, and the absence of coherent policy and the lack of planning for publicly financed health care. Indeed, the data imply the lurching of a system seeking to find its grounding and are consistent with the description above of the waves of reform, lack of clear policies regarding responsibilities, and the vague stages of decentralization.

The commitment of states and their role vis-à-vis the federal government are clearly shown in figure 12.3. The graph compares "total state spending" with own revenue expenditures with the difference because of federal transfers. States' allocations to health complement or in some cases compensate for federal revenue-sharing levels. In 1988, when federal transfers reached a new high and municipalities picked up spending, states spent virtually nothing of their own revenue, relying instead on other levels of government. The resulting patchwork of funding that has taken place in recent years suggests a disjoint in health delivery. Sources and levels of funding are unreliable, and no one is in charge. Decentralization has not taken hold for a clear decentralization policy requires a systematic divestiture policy, budget and follow-through. This has not yet been fully resolved. The PPS has impeded this to some degree, but the irregularity of transfers and the confusing roles also play an important part.

Further adding to the confusion is the malfunctioning of PPS. As shown in figure 12.2 the number of discharges (AIHs) is increasing but the average and total expenditures, while rising, are not keeping pace. A comparison of MOH/INAMPS reimbursement levels and actual costs for six diagnoses sheds light on how the government has chosen to cope with underfunding of political promises. Using a sample of hospitals from three major Brazilian cities and reimbursement payments for three consecutive months at the end of 1990 and beginning of 1991, the study results (figure 12.4) show that, on average, reimbursements only covered a fraction of average hospital costs. Particularly important in the figure is the reimbursement for normal deliveries, the most common reason for hospitalization (12 percent of total admittances). The total reimbursement of $130 does not come close to the cost of $576. Hospitals can reduce the average length of stay of three days to save money, and length of stay have been declining. However, unless techni-

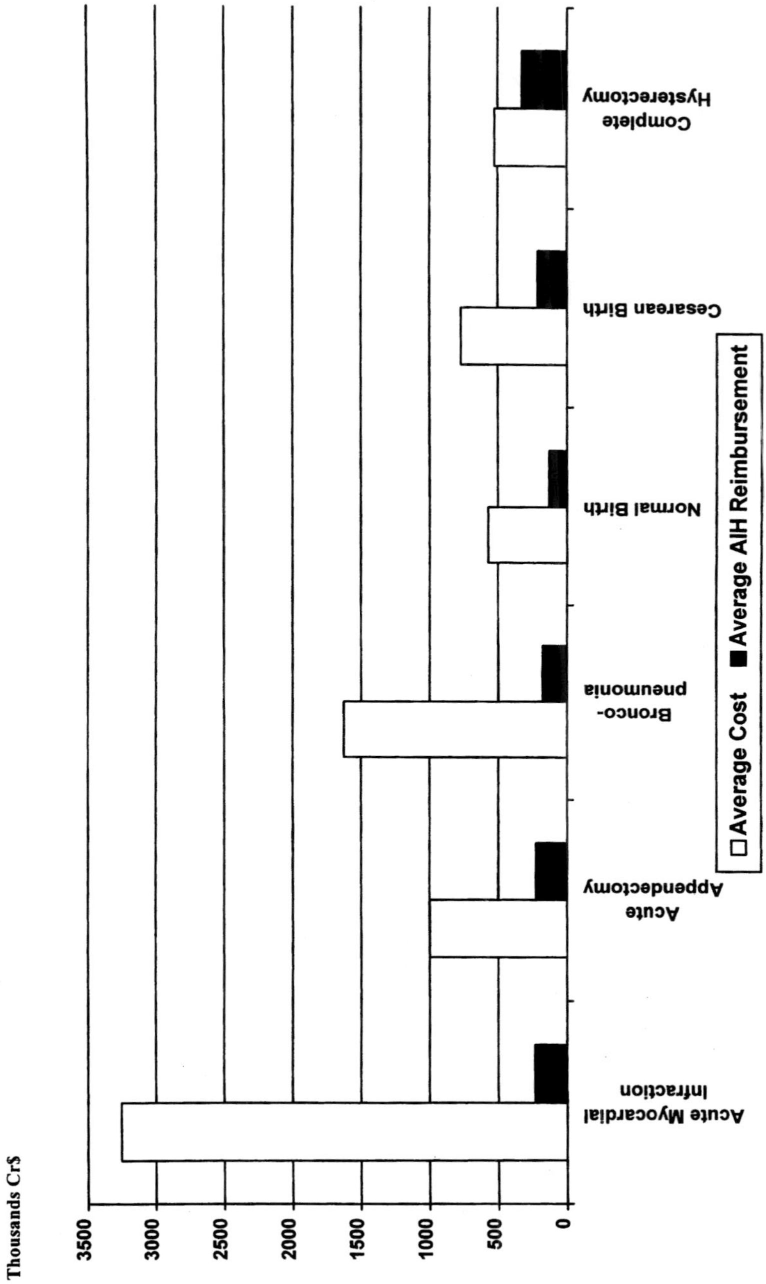

Figure 12.4 Private Costs and INAMPS Payments for Selected Procedures, December 1990

Source: Matos 1991.

cal efficiency can be improved, quality is likely to suffer in adjusting to grossly inadequate payments. It should also be noted that some diagnoses are overcompensated; these are largely high-tech procedures, which are therefore attractive to providers (World Bank 1994).

Ultimately, the incentives are to favor patients whose diagnoses are adequately reimbursed; to refer to other (public) hospitals those that are not (public hospitals are financed through direct wage payments supplemented by AIH reimbursements); and to reduce lengths of stay and any elective diagnosis or procedure that will raise costs. (Hospitals survive through a combination of favoring adequately reimbursed diagnosis; fraud; financial creativity, in high inflation periods particularly; private billings, periodic general public transfers from state and municipal government.) The problem is because the federal government has paid inadequate attention to fundamental questions such as costs and has neglected opportunities for oversight and sensible adjustment of reimbursements. Part of this is attributable to the virtual absence of cost data, but there has been no attempt to responsibly align relative costs and reimbursement levels for many years (World Bank 1994).

IMPLICATIONS FOR PHASE TWO

The Brazilian health care system is an amalgamation of different financing and delivery mechanisms. The range of experimentation and activity is impressive, and the innovation across these many initiatives reflects both creativity and courage—to design and implement the untested. Achievements of this decade of reform include significant steps toward decentralization, an important element in a federal country, especially one the size of Brazil; promotion of private sector alternatives to delivery and finance health care; development of a nationwide public insurance system based on prospective payment for outpatient and inpatient services; existence of a full range of services from the most basic to tertiary care; and an effort to address legislated equity through universal access to publicly financed services, paid for through a largely progressive payroll tax system.

Many of these engender costs and difficulties but still represent significant achievements. The unfinished agenda includes sorting out the specific roles of different government levels, and assessing and accommodating the capacity of some states and most municipalities to handle expanded obligations. The role of states in particular is unclear, with implicit accountability for health but no leverage over municipalities.

Although equity has been attained in law, its affordability is not yet clear, nor is it evident how the government proposes to adjust its responsibilities and its available revenues to maximize returns for the population at large. The public insurance system was designed to address some of the most egregious problems of the previous payment systems; but with gross mismanagement, uncontrolled expenditures, and the inability to project spending needs, it has not taken advantage of the built-in incentives to improve efficiency. It has not lived up to its potential. Any financing system requires careful monitoring; and costs, the backbone of the systems, were never systematically collected, hospitals were never required to demonstrate improved efficiency, and abuses and problems were left unidentified and therefore unaddressed.

The outcome of the subsequent deterioration of the system is that 25 percent of the population, all of whom pay social security taxes, also purchase or receive from employers health insurance coverage. This group does, however, consume costly tertiary care. What this implies for equity is not clear. On one hand, since it is the only service consumed by the payers of the system, it may be a necessary investment for their political and financial support for universal care, and for effective pressure to maintain basic levels of quality and access. On the other hand, what proportion of total resources are spent on the consumption of these services? Lack of data prevents even analyzing the question, but it is an important political issue.

Unregulated competition and inadequate regulation of the private sector delivery has led to abuses, from exclusion of common conditions in health care plans to patient "dumping" (sending patients whose treatment promises to be costly to public facilities). To ensure fairness, access, cost containment, financial accountability, and basic quality of the delivery of care, some role for government and hospital/medical provider associations are needed to regulate the delivery of services and to provide the public with information on the provider options and their quality. Such regulation offers a "seal of medical approval" to potential patients, an element that is currently absent. But its existence would compensate for the absence of public oversight and prevent serious deterioration in the quality of publicly financed health care.

A related issue is that public costs are closely tied to price rises in the private sector. This limits government's ability to contain costs without losing its participating hospitals and physicians, because reimbursing below market levels leads to fewer providers who are willing to take publicly insured patients. Indeed, this has occurred both in Brazil, where the number of participating hospitals in AIH has declined recently, and in the U.S. Medicaid program for the poor whose patients face a limited supply of providers.

This summary of the problems stemming from the Reforma Sanitária and the financial reforms of the 1980s define the priority areas for the second phase of reform. First, there is a strong need to consolidate institution reforms. In particular, states require a pivotal position to ensure that their populations' needs are defined and met. Priorities should be to reconsider and refine the respective functions of each level of government; to standardize revenue-sharing formulas and tie this to some performance measures; and to address diverse priorities across regions, states, and municipalities. Second, unbiased empirical policy formulation is needed for public decision making, and to provide feedback on implementation. Are the policies and programs meeting goals, is the system working properly? These are keys to effective, affordable program management.

Third, serious cost containment is essential. Faltering budgets, a broader target population, rising expectations, and the growing cost of medical technology have become central concerns and are likely to persist. The implications point to the need to function within budget constraints, which implies raising efficiency, rationing care, and controlling the volume of care—all subjective, politically difficult steps. But without an effective cost containment policy, Brazil will not be able to extend health care services to the entire population at an acceptable level of quality.

Finally, the government must step in to ensure accountability of public and private providers and payers of service. If they do not, the cracks in the quality of care that are already apparent will only deteriorate further. Quality assurance in hospitals, essentially a self-monitoring system of sentinel (deaths, for example) and routine (infection rates) events; accreditation of physicians and hospitals and regulation of technology acquisition; insurance companies and provider behavior; all are functions of government in a hybrid system like that of Brazil. There are lessons for other countries in Brazil's experience, but the findings at this juncture should also provide the basis for a consolidation of the reforms in the 1980s and early 1990s, to implement and make them viable. This is the challenge for the remainder of the decade—to maintain momentum, but to use the new openness in the country to adjust the reform and finalize it.

Note

We would like to thank Julio Frenk for helpful comments. All views are those of the authors and do not represent the policies of the World Bank or the IADB. All references to dollars ($) are to U.S. dollars.

References

Couttolenc, Bernard F. 1991. "Change in the Brazilian Health System: Key Issues for SUS." Background paper for the project Issues in Health Care Delivery and Finance in Brazil, prepared for the World Bank. October.

Czapski, Julian. 1993. "Assistência ambulatorial no Brasil: História, qualidade, problemas." Background paper commissioned by the World Bank. September.

Gentile de Mello, C. A. 1983. *Medicina e realidade brasileira.* Rio de Janeiro, Achiame.

Hurst, Jeremy W. 1991. "Reforming Health Care in Seven European Nations." *Health Affairs* (fall): 7–21.

IBGE/AMS. Multiple years. *Annual Medical Supply Survey.* IBGE.

Iunes, Roberto. 1991. "Access and Health Care Utilization in Brazil: The Data from the PNAD." Background paper commissioned by the World Bank. December.

Levcovitz, Edwardo. 1992. "Analysis of the Public Reimbursement System in Brazil." Background paper commissioned by the World Bank. April.

Lewis, M., and A. Medici. 1995. "Private Payers of Health Care in Brazil: Characteristics, Costs, and Coverage." *Health Policy and Planning* 10:4.

Medici, A. C. 1990. *Ecónomia e financiamento do setor Saúde no Brasil.* São Paulo, Brazil: Faculdade de Saúde Pública.

Pesquisa Nacional Anual Domiciliario (PNAD). Multiple years. *Nacional Annual Household Survey.* IBGE.

Piola, S. F., and S. M. Vianna. 1991. "Políticas e prioridades do sistema unico de Saúde-SUS." Background paper commissioned by the World Bank.

Silver, Lynn D., Vera Travassos, and Cláudia Maria. 1992. "Estudo da validade dos Diagnosis Related Groups (DRG) para internações hospitalar no Brasil." Fundação Oswaldo Cruz, Rio de Janeiro. December.

Veras, C. M. T. 1989. "Diagnosis Related Groups—DRG: Avaliação do uso de uma metodologia de mensuração do produto hospitalar com utilização de base de dados de SAMHPS/AIH na cidade do Rio de Janeiro." Paper presented at Congresso de ABRASCO, São Paulo.

Vianna, S. M., S. F. Piola, A. J. Guerra, and S. F. Camargo. 1991. "O financiamento da descentralização dos servicos de saúde." Documents de Política no. 03. IPEA.

World Bank. 1989. *Adult Health in Brazil: Adjusting to New Challenges.* Brazil Department. Washington, D.C.: World Bank.

———. 1994. *The Organization, Delivery and Financing of Health Care in Brazil: Agenda for the 1990s.* World Bank Report No. 12655-BR. Brazil, Peru, and Venezuela Department. Washington, D.C.: World Bank.

three / Reforms Under Study

13 / Reforming the Brazilian Pension System

Cheikh T. Kane

Brazil has a long tradition in the provision of social insurance, which can be traced back to early 1923, with the creation of insurance funds for railway workers. Today, the pension system is comprised of three pillars. The first and largest pillar is a mandatory and contributory defined-benefit scheme covering workers in the private sector and state-owned enterprises (SOEs), which is centrally managed by the Instituto Nacional do Seguro Social (INSS). The second pillar is a mandatory defined-benefit scheme covering civil servants. In contrast to workers affiliated with the first pillar, civil servants for all intents and purposes do not contribute for their retirement benefits. An important feature of the Brazilian pension system is that the pension promises under both pillars are constitutionally guaranteed. As we shall see this brings considerable rigidity to the reform process.

The third pillar comprises voluntary open and closed pension funds. Open pension funds are voluntary savings schemes offering both group plans and individual plans. Open pension funds play a minor role in the Brazilian pension system and are dominated by two companies that account for 84 percent of total assets. Closed or occupational pension funds are company based; they are limited to the company or group of companies that are sponsoring the pension plan. Closed pension funds are dominated by defined-benefit plans, although a number of companies offer defined-contribution or mixed pension plans. Closed pension funds have important fiscal implications for two main reasons. First, collectively, SOEs manage the majority of closed pension fund assets, and most of these assets are managed in-house. Second, many SOEs explicitly design their closed pension plans to meet a target replacement rate for both pillars. As such, a reduction in the benefit in the first pillar, ceteris paribus, would be partly offset by a higher replacement rate in the third pillar.

Although the first pillar of the Brazilian pension system is the one that has attracted the most attention, a comprehensive approach is needed to understand the magnitude of the problems and identify reform options. Brazil is one of the few middle-income countries in Latin America that has not embraced radical pension reform. The discussion that follows provides evidence that this slowness to change contrasts with the looming fiscal crisis of the two main pillars of the system. The rest of the chapter is organized as follows. The first section is devoted to the first pillar and focuses particularly on fiscal sustainability, efficiency, and equity issues. These three themes are revisited in the next section for the civil servant pension scheme. The next section explores the main issues arising with the voluntary or third pillar. The discussion then turns to reform options, including the 1996 constitutional amendments, and conclusions.

THE FIRST PILLAR FOR PRIVATE SECTOR AND STATE-OWNED ENTERPRISES

This is by far the largest pillar of the Brazilian pension system with about 31 million contributors, or roughly 48 percent of the labor force, and 12 million beneficiaries. Affiliation to the first pillar is mandatory for non–civil servants, except self-employed who join on a voluntary basis. As in many Latin American countries, Brazil's main pension pillar has gradually shifted from a partially funded to a pay-as-you-go (PAYG) system. Under this scheme, current resources are used to finance current expenditures. These resources come mainly from contributions and federal transfers. Employee contributions vary across income groups according to a progressive schedule from 8 to 10 percent. Rural workers, however, do not contribute but are entitled to the same benefits as the rest. Urban employers face a uniform contribution of 20 percent. The total contribution of 28–30 percent is very high by Latin American standards, where the average contribution is 10 percent. Only Uruguay, which has a much older population, has a higher contribution of 29.5 percent.

Functioning and Main Programs

The main retirement plans that are offered include old age, disability, length of service, special retirement, and survivor.

Old Age

Under this program urban workers can retire at age sixty-five for men and sixty for women and, until 1992, required participation in the system for only five years. The number of years of participation is being raised gradually (by six months each year) from six in 1994 to fifteen by the year 2012. Rural workers can retire five years prior to their urban counterparts. This is the only program for which there are more rural than urban beneficiaries. The replacement rate varies between 75 and 100 percent, subject to a minimum and maximum benefit. The minimum benefit is set at one minimum wage and the maximum benefit at ten minimum wages.

Disability

The permanent disability program requires only one year of affiliation with the system. This minimum affiliation period is waived when disability is caused by a work-related injury. The replacement rate varies between 85 and 100 percent, subject to the same minimum and maximum pension as the old age program. Given the loose eligibility conditions, the disability program is subject to a substantial amount of fraud. More than half of beneficiaries of newly granted disability pensions are younger than fifty-five years.

Length of Service

The length of service program allows workers who can document thirty years of service for men and twenty-five years for women to retire with a full pension. This program is also expensive, with a replacement rate varying between 70–100 percent and an average pension that is about twice higher than that of the old age program.

Special Retirement

The special retirement program enables workers in certain professions (such as pilots) to retire after fifteen, twenty, or twenty-five years of service. The starting replacement rate of 85 percent is the highest among all the retirement programs.

Survivor

The survivor program grants benefits that vary between 90 and 100 percent of the pension that the deceased would have been entitled to. This program accounts for 27 percent of total benefits and 21 percent of total expenses.

Actuarial Imbalance

Like many PAYG schemes, the main Brazilian pension scheme faces important fiscal imbalances. In 1988 only 54 percent of social security contributions were necessary to finance pensions. The rest was channeled to health benefits. By November 1995 pensions expenditures had risen to 115 percent of contributions, leading to a monthly cash flow deficit of US$431 million. The system's structural imbalance was worsened by the 1988 Constitution, which doubled the minimum pension from half to a full minimum wage while reducing the retirement age for rural workers by five years. As the new rules became effective, the flow of new retirees increased by an unprecedented 34 percent in 1992. From a fiscal standpoint, the 1988 Constitution has been thus described as unrealistic or unfeasible (Simonsen 1992).

Until the adoption of the stabilization plan in 1994 (*plano Real*), inflation eroded benefits and the structural imbalances were somewhat hidden. Interest income became an important source of financing, as nominal interest rates more than compensated for the double-digit monthly inflation rates. As monthly inflation fell from 45 percent during the second quarter of 1994 to 3 percent in August of 1994, interest income also fell from US$486 million to US$86 million. Double-digit monthly inflation rates combined with bimonthly adjustment of benefits implied an erosion of real pension expenditures by about 20 percent. The irony for Brazil is that the early success of the stabilization program has revealed the true dimension of the fiscal imbalances. Actuarial projections show that these imbalances would worsen in the future, as the ratio of pensioners to workers increases. Depending on assumptions about GDP growth and the minimum wage relative to the average wage, the deficit could climb to 2–5 percent of GDP by the year 2015 and 7–9 percent by the year 2025. (These projections do not take into account the 1996 Constitutional amendments, but very little fiscal relief should be expected from these changes.)

One of the main reasons behind the first pillar's actuarial imbalance is that the ratio of pensioners to contributors stands at 40 percent, whereas the population dependency rate (that is, ratio of population over sixty to population between twenty and fifty-nine) is only 15 percent (see table 13.1). This is the direct result of early retirement provisions and low coverage. Another indicator of the system's imbalances is the implicit pension debt, which captures liabilities toward current pensioners and workers. The implicit pension debt, using a 4 percent discount, is estimated at 188 percent of GDP (see table 13.1). Even after deducting from these liabilities future contributions, the net present value of liabilities would remain at 113 percent of GDP (1994). By way of comparison, unfunded net liabilities in the United States, which has a much older population, are estimated at 43 percent of GDP (Van der Noord and Herd 1993).

Efficiency

The combination of loose linkages between contribution and benefits and high marginal taxes create significant distortions in the labor market. Loose linkages are a direct result of the benefit structure, which, for instance, allows workers to retire after one year of contribution for disability. This is compounded by weak administrative capacity. There is no reliable central record keeping; workers are responsible for keeping booklets in which wages are recorded as evidence of their eligibility for retirement benefits. The situ-

Table 13.1 Brazil's Cost Rate and Implicit Pension Debt, 1994–1995 *(in percentages)*

	Cost Rate Pensioners/ Workers	*Pension/ Wage*	*Cost Rate*	*Implicit Pension Debt/GDP* D=4%[a]	D=6%
First Pillar: INSS[b]	40	26	10	188	n.a.
Second Pillar: Civil Servants[c]					
Minas Gerais	29	178	52	83.9	55.3
Rio de Janeiro	38	153	92	81.9	54.0
Rio Grande Do Sul	78	153	119	297.0	195.1

Source: Author.
Note: Data for civil servants exclude workers from state-owned enterprises.
a. D = Discount rate.
b. Implicit debt is relative to Brazil's GDP.
c. Implicit debt is relative to the state's GDP.

ation is worst for rural workers since labor unions are granted the authority to decide on workers' eligibility. For these reasons, the benefits fraudulently extracted from the pension system are believed to be significant. Corroborating this belief is a task force's finding that 10 percent of benefits reviewed in the state of Rio de Janeiro were invalid.

Another shortcoming of the Brazilian social security is that it relies on high marginal tax rates on payroll, which have become an open invitation to evasion and are inducing major distortions in the sectoral allocation of labor. Payroll taxes in Brazil vary across wage brackets and sectors between 38 and 45 percent. These rates are much higher than the average in Latin America or even that of OECD countries. Such a high penalty on the use of labor induces a shift of unskilled labor away from the formal sector.

Empirical evidence points to the adverse effects of increased contribution rates on revenues. For instance, although inflation and recession contributed to the 21 percent revenue decline in 1983, econometric analysis suggests that more than half this loss was caused by an increase in payroll taxes the preceding year. This is corroborated by the finding that, regardless of gender and across different age brackets, an increase in the payroll taxes leads to a reduction in the probability of contributing to the social insurance system (see World Bank 1995). It should be emphasized that the widespread evasion from payroll taxes, more than a simple leakage, induces a social cost similar to a deadweight loss (see Slemrod and Yitzhaki 1996 for the social costs of taxation). This cost will rise with the resources that are used up to conceal or misrepresent the tax base. The most conservative estimate on evasion, as a proportion of the declared wage bill, is 15 percent (in 1988). In labor-intensive activities such as civil construction and agriculture, the figures exceed 90 percent.

Equity

The intragenerational redistribution induced by the main public pension scheme can be gauged by deriving the rates of return that are implicit in the contributions paid and the benefits received. These rates of return for urban pensioners are derived by pension program and for different socioeconomic groups. Table 13.2 summarizes the results.

A very important finding is that the general wisdom that the length of service program is the main culprit to the social insurance financial difficul-

Table 13.2 Implicit Rates of Return for Urban Workers, by Program, Sex, and Income Group, 1994

(in percentages)

First Pillar: Urban Workers	*Men*	*Women*	*All*
Old-Age Pension			
5 years' contribution	45.94	52.75	50.81
12 years' contribution (min. wage)	14.68	18.30	16.26
Less than 2 years (min. wage)	16.66	17.91	17.60
2–3 years (min. wage)	16.52	19.07	17.99
3–4 years (min. wage)	14.94	19.28	16.91
More than 4 years (min. wage)	14.57	13.50	14.67
Length of service 25–30 years	7.04	9.70	7.73
Less than 2 years (min. wage)	7.15	9.59	8.77
2–3 years (min. wage)	7.64	10.20	8.52
3–4 years (min. wage)	6.98	9.80	7.79
More than 4 years (min. wage)	7.15	6.84	7.22
Length of service 30–35 years	6.25	8.79	6.95
Special retirement, 25 years	11.10	11.32	11.19

Source: Rofman 1995.

ties overlooks the fact that the old age program offers even better returns to some of its beneficiaries. This arises because most old age pensioners have had less than twenty years of contributions, which is the threshold level to ensure parity between old age and length of service. The message is simple: it is an illusion that eliminating early retirement alone would solve the problem. This message is worth emphasizing because, more often than not, discussions about pension reform in Brazil tend to stress the generosity of early retirement provisions and leave aside the structural problems of the remaining programs.

The system redistributes in favor of women because of the combination of preferential eligibility rules and higher life expectancy. As a result, women who in the past retired with five years of contribution under the old age program received an average return that was 7 percentage points above that of their male counterparts. This difference narrows with an increase in the number of years of contribution. This gender gap in rate of return has obvious actuarial implications: since the female labor participation is expected to continue rising, the associated fiscal burden will follow. For the old age program the rate of return gap between these two regions is estimated at 1.40 percentage points (see Rofman 1995).

THE SECOND PILLAR FOR CIVIL SERVANTS

Functioning and Main Programs

Under the federal constitution all civil servants are subject to the Regime Juridico Unico (RJU), as opposed to the Consolidacao das Leis do Trabalho (CLT) for workers affiliated with the private sector or SOEs. Each Brazilian state has its own constitution, which has to be consistent with the federal constitution. All the parameters about pension benefits that appear in the federal constitution are adopted by all states. There are minor differences across states, mainly with respect to survivor benefits. A common denominator to all states is that workers do not contribute for their old age pensions. A recent exception is Rio Grande Do Sul, which introduced a 2 percent contribution rate in March 1996. Whereas retirement pensions are treated like wages and paid directly by the state treasury, survivor benefits are typically managed by a separate agency to which workers contribute. In some cases, the survivor benefit agency also provides social assistance and health benefits.

Normal Retirement

This occurs after thirty years of service for men and thirty-five years for women, with 100 percent of final salary. Workers are allowed to retire five years prior to the normal retirement but with a reduced replacement rate of 86–97 percent of final salary. Workers who reach the statutory retirement rates prevailing in the first pillar for urban workers (sixty-five for men and sixty for women) may also retire with a pension proportional to their years of service. For civil servants reaching the age of seventy, retirement becomes mandatory. In some cases, the mandatory retirement age is reduced to sixty-five for politicians.

Special Retirement

Teachers and politicians are allowed to retire with a full pension after thirty years of service for men and twenty-five years for women. This is often one of the most expensive programs for states, because teachers account for a large proportion of civil servants. In the state of Minas Gerais, for instance, teachers account for more than three-quarters of workers and pensioners. Moreover, the majority of teachers are women, which further reduces the average retirement age.

Disability Retirement

Workers subject to a permanent disability are entitled to a full pension. Typically, this program is very small, as civil servants are less exposed to work-related injuries than their counterparts working in the manufacturing sector.

Survivor Benefit

This benefit is often set at a 100 percent of the salary or pension. In some states, such as Rio Grande Do Sul, the survivor replacement rate has fallen to 50 percent (the legality of the 50 percent replacement rate is being challenged in court). Typically, this program is managed by a separate agency rather than paid directly out of the treasury. Unlike the other programs, which are noncontributory, civil servants do contribute to be eligible for survivor benefits. The contribution rate varies across states; it is 9 percent in Rio de Janeiro and Rio Grande Do Sul, and 8 percent in Minas Gerais. In the case of Rio Grande Do Sul, the law stipulates that 60 percent contributions should finance survivor benefits and the rest for medical assistance.

Actuarial Imbalance

Cost Rate

Because of its noncontributory nature, the civil servant pension scheme has a prohibitive cost. This is compounded by early retirement provisions, a 100 percent replacement rate applied to final salary, and an implicit indexation of pensions to wages. Table 13.1 shows the cost rate for the civil servant pension schemes in three selected states. The ratio of pension expenditures to the wage bill (cost rate) is 92 percent in Rio de Janeiro, 52 percent in Minas, and 119 percent in Rio Grande Do Sul. This is, above all, the result of a very high (153–178 percent) average pension relative to the average wage (that is, benefit ratio). The average pension relative to the average wage is roughly four times higher for civil servants compared with workers in the private sector.

Unfunded Liabilities

The short-term liquidity problem captured by the high pension cost rate is compounded by significant longer-term unfunded liabilities. The present value of these liabilities—using a 4 percent discount—vary between 82 percent (in Rio de Janeiro) and 297 percent (in Rio Grande Do Sul) of the state's GDP.

Efficiency

The noncontributory civil servant pension scheme creates many perverse incentives. One such incentive is for workers to join the civil service toward the end of their career and benefit for the more generous pensions. This occurs because periods of activity in the private sector can be combined with years of service in civil administration when claiming a pension. Lifetime civil servants also have an incentive to negotiate abnormal salary increases prior to retirement. As a result, the Brazilian administration is more an island of privileges than a center that efficiently delivers public service.

Equity

The civil servant pension schemes violate both horizontal and vertical equity norms. Horizontal equity is violated because civil servants earn much higher returns than workers of the same income group who are affiliated with INSS. Pensions relative to the average wage are four times higher for civil servants compared with other workers, and such a gap cannot be justified by the often used argument of lower salaries in the public sector. This is compounded by the fact that civil servant pensions are mostly financed out of general revenues, hence by workers who are not covered by any pension scheme. Vertical equity is also compromised because the use of final salary to determine pensions favors high-income earners, who typically have steeper earning profiles. Civil servants are such a powerful and often well-organized interest group that attempts to cut down on these privileges run into formidable obstacles.

THE THIRD PILLAR: CLOSED OR OCCUPATIONAL PENSION PLANS

The third pillar of the Brazilian social security system is voluntary and comprises open and closed private pension funds. Open funds are managed by independent financial or insurance companies and are open to the public. By contrast, closed pension funds are used exclusively by employees of companies, which sponsor these funds. Closed pension funds manage more than 90 percent of the assets of all private pension funds. In general, in 1994 private funds remained underdeveloped in Brazil, with assets representing 3.5 percent of GDP. By way of comparison, the corresponding asset GDP ratio was 34 percent in the United States and 41 percent in Chile.

The market for open pension funds in Brazil is dominated by two companies, which account for about 84 percent of total assets. Open funds offer both group plans and individual plans. Unlike closed pension funds, open pension funds are subject to flexible investment rules: mainly subject to maximum asset shares. There is no constraint on the number of participants. These funds are structured as annuities and are required to provide a real return of 6 percent. Lately open pensions have been offering an option plan, which grants 100 percent of realized returns, minus the management fee. There are two major limitations to the development of open funds. First, because of past bankruptcy problems, they suffer an image problem. Second, contributions to the plans are not tax deductible.

Closed pension funds have about 2 million participants of which 92 percent are contributors and the rest beneficiaries. This leaves the system with a relatively low dependency rate of 9 percent, compared with 40 percent for the mandatory first pillar. Closed pension funds are dominated by the publicly sponsored ones. Privately sponsored closed funds, however, are growing faster and are expected to dominate the industry in the future. Closed pension funds offer defined-benefit (12 percent), defined-contribution (28 percent) and hybrid plans (60 percent). It is interesting to note that publicly sponsored companies do not offer any defined-contribution plans, which partly explain some of the difficulties they face. Unlike open funds, closed funds are subject to a minimum level of participants, which is currently set at one hundred.

REFORM OPTIONS AND CONSTRAINTS

The Case for Reform

Although in the 1990s Brazil has a relatively young population, aging will occur much more rapidly than in OECD countries. This is the direct result of fertility decline combined with increased life expectancy. It took France about 140 years for the proportion of its population over sixty to double from 9 to 18 percent. In Sweden this transition took eighty-six years, and in the United Kingdom forty-five years. For Brazil in sharp contrast such doubling of the old population will take place in about twenty-eight years.

Aside from the longer term need to equip the country with a pension scheme that can sustain rapid aging, Brazil needs to consolidate its ongoing stabilization plan with deep structural reforms. Pensions play a very important role because of their far-reaching fiscal implications on both the state and the federal fiscal accounts. Another rationale for profound reform of the Brazilian pension scheme is that it has very regressive features, in particular the civil servant scheme financed out of general revenues.

The Failed Reform in 1996

After an initial defeat, one of the houses in Congress passed a social security amendment in May 1996. Unfortunately, this amendment would not introduce a new pension system with a capitalization component in line with the reforms adopted in Latin America (for example, Chile, Peru, Colombia, Argentina, Uruguay). In fact, the new text under Article 202 specifically emphasizes that affiliation to any other scheme than the public PAYG would remain optional.

The proposed amendment also fails to address issues related to the system's actuarial imbalance of the first two pillars. Despite having added a paragraph calling for the need to achieve such balance, the changes adopted hardly move in that direction. For the dominant scheme covering private sector workers, the normal retirement age and the replacement rates are unchanged. The only important change introduced is the substitution of years of service with years of contribution. In principle this substitution, rightly applied, could reduce unfunded liabilities, in particular for future entrants. However, because the definition of years of contribution is very loose, little actual fiscal improvement should be expected. For instance, the amendment defines years in activity in the rural area as years of contribution. What makes this provision so costly is that the new rules still allow rural workers to retire five years prior to their urban counterparts.

For civil servants, the replacement rate remains at 100 percent, retirement eligibility conditions are also maintained, and pensions are still fully indexed to wages. The only changes introduced are (1) the requirement to have ten years of effective service in the civil service to be eligible for retirement; and (2) substituting final salary with a five-year average for workers retiring with less than five consecutive years in their preretirement job. The second measure is designed to curb abnormal wage increases prior to retirement.

As far as occupational pension plans of the third pillar are concerned, the amendment stipulates that for plans sponsored by SOEs and public agencies, the government as an employer should not contribute more than the employee. Previously public institutions sponsoring occupational pension plans were allowed to contribute up to twice the employee contribution. Occupational pensions have two years to comply with the new rules. The extent to which this new rule will be followed can be questioned, considering that the previous ceiling of two-thirds of total contribution was often violated. (These violations were documented by a 1994 congressional report. In 1992 Telebras pension contributions to its occupational plan accounted for over 75 percent of total contributions, well above the two-thirds rule.)

Reform Options and Sequencing

All recent Latin American reformers have rightly introduced a capitalization scheme. What varies across these reformers is whether and how this is combined with a public pension pillar. For Brazil the dual objectives are (1) to rationalize the current first two pillars, and (2) to introduce a mandatory defined-contribution scheme. One should recognize, however, that the government's inability to implement any meaningful change through the 1996 amendment is indicative of the formidable forces against reform. Future changes would have to take place in a context of another constitutional referendum, which is not likely to take place soon.

Reforming the First Pillar

There are many compelling reasons for reforming the existing first pillar before introducing a mandatory capitalization regime. Chief among them is that it would lead to a reduction of the implicit pension debt Brazil would need to finance, by introducing a defined-contribution scheme. Measures that would reduce the implicit pension debt include adopting a uniform retirement age of sixty-five for all, hence eliminating all preferential retirement. Alternatively, any retirement prior to the normal retirement age should be associated by a corresponding reduction in the pension level.

The pension system for rural workers also needs rethinking. Strictly speaking, it should be considered a social assistance program since virtually all benefits are set at the minimum wage and rural contributions are neither significant nor related to labor earnings. Therefore, a case can be made for financing rural pensions out of general revenues. Irrespective of source of financing, however, cost containment considerations call for raising the retirement age of rural workers closer to that of their urban counterparts.

Reforming the Second Pillar

Short of implementing a fundamental reform, which would require a constitutional amendment, states can take a series of measures to contain pension costs. First, states should follow the example of Rio Grande Do Sul and introduce a contribution for civil servant pensions. This would somewhat reduce unfunded liabilities, but more important it would facilitate the future introduction of an actuarially balanced pension scheme for civil servants.

Probably the most effective way of reducing pension liabilities would be by downsizing. This is because severance pay typically amounts to one month of salary per year of salary and does not take into account acquired pension rights. (As an incentive for early voluntary separation Rio Grande Do Sul offers a severance pay that starts at 1.25 months of salary per year of service for workers who opt for the program within two weeks after its beginning. The severance pay then gradually falls to 1 percent three months later.) Considering that in Rio, for instance, active civil servants account for about two-thirds of total pension liabilities, the savings induced by downsizing can be significant.

One area with considerable room for curbing the generosity of the pension system within the boundaries of the existing constitution is the survivor program. The reason is that many states' laws have granted more liberal survivor pensions to certain groups without any clear social justification. States should therefore consider rolling back preferential survivor benefits and tightening orphan benefits to women. Often, these orphan benefits are not subject to a uniform and rigorously applied age limit. Cases of women who decide not to marry officially in order to preserve a previously acquired orphan benefit are believed to be numerous. For all these reasons states should consider not only eliminating preferential survivor benefits but also contracting out disability and life insurance to the private sector. The cost of running the state-managed survivor programs by far exceeds the cost incurred by countries that have privatized these programs (such as Peru, Chile, Argentina). The ultimate goal, however, ought to be to bring the civil servant scheme closer to the private sector one. The U.S. experience of merging both schemes while creating a savings scheme is worth considering.

Reforming the Third Pillar

There is considerable room for improvement in Brazil's voluntary savings pillar. A critical area to reform is the supervision of this pillar. The Secretariat of Complementary Social Security is responsible for overseeing closed pension funds. This unit, comprised of thirty-six employees and four inspectors, is seriously understaffed and lacks the technical skill to operate efficiently. The regulatory agency lacks the resources to computerize its operations, in particular for disclosure reporting. There is some potential conflict of interest, because some of the agency's staff members were previously affiliated with the association of closed pension funds. It is recognized that the regulatory agency needs at least one hundred well-qualified inspectors. All funds found violating the investment regulations with impunity should be fined, thereby forcing compliance while increasing the agency's resources. Although some of the investment rules leave much to be desired, the failure to abide by good rules, such as the maximum share of real estate assets, has affected the profitability of some funds.

Setting up an efficient regulatory body should be complemented with improved investment regulations. Compared to international standards, Brazil's investment regulations of closed pension funds are very restrictive. Asset allocation for these funds are usually subject to both minimum and maximum provisions. Foreign assets have been permitted only recently but were restricted to Mercosul countries and to a 1 percent share. Most countries have far more liberal provisions for foreign assets; Chile has a 9 percent maximum, and more recent reformers such as Colombia and Argentina have a ceiling of 10 percent on foreign securities. In general, Brazil should move toward the "prudent man" approach that prevails in the United States, the United Kingdom, and the Netherlands. As a first step, assets shares should be subject to ceilings only. For foreign assets the 1 percent ceiling, which applies to Mercosul countries only, should be raised gradually to 10–15 percent and extended to all countries. International experience demonstrates that, for pension funds, investment in foreign securities is an effective tool to diversify portfolio risk.

Allowing pension funds to operate under flexible investment regulations is not sufficient to guarantee an efficient risk-return combination. In addition, pension managers should compete for funds. Currently workers cannot transfer their accumulated assets to better performing funds. Adding to this lack of portability rights is that vesting requirements are either nonexistent or very restrictive. A few companies have managed to introduce some competition by relying on more than one firm for the management of their pension fund's assets. Competition would be improved by allowing workers and companies to switch to a new pension manager every year, for instance.

In order to encourage voluntary savings, it is also important to ensure an adequate tax treatment of contributions and benefits. Such treatment is compromised in Brazil because employee contributions to both closed and open pension funds are not tax deductible. Providing such a deduction has proved an important incentive. It should be noted that deducting for contributions while taxing benefits would not change the intertemporal budget constraint. This change, however, has cash-flow implications that need to be examined.

Introducing a Mandatory Fully Funded Scheme

It is worth mentioning that Brazil, more than any other country in the region, has the financial market that is ready to absorb and grow from a mandatory capitalization regime. Market capitalization of the Brazilian stock markets accounts for 34 percent of GDP (in 1994); and despite the significant portfolio shift associated with past high inflation episodes, broad money represents 14.25 percent of GDP. Latin American reformers had much smaller equity markets when the capitalization regime was introduced. Indeed, market capitalization was 12 percent in Chile in 1985 and 6 percent in Peru in 1992. The real challenge hinges on implementing a strong regulatory body to supervise private pensions and finding a way of financing the implicit pension debt.

CONCLUDING REMARKS

Following the generous pension promises granted by the 1988 Constitution, the actuarial imbalance of the pension system has accelerated. Prior to the stabilization plan, these imbalances were hidden by inflation erosion of benefits and unusually high interest income. Since the third quarter of 1994, however, the early success of the stabilization program has uncovered the true dimension of the fiscal crisis. States are finding it very difficult to meet pension and wage expenditures for civil servants, and the main pension scheme covering private workers and SOEs is facing growing operational imbalances. The amendments for social security in the 1996 Constitution do not address the fundamental causes behind the deteriorating fiscal posture, which is also combined with significant labor market distortions.

Outlining directions for genuine change, as attempted in this chapter, is probably the easiest step. Finding ways of implementing changes of such magnitude despite the powerful vested interests for the status quo remains the true challenge. But nothing less than meeting this challenge will make Brazil join the club of true reformers in Latin America and face the rapid demographic transition that will take place in the next decades.

References

Rofman, R. 1995. "Effects of Social Security on Lifetime Income Distribution in Brazil." PSP Discussion Paper Series No. 74. World Bank Poverty and Social Policy Department.

Simonsen, M. 1992. "Economic Concepts and the Taxation System: Brasilia, Brazil." Paper presented at the Senior Policy Seminar "The Politics and Economics of Public Revenues and Expenditures." Brasilia.

Slemrod, Joel, and Shlomo Yitzhaki. 1996. "The Cost of Taxation and the Marginal Efficiency Cost of Funds." *IMF Staff Papers* 43.1 (March).

Usher, D. 1986. "Tax Evasion and the Marginal Cost of Funds." *Economic Inquiry* 24 (October).

van der Noord, Paul, and Richard Herd. 1993. "Pension Liabilities in Seven Major Economies." OECD Working Paper No. 1142. Paris.

World Bank. 1995. "Brazil: Social Insurance and Private Pensions." Report No. 12336-BR.

14 / Social Security in Ecuador

Mixed or Substitutive Reform?

Rubén M. Lo Vuolo and Carmelo Mesa-Lago

Ecuador's social security system has evolved in a fragmented manner, creating a stratified system along occupational lines. Unification under the Ecuadorian Institute of Social Security (Instituto Ecuatoriano de Seguridad Social, IESS) has not changed the significant degree of stratification and differences among the insured groups. Nowadays the majority of the salaried labor force as well as a few pockets of the self-employed are covered by the law on a compulsory basis. Legally excluded are unpaid family workers, workers in the home, most temporary workers, and the unemployed; however, any person eighteen years or older is entitled to voluntary coverage.

Ecuador shows one of the lowest rates of population coverage in Latin America and ranks the worst among the group of *intermediate* countries (Mesa-Lago 1989b). Reasons for such a low coverage are various. (1) In 1980, Ecuador was the country with the second-smallest formal urban sector (22.7 percent) in Latin America and also with the second smallest (after Bolivia) combined formal urban/rural modern sectors (36 percent). (2) In Ecuador's three regions (Coastal, Andean, and Amazonian) respectively, 52 percent, 40 percent, and 76 percent of the regional populations are rural. (3) In 1987 agricultural workers represented over one-third of the workforce.

Even though the system is administered by a central institution (IESS), its normative problems, privileges, and cumbersome rules much resemble those of the pioneer countries of the Southern Cone of Latin America. The Ecuadorian social security legislation has become a labyrinth of often contradictory and arbitrary regulations; attempts to reform it have not accomplished the task (Thullen 1987). The IESS suffers from massive overstaffing, high administrative costs, low investment returns, misused reserves for housing and consumer loans, and transfers from pension reserves to the health/maternity program. IESS has been recently hit by several scandals of fraud and mismanagement. There is a significant state debt to IESS, mostly because the state has not paid its legal obligation to transfer 40 percent of total pension costs. The IESS health/maternity program is out-of-step with the needs of the country, concentrated on urban areas, curative medicine, and the age groups with the least sickness incidence. The overall inefficiency of such programs is reflected in excessively long hospital stays, low occupancy rates in most hospitals, and obsolete and inoperative equipment, all of which prompts patients to use other services.

Ecuador has not yet implemented social security reform but there has been much discussion on the need for and type of such reform. There is an agreement on the technical problems of the system, but not on the model and concrete measures to solve them. At the beginning of 1995 the governmental agency in command of social security reform published a proposal for a substitutive type of reform, and discussion began on it (CONAM 1995), but a national referendum rejected the privatized pension program. Furthermore, the institutional crisis that led to the removal of the president and his replacement in 1996 resulted in a weak executive, and the reform process was halted at least until the end of 1997.

This chapter will first of all summarize the organization and problems of the Ecuadorian social security system. It will then consider the issues involved in the discussion on the reform. At this stage, no conclusion can be reached regarding the final result of the reform process.

THE ECUADORIAN INSTITUTE OF SOCIAL SECURITY (IESS)

Organizational Structure

The IESS manages several programs: old age, disability, and survivor pensions; sickness/maternity; occupational accidents and diseases; funeral aid; and severance pay (Mesa-Lago 1984, 1989a, 1992). In addition, the IESS administers the Peasant Social Insurance Fund (SSC), as well as special programs for mortgage, personal loans, various groups of insured, and so on. In

February 1993 the Social Security Law for the Armed Forces was enacted; the pension and health programs were separated from the IESS and an independent institute was created (ISSFA); the armed forces remained in the IESS.

There are divergent contributions and conditions for entitlement among the multiple groups insured by IESS, as well as several units performing similar functions. In 1963–1964 the separate public and private funds were unified under one central administration. However, the two funds became quasi-independent departments, lacking overall coordination and leaving intact the privileged treatment of special groups (information is still gathered separately from twenty-seven or thirty schemes). A plan to regionalize the IESS administrative functions was not implemented, thus contributing to disorganization and disarticulation of the administrative process and the sources of information.

The IESS has its own health facilities (such as hospitals, rural posts, medical staff, pharmacies), although in isolated areas it subcontracts from other institutions for the use of existing facilities. Other health facilities are operated by (1) charity institutions and municipalities; (2) the Ministry of Health (MOH), the largest health network in charge of preventive medicine; and (3) the Ministry of Defense, which administers facilities (reportedly the best in Ecuador) for military personnel and their dependents. There is no coordination among the various public health institutions in Ecuador. Duplications and significant gaps are common, especially between the IESS and MOH facilities.

Founded in 1968, the SSC provides basic protection to a segment of the rural population (mostly peasants) against the risks of sickness, maternity, old age, and invalidity. Financed mainly through a payroll tax levied on urban-based IESS insured and their employers, SSC is expected to provide primary health coverage to rural inhabitants enrolled through cooperatives, agricultural firms, producer associations, and traditional community groups. Although SSC is organizationally a dependency of the IESS, it retains considerable decision-making autonomy in terms of planning, investment, and operations. Essentially the SSC represents a separate social security scheme within the more generous overall IESS system. The SSC provides a limited package of primary health care while the IESS grants comprehensive coverage. Unlike the IESS, however, the SSC provides health coverage to the entire family, which is the principal enrollment unit. The head of household is responsible for paying the monthly premium.

Population Coverage

Ecuador is far behind the population coverage levels achieved by Latin American countries in a similar stage of development. Despite some modest advances, the rate of expansion of coverage is slow and largely determined by structural factors. According to Lo Vuolo (1993), once corrections are made the coverage may be estimated around 29–30 percent of EAP, 60–70 percent of salaried labor force, and 17–18 percent of total population.

In 1990 the labor force participation rate was 32 percent (CELADE 1992), far below those Latin American countries with mature social security systems. There is a large difference in rate between males (49.8 percent) and females (only 14.2 percent). According to the latest population census (in 1990), the percentage of wage earners in the EAP was one of the lowest in Latin America (42.5 percent); the percentage of self-employed (39.2 percent) combined with that of unpaid family workers (4.4 percent) was among the highest.

Ecuador has a large service sector (around 45 percent), an indication of significant informal employment, which is normally not insured. Another impediment to the expansion of coverage is the low population density and isolation of the Oriente (Amazonian) region. The more urban and developed region, the higher its social insurance coverage. However, inequalities in IESS coverage among Ecuadorian provinces are changing largely because of the impact of SSC, which now extends to all provinces.

Coverage of EAP accelerated in the 1970s but slowed thereafter. The most important step taken to break the structural barrier to universalization of coverage has been the SSC program. The coverage of this program is still very small but growing fast: in 1991 the SSC registered approximately 15 percent of Ecuador's rural population. A significant number of wage earners is actually not covered by social insurance because of evasion: in 1990 only 58 percent of salaried workers were insured.

Coverage of the total population grew slowly in the 1960s as new groups were incorporated into the system. This growth accelerated in the 1970s as a result of the SSC and, after a slowdown in the early 1980s, accelerated again after 1983 through the expanded coverage of peasants and other groups. A major reason for the low coverage of the total population is the virtual exclusion of dependents of the insured; their coverage is one of the two most restricted in Latin America.

Financial and Actuarial Balance

The IESS is basically financed by (1) wage contributions from the insured and the employer; (2) state contributions as a third party in addition to state contributions as employer; and (3) investment returns. Major causes of IESS financial disequilibrium are evasion, state and private debts, and payment delays. The current total percentage of wage contributions to the general system is 20.5 percent, which is excessively high if the low population coverage and the high dependency rate is taken into account. The general wage contribution assigned to SSC is only 0.7 percent, whereas the one paid by the peasants is based on the minimum agricultural wage. Since peasants are basically self-employed, they do not benefit from but are negatively affected by increases in the minimum wage.

The wage contribution varies significantly among insured groups and the scope of the salary tax base is not always the same. For instance, in the private sector the base includes all fringe benefits except the four "extra" monthly salaries paid annually, but in the public sector it includes only the basic salary. Therefore, the effective contribution rate is much smaller than the potential rate. On the other hand, the effective salary replacement rate is lower than the potential rate.

The law imposes several fiscal obligations on the state, in addition to its contribution as employer: (1) to finance 40 percent of the cost of pensions in the general system, both sections; (2) to pay military pensions; and (3) to finance special (additional) pensions for some occupational groups, including SSC. The nonfulfillment of most of these obligations resulted in a significant agreed-upon state's debt to the IESS. This amounted to $296 million for 1985–1993 alone.

There have been payment agreements signed in the past that acknowledged state debts. However, these agreements were systematically violated. The real value of the total debt is a matter of permanent discussion; in a 1993 actuarial balance, it was estimated at $508 million dollars in only the pension program (IESS 1993). According to this actuarial balance, which has been criticized because of its controversial assumptions, this amount represents more than the actual value of total receipts expected in the next ten years.

In addition, private and other public employers (including provincial and municipal governments) evade their obligations to the IESS (the private debt was estimated at the end of 1994 as $66 million). In practice, the IESS failed to use the numerous legal and administrative avenues to control evasion; high inflation rates stimulate noncompliance because interests and sanctions charged by IESS in the past were well below the market interest rates and inflation. Another problem is that the corresponding departments did not effectively control the obligations. Despite some progress in improving control of payment delays and collection of payments, the central government debt has not been paid off and crucial evasion and payment delays continue. At the end of 1994, however, the minister of welfare announced that 60 percent of the private debt had been collected. This point, however, could not be confirmed.

The law mandates that IESS must periodically fix contributions based on actuarial principles, but this has not been done. Since the same law leaves to the superior council of IESS the power to determine—in the annual budget—the necessary resources for each program, in practice IESS works with a global financial fund for the whole set of programs. A fundamental problem in evaluating the actuarial status of the IESS is the absence of adequate data. The most serious obstacle is the lack of reliable information regarding transfers from programs that generate surpluses (traditionally, pensions and occupational hazards) to those with deficits (sickness/maternity).

Initially, the pension program was a fully funded collective, that is, it applied the general-level-premium method and the solidarity principle. But in 1971 the IESS actuary recommended a shift to the scaled-premium method, which has been in practice ever since. Ecuador's legislation mandates an actuarial balance of the pension fund every three years, an obligation that has not been fulfilled. In fact, the pension system of Ecuador has never been properly funded. The sickness/maternity program is financed by a pay-as-you-go (PAYG) method, systematically generates a deficit, and did not have an actuarial evaluation for about fifteen years.

In 1993 actuarial analyses were undertaken at the IESS under the supervision of an internationally known actuarial expert (Bayó 1993). He projected that the sickness/maternity program will have an actuarial deficit of $146 million by 1998. To correct this deficit the current wage contribution for that program would have to be increased twofold: from 3.4 to 7 percent in 1993 and to 8 percent in 1998. The review of the IESS pension program revealed a more alarming deficit for the period 1992–2003, under various premises: (1) $512 million requiring an increment of the contribution from 7.39 to 12.5 percent, not taking inflation into account and assuming that the state would pay 40 percent of the cost of pensions; (2) $898 million and an increase of the contribution to 13.6 percent, taking inflation into account and assuming state payment of 40 percent of pension; (3) $1.9 billion and a raise of the contribution to 13.6 percent, taking inflation into account but assuming the state will not pay 40 percent.

All three estimates were based on the premise that new generations would be incorporated into the IESS, but if it were to be closed (in a privatization model of reform à la Chile), the deficit would increase by $2.2 billion and the contribution would need to be increased to 32.9 percent. A combination of the above two programs with the remaining ones—administrative costs, dismissal, sick leave, occupational risks, funeral aid, and peasant insurance—would, to achieve global actuarial equilibrium in the IESS in 1992–2002, require increases in the total contribution from a current 20.5 percent to 29.2 percent, 30.3 percent, or 39.3 percent according to divergent assumptions.

Investment

Regarding portfolio investment, the data are fragmentary and often contradictory. There are serious problems in reconstructing a series of total net assets, mainly with respect to investment returns, but available estimates suggest that it was equal to 5 percent of GDP in 1990, while invested assets equaled 1.4 percent (Mesa-Lago 1992). A recent study estimates that, at the end of 1993 and if the state debt is added, the total amount of IESS investments was equivalent to $1 billion (Pardo 1994).

Most investment benefits the actively insured and not the whole population, another example of the use of the IESS in favor of selected interest groups. The IESS investment is classified in two broad categories: (1) investment that is directly beneficial to the insured (*privativas*), such as personal and mortgage loans and hospital construction; and (2) investment that is not directly beneficial to the insured (*no-privativas*), such as bonds, bank deposits, shares, and real estate. *Privativas* investments have traditionally had considerably lower yields (normally negative) than yields generated by *no-privativas.* The percentage distribution of investment by the two types in 1989–1993 showed a decline in *privativas* from 67 to 47 percent in 1991 but an increase to 89 percent in 1993. Conversely, *no-privativas* grew from 33 to 53 percent and then decreased to 11 percent. In 1993 53 percent of total investment was in personal loans with a negative real yield of −16.5 percent; another 29 percent was in mortgage loans with a −24.3 percent yield. Because of these reasons, the annual real yield in 1980–1987 averaged −10 percent; it was −13 percent in 1991 and −20 percent in 1993. Possibilities for profitable investment in private stock has been very limited in Ecuador because only a few enterprises qualified to enter and trade in the stock market and there was no risk classification of firms. These and other circumstances led to a 46 percent decline in the real value of the IESS reserves in 1974–1990. Furthermore the amount invested (in constant sucres) decreased by a further 64 percent in 1991–1994.

The IESS lacks flexibility to take advantage of relatively safe and profitable opportunities for investment. The enactment of the law regulating the capital market in 1993 was a positive step. The law also created a monetary unit of constant value, which should stimulate investment in the market, but it would take time to generate alternative profitable investment instruments.

Investments are regulated by the IESS statutes and rules, which are based on the Social Insurance law. Additional regulations are: (1) the law of public budget; (2) the law of Monetary Regime and State Bank; and (3) the Law of Capital Markets. The budget law mandated that the minister of finance has control over all financial investments of public institutions, including the IESS, but in November 1992 the IESS was excluded from such a norm. Therefore, at least legally, IESS investments are now out of fiscal control.

However, the monetary authority (Junta Monetaria) had the right to regulate IESS financial investments. As a public institution IESS was mandated to present an annual plan of investments, under the provision that investments cannot last more than 180 days and less than 30 days. Thus, IESS was required to have large amounts of liquidity and virtually all its funds deposited in a current account in the Central Bank, which paid no interest. However, the Law of Capital Markets established that under no circumstances could the Central Bank freeze IESS deposits. But in practice the solution is political and subject to dispute; the liberalization of IESS deposits in the Central Bank or the eventual payments of the state's debt are regularly used by the government to exercise pressure on the IESS in order to force changes in that institution.

Benefits

The IESS insured are protected against practically all social risks and enjoy more favorable entitlement conditions than in most countries of the region. Benefits and entitlement conditions are generous or meager and strict, according to the power of pressure groups. Preferential treatment is given through legislation or contracts signed with the IESS. Insured groups with the best benefits are the most powerful and best organized and enjoy higher incomes (the military, teachers, miners, communications employees), while insured groups with the worst benefits have little political influence and lower incomes (domestic servants, the self-employed, artisans). In recent years, there has been some standardization of benefits and entitlement conditions, but significant and nonjustified inequalities still persist among insured groups.

The pension program not only covers old age, disability, and survivors, it also adds seniority pensions, four annual extra monthly pension payments, and a supplemental pension program for privileged groups. The overall age of retirement is fifty-five (for both sexes) with thirty years of contributions (this declines with age, for example, ten years of contribution at seventy years of age). Furthermore, one can retire with thirty-five years of work at any age and receive 81 percent of the average salary earned in the best five years. An insured who is dismissed with twenty-five years of work can retire at forty-five years of age with a reduced pension. The number of dependents with a right to survivor pensions is quite large and the maximum age of orphans with a right to pensions is twenty-five years, even if they are not students. Finally, all pensions can be accumulated with a paid job, and when the insured retires from the second job he or she is entitled to an increment in the pension.

Under the sickness/maternity program, in addition to medical-hospital-dental care the insured enjoys generous benefits such as part of the costs of dental prosthesis and contact lenses. Services received at facilities outside of IESS are fully compensated in most cases, and when prescribed medicines are not available at IESS, the insured can buy them in private pharmacies and be reimbursed. The insured has also the right to travel and receive medical treatment abroad when not available at home (few insured, however, are granted this right and the decision is arbitrary). In contrast, immediate family dependents are eligible for very few benefits: neither the wife nor the children of an insured male are entitled to any benefits. Until recently, the infant of a female-insured below one year of age was eligible for medical care but not for surgery and medicines, and children above one year of age still are not entitled to benefits. Ecuador is one of two countries in Latin America that does not provide full health care coverage to dependents.

Health statistics show significant gains in health status during the 1980s (La Forgia and Cross 1993). Infant mortality decreased from 72 to 53 per 1,000 births, with rural infant mortality falling from approximately 70 to 63. Maternal mortality declined from 2 to 1.6 (per 10,000 births). The total fertility rate declined from 5.35 (in 1979) to 3.83. Mortality rates because of transmissible and infectious diseases fell from 3.83 to 2.12. Mortality because of preventable disease (representing nearly 50 percent of total deaths in 1980–1981) was reduced to 37 percent by 1990–1991. The average number of days lost because of premature death decreased from 259 to 134.

Despite a significant improvement in health standards, Ecuador still does not compare favorably with other Latin American countries at a similar level of development. This is partly because of inequalities in access to health care services, particularly in marginal urban and rural areas. The philosophy of the IESS health program is incompatible with the current situation: it stresses predominantly curative medicine, focuses mainly on urban groups in the productive age bracket (the group with the lowest health risk), and emphasizes high-tech costly medicine. Little is spent on preventive medicine and—despite Peasant Social Insurance—coverage of the rural population is still minimal. Several indicators suggest overbuilt capacity, as well as overutilization and inefficient use of health facilities (Mesa-Lago 1992). In 1980 the cost of per capita health care at IESS was seven or eight times higher than the Peasant Insurance and the MOH. However, SSC epidemiological records suggest that it has had little impact on health conditions in the communities served by the SSC and that part of the problem rests in SSC's overemphasis on curative services (La Forgia and Cross 1993).

Although data on IESS current expenditures are not always consistent, expenditures are among the highest in Latin America if one takes into account that it has one of the lowest population coverages. This situation is partly explicable by liberal benefits and entitlement conditions, particularly in relation to pensions, which take the largest share of total benefits. Most of the investment for construction and equipment of IESS hospitals is allocated to provinces with the highest population coverage and number of hospital facilities. Studies of health demand show that IESS health beneficiaries are the least satisfied with the health system and that at least 180,000 of IESS insured have duplicate health coverage through the private sector (La Forgia and Cross 1993).

Administrative Costs

IESS administrative costs are also among the highest in Latin America and the world. The law mandates that no more than 5 percent of contributions is used for administrative expenses but, in practice, about 8 percent is actually spent. Between 1975 and 1990 the percentage of IESS administrative expenditures over current expenditures climbed from 11.2 to 41 percent (the third highest in the region); from 6 to 26 percent if total expenditures are taken into account. Although both real benefit expenditure and investment declined sharply in 1980–1990 (by 62 percent and 71 percent, respectively), real administrative expenditures rose by 93 percent.

The main reasons for the high administrative costs are excessive personnel, generous compensations, overall administrative deficiencies, and the high costs and inefficiency of the health program. There are 108 trade unions within the IESS who have salaries and fringe benefits well above those of the average insured. Nonmedical personnel increased 65 percent in 1981–1987, raising its share of total personnel to 48 percent. The number of IESS employees increased 56 percent in 1980–1992, but the rates of employees per 1,000 insured declined from 13.7 to 9.3. However, if peasant insurance is excluded, the ratios were 16.7 and 13.4. In spite of this decline such ratios are among the highest in the region (Mesa-Lago 1992). Until now IESS has not been much affected by the general policy of public employees reduction.

Bidding procedures are extremely cumbersome and they also favor big business and pushes prices up. There is no integrated system of accounting, and other administrative resources are seriously underutilized. Finally, because there is not a single ID for social security, taxes, or other fiscal activities, it is not possible to cross check data and to effectively control evasion.

THE REFORM PROCESS

Difficulties in Deciding the Reform

In May 1992 prior to the presidential election, there were no specific proposals in Ecuador to reform either the pension or the health care programs. There was, however, increasing polarization. At one extreme were those who argued that the IESS needed only a few partial reforms and who blamed external factors for the crisis (IESS bureaucracy, trade unions, leftist parties).

At the other extreme were those who wanted full privatization (entrepreneurs, conservative parties, and some international financing agencies). Building a consensus in the middle (for example, a mixed pension system) was an extremely difficult task. Some argued that the reform should be instituted in one quick step and that IESS should be dismantled. Another idea was to eliminate the IESS sickness/maternity and the SSC and to integrate the latter into the MOH. Propositions on privatization ranged from the privatization of all hospitals (both IESS and MOH) to the maintenance of public sector health programs, but permitting the subcontracting of the proper services with the private sector and gradually reducing the public sector role (Mesa-Lago 1992).

Even when there seems to be a general consensus with respect to the crisis of the social security system, there is no agreement about what kind of reform and regime should be established to replace the one functioning under the guidance of the IESS. Moreover, it is apparent that some of the pressure groups favor a reform by "default," that is, let the IESS fall down by itself and leave market forces to adjust the situation. Behind this idea is a strategy aiming to surpass the political constraints by means of isolating the IESS problem from the reform problem.

Instability and high turnover in the IESS leadership is an important element of the political turmoil over the matter. For example, between August 1992 and the end of 1994 IESS went through six executive directors. As a result, every matter related to the social security problem was discussed again and again, and the director did not have time to develop and apply policies.

The autonomy of IESS is a key element in the political environment of the reform. The director of IESS does not necessarily represent the government interest; furthermore, it is common that, once in office, the director will oppose the executive by assuming the representation of the interest groups within IESS. Any time the government advances a proposal to control the administration of IESS or to change the legislation, there is frank opposition from the bureaucracy, the unions, and the direction of the institute. As a result, the director usually leaves office in the middle of an open confrontation with the government. Some people argue that, because the government does not give the director any political support, he needs to get such support from the unions and the bureaucracy.

Given the autonomy of IESS, a central question in the reform process is, Who within the executive should take the command of the reform process? In Ecuador, the reform of the social security system is not limited to one department of the executive but a group of them; hence much of the discussion relates to the political appointment of the official responsible for the reform process. The government answer was to have a "collective" approach.

At the beginning of 1993, an executive committee of reform was established made up by the general secretary of public administration, the president of CONADE (planning agency), the ministers of finance, public health, and social welfare, the president of the Monetary Board, and the IESS director. The committee was not able to develop a proposal. The most important action was taken in October 1993, when the committee designated a technical commission to coordinate international technical assistance and to elaborate such a proposal. When this commission produced the first proposal of pension reform, it was not endorsed by the committee but was taken as merely one more working paper. Members of the committee, in turn, hired other domestic and foreign experts, who then produced other proposals.

Meanwhile, many changes in the economic, political, and social environment are degrading IESS services and the very legitimacy of the institution. For instance, the separation of the armed forces from IESS means that the deficit of this privileged group—the one with the best benefits—must be covered by the Treasury. Also, the armed forces may be separating from the regime to maintain their privileges in case privatization occurs. Another important element in the process of reform is the Law of the Capital Market enacted in May 1993, which authorizes the creation of private pension funds on a voluntary basis.

At the same time, the government gradually advanced its thought in the matter. In June 1993 it published the "Agenda para el Desarrollo," which set a development plan for 1993–1994. This document explained IESS problems as a result of its constitutional "monopoly": the problem was lack of competition, hence the need to create private enterprises in order to administer pension funds and health insurance. The document does not clarify the role of IESS in the new scheme but affirms the need to radically reform it.

The political determination to reform social security seemed to gain strength when the National Council for the State Modernization (Consejo Nacional de Modernización del Estado, CONAM) took command of the matter. CONAM is responsible for the coordination and supervision of the whole process of state reform. This council was created by the Law for the State Modernization, enacted at the end of 1993. The president of CONAM is an independent figure coming from the private sector.

In May 1994 a presidential decree created a new smaller social security commission with, as members, a representative of the president, the executive director of CONAM, the minister of finance, and the executive director of IESS. Almost immediately, the commission approved the main lines of an official proposal for a pension reform. At the beginning of 1995 CONAM published its social security reform proposal divided in two parts: pension and health reforms (CONAM 1995).

At the same time, there was another official group working on a health reform proposal—the Comisión Interinstitucional de la Reforma del Sector Salud (Comisión), headed by the MOH. This Comisión was an interinstitutional group, convened in 1994, made up of the representatives from the major groups both public and private currently providing health care in Ecuador. One striking aspect was that the appointed bodies—the Comisión and CONAM—were similar in terms of the overall structure and guiding principles, but they developed independent proposals. More limited (and very preliminary) plans have been put forward by IESS and some private groups.

Reform Options

The existing technical proposals agree that the social security system of Ecuador must be drastically reformed. The recent actuarial reviews indicate huge actuarial deficits in the two major programs (pension and sickness/maternity). The few programs with potential surpluses lack an actuarial evaluation and do not appear able to compensate for the financial and actuarial problems of the major programs. The needed increases in contributions to restore equilibrium are politically nonfeasible unless a radical reform of the whole system is implemented.

There are three alternatives or options for a pension reform in Ecuador. First is the maintenance of a radically transformed IESS as the fundamental social security institution of the country. Second is the creation of a mixed system combining a reformed IESS with various degrees of private-sector participation. Third is full privatization of the system (shutting down the IESS and substituting it with an FFI privately managed system) combined with a welfare program of minimum pension. There is not much support for the first option and the discussion seems to be confined to the latter two (Mesa-Lago 1992; Lo Vuolo 1993; Primamérica Consultores 1994a, b; CONAM 1995; Vittas 1992).

Technical reports and reform proposals commonly suggest the restructuring of IESS in order to make it financially viable. Because the contribution burden is already heavy, the advice is to reduce expenditures through various measures: (1) the elimination/reduction of some pension benefits such as seniority pensions, extra monthly pensions, payment of minimum wage to the special retirement pension, rights of parents and brothers and sisters to survivors pension; (2) the termination of privileged programs available to a few insured groups; (3) the standardization of entitlement conditions for all insured groups and the increase of the retirement age; (4) the suppression of generous health care benefits; (5) a drastic cut in administrative expenditures, including reduction in personnel; (6) a change in the predominantly curative orientation of health care to give more resources to preventive care as well as to repairs and reequipment of existing facilities over construction of new facilities. There are also various suggestions as to how to raise revenues: (1) to make uniform the percentage contribution paid by all insured and to use the full salary as a contribution base; (2) to control evasion and payment delays and to fix the overall state contribution to IESS, based on a more realistic fiscal capacity; (3) to increase the real yield of investment by changing the composition of the IESS portfolio and to maximize investment in high yield instruments (4) to establish the needed contribution for each program in order to transfer part of the premium from those with superavits to the ones with deficit; (5) to sell unprofitable enterprises; and (6) to modernize the capital market to allow investment in stock.

The proposals aiming to maintain a pillar on a PAYG basis take into account the demographic data of Ecuador. Given the young age of the population, there is no demographic aging problem in this country; EAP is actually increasing at a very high rate. During the 1960s and 1970s, it was growing less than the total population but still at an average rate of 2.5 percent. In the 1980s, the average rate increased to 4.5 percent (Sierra 1994a, b).

The problems of the Ecuadorian pension program cannot be compared with those of the most mature pension programs in Latin America. The latter show "systemic" crisis, mainly caused by universal coverage and deep financial deficits based on the low ratio between active insured (contributors) and pensioners. In these countries, apart from generous benefits and entitlement conditions (as in Ecuador), pressures arise mostly from (1) the erosion of the pension fund's reserves and the impossibility to run on a PAYG system, given the fall of the active/passive ratio; and (2) the political power of urban pensioners (because peasants constitute a weak force). These problems are not present in the case of Ecuador. In 1990, pensioners represented only 15 percent of the population fifty-five years or older; 7.2 percent among those sixty-five years or older. No more than 30 percent of the EAP is effectively insured. Therefore, the crisis of the Ecuadorian system cannot be explained by "maturity" of the system but it is related to the irrationality of the model in force.

The crisis of the Ecuadorian pension system is the result of a combination of factors: faulty design features, inefficient administration, and exogenous factors (government debt and interference, inflation, lack of profitable investment alternatives, and so on). This explains why the system dependency rate is much higher than the demographic one: many workers evade contributions and many pensioners are below the normal retirement age. Here seems to be another agreement: the internal flaws of the system and the macroenvironment (stability, modernization of capital market, and so on) should be corrected before any more fundamental reform is undertaken in order to lower the burden toward future pensioners.

The case of health care is different from that of pensions. First, there is a disconnection between MOH (in charge of primary care and public hospitals) and IESS facilities. Second, there is not an IESS monopoly in this area but various actors providing health services (MOH, armed forces, private sector, for example). Furthermore, the IESS has lower coverage than the MOH.

In Ecuador mortality and morbidity because of infectious diseases and nutritional deficiencies remain the main killers of children, specially in rural areas and among indigenous subpopulations (La Forgia and Cross 1993; Rand 1995). At the same time, the country is undergoing the process of morbidity/pathological transition, and the incidence of noncommunicable diseases has risen significantly. Cardiovascular diseases and cancer are the main causes of adult mortality and constitute a rising share of hospital admissions. Therefore, more pressures from the cost side of the health problem should be expected.

The technical reports addressing the Ecuadorian health sector problems are in agreement: (1) health outcomes vary, more than they should, between rich and poor as well as between regions; (2) the quality of service delivery should be improved; (3) major inefficiencies exist; (4) the costs and unmet demands on the present system exceed current sectorwide resources (Mesa-

Lago 1992; La Forgia and Cross 1993; Rand 1995). The discussion regarding health reform seems to be confined to how to provide a framework for integrated planning of health care through creation of a single mechanism for distribution of funds. In principle, the major proposals do not support the alternatives of single-payer or multipayer systems.

The Official Proposal

At the end of May 1994 the Social Security Commission approved a document entitled The Main Lines to Reform the Ecuadorian Pension System (*Lineamientos para la reforma del sistema de pensiones de Ecuador*). The document was very general and identified two mutually consistent projects. One was the reform of the current IESS pension program and the other was the creation of a new system with two integral components: a basic pension and a complementary pension based on individual capitalization. The document stressed the need to separate the pension and the health/maternity programs and briefly pointed out that an alternative to the latter would be based on private management. It also suggested a set of measures to improve IESS investments. Even when the document did not select a specific model to be adopted, it specified two options to be studied: a mixed system (with two pillars, as in Argentina and Uruguay) and a substitutive system (FFI with a guaranteed minimum pension, as in Chile). In both options, the administration of individual accounts should be done by private corporations. Affiliation to the new system would be mandatory, and any kind of compensation to current IESS insured would be a matter of future analysis.

When CONAM published its proposal in January 1995, it was clear that the official option for pension reform was a substitutive model à la Chile (CONAM 1995). This document rejected any other alternative and assumed that an FFI privately managed system would have positive effects on the capital and financial markets, less political influence, more specialization, and better incentives to save. The main source for this proposal was the work done by Primamérica, a private Chilean corporation that had been advising the commission since the very beginning (Primamérica Consultores 1994a, 1994b). The main features of CONAM's proposal were: (1) separation of pension and health within the IESS as a first step; (2) shutting down the public pension program (IESS) and transferring all insured under thirty (as well as mandatory incorporation of future generations) to the new FFI system managed by private corporations in competition; (3) guarantee of a minimum pension by means of a payroll tax of only 0.5 percent, which will be under public control but administered by the same private corporations (this is the main difference with the Chilean model); (4) recognition of past contributions to IESS issuing a public bond, which will pay 4 percent real interest rate and will be charged against the state's debt; (5) transfer of the SSC's contributions to the health sector, so this program will not have contributions for pension benefits; (6) financing would be increased by means of raising the payroll tax and applying the tax to the worker's entire salary. This proposal is for an extreme reform for Ecuador; much of the data used to support the arguments were based on assumptions that were highly disputable and projections that have not been publicized.

CONAM has elaborated a proposal for health reform, too. At the same time, another proposal was elaborated by the Comisión Interinstitucional de la Reforma del Sector Salud. This proposal was not formulated in an official document but in different papers sponsored by the Comisión that did not clearly represent a consensus position of its members (which include representatives of various institutions). In summary, there were two official bodies working on different proposals for health reform.

The health reform proposals developed by the two appointed bodies were similar in terms of the overall structure and guiding principles (Rand 1995). Both groups proposed a national health insurance system that would completely restructure the health care sector through the introduction of a new financing system, reconfigure and greatly expand the insurance system and create a new delivery system. Just as the proposal to reform the pension system resembled the one undertaken in Chile, the proposals on health care reform drew heavily from recent reforms in Colombia (a group of Colombian experts in fact advised both the Comisión and CONAM). The CONAM and Comisión proposals differed in some key operational details, such as in the specification of the cross-subsidy mechanisms, design of the benefit package, and calculation of the capitation rate.

Given the similarities between the two proposals and the fact that the CONAM proposal was the proposal attached to pension reform, we refer to it in order to highlight the main features. (1) As in the case of pension, financing would be increased by raising the tax and applying the tax to the worker's entire salary but also, in the case of health, by broadening the population base of insured who are contributing to the system. (2) The population coverage would be extended to the worker's dependents. (3) The financing scheme involves two components: the contributive regime (that sector of the population that would directly pay for their health benefits) and the subsidized regime (those whose care would be subsidized by other sources). (4) The transfer of resources within the contributive regime and between the contributive and subsidized regimes will be handled through a national health fund. (5) A new health insurance infrastructure would be created, wherein entities called *organizaciones promotoras de salud* (OPS) would function as insurance companies. (6) Instead of paying the obligatory contribution to the IESS, contributors would pay it to an OPS of their own selection, one of which could be IESS. (7) The OPS would sign up a provider network and must offer a predetermined standardized minimum benefit package to all members and could decide to supplement this minimum package. (8) The activities of the OPS would be controlled through an independent agency. As in the case of pension reform, rather than engage in a process of incremental and piecemeal reform, CONAM's health proposal chose a far more comprehensive and sweeping course. It fashioned an integrated reform that addressed multiple aspects of reformation of the governance and administrative structures, financing mechanisms, the devising of the insurance benefit package, and the creation of new delivery systems that could reconfigure provider practices.

FINAL COMMENTS

In 1995 it was clear that political commitment to go for a reform of the Chilean type in the case of pension and of the Colombian type in the case of health had gained strength. However, the proposals in both areas left out several important technical and political issues that need to be addressed. For instance, in the case of pension, Would it be possible to impose a mandated private system or should the new system be optional? Could the state pay the fiscal burden of the proposed change? Could the new system expand the low coverage of Ecuador? Would it be an assistance program? How much would it cost, given the low coverage of Ecuador?

In the case of health, the proposals would nearly double the portion of GDP devoted to the health sector. Here the questions dealt with assumptions regarding incentives, contributions, and the financial sustainability of the reform effort. The level of decentralization entailed in having the OPS collect the tax would make it difficult to monitor payments and create a substantial potential for evasion/graft in the transfer of surplus revenue to the national fund. Also, would the contributive regime be broad enough to generate sufficient revenue to fund the subsidized regime? The population covered by the subsidized regime and the benefit package extended to them would determine the extent to which the public sector can withdraw from the provision of supply-side subsidies.

These and other questions demand an answer before it is possible to have a clearer picture and to judge the rationality of the official proposals for social security reform in Ecuador. In addition, the executive did not have control of Congress, and its minority was even further reduced after the 1993 elections. The executive lacked power to pass a radical reform of social security in Congress and on November 26, 1995, called a referendum about constitutional reforms in an attempt to get direct support from the population. The referendum questionnaire included the de-monopolization of social security but the population rejected it by a majority. Furthermore, the major pusher of the substitutive model, the vice-president, was involved in a financial scandal and left the country. The election of the erratic and unpredictable President Abdalá Bucaram Ortiz in August 1996 led to considerable political instability and uncertainty and paralyzed the reform process. The removal of the president in February 1997 and the ensuing institutional crisis concerning his successor made the situation worse. Eventually the new president selected by Congress became an interim caretaker devoid of real power to undertake the reform.

At the end of 1997 there was no clear picture about the orientation of the social security reform in Ecuador. It could be either a substitutive-private system (as in Chile) or a mixed system (as in Argentina and Uruguay) in the case of pensions; and either an integrated system combining a public sector and a private sector managed by HMOs (as in Chile) or a mix of multiple providers (as in Colombia) in the case of health. What was certain is that for two years (1996–1997) the reform process was paralyzed and the IESS continued its deterioration. This deterioration could have been either a deliberate policy to facilitate a later drastic reform or the simple outcome of government inertia because of the political stalemate in those years. A commission of the World Bank in late 1997 began to explore the viable reform options again, in anticipation of the election of a new president in mid-1998, hopefully with sufficient power and commitment to get approved and implemented a social security reform protracted for seven years. It is hoped that the president will have the power and commitment to approve and implement a social security reform that has been under discussion for seven years.

Note

All references to dollars ($) are to U.S. dollars.

References

Bayó, Francisco. 1993. Informe de la valoración actuarial del régimen de enfermedad-maternidad. Quito: IESS, October. Mimeo.

CELADE. 1992. "América Latina: Población económicamente activa, período 1970–2000." *Boletín Demográfico* 25.49 (January).

Consejo Nacional de Modernización del Estado (CONAM). 1995. *Ecuador: Propuesta de reforma a la seguridad social.* Quito: CONAM. January.

Instituto Ecuatoriano de Seguridad Social (IESS). 1993. *Valuación actuarial del seguro de invalidez, vejez y muerte.* Quito: Dirección de Asesoría Matemático Actuarial, December. Mimeo.

La Forgia, Gerard, and Harry Cross. 1993. *Health Financing in Ecuador—A Challenge for the 1990s: A Strategy for USAID/QUITO.* Quito: The Urban Institute, August. Mimeo.

Lo Vuolo, Rubén. 1993. *Apoyo a la reformulación del sistema de pensiones de Ecuador.* Asistencia técnica para la preparación del programa sectorial financiero. Quito: BID, November. Mimeo.

Mesa-Lago, Carmelo. 1984. *Social Security in Ecuador: Final Report to the World Bank Public Investment Mission.* Washington, D.C., December. Mimeo.

———. 1989a. *Financial and Economic Evaluation of Social Insurance (IESS) in Ecuador.* Washington D.C.: World Bank. November 20.

———. 1989b. *Ascent to Bankruptcy: Financing Social Security in Latin America.* Pittsburgh: University of Pittsburgh Press.

———. 1992. *The Ecuadorian Social Security Institute (IESS): Economic Evaluation and Options for Reform.* Health Financing and Sustainability (HFS) Project. Quito: AID, September.

Pardo, Claudio. 1994. *Propuesta para el mejoramiento de inversiones del Instituto Ecuatoriano de Seguridad Social.* Asistencia técnica para la preparación del programa sectorial financiero. Quito: BID, February. Mimeo.

Primamérica Consultores. 1994a. *Diagnóstico del sistema de pensiones.* Santiago de Chile: Fundación Ecuador. Mimeo.

———. 1994b. *Propuesta de reforma al sistema de pensiones de Ecuador.* Santiago: Fundación Ecuador. Mimeo.

Rand. 1995. "Advancing Health Care Reform in Ecuador: Analysis of Current Options." Prepared for the IADB, January. Mimeo.

Sierra, Enrique. 1994a. *Ecuador: Población y tendencias demográficas.* Quito: BID, March. Mimeo.

———. 1994b. *Ecuador: PEA—Tendencias, estructura y características.* Quito: BID, April. Mimeo.

Thullen, Peter. 1987. *Informe sobre aspectos escogidos del seguro social ecuatoriano.* Quito, December. Mimeo.

Vittas, Dimitri. 1992. *Strategy for Pension Reform.* Informe al Secretario General de Planificación. Quito: CONADE, October. Mimeo.

15 / Poverty of Social Security in Guatemala

The Need for a Structural Reform

María Amparo Cruz-Saco Oyague

In contrast to most recent evidence that social security crises in Latin America are largely an outcome of disequilibria in the pension scheme (Mesa-Lago 1994), the crisis of the Guatemalan social security system is of a rather different nature. Admittedly, the pension fund of the Guatemalan Institute of Social Security (IGSS) will face an actuarial unbalance by the year 2000 because of the very limited expansion of active affiliates and the steady growth of pensioners. This process is aggravated by the historical depreciation of the pension fund because of negative real returns. However, presently, the crisis of the social security scheme is essentially its failure to protect the working classes and their relatives. The actual coverage of the population is 10 percent. Meanwhile two-thirds of Guatemala's people live in poverty. Thus, after several decades of a Bismarckian social security scheme it is obvious that the model is ill-suited to an extremely poor country. What is the type of social security reform most appropriate for Guatemala?

The purpose of this chapter is to provide a broad understanding of the reasons why social security in Guatemala needs to be structurally reformed. To this purpose in the next three sections we analyze coverage, benefits, and the financial balance of the IGSS. Then in the next two sections we suggest some general ideas for both a health care reform and a pension fund reform. We believe that the social security reform in Guatemala (which implies a health care reform and a pension fund reform) should continue to be articulated around a stronger and restructured IGSS in close coordination with the ministry of health (MSPAS) and the supplementary role of the private sector in both the provision of health care and the administration of additional pension programs. As a corollary we recommend solutions of the "reformed public" type or the "mixed" schemes type, instead of the adoption of a fully substitutive private solution. This belief is based on several arguments, including the extended poverty and extremely low coverage, the small size of the private sector's supply of medical health care in the interior, the incipient financial market, and the state's consistent evasion of its legal contributions to affiliates.

Fifty years have elapsed since the creation of the IGSS in 1946. Its mandate was to protect the working classes against occupational, health-related, and old age risks (Congreso 1946). Health care in Guatemala is provided by the private (modern and traditional practitioners) and public sectors, nongovernmental institutions, international agencies, and a handful of enterprises; the IGSS and the MSPAS are the most important providers. However, their coverage is one of the lowest in the region. Combined, the IGSS and the MSPAS spent less than 2 percent of GDP to provide health care to a population of 9.5 million, which translates as roughly $25 per person per year and which, evidently, is not enough to fund preventive and primary care, outpatient and hospitalization services, as well as investment expenses (Banco de Guatemala 1990, 1992). The IGSS and the MSPAS administer all existing health posts and centers, 80 percent of the beds, 55 percent of medical and auxiliary personnel, and 40 percent of hospitals. Almost all private clinics and hospitals are located in Guatemala City.

Despite some improvement in demographic indicators (MSPAS et al. 1992), Guatemala is still one of the three poorest countries in Latin America (the others are Haiti and Bolivia). According to the Estudio Básico del Sector Salud in Guatemala in 1991 (MSPAS et al. 1992), infant mortality rate was forty-one per thousand, although other estimates suggest a rate closer to fifty (CEPAL 1991). This rate—which is higher for the rural, indigenous population—is still the highest in Central America. Physical and human medical resources are insufficient, inefficient, and centralized in urban centers, Guatemala City in particular. Further, IGSS approach to health care is extremely curative and prescriptive, which generates high-cost services benefiting only a very small proportion of its affiliates.

The Guatemalan pension fund system is underdeveloped and stratified. It consists of a dozen funds with a broad range of different benefits and acquisition conditions. The IGSS's pension fund is fairly recent and the most important. It was implemented in 1977 and had 300,000 pensioners in 1992.

Next in importance is the public administration employees pension fund, with 120,000 affiliates and 30,000 pensioners. Third is the armed forces pension fund with 12,000 affiliates and about 1,500 pensioners. The rest of the system is made up of very small funds for journalists, artists, Central Bank employees, university professors, and so on. There are a few privately run pension funds for upper-income families, mainly through Guatemala's major banks.

COVERAGE

IGSS operates two programs: sickness, maternity, and accidents (EMA) and invalidity, old age, and survivors (IVS). IGSS evolved very slowly since its creation in 1946. The first program (accidents) was implemented in 1948 in five departments—Guatemala, Izabal, Sacatepequez, Escuintla, and Quetzaltenango. This program was gradually extended to the rest of the country. Three decades later, in 1978, its coverage was national. The next program to be introduced was maternity care in the department of Guatemala in 1953. With the introduction of medical care, the department of Guatemala, where the capital city is located, enjoyed full EMA coverage in 1968 (IGSS 1991).

By the end of the 1970s, EMA was also extended to eight new departments —Zacapa, Chiquimula, Baja Verapaz, Totonicapan, Sacatepequez, Jalapa, El Quiche, and Solola. Extension of EMA to these eight departments was based on purely political reasons.[1] A decade later, EMA was introduced in Escuintla. Here, the coverage was recommended by the International Labor Organization (ILO) and the InterAmerican Development Bank (IADB) after careful consideration of a new health model based on primary care.

Only ten departments out of twenty-two are currently covered for sickness and maternity. Medical care in the remaining twelve departments is left to traditional medicine and to the meager financial possibilities of the MSPAS. In these departments, the private sector is very small. In contrast to EMA, which operates in only ten departments, the IVS program has been implemented nationally ever since its creation in 1977.

IGSS defines its coverage in affiliates, pensioners, and beneficiaries (which include affiliates, pensioners, and their relatives: spouses, partners,[2] small and disabled children, and disabled parents). Table 15.1 shows that in twenty-five years population coverage (column 7) has increased only 7 percent points.[3] At an annual rate of coverage extension of 2.6 percent (accomplished

Table 15.1 Population Coverage under IGSS in Guatemala, 1950–1991

	(1)	*(2)*	*(3)*	*(4)*	*(5)*	*(6)*	*(7)*	*(8)*	*(9)*
1950	2,969.0	n.a.	184.2	—	184.2	n.a.	n.a.	n.a.	—
1965	4,568.4	n.a.	345.5	—	345.5	438.6	9.6	n.a.	—
1975	6,081.6	1,856.2	550.2	—	550.2	740.9	12.2	29.6	—
1985	7,963.4	2,360.4	631.7	44.3	676.0	1,025.6	12.9	26.8	70.1
1986	8,195.2	2,433.4	660.4	50.0	710.4	1,064.1	13.0	27.1	75.7
1987	8,434.3	2,508.7	679.0	55.3	734.3	1,102.5	13.1	27.1	81.4
1988	8,680.9	2,463.9	779.6	59.6	839.2	1,316.3	15.2	31.6	76.4
1989	8,935.2	2,542.5	788.4	65.1	853.5	1,531.0	17.1	31.0	82.6
1990	9,197.3	2,624.5	785.8	70.8	856.6	1,558.3	16.9	29.9	90.1
1991	9,467.0	2,712.5	786.9	77.9	864.8	1,555.2	16.4	29.0	99.0

Source: IGSS, Informe de Labores, various years.

Key:

1. Total population (in thousands)
2. EAP (in thousands)
3. Active affiliates (in thousands)
4. Pensioners (in thousands)
5. Total insured (active and pensioners, in thousands)
6. Beneficiaries (in thousands)
7. % coverage [(6):(1)]
8. % EAP coverage [(3):(2)]
9. % demographic pressure [(4):(3)*1000]

in 1965–1991), and considering a demographic growth rate of at least 2.8 percent, the IGSS would never reach full coverage unless the model of social security were dramatically changed.

Coverage of the economically active population, EAP, is presented in column 8. In forty-three years only one-third of the EAP has been covered. Reasons for this failure are explained partially by structural constraints. The EAP comprises one-third of Guatemala's total population, 2.7 million inhabitants in 1991. Only 37 percent of the population is adequately employed, that is, laborers working eight hours a day, or less if they choose to do so, and who receive a salary that is at least equal to the minimum salary in the designated economic activity. The rest—two-thirds of the labor force—is underemployed. By occupational categories, the EAP comprises 1.3 million salaried workers (48.4 percent), 0.9 million self-employed (33.4 percent), 0.5 million household or family workers (*trabajadores familiares,* 16.5 percent), and 40,000 business owners (*patronos,* 1.5 percent) (INE 1990). The proportion of salaried workers is low by Latin American standards.

According to the Bismarckian model, if only the salaried labor force were to be covered by IGSS, the deficit of coverage would amount to 40 percent (since 787,000 affiliates out of 1.3 million salaried workers are covered). If workers in all occupational categories of the EAP were to be covered, the deficit would amount to 70 percent (since only 787,000 affiliates out of 2.7 million EAP are covered). Employers and employees evade or at least delay their obligatory contributions to the IGSS at an increasing rate. An estimated 50 percent of private employers registered with the IGSS fail to contribute to the IGSS. Evidence suggests that this situation is related to several reasons, including the worker's urgent need for more additional income on a current basis; the perception that social security contributions are only a tax; the limited access to IGSS providers; and the perceived low quality of care and pensions.[4]

Based on the latest sociodemographic survey (INE 1990), we have estimated IGSS coverage's deficit for 1989. In table 15.2, our national estimate for the deficit is 92 percent, which in turn implies that IGSS's coverage of the total population is only 8 percent—rather than the 17.1 percent IGSS estimate for population coverage in 1989 (see table 15.1). Our estimate, however, is fairly close to projections by a Guatemalan independent research center, the Centro de Investigaciones Económicas Nacionales (CIEN), projections that give a figure of 10 percent for IGSS population coverage (CIEN 1992a, 1992b). IGSS do admit that their figures for total affiliates are probably inflated; evidence suggests that overestimation may be of the order of 40–50 percent.[5]

BENEFITS

The IGSS medical care program provides outpatient medical care, hospitalization, dentistry, medicines, and other services to affiliates. A monetary subsidy amounting to two-thirds of the salary is also provided. If hospitalization is for maternity care, the worker receives full compensation. Affiliates' relatives also receive coverage, that is, spouses, partners, and children (two-year-old children in Guatemala, five-year-old children in the next eight departments covered with EMA, and six-year-old children in Escuintla). Any injured worker is covered by the IGSS with medical service and a monetary subsidy when applicable. If the worker was not an affiliate, both the employer and the employee have up to three months to comply with their obligatory contributions. If the accident leads to physical disability or death, the worker or the worker's family is entitled to a pension or a survivor's pension. This legislation has led to "moral hazard" since the number of simulated accidents

Table 15.2 Estimates for the Uncovered Population in Guatemala, ca. 1989

	No. of Uncovered Persons (in millions)	*% of Population*
Uncovered persons ten years old or more	5.9	66
Inactive *(inactivos)*[a]	2.9	33
Underemployed (*subempleados*)[b]	1.8	20
Openly unemployed (*desempleados abiertos*)[c]	*	*
Subtotal	4.7	53
70% of uncovered EAP[d]	1.7	19
Minus correction for beneficiaries[e]	(0.5)	(6)
Subtotal	1.2	5
Uncovered children less than ten years old	2.3	26
Uncovered children five years old or younger[f]	1.0	11
Uncovered children between five and ten years old[g]	1.3	15
Subtotal	2.3	26
Total no. of uncovered persons	8.2	92

Source: Author's estimates based on INE 1990 and IGSS 1992c.

a. The economically active population includes all persons ten years old and more (INE, 1990). Note, however, that the Constitution dictates that children fourteen years old and less cannot be employed at all (República de Guatemala 1985, Constitución Política, art. 102, l.). "Inactive" are persons ten years old or more who are unemployed, do not actively seek a job, and are willing to be employed. They are basically self-employed, household or "family" nonsalaried workers, or are paid in kind, "informally." The survey uses "inactive" and "underemployed" to basically represent "informality."

b. Includes visible and invisible underemployment. Visibly underemployed persons work less than forty hours a week and wish to work more. Invisibly underemployed persons work forty or more hours a week with incomes less than the minimum wage in their designated activity.

c. The openly unemployed are a mere 58,000.

d. The remaining 30% is covered by IGSS.

e. This figure excludes spouses, partners, children, and parents of affiliates who are entitled to benefits.

f. Only 25% of children in this segment receive coverage through their parents. Approximately 15% of the population is under five years of age.

g. About 15% of the population is totally uncovered.

and incapacity certificates has risen substantially because of rent-seeking behaviors of workers.

Under the medical care program, if medicines can not be provided by IGSS's pharmacies, the insured pays for them and claims a refund from IGSS. Similarly, if the medical service can not be provided in Guatemala, affiliates or their beneficiaries can receive the treatment abroad. However, IGSS can refund only up to $25,000.

When the IVS program was implemented, the retirement age was set at sixty-five years. Based on the perception, however, that life expectancy was sixty-five, in March 1988 organized workers exerted pressure to reduce it to sixty years. (Note that retirement age should be based on life expectancy after retiring, rather than life expectancy in general.) The benefits of the IVS program include pensions and medical services. It covers three risks: invalidity, old age, and survivors. Eligibility for disability pensions includes payment of contributions for at least thirty-six months in the six years previous to the first day of disability and being less than sixty years old. The right to a retirement pension is obtained when the insured has made at least 180 contributions (fifteen years) and is sixty years old. Eligibility for a survivor's pension requires that an affiliate has contributed at least thirty-six months in the six years previous to the affiliate's death or that the affiliate was receiving a retirement or a disability pension. In the case of accident, eligibility is obtained if the contributor fulfilled the requirements for a monetary subsidy for accident. Funeral allowances can not exceed Q 125 (about $24). Survivors include widow or partner, children up to eighteen years (or more if they are disabled), and parents if they are disabled. Invalidity and survivors' pensions are based on the average of salaries paid in the last thirty-six months, while retirement pensions are based on the average of salaries paid over the last sixty months.

This average salary is called the base salary. Retirement pensions are subject to increases, which are calculated with reference to the total time of service. The pension can never exceed 80 percent of the base salary. In 1992 the minimum monthly pension paid amounted to Q 70 (ca. $13) and the highest pension, Q 1,800 (ca. $340) (IGSS 1992b). When contrasted with average salaries recorded by the Instituto Nacional de Estadísticas (INE 1992) for the same year, we found that the lowest monthly salary (Q 238) was paid in agriculture, silviculture, and fishing. Thus, the minimum IGSS pension was one-third the lowest wage in the formal sector.

In 1980–1991 the real value of the per capita pension decreased by almost 25 percent (see table 15.3). The annual average pension was Q 1,097.3 ($207) or Q 91 ($17.25) a month. This average is only 30 percent higher than the minimum pension of Q 70, which reveals that a vast majority of retired workers are located on the lower end of the pension's range. Analogously, in 1980–1991, per capita real expenses of the EMA program fell by 11.6 percent (Cruz-Saco 1993, table 17), which reflects a deterioration of services rather than gains in efficiency.

One of the main features of IGSS is the exclusion of twelve departments from the benefits of EMA. Consequently, potential beneficiaries have migrated to covered departments and their presence contributes to the shifting out of the demand curve for medical care in the ten departments where

Table 15.3 Average Pensions in Guatemala, 1980–1991

	Pension Payments[a]	*No. of Pensioners*	*Per Cap. Average Pension (in Q)*	*Nominal Pension*	*Inflation*[b]	*Real Pension*
1980	2,641.9	9,334	283.0	100.0	100.0	100.0
1981	4,893.5	15,823	309.3	109.3	111.4	98.1
1982	7,834.5	25,831	303.3	107.2	111.7	96.0
1983	12,476.2	32,611	382.6	135.2	116.9	115.7
1984	16,837.7	39,297	428.5	151.4	120.9	125.3
1985	20,023.2	44,251	452.5	159.9	143.4	111.5
1986	25,967.2	49,963	519.7	183.6	196.4	93.5
1987	30,064.8	55,301	543.7	192.1	220.6	87.1
1988	42,234.6	59,568	709.0	250.5	244.5	102.5
1989	51,239.2	65,087	787.2	278.2	272.4	102.1
1990	70,735.0	70,746	999.8	353.3	384.7	91.8
1991	85,521.9	77,940	1,097.3	387.7	512.3	75.7

Source: IGSS, Informe de Labores, various years.
Note: Inflation index: 1980 = 100.
a. Quetzals in thousands.
b. Average national inflation rate.

EMA is provided. There are important differences in physical infrastructure and medical coverage by departments (IGSS 1992c). Table 15.4, for example, shows coverage by department and some health production ratios. As can be easily recognized, the departments of El Progreso, Chimaltenango, Santa Rosa, Alta Verapaz, Petén, and Juliapa have received little medical attention.

The evolution of the EMA shows that urban salaried workers and public administration employees enjoy higher coverage than peasants and other rural workers in areas of less relative development. Urban workers, particularly in the department of Guatemala, enjoy the highest levels of coverage because of their ability to organize and exert political pressure. On the contrary, in the least favored departments the IGSS is absent. Notice in table 15.4 that over 50 percent of all affiliates reside in the department of Guatemala. Workers in the altiplano are excluded from the benefits of social security. Plant and equipment are deteriorating at a fast rate because of budgetary cutbacks and bureaucratic obstacles. In general, EMA operations are limited by often chaotic and centrally controlled procedures regarding procurement and distribution of medicines, drugs, and supplies, regarding the preparation and authorization of service contracts and administration of personnel, as well as by decisions regarding equipment purchase and repair.

The IGSS administrative costs have fluctuated around 15 percent of the

Table 15.4 Health Coverage in Guatemala, by Department

	Affiliates (in 000)	*Total Pop. (in 000)*	*Coverage (%)*	*Beds per 1,000*	*Doctors per 1,000*	*Occupancy Rates (%)*	*Av. Days of Stay*
Guatemala[a]	409.0	2,018.2	20.3	3.5	85.9	64.0	5.5
El Progreso	3.7	108.4	3.4	n.a.	8.0	n.a.	n.a.
Sacatepéquez[a]	15.2	180.2	8.4	3.2	24.3	33.1	2.9
Chimaltenango	14.3	343.8	4.2	1.4	6.3	8.9	7.2
Escuintla[a]	85.3	542.1	15.7	3.0	65.7	61.2	4.2
Santa Rosa	23.6	267.8	8.8	0.6	5.9	10.3	6.2
Sololá[a]	5.6	242.1	2.3	5.3	47.8	25.6	3.8
Totonicapán[a]	2.7	297.5	0.9	3.0	48.8	17.5	3.5
Quetzaltenango	34.1	557.8	6.1	3.1	26.4	38.2	7.7
Suchitepéquez	37.0	361.7	10.2	2.1	24.8	46.5	6.1
Retalhuleu	21.6	238.9	9.0	2.3	22.6	17.4	6.1
San Marcos	25.3	702.3	3.6	2.9	22.1	25.2	7.2
Huehuetenango	8.2	716.7	1.1	1.2	13.4	16.8	3.2
El Quiché[a]	7.2	574.7	1.3	2.7	32.1	22.2	4.6
Baja Verapaz[a]	4.3	184.5	2.3	4.6	55.4	33.1	3.4
Alta Verapaz	22.3	591.9	3.8	1.0	8.5	27.0	5.7
Petén	5.7	253.3	2.3	2.5	7.0	4.3	5.0
Izabal	37.9	326.4	11.6	1.5	13.2	29.2	5.5
Zacapa[a]	7.1	161.6	4.4	4.2	47.7	34.8	3.4
Chiquimula[a]	6.9	252.1	2.7	5.8	40.3	21.4	3.3
Jalapa[a]	3.6	190.8	1.9	6.7	47.3	28.1	3.0
Jutiapa	5.8	354.3	1.6	1.2	6.9	6.9	5.9
Total	786.7	9,467.1	8.3	—	—	—	—

Source: IGSS, Boletín Estadístico, 1992.
a. Department is covered by EMA.

total. There is an excessive growth of temporary workers. Some areas have excess personnel, while others have a shortage, which shows the need to reallocate personnel among different offices. Administrative procedures are very slow and information processes do not work. Most medical care production indicators show inefficiencies and excessive costs.

In terms of the gender composition of affiliates for the IVS program, the probability that a woman is covered is 1:2 (Cruz-Saco 1993, table 7). In the best scenario, it takes five months to initiate payment of pensions after fulfillment of conditions for eligibility. Monthly payments of pensions are made directly in the main office of IGSS in Guatemala City or through the department offices in the rest of the country. On payday, from very early in the morning, several hundred old, sick pensioners line up and wait for their checks, which are then cashed next door at the Banco de Guatemala, the Central Bank.

FINANCIAL BALANCE

The IGSS is funded with legal contributions—fixed percentages of wages—from the employee, the employer, and the state. The wage tax base excludes special supplements to salaries, which the state has granted in the past to compensate for real losses in income because of inflation. Such supplements represent some 30–40 percent of the affiliate's total wage. Only in the case of the IVS program can self-employed workers continue their affiliation through payment of both the employee's and the employer's contribution. The state does not collect any special taxes to supplement social security funding. Legal contributions (see table 15.5) have remained unmodified since the creation of the system. The total wage contribution, 17.5 percent, seems relatively high considering the IGSS's low coverage.[6]

Despite its legal obligation to contribute to the social security system, the government has amassed a huge debt with the IGSS. This debt amounts to approximately $170 million and represents twice the IGSS total expenditures (considering both programs and administrative costs) and 1.2 times the IGSS's pension fund. Similarly, the private debt—which includes unpaid obligations from the private sector, municipalities, and public enterprises (parastatals)—amounts to 40 million dollars, which, added to the government's debt, makes a total of $210 million, or 91 percent of the IGSS total assets (Cruz-Saco 1993, table 10).

Reasons for poor collection of revenues include the absence of administrative procedures to maintain and update the listing of registered establishments, and the lack of effective policies to enforce obligatory contributions in all establishments with at least three workers in the department of Guatemala and at least five workers in the rest of the country. According to

Table 15.5 Legal Contributions to Social Security Funding in Guatemala, by Program

(percent of wage or income)

Program	*Worker*[a]	*Employer*	*State*	*Total*
IVS	1.5	3.0	—[b]	4.5
Sickness, maternity	2.0	4.0	3.0	9.0
Occupational risks	1.0	3.0	—[c]	4.0
Total	4.5	10.0	3.0	17.5

Source: IGSS, Informe de Labores, 1992.

a. Voluntary contribution for independent workers is 4.5%

b. The state pays 25% of IVS payments and contributes as employer.

c. The state pays 3% of EMA expenses (the program for sickness, maternity, and accidents).

interviewed officials, some of these deficiencies could be prevented if IGSS were appropriately managed.

In addition to employers' and employees' contributions, which make up most of IGSS's revenues, another 20 percent is made up of financial returns mostly from the pension fund. Table 15.6 presents the evolution of the pension fund over 1980–1992. In 1992 the pension fund amounted to $133 million, 62 percent of IGSS's total assets and 17 percent of Guatemala's monetary base. In 1986–1991 the Banco de Guatemala kept these resources as deposits at fixed negative real interests. The opportunity cost the IGSS a loss of $80 million, the cumulative return that the IGSS could have made if the funds had been deposited in the financial system at competitive rates.

Beginning in 1992 the Banco de Guatemala gradually freed up these resources. But in November 1992, because of inflationary pressures generated by the additional liquidity implied by the transfer, the Banco de Guatemala managed to "recapture" these resources, this time paying competitive rates. The IGSS's lack of financial autonomy has affected the real value of the pension fund, which in over a decade has grown only 1 percent annually in real terms over 1980–1992 (see table 15.6).

There are at least two reasons why the Banco de Guatemala will prefer to keep the pension fund under close control. First, in 1992, freeing up those resources generated immediate inflationary pressures that the Banco de Guatemala wants to avoid in the future, even at the cost of incurring losses to pay a financial subsidy. Second, inflationary pressures are in themselves destabilizing, and end up in deflationary pressures on the exchange rate, which the Central Bank is also trying to avoid. The Bank will not jeopardize its stabilization program, now running successfully in its third year, with the approval of the International Monetary Fund (IMF) by letting the IGSS make portfolio investments with their pension fund.[7] The decision is therefore to keep those resources under tight control.

In 1983–1991 both programs—EMA and IVS—mounted to 84 percent of IGSS's total expenditures; administrative costs made the remaining 16 percent. In the total expenditures (net of administrative costs), medical services represented 60 percent on average, and pension payments 40 percent, which shows that the pensions scheme—though relatively young (it was implemented in 1977) had begun to mature. IGSS's total allowances for both programs represent 1 percent of GDP, and on average the MSPAS's current expenditures amount to approximately 1.2 percent of GDP. If we consider

Table 15.6 Growth of the Pension Fund in Guatemala

	Pensions Fund (millions $)	*Growth Rate*[a] *(%)*	*Pensions Fund/ Total Assets (%)*	*Nominal Yield (%)*	*Inflation*[a] *(%)*	*Real Yield (%)*
1980	119.0	—	57.0	9.0	10.7	(1.7)
1981	154.3	29.7	61.1	10.0	11.4	(1.4)
1982	185.3	20.1	72.1	10.0	0.2	9.8
1983	204.1	10.1	71.1	8.0	4.7	3.3
1984	228.2	11.8	70.9	8.0	3.4	4.6
1985	259.9	13.9	73.2	9.0	18.7	(9.7)
1986	118.5	(54.4)	70.0	10.0	37.0	(27.0)
1987	138.5	16.9	68.5	10.0	12.3	(2.3)
1988	149.9	8.2	64.6	10.0	10.8	(0.8)
1989	136.8	(8.7)	63.7	11.0	11.4	(0.4)
1990	106.8	(22.0)	65.2	13.0	41.2	(28.2)
1991	127.5	19.4	62.2	14.5	33.2	(18.7)
1992[b]	133.0	4.3				
1985–92	—	(48.8)				
1980–92	—	11.7				
Annual increase, 1980–92	—	1.0				

Source: IGSS, Informe de Labores, various years.

a. Figures in parentheses represent negative growth rates.

b. August 1992 only.

IGSS's medical care expenses only and if we adjust for population covered, IGSS spends about four times more on its 1.5 million beneficiaries (health care only) than the Ministry of Health spends on its 7.7 million, theoretically covered.[8]

In 1986–1991 IGSS's financial balance remained relatively stable, for two reasons: budgetary cutbacks in the provision of services and the absence of any substantial increase in coverage. The production of outpatient visits, outpatient drugs, and occupancy rates have dropped markedly. Allegedly, patients complain about the poor quality and ineffectiveness of IGSS's health services. At the same time, the number of pensioners is rising steadily (over 10 percent per year), which in less than a decade will affect the actuarial balance of the IVS program. Therefore, without even considering the extension of coverage, IGSS must inevitably face the need to restructure in order to extend coverage to currently uncovered working classes, to improve the quality of its services and, consequently, its institutional image, and to acquire financial autonomy to serve its affiliates and relatives.

A MODEL OF HEALTH CARE REFORM

Guatemala's first experience with a very basic primary health care model began in 1989 when coverage was extended to the department of Escuintla. This department is located on the southwest coast; it is highly populated, and it specializes in the production of coffee. With a 70 percent rural population, 80 percent illiteracy, 67 percent deficit in housing, and 74 percent of the children less than four with some level of malnutrition, Escuintla's population became the target for a primary health care approach to the extension of coverage (IGSS 1987a, b, c, 1988). Health care services were provided to affiliates and their beneficiaries (spouses, partners, and children six years old or less) at the same contribution rates that were applicable in the rest of the country.

The Escuintla model is based on four health care levels. The first level consists of ambulatory health teams who visit communities and households. Each team is led by a community health doctor and is made out of health promoters, sanitary inspectors, hygiene promoters, trained and auxiliary nurses, and social workers. Personnel is paid by the IGSS to act as liaisons between the IGSS and each municipality. They initiate contact with clients. Visits are cost efficient because several services are provided with one visit to the household, such as regular checkups and vaccinations for family members, sanitary education, or the promotion of hygiene in food preparation. The second level is represented by the habilitation of a medical office or health post for outpatient visits and short-term hospitalization only. The third level implies the referral of patients to the regional hospital. The fourth consists of the referral to specialized hospitals in Guatemala City (only fifty-eight kilometers away).

It turned out that the demand for health care services had been sharply underestimated. The new hospital in Escuintla, inaugurated to become the instrument for third-level health care, rapidly became very congested in spite of efforts to intensify preventive and primary care at the first and second levels. Additional health promoters and auxiliary nurses were hired at an extra cost. Medical supplies, medicines, drugs, and vaccines had to be reordered constantly. After several months the program seemed to be out of control. Costs doubled, while revenues were cut in half because of evasion and poor collection.

Administrative and financial problems notwithstanding, population coverage rose in Escuintla to 47.7 percent, much higher than the national average of 10 percent and the infant mortality rate dropped from seventy-seven per thousand in 1989 to fifty-eight per thousand in 1992 (PAHO 1991). Of all beneficiaries, 89 percent used IGSS services and the rate of vaccination reached 80 percent (it is only 60 percent on average for the country). In 1991–1992, the cholera epidemic (expected to infect several thousands) generated twenty-five hundred cases with a fatality rate of 0.2 percent. And yet the program reported the absence of any information system to perform planning, organization, administration, and control; the lack of means of transportation; the lack of literature and manpower to maintain the subprogram of continuous education; and very poor coordination with the MSPAS.[9]

The most important lesson learned from the model of Escuintla was that civil society could get organized under the auspices of the IGSS to provide an effective preventive health care system based on provider-initiated health services. Next, it was realized that the IGSS can provide this type of service with the support of the community and the participation of health teams under the leadership of a community health doctor. Important improvements in health indicators showed that the model was relatively successful, but that it needed some readjustments. In the first place, any future attempt to extend coverage should be closely coordinated with the MSPAS to avoid duplication of functions and the full use of their joint medical infrastructure. Second, extensions have to be demand-driven and based on sound estimations of the demand side to prevent bottlenecks. Third, cost estimations have to be on the conservative side to avoid cancellations of programs because of the absence of financial resources. And finally, the project requires a comprehensive information structure for planning and monitoring.

The type of reform that is proposed here considers as a precondition the restructuring of the IGSS and the MSPAS and the abandonment of a health approach based on the construction of hospitals and the expectation that clients will visit facilities when they feel the need for treatment. In view of the demographic and epidemiological profiles of Guatemala, the World Bank's recommendation for the implantation of a basic health package (World Bank 1993) seems effective because of the presence of a large indigenous population (37 percent), which has historically exhibited the worst health indicators (INE 1990), and because of the youth of Guatemala's population (45 percent of the country's total population is less than fifteen years old; less than 5 percent is above sixty years [Dirección General de Estadística

1985]). Efforts to lead Guatemala through its health transition are expensive, because health care services have to be provided to the rural 65 percent of the population that currently has very limited access to those services.

Implementation of the new model will inevitably face financial constraints that need to be overcome with enormous productivity and efficiency gains on the part of health administrators. As a share of GDP, for example, allocations to the MSPAS have never surpassed 1.2 percent. As a goal we could realistically expect a rate of 2–3 percent to be reached in the next few years with an extraordinary effort to support a health support program. At the same time, funding from external sources and donors can supplement governmental efforts but must never substitute them. The MSPAS would require a profound restructuring to address the needs of an approach that relies on preventive and primary health care based on the effective roles of health posts and centers and in coordination with the Ministry of Education. The basic program, which can be implanted at the first and second levels, entails essential public health care—expanded programs of immunizations, school health programs to treat worm infections and micronutrient deficiencies, provision of health education, sanitation, family planning, nutrition, educational programs to reduce the consumption of alcohol and drugs in general—and clinical services targeted at pregnant women (prenatal, delivery, postnatal care), treatment of tuberculosis, diarrheal diseases, upper respiratory infections, measles, and malaria.

For an efficient use of human and physical resources pertaining to the MSPAS and to IGSS, we propose that both institutions closely coordinate their activities and decide on specific areas of influence. It is understood that implantation of a new health model in Guatemala requires a substantial restructuring of the IGSS also, along the lines set forth in Cruz-Saco (1993). Based on the demographic and socioeconomic characteristics of the country, we have identified four subregions or markets: Guatemala City and its surrounding areas, the southern coast, the Altiplano, and the ladino East.

In Guatemala City a stronger IGSS could continue to provide curative outpatient visits, emergencies, and hospitalizations to its affiliates and their relatives. The IGSS should aim at full coverage of the salaried labor force and could, eventually, hire external providers to supplement coverage when a cost/benefit evaluation suggests that the opportunity cost of hiring services is lower. In coordination with the MSPAS, the IGSS should actively seek the provision of a basic health package to currently uncovered urban groups, particularly independent workers and the so-called urban "inactive" population, which amounts to over 2 million individuals, about one-third of the country's population. These sectors live in urban-marginal settlements, and expansion of coverage should include, initially, only the provision of preventive and primary health care attention.

In the south coast, extension of coverage should be monitored again by the IGSS (in coordination with the MSPAS), the employer or agro-exporting *finca* (farm) and private health care providers. Still under the scheme of health care insurance, preventive and primary health care attention should be delivered directly at the job center or in the settlement where workers and their families are living (*cuadrillas*). The Escuintla model with the four referrals should be basically followed. However, two important amendments should be introduced. First, employers (*finqueros*) should provide some minimal space and infrastructure for the implementation of the health post or more posts according to the perceived demand for services. Second, services could be provided by the IGSS or by any other private caretaker. Decisions should be based on the cost-effectiveness of each alternative. When a private caretaker is hired, the IGSS should make sure that services are of the quality and frequency required by affiliates and their relatives.

In the Altiplano, the health care insurance scheme is suboptimal because of extreme poverty and migration flows. We suggest that the MSPAS closely coordinates and monitors organized communities (either municipalities, nongovernmental agencies, or Indian community *asambleas*) and staffs them with teams of health promoters, nurses, sanitary inspectors, and so on, under the supervision of a community health doctor, who should work in approximately the same way that health teams work in Escuintla. MSPAS will also provide technical assistance, medical supplies, medicines, drugs, and vaccines. The existing IGSS and MSPAS facilities, health posts, centers, and clinics should be integrated under one administration; they should be reequipped; and the referral system to regional and specialized hospitals should be strengthened.

In the east ladino subregion, with a scattered population, the IGSS, the private sector, and the MSPAS should coordinate the provision of the basic health package. We suggest that the IGSS specializes in curative care, emergencies, and hospitalizations. Further, the private sector should supplement IGSS's functions, and the MSPAS should specialize in preventive and primary health care only.

Basically, what this proposal does is redefine the roles of the IGSS, the MSPAS, and the private sector. It relies on a stronger IGSS for health care in the capital city and for the coordination of health care in the south coast. It limits the IGSS influence in the Altiplano and it relegates it to a more specialized role in the ladino area. The private sector supplements the IGSS anywhere in the country. To the extent that the private sector can achieve higher levels of cost-effectiveness, the IGSS could be detracting from the direct administration of such services. Finally, the MSPAS should also be restructured and strengthened. As "head" of the sector, it possesses regulatory functions to normalize the articulation and transparency of the health sector. At the same time, it assumes the cost of extending preventive and primary health care to the Altiplano.

ISSUES IN THE PENSION REFORM

The debate on the need to reform the pension fund system in Guatemala began in 1992, when CIEN proposed the adoption of a fully private pension fund scheme (CIEN 1992c). However, in 1993 central attention was given to the constitutional reform. Thus, public interest shifted away from the issue of the privatization of pensions.

There are several reasons why a fully substitutive pension system in Guatemala would face structural obstacles. First, Guatemala is a fragile democracy that will make the adoption of a privatization model very difficult because of opposition from strong interest groups (unions and workers' organizations, university professors, institutional opposition from agencies such as the IGSS, and current pensioners) to the reform, in similar ways to what have been seen in the rest of the region. An enormous distrust in government suggests that it will not honor recognition bonds or contribution years or measures to compensate low individual pension funds that cannot pay decent pensions at retirement.

Second, the cost of the transition from one scheme to the other represents a substantial fiscal effort because the state will have to honor affiliates' pension contributions and a minimum annual return. The Guatemalan state, however, has traditionally failed to comply with its legal contribution and has amassed a phenomenal debt with the IGSS (1.7 percent of GDP). What is the probability that it will honor payment of pensioners' funds?

Third, when Chile adopted its substitutive private scheme, health care coverage of the population was almost universal. In Guatemala the exception is covered. When social security is privatized, it loses its solidarity component. Since the majority of the population will not have access to private insurance, will the state increase the availability of public funds for public assistance, primary care, regular health care, and so on for the vast majority?

Fourth, privatization of pension funds rely on a stable, relatively well developed financial market that offers long-term instruments to pensions administrators. Guatemala's financial market is tiny and needs to undergo an institutional reform too. Should the privatization of pensions await the successful completion of the financial reform, which would help develop long-run instruments, could it be simultaneously implemented?

Fifth, the Banco de Guatemala kept the IGSS pension funds captive for several years. When part of the funds were freed and the IGSS deposited them in the banking system, inflation rate rapidly surged. Immediately, the Central Bank called those funds back. What are the conditions that the Central Bank will impose for a full privatization of pension funds: higher economic growth rates or investments in foreign denominated financial assets?

Finally, the Chilean economy underwent extensive institutional reform and modernization over more than five years before its pension reform was introduced. Before the reform was introduced, benefits and acquisition conditions were standardized. Similarly, in the case of Peru's social security reform (adopting the substitute private scheme), the economy is also undergoing substantial institutional reform. Is it possible for Guatemala to initiate a dramatic change in its pensions regime that is not seconded by similar changes in its economic context?

It is too early to anticipate the sort of reform that Guatemala will implement. However, in view of the questions that we raised, the best solution should be a feasible and sustainable one, a compromise between various different institutions (see also recommendations laid out in chapter 17) that lies somewhere within the range of a reformed public scheme or a mixed scheme with supplemental pensions. For example, the IVS program should continue to be mandatory and the state should guarantee a universal minimum basic pension. At the same time, privately administered pension funds could be voluntary and supplement the basic pension regime. Guatemala may consider the initial Mexican experience of introducing a supplemental voluntary system of individual capitalization to begin to develop a private program in a straight and regulated manner. We do recommend that the pension reform encourages the development of a private market for pension funds.

CONCLUSIONS

In order to reduce the incidence of poverty, Guatemala needs to formulate a new health care model, one that addresses the problems of the very poor: preventive and primary health care, and the needs of its very young population. The IGSS has had a limited expansion of coverage. It needs to be restructured and strengthened to support the MSPAS's agenda for a healthier Guatemala. We have suggested that the new health model should be based on the participation of both the IGSS and the MSPAS. The IGSS should become the main supplier of a basic health package in Guatemala City, its surrounding areas, and in the south coast. The MSPAS should lead the provision of a similar package in the Altiplano and in the ladino region with participation of organized communities. While both the MSPAS and the IGSS should coordinate their functions, the regional segmentation of the markets will induce a more rational use of existing infrastructure and will minimize duplication of functions. The new approach should be based on a provider-initiated health service and the effective use of four levels of attention: health posts, health centers, regional hospitals, and specialized hospitals.

The private sector should be allowed to operate at any level. The IGSS should seek to compete with external services. Decisions for the provision of medical care should be based on a cost/benefit analysis of IGSS's services as opposed to the private sector's services. If the private sector is more competitive, the IGSS should detract from the administration of medical services. However, the IGSS should continue to supervise and evaluate the quality of the attention received by its affiliates.

Although the IGSS's pension fund is not facing a crisis now, a crisis will surely hit in another ten years or less. Full privatization of the IGSS's pension fund faces some difficulties because of the smallness of the financial sector, the poverty of the working classes, very small coverage, the fact that the democratic process is still unstable and fragile, and the lack of financial support on the part of the state. We believe that a mixed solution is optimal. It will maintain the administration of the pension funds with mandatory contributions by the IGSS, but at the same time, it would create the necessary conditions for the development of a parallel market for private supplemental pension funds.

Notes

1. Interviews with Alfonso Morales Sandoval, director of Medical Health Care Services, IGSS, on November 24, 1992; and Héctor Colindrés, advisor to MSPAS, on November 24, 1992.

2. OGSS covers the female partner *(compañera)*, often the mother of the affiliate's children. Female partners are covered but not male partners.

3. There are at least three sources for the overestimation of affiliates and the total figure of beneficiaries. First, estimates of affiliates are formulated by IGSS based on a sample of payrolls and surveys taken each January. Because of seasonal labor requirements in agroexporting activities (coffee, cotton, sugar), payrolls in January are inflated with respect to the annual average. Second, this estimate is not corrected for duplicate entries, laid-off workers, deaths, partially or totally disabled workers, and so forth. Third, figures for spouses, partners, children, and parents are estimated by a fixed ratio. An updated, electronically operated register of affiliates does not exist.

4. Interviews with Juan Francisco Ramírez Alvardo, director of Financial Administration, IGSS, on December 15, 1992; Victor Hugo Ramos, Collections Department, IGSS, on November 22, 1992; and Walter Enríquez, Inspections Department, on November 19 and December 14, 1992.

5. Interviews with Maria del Carmen Aceña, CIEN, on December 16, 1992; and Raúl Sosa, Actuarial and Statistics Department, IGSS, on November 22 and December 15, 1992.

6. Guatemala ranks thirteen in twenty-five countries regarding contributions (as a percentage of wage or revenue) to social security and ranks among the five countries with the lowest coverage in Latin America. See McGreevy 1990, annex tables 2, 9.

7. Interview with Maria del Carmen Bonilla, vice-president, Banco de Guatemala, on January 24, 1994.

8. Technically we should exclude about 0.5 million people who are covered by the private sector and nongovernmental organizations. As expected, funds available to the Ministry of Health (about Q 44 or $8 per person per year) are totally insufficient to pay for basic primary health care. There is some external aid; however, it is very small in terms of need.

9. Interview with Héctor Colindres, advisor to MSPAS, on November 24, 1992.

References

Banco de Guatemala. 1990. *Estadísticas de las finanzas públicas, 1960–1989.* Guatemala: Banco de Guatemala.

———. 1992. *Estadísticas monetarias varias.* Guatemala: Banco de Guatemala. Mimeo.

Centro de Investigaciones Económicas Nacionales (CIEN). 1992a. "Salud, lineamientos de política económica y social." Part of the project "Lineamientos de política económica y social para Guatemala, 1991–1995," July. Guatemala: CIEN. Mimeo.

———. 1992b. "Previsión social, lineamientos de política económica y social." Part of the project "Lineamientos de política económica y social para Guatemala, 1991–1995," July. Guatemala: CIEN. Mimeo.

———. 1992c. "Informe al Congreso, no. 19." El sistema de previsión social en Guatemala. September. Guatemala: CIEN.

Comisión Económica para América Latina (CEPAL). 1991. *Anuario estadístico de América Latina y el Caribe, 1991.* Santiago de Chile: CEPAL.

Congreso de la República. 1946. *Ley orgánica del Instituto Guatemalteco de Seguridad Social, decreto no. 295 del Congreso de la República del 30 de octubre de 1946.* Guatemala: Congreso de la República.

Cruz-Saco Oyague, María Amparo. 1993. *El Instituto Guatemalteco de Seguridad Social (IGSS): Evaluación económica y alternativas de reforma.* Informe Final de Misión IDB. Guatemala: Banco Interamericano de Desarrollo.

Dirección General de Estadística. 1985. *Guatemala: Estimaciones y proyecciones de población, 1950–2025.* Centro Latinoamericano de Demografía and Agencia Canadiense para el Desarrollo Internacional. San José, Costa Rica: Edit. Texto.

Instituto Guatemalteco de Seguridad Social (IGSS). 1987a. *Resumen de conclusiones y recomendaciones I Seminario Taller "Nuevas estrategias de salud para la extensión de los programas de enfermedad maternidad a la costa sur occidental del país."* Antigua, Guatemala: IGSS. October.

———. 1987b. *Marco de referencia para la extensión de los programas de enfermedad maternidad a la costa sur occidental del país con énfasis en nuevas estrategias de atención en salud.* Comisión de extensión de los programas de cobertura a la costa sur (enfermedad común y maternidad). II Seminario Taller "Nuevas estrategias de salud." Antigua, Guatemala: IGSS. October.

———. 1987c. *Análisis de las prestaciones en servicio (salud) y de la situación económico financiera del régimen de seguridad social.* Anexo. Solicitud de cooperación técnica para la factibilización de la extensión de los programas de enfermedad y maternidad a la costa suroccidental del país. Guatemala: IGSS. May.

———. 1988. *Diagnóstico situacional costa suroccidental de Guatemala.* Informe final. Comisión específica para el estudio de la extensión del programa sobre protección relativa a enfermedad y maternidad a la costa suroccidental del país. Guatemala: IGSS. April.

———. 1992a. *Estados financieros 1985, 1986, 1987, 1988, 1989, 1990, 1991, al 31 de agosto 1992.* Guatemala: IGSS.

———. 1992b. *Informe de ejecución presupuestaria 1985, 1986, 1987, 1988, 1989, 1990, 1991, al 30 de junio 1992.* Guatemala: IGSS.

———. 1992c. *Boletín estadístico 1992.* Guatemala: IGSS.

———. 1987–1992. *Informe anual de labores 1987, 1988, 1989, 1990, 1991, 1992.* Guatemala: IGSS.

Instituto Nacional de Estadística (INE). 1990. *Encuesta nacional sociodemográfica, 1989.* Vols. 1, 2. Guatemala: INE.

———. 1992. *Indice de precios al consumidor,* no. 62. Guatemala: INE.

McGreevey, William. 1990. *Social Security in Latin America: Issues and Options for the World Bank.* World Bank Discussion Papers, no. 110.

Mesa-Lago, Carmelo. 1994. *Changing Social Security in Latin America: Toward Alleviating the Social Cost of Economic Reform.* Boulder, Colo.: Lynne Rienner.

Ministerio de Salud Pública y Asistencia Social (MSPAS), Banco Interamericano de Desarrollo (BID), Organización Panamericana de la Salud/Organización Mundial de la Salud (OPS/OMS). 1992. *Estudio básico del sector salud, Guatemala, 1991.* Publicaciones científicas y técnicas de la Organización Panamericana de la Salud. Guatemala: MSPAS. October.

Pan American Health Organization (PAHO). 1991. *Primera evaluación del programa de extensión de los servicios de enfermedad y maternidad del departamento de Escuintla.* Guatemala: PAHO. April–July.

República de Guatemala. 1985. *Constitución política.* Decree by the Asamblea Nacional Constituyente. Guatemala: Asemblea Nacional Constituyente. May 31.

World Bank. 1993. *World Development Report, 1993: Investing in Health.* Washington, D.C.: World Bank.

16 / Social Security in Venezuela

Diagnosis and Reform

Carmelo Mesa-Lago and Mariela Arenas

HISTORICAL EVOLUTION AND CURRENT ORGANIZATION

The Venezuelan Social Security Law was enacted in 1940 and was regulated in 1944. At the beginning, the system covered only sickness, maternity, and disability pensions from occupational accidents. The reform of 1966 established the Venezuelan Social Security Institute (Instituto Venezolano de Seguros Sociales, IVSS) and introduced the program of pensions for old age, disability, and death. It also extended the benefits of social security to public employees, domestic servants, members of cooperatives, and union leaders. The reform established two regimes: (1) the general regime, which offers cash benefits, provides health care, and covers the salaried workers of the private sector and blue-collar workers of the public sector, including their dependent family members; and (2) the partial regime, which offers only long-term cash benefits for partial incapacity, disability, old age, and death. The partial regime is especially geared to public employees. Workers can choose between the two regimes, subject to geographical restrictions: the general regime can only be adopted in areas where the IVSS has health care facilities.

In 1986 the Public Employees Retirement and Pension Fund (Fondo de Jubilaciones y Pensiones de Empleados Públicos, FJPEP) was created as a separate organization from the IVSS, offering the same pensions as the IVSS plus one for seniority regardless of the worker's age. The actual operation of the fund started in 1991. In 1989 the IVSS began administrating an unemployment insurance program, which covers salaried workers in both public and private sectors.

According to Venezuelan law, any public employee that before 1986 had a more favorable regime than the general one (mostly because of previous collective agreements) can keep his or her old regime and be exempted from registering in the new program. There are over four hundred of these special regimes. In addition to the IVSS there are several other social security programs for the armed forces, police, Ministry of Education, Venezuelan Central Bank, and other institutions.

POPULATION COVERAGE

According to current legislation, salaried workers in the public and private sectors, domestic servants, members of cooperatives, union leaders, and taxi drivers must be covered by either the IVSS or any other system, although the actual incorporation of some of these groups has not taken place yet (IVSS 1994a). Self-employed workers will be able to voluntarily affiliate with the IVSS system as soon as the executive enacts the relevant regulations. Temporary and household workers are not covered by unemployment insurance. People who benefit from the unemployment insurance can also keep some of the other benefits (Márquez 1993; ILO 1994a; US-SSA 1994).

The percentage of the economically active population (EAP) covered by the IVSS general regime increased from 22.5 to 25.9 percent in 1980–1993, at an average annual growth rate of 0.26 percent. This group is covered against all risks. If we add the workers included under the partial regime, coverage increases by ten percentage points. If we consider all the workers included in the general regime and the pensioners, the health coverage of the total population rises from 28.4 to 34.4 percent, at an annual average growth rate of 0.46 percent (authors' calculations based on IVSS 1994a, b, 1995). The problem is that IVSS does not know how many dependent relatives are covered; these are calculated assuming a ratio of 2.5 relatives per each pensioner, and since family members represent 71 percent of all the insured people under the general regime, the total figure of coverage is questionable. Recently, IVSS extended (at least, legally) the access to health services to workers in the partial regime; this may add approximately 4 percent to the total population's health coverage. In 1984 a presidential order required IVSS hospitals to treat nonpensioners; according to the president of IVSS this order has increased the health coverage for 3 million people (La Fuente 1995) but further research is needed to verify if these two sectors have real access to the system.

Coverage by other institutions is impossible to estimate. The FJPEP has around 650,000 members (Mesa-Lago 1995) and there is no available information about pensioners in other programs. In any event, social security is very unlikely to cover one-half of the population. IVSS coverage data for 1968–1993 indicate that the percentage of the EAP increased from 23.3 to 34.7 percent; meanwhile total population coverage increased from 18.2 to 34.3 percent (Malagardis 1994). At this slow rate of increase, from seventy to one hundred years will be needed for the IVSS to cover 80 percent of the population.

Only salaried workers of the formal private sector and public sector can belong to the IVSS, and not all of them are currently active contributors. As income increases so does the percentage of insurable workers; for example, in 1990, only 35 percent of the population in the lowest income decile was potentially insurable, while this percentage was 67 percent in the wealthier ninth decile. This tendency is explained because people with the lowest income either work in small businesses, which customarily evade the registration and social security contributions, or are self-employed and do not yet have the right to voluntary affiliation. Moreover, the effective tax rate for these two groups is very heavy, which adds another restriction to their enrollment. Finally, as the labor market has become more informal, evasion has increased (Márquez 1993; Mesa-Lago 1990).

Coverage in certain geographic areas is still not effective (IVSS 1994a). There are also tremendous differences in the types of coverage among states and regions. For example, in 1990, 48 percent of all beneficiaries were concentrated in the capital region (IVSS 1993a). The least urbanized and poorest regions and states have the lowest coverage level and vice versa (Malagardis 1994).

FINANCING

Revenues of the IVSS come from four sources. They include: (1) contributions from employers and workers, which showed a decreasing trend between 1970 and 1994, from 83 to 71 percent of total revenues; (2) government contributions, which fluctuated markedly in this period, showing a decrease from 11 to 8 percent; (3) investment returns, which increased from 6 to 21 percent; and (4) other revenues, which are less than 1 percent of the total. IVSS revenues as a percentage of GDP have been constant around 1.5 percent in the last twenty-five years (Márquez 1993; IVSS 1994b, 1995).

Contributions

Contribution rates were frozen for twenty-two years. In 1989 the employer's contribution increased, while the worker's contribution remained constant. In the general regime, workers pay the equivalent of 4.5 percent of their salaries, while employers pay 10.7–12.7 percent, according to the degree of risk (this risk is associated with occupational risks). The total contributions are therefore between 15.2 percent and 17.2 percent of the worker's salary. In the partial regime this rate is much lower (2.5 percent for the worker and 5.7 percent for the employer, making up a total of 8.2 percent). Payments are lower in this regime because it includes neither health care nor some cash benefits. The government must theoretically contribute with an additional 1.5 percent but it is usually delinquent in these payments. The average IVSS contribution (16 percent) ranks seventeenth among twenty Latin American countries. If we consider that Venezuela ranks ninth in terms of coverage, it may be concluded that the contribution level is probably too low. The maintenance of such low contribution rates (and the stagnation of the IVSS revenues as a percentage of GDP) has been possible only by the strong erosion in the real value of pensions and the price control of medicines (Márquez 1993).

The taxable wage for the contributions has a cap that was frozen at 3,000 bolívares per month until 1989 and was gradually increased to 75,000 bolívares in 1994. This level is equal to five minimum wages, or $440. The national average wage is 21,000 bolívares; 72 percent of the affiliates earn the minimum wage (15,000 bolívares, or $88) and only 3 percent of the affiliates earn more than the cap.

The cap has a regressive effect on distribution. For example, the lowest income decile group pays 13.5 percent of its wage, whereas the highest income decile pays only 10.6 percent. Therefore, abolishing the cap should significantly increase the revenues for IVSS and produce a progressive effect. An expert has calculated that if the cap is abolished the IVSS revenues will increase by 150 percent, while an increase in the contribution rate without changing the cap would increase revenues by only 20 percent (Márquez 1993). On the contrary, the current IVSS president points out that because of the recent increase in the cap, its elimination will not result in a significant increase in revenues, given that only 3 percent of insured workers earn wages above it. Therefore, he proposes doubling the contribution rate (La Fuente 1995; see the section "Financial and Actuarial Equilibria," below).

The premium set by law for the FJPEP is 3 percent for the worker and 3 percent for the government-employer. In practice, 30 percent of the revenue comes from the government and 70 percent from the workers. This situation shows a significant degree of delinquency in the government's payments (Mesa-Lago 1995).

Evasion, Payment Delays, and Debt

The employers' evasion and payment delays are high. The gap between the invoicing and the collection has been increasing from 8 percent in 1975 to 39 percent in 1993. In 1994 it was 25 percent and a record of 40 percent was projected for 1995. In 1990, the gap was 57 percent in the public sector and 22 percent in the private one. In 1994, these rates were reduced to 45 percent and 18 percent in the public and private sectors respectively (IVSS 1995).

There are various reasons for the evasion and payment delays. First, the interest rate and the penalty for late payments are very low. Penalties were historically 1 percent and have recently been increased to 12 percent; but since the average inflation rate for the 1988–1994 period was 50 percent, the penalty rates were negative (–38 percent) in real terms (CEPAL 1994). Second, all the IVSS record-keeping is done by hand; therefore the control over revenue collection is very poor. IVSS has estimated that with a modern control system, revenues could increase by as much as 40 percent. Third, it has been observed that, as wages decrease, the coverage and the potential contribution decrease as well, while the opposite happens when the wages increase. Fourth, the decrease in real wages and the increasingly informal labor market have stimulated the delinquency. Lastly, the erosion of the real value of the benefits and the quality of the health care services provided by IVSS have also encouraged the evasion of social security contributions. In all, the private employers' debt is estimated at around 52 billion bolívares ($308 million).

If the behavior of the private sector leaves much to be desired, the public sector is even worse. The government debt is only partially documented, but it is calculated to be at least 473.4 billion bolívares ($2.8 billion). In its contribution as employer, the government has a debt of 60 billion bolívares ($355 million). Furthermore, government has borrowed money from the IVSS for as much as 403 billion bolívares ($2.4 million). On top of this, we must consider the losses related to deposits at the Venezuelan Central Bank (Banco Central de Venezuela, BCV), at an interest rate lower than the market rate, estimated at 22.7 billion bolívares ($134 million). Finally, the government is required by law to pay to the IVSS the equivalent of 1.5 percent of each affiliate's salary, for management and maintenance, which it has never done. There are no records of the government's debt associated with the nonpayment of this contribution. In order to increase its revenues, the IVSS is currently demanding by trial the payment of both the private and the public employers' debts, concentrating its efforts on the largest debtors. (In contrast to its practice with regard to the IVSS, government usually pays its contributions to some of the other independent public-sector funds or institutions. Government subsidizes the armed forces but not the police, the Venezuelan Central Bank, or the Ministry of Education.)

Investment

Investment income as a proportion of total IVSS grew from 5.6 percent in 1970, to 12.7 percent in 1980, and 26.3 percent in 1986 (Mesa-Lago 1994b). There is no detailed or consistent information for the years after 1986. Therefore, any analysis for more recent years is necessarily very rough.

The real yield of the IVSS pension fund investment depends mainly on the amount invested on public securities. In 1970–1973 the fund invested 47 percent of its reserves in public securities. This percentage increased from 89 to 100 percent in 1974–1988 and then decreased to 83 percent in 1989. From 1970 to 1974 the real yield on public securities averaged 4.2 percent, partly because of the low inflation rate. As the inflation increased in the 1980s (and especially in 1989–1994), the real yield turned negative (except in 1983 and 1986) and the average for the decade was −13.5 percent. This adverse performance resulted in the erosion of pension fund value, which between 1980 and 1988 fell in real terms by 63 percent. The dramatic increase in the inflation rate to 84 percent in 1989 had devastating effects in the fund. IVSS estimates indicate that the real yield in 1993 was also negative (−9.9 percent) but it turned positive in 1994 (5.1 percent). The latter figure is dubious because the inflation rate almost doubled that year (Mesa-Lago 1995).

The negative investment performance in 1970–1989 was the result of the concentration of the portfolio in government securities. Except for seven years (1980–1985 and 1989) these securities represented between 80 and 89 percent of the total investment. Government securities were long-term investments whose principals were not indexed to inflation and whose real interest rates were negative. The investment in private securities generally represented between 12 and 43 percent of the total fund, except in 1970 when it was under 6 percent. These private securities were also long-term investments, mostly mortgage bonds with an interest rate lower than both the market and the inflation rates. The remainder of the portfolio was invested almost completely in bank term deposits, whose share of the fund reached a maximum level of 27 percent in 1982, then fell until almost disappearing in 1989. The investment in other securities was insignificant (Márquez 1993).

The concentration of investment in government papers was caused by a law that forced the IVSS to deposit its funds at the BCV. This institution had the authority to determine which instruments and amounts the IVSS pension fund should be invested in. The BCV used the IVSS funds as monetary policy instruments to contain inflationary pressures by covering the fiscal operational budget deficit. This policy led to a significant depletion of the fund. In 1993 the BVC's new regulatory law ended its control over IVSS investment and forced the BCV to return to the IVSS 45,000 million bolívares ($266 million). The capital was returned in the following way: 64 percent in public debt bonds that do not pay interests and have virtually no value; 25 percent in private debt with no market demand and paying an 8.5 percent nominal interest, which means negative rates of –37 percent and –62 percent in 1993–1994; and only 11 percent in cash. The sum of 5,859 million bolívares ($35 million) was deposited in banks with a higher return (26 percent) than any of the previously mentioned, but the rate is still negative.

The actual share of the IVSS reserve that was deposited at the BCV fluctuated significantly but averaged 72 percent in 1967–1991, and the return from these deposits was (except for a brief period in 1985) well below market rates. Between 1970 and 1975 the share of the reserves deposited at the BCV increased from 54 to 92 percent, and the difference between the BCV and the market rates decreased from –1.2 to –1.8 percent. By 1980 the difference in return had fallen to –4 percent and the share of compulsory deposits decreased to 79 percent. In 1985 100 percent of the reserve was deposited at the BCV, earning returns that were slightly above market rates (by 0.3 percent). From then on, the share slowly decreased to 46.1 percent in 1991, while the return differential worsened, reaching a staggering –22.2 percent in that year. The IVSS estimates that the accumulated losses attributed to these obligatory deposits at the BCV amounted to 22.7 billion bolívares or $134 million (IVSS 1995). Senior executives at IVSS point out that if the institute had been allowed to freely invest its resources, the fund would probably now be ten times larger (Mesa-Lago 1995). This assertion has not been documented though.

The information regarding the FJPEP is more scarce. One advantage of this fund over the IVSS is that the law did not require the FJPEP to deposit its resources at the BCV. In 1996 the fund stood at 32 billion bolívares ($190 million) and its executives declared that two-thirds of the fund's growth in the last fourteen months came from the investment yield. It is said that the nominal yield in 1993 was 61 percent, almost twice as high as the return on the IVSS portfolio, which represented a real return of 23 percent. In 1994 the nominal yield fell to 42 percent, the inflation rate almost doubled, and the real yield was –28 percent (Mesa-Lago 1995). In March 1994 the fund was invested as follows: 47 percent in commercial banks, 31 percent in BCV bonds, and 22 percent in private sector securities.

Investment alternatives currently existing in Venezuela are very limited. The stock market is very small and has deteriorated because of the domestic bank in 1995. Less than twenty shares were traded in the stock market that year. Fixed income securities show all negative real returns ranging from –20 to –40 percent; and the government papers of variable yield, as well as bank deposits, also offer negative real returns. There are also mortgage bonds, which used to have fixed interest rates (and were a very bad investment for IVSS) but now offer floating rates.

The previous analysis shows that the social security reform cannot be done in an isolated way but in the context of macroeconomic reforms aimed at reducing inflation, restoring the confidence in the banking system, and regulating, consolidating, and expanding the stock market. There is a project for a partial reform of the Capital Markets Law, which has broad consensus. This project grants the National Securities Commission independence from the government; creates the Centralized Security Deposit; modernizes the National Securities Registry; regulates the investment funds, their management companies, and the operation of securities brokers (Ministerio de Hacienda 1994). The enactment of this reform would be a first step toward providing social security funds with profitable alternative securities.

EXPENDITURES

Overall Expenditures: Magnitude, Composition, and Trend

In the analysis of the expenditures of the Venezuelan social security we will have to be restricted to the IVSS, given the insufficient statistical information on other pension and health programs. According to information published by the International Labor Organization (ILO), social security expenditures as a percentage of GDP increased from 3.1 percent in 1965 to 3.9 percent in 1975. These data also show that in 1980 such percentage decreased to 1.3 percent and then remained stable until 1986 (the last year statistical data are available; ILO 1994b). In terms of such percentage, Venezuela ranked fifteenth among the countries of the region (this ranking excluded Haiti). The lowest-ranked countries were El Salvador, Honduras, Guatemala, and the Dominican Republic, all of them with population coverage that was lower than in Venezuela (and with younger systems as well).

Other sources show that the proportion of IVSS expenditures to GDP increased from 1.3 to 1.5 percent in 1980–1983. From 1984 to 1992 this proportion decreased slowly (the average for the period was less than 1.1 percent) and rose in 1993 to 1.3 percent, because of the increase in the minimum pension. Taking into consideration the Venezuelan level of development, this proportion is extremely low (Márquez 1993; Malagardis 1994; IVSS 1993a, b; IMF 1994).

Benefits, as percentage of total costs, have fluctuated between 77 and 91.4 percent with administration costs accounting for the remainder (see "Administration" section). Within the benefits component, we observe two definite trends: a relative decrease in health care costs and a proportional increase in pensions and other monetary benefits. In 1970, health care costs accounted for 63.7 percent of total expenditures, while pensions represented only 4.1 percent. In 1980 the share of health care costs had fallen to 47.9 percent, while that of pensions had increased to 28.9 percent. In 1994 it was estimated that the share of the former was 36.3 percent of the total, while the share of the latter was 42 percent. This trend—which is the natural consequence of both the aging of the insured population and the maturity of the pension program—was offset in the period 1985–1992 by the severe reduction in the real value of pensions during those years. The increase in the minimum pension in 1993 eliminated this distortion.

The share of pensions in total expenditures rose from 21.4 percent in

1992 to 42 percent in 1994. In 1986 the percentage of health care in Venezuela ranked fifth highest among Latin American countries. The four countries ranking ahead of Venezuela were El Salvador, Guatemala, Honduras, and the Dominican Republic, all of which had "younger" pension programs, and a lower pensions burden (Mesa-Lago 1994b). In Venezuela, as in other countries of the region, the pension fund has transferred massive resources to the health care program to fund its operational deficits. This transfer is only possible during the early stages of the pension program. When the pension program reaches maturity, transfers are no longer possible because the accumulated resources of the fund are insufficient to pay pensions and support the health care program at the same time.

Pensions

The conditions for retirement in the IVSS system are relatively generous compared to other countries in the region. The retirement age is sixty for men and fifty-five for women, and only fourteen and a half years of service are required. The FJPEP has similar retirement ages but also offers the possibility of early retirement, regardless of age, after thirty-five years of service. Other independent programs offer even more favorable conditions. The retirement ages in the IVSS system are among the lowest in the region: only Bolivia, Haiti, Paraguay, Ecuador, and Panama have lower retirement ages, but life expectancy in the first four is inferior. Life expectancy in Venezuela is currently the fourth highest in the region; Cuba, Panama, and Uruguay have higher life expectancies (their pension programs are in crisis). Argentina, Colombia, and Costa Rica whose retirement ages were similar increased them in the early 1990s (Mesa-Lago 1994b).

In 1994 the government decreed that the minimum pension should equal 95 percent of the minimum salary (14,460 bolívares or $86). This raise was enacted against the advice of the IVSS actuary, who warned that such increase would only be possible through a raise in contributions. Contributions remained constant, and apparently, government is currently funding the actuarial deficits (Mesa-Lago 1995).

The generous retirement conditions and the erosion in the value of the IVSS pension fund forced a reduction of 40 percent in the real value of pensions between 1972 and 1979 (Márquez 1993). This situation deteriorated in the 1980s. In 1990 the real pension equaled 26 percent of that in 1980. The increase in the minimum pension decreed in 1993 resulted in a slight recovery; in 1994, however, the real monthly pension was in real terms only 14 percent of the 1974 pension. Moreover, the IVSS has tried to reduce its pension expenditures by delaying the granting of benefits: there were fifty thousand applications waiting to be processed in 1994 (Mesa-Lago 1995).

Health Care

The IVSS health care program combines sickness, maternity, and occupational risks with requirements that are generally more lax than the Latin American average (Mesa-Lago 1993). There are some highly expensive special programs, such as dialysis, pacemakers, prosthetics, and medicines for diabetes and hemophilia (IVSS 1993b). From the workers' point of view, the most beneficial aspect of the program is that there is no "waiting period" to receive health care. Besides, government has recently decreed that the uninsured poor population can also have access to health benefits administered by the IVSS.

The contributions for the IVSS health care program equals only one-fourth of the premium to a private insurance company for a similar service. This low contribution was possible because of price controls on medicines and other supplies (and low inflation rates), and by the transfer of massive resources from the pension fund. In the 1980s and early 1990s, however, higher inflation rates raised the costs of health services, worsening the program's deficit. In order to limit the costs, IVSS has reduced the quality of health services and the waiting list to consult with a doctor has increased dramatically, especially for the insured sector with the highest income. The recent incorporation of the uninsured poor has made the problem worse (Márquez 1993; Mesa-Lago 1995).

Unemployment

Venezuela is among the six Latin American countries that have unemployment insurance. This program covers all the active IVSS affiliates, but since 1993 it has been restricted to dismissed workers. The waiting period is less than a month and the replacement rate is 60 percent. It is questionable whether the introduction of this benefit is socially optimal; an alternative use of the resources could have been the extension of health coverage to the presently uncovered population (Mesa-Lago 1994b).

The unemployment insurance program was introduced when unemployment stood at 9 percent consistently for many years. When the program started operating in 1990 the unemployment rate increased to 11 percent, and it later decreased to 6.6 percent, only to increase again to 9 percent in 1994 (CEPAL 1994). The costs associated with this program have fluctuated around 8 percent of total IVSS expenditures. The contribution for the program was originally set at 1.1 percent but had to be doubled in 1991 (IVSS 1994a).

ADMINISTRATION

Administrative Costs

As a percentage of total expenditures, administrative costs behaved quite erratically, falling from 21 percent in 1970 to 12 percent in 1986, only to grow later to 23 percent in 1993. The IVSS management points out that a significant portion of these expenditures consists of health care costs and should not be considered administrative cost. Following this interpretation, the non–health administrative cost fluctuated between 6.9 and 8.8 percent during 1981–1988 but rose sharply after 1989 to 16 percent. There is no official information available after 1990, but the current share of administrative expenditures (including both health and non–health administrative expenditures) should be around 12 percent.

Overstaffing

The main component in administrative expenditures is labor costs. The total number of IVSS employees rose by almost 70 percent between 1986 and 1993, while the total number of people with IVSS health care coverage increased by only 29 percent. Therefore, the ratio of employees to every thousand insured grew from 6.4 to 7.8 (IVSS 1994b). In the late 1980s, Venezuela's ratio of employees to insured people was close to the Latin American average (Mesa-Lago 1993). But the information available about the number of IVSS employees is not accurate. In March 1993 there were supposedly 66,111 employees, which included both permanent positions, vacancies, and also excess personnel. According to IVSS statistics, in 1993 the number of employees was reduced by 5,290. An additional reduction of 7,167 was made in 1994, totaling 12,457 in two consecutive years (IVSS 1995). In 1994 there were 54,341 employees, out of which 47,198 were permanent (IVSS 1994b). For 1995 the IVSS projected a range of employees between 28,399 and 48,399. The deficit resulting from the cost of removing the excess personnel (and subsequent transfer from the government) could range from 13.5 to 21.6 billion bolívares, or from $80 million to $128 million (IVSS 1995).

There are thirty-three labor unions, one in each hospital and in other areas. Before 1995 the collective agreement was reviewed and signed every three years, but now it has to be revised annually and strikes are frequent. Between 1992 and 1994 five important collective bargaining agreements were signed that gave enormous concessions (IVSS 1993b). The management at IVSS points out that the basic wage of 90 percent of the employees is below the basic consumer basket, but this is compensated with several additional benefits, like transportation bonuses, bonuses per child, overtime wages, and a seniority retirement plan that pays 100 percent of the last salary and is additional to the IVSS retirement pension. The global wage of the employees, including additional benefits, is higher than the average wage of the insured population (Mesa-Lago 1995). The IVSS president declared that, in the past, the institute had never been managed in an efficient way, that it was an appendage of the political parties, and that many of its directors prospered at the institute's expense (La Fuente 1995).

IVSS employees are protected by the Labor Law, the Civil Service Law, and their collective bargaining agreements, which makes it very difficult to fire employees. Any resignation requires the payment of social benefits; if the worker is fired with no proved reason, the payment must be double. IVSS has used a special fund of 8 billion bolívares to fire unneeded or incompetent employees, but this fund is almost exhausted and it was very difficult to get rid of any additional employees in 1995. Some authorities, including the IVSS president, recommended radical actions to (1) suspend the Civil Service Law; (2) fire any corrupt, incompetent, or unnecessary personnel; (3) restrict the additional benefits (paying an adequate salary); (4) make effective the eight-hour workday that is rarely observed; and (5) privatize some services, as it has already been done with the security systems. This decision will require strong support from the government and will carry political costs. On the other hand, there is a high personnel rotation and it is very difficult to find experts such as actuaries (Mesa-Lago 1995).

Other Administrative Problems

Many IVSS inefficiencies and management problems are the result of primitive administration methods and obsolete equipment. The accounting system suffered a thirty-three-month delay because of inadequate procedures. The treasury and auditing have the same problems. The computer system is sixteen years old, and only ten out of nearly two hundred employees are capable of operating it. Similar situations occur with other equipment although it was planned that new systems would begin operation in 1996–1997 (Mesa-Lago 1995).

Hospital Efficiency

Venezuela's health services in the mid-1980s ranked fourth among Latin American countries in physicians per ten thousand inhabitants, and eight in hospital beds per one thousand inhabitants. Venezuela ranked fifth in terms of life expectancy, and seventh in infant mortality rate (Mesa-Lago 1993). These ratios have remained constant in recent years with the single exception of the infant mortality rate, which has fallen from thirty-seven per one thousand infants born alive in 1985 to twenty-five in 1994 (MSAS 1994).

IVSS hospital efficiency is low. The ratio of bed occupancy shows an increase from 66 to 69 percent between 1989 and 1992, and a sudden increase to 81 percent in 1993, probably because of the broadening of the services to the uninsured population. Strangely, this indicator decreased to 73 percent in 1994. According to international standards, a bed occupancy ratio of 81 percent is adequate, whereas a ratio of 73 percent is somewhat low and levels of 63–69 percent are very low. As to the average length of stay in hospitals, this has oscillated between 8.5 and 10 days, which is considered too high. If the average stay could be reduced to 6 or 7 days (a more adequate level) the bed occupancy ratio would also decrease to levels closer to 50 percent. Another indicator, the average annual number of outpatient consultation per beneficiary increased from 1.55 to 1.93 in 1989–1992, only to fall to 1.25 in 1994.

IVSS provides health care services in its own hospital as well as in private clinics. The ratio of IVSS-owned beds to total beds increased from 67.7 to 71.8 percent in 1989–1991 but fell to 68.6 percent in 1993. According to IVSS, 2,939 private beds were contracted in the major Venezuelan cities, which served an average of 6,000 people monthly at an average cost of 6,000 bolívares ($272). In the Latin American context this cost is too high; IVSS points out that the cost in its own hospitals is lower. Further independent studies are needed to determine the real hospital costs, to find any inefficiencies and decide the convenience of the hospital services' privatization.

In the past Venezuelan health policy has emphasized costly curative medicine such as hospital care and the use of high-tech treatment and physicians. On the other hand, preventive and primary health care, ambulatory service, and paramedic personnel received scant attention. In the last ten years the control of endemic diseases, immunizations, and mother-infant health care programs have suffered strong budgetary cuts. Meanwhile, the share of the budget assigned to personnel and administration increased.

Pensions

In 1978–1989 the pension fund generated an accounting financial surplus (between 0.1 and 0.5 percent of GDP) but with a declining trend. Since 1985 the accumulation of reserves turned negative, and in 1989 25 billion bolívares were needed just to keep the real reserves from falling; the deficit was equivalent to 2 percent of that year's GDP (Márquez 1993). The situation deteriorated rapidly in 1990–1995 as the fund suffered growing financial deficits, leading to a significant increase in the actuarial deficit.

The analysis of the actuarial reserve (the resources needed to pay for all the future pension obligations) showed the critical situation of the pension fund. Defining the potential reserve as the money there should be to cover all future pension obligations, and the actual reserve as the money there actually is, the gap between the two grew from 24 to 75 percent in 1970–1991. In the last year, actual reserves were 39.3 billion bolívares, and the potential reserves were 252.3 billion. Even worse, actual reserves in real terms have been falling since 1983, leading to an accumulated loss of 56.8 percent between 1983 and 1991. Recent figures are not available, but the declining trend probably continued.

The Venezuelan population is very young: in 1995 only 7.7 percent was at the retirement age. In the year 2025, this percentage will increase to 13.8 percent, still relatively low compared to the region's average. However, the ratio of active workers to pensioners has dropped from 28.8 in 1977 to 6.8 active workers per pensioner in 1993 (IVSS 1993b). Compared to the pioneers, the Venezuelan ratio is still high. Nonetheless, if the IVSS coverage does not grow at a sufficient speed and if the retirement ages are kept low, this ratio will continue to fall as the program matures and the population ages.

The government is well aware of the fund's financial imbalance. The 1992 Public Credit Law assigned 21.4 billion bolívares to the pension fund; half these resources were assigned to pay the IVSS debt with the fund and the remainder were assigned for capitalization of the fund. The Venezuelan Investment Fund was put in charge of the administration and payment of the resources (Malagardis 1994). In 1995 IVSS requested 134.4 billion bolívares from the government in order to cover the deficit (IVSS 1995).

Health Care

Since its creation the health care program has had continuous deficits because of its low contribution rate (6.25 percent). Approximately 35 percent of the IVSS's income is assigned to health care; it would have to be 60 percent in order to cover operation costs. The operational deficit has been routinely financed by transfers from the pension fund. The extension of the IVSS health services to the partial regime affiliates and to the uninsured poor, without corresponding financial support from the government, increased the deficit (IVSS 1993b).

Unemployment

This program started with a contribution of 1.1 percent. This contribution was insufficient because of an increase in the unemployment rate, a high degree of evasion and delayed payments, and relatively liberal entitlement conditions. The contribution was raised to 2.2 percent, but the current financial status of the program is still unclear.

Administration

The administration fund should be financed from a government contribution equivalent to 1.5 percent of wages. Some IVSS sources say that the government has never paid this obligation, while others note that it has paid one-half of what it should have. This program's deficit has apparently been covered through transfers from the pension fund (Malagardis 1994).

SUMMARY OF STRENGTHS AND WEAKNESSES

Although there have been several improvements, the Venezuelan social security system is very fragmented and unequal. An immediate unification and standardization process is imperative. This process should suppress inequalities and privileges, reduce costs, and eliminate government subsidies with regressive effects.

In the late 1980s Venezuela ranked ninth among Latin American countries in terms of total population coverage. Although its ratio is above the regional average, other countries with less resources and a lower degree of development than Venezuela (Chile, Costa Rica, Panama, Uruguay, for instance) had higher coverage rates (Mesa-Lago 1994b). The recent evolution of coverage shows a very slow increase: almost a century will be needed to reach universal coverage. Finally, the differences in the degree of coverage vary remarkably according to the levels of income, degree of urbanization, and geographical location.

Financing

The IVSS contribution rate is one of the lowest of the region and has been kept frozen until recently. Even though the population coverage is above the average for Latin American countries, revenues are insufficient to cover expenditures because of benefits that are too generous and the insured's wages, that are too low. Around 70 percent of the affiliates earn minimum wages and therefore contribute very little. The cap on the taxable wage has recently been increased, and only 3 percent of the insured population earn wages over it. Top officials at the IVSS have pointed out that only by doubling the contribution rate would the institute's revenues be sufficient. Evasion and delays in the contribution payments are too high. For instance, the difference between expected and actual revenues was 25 percent in 1994 and was projected to be 40 percent in 1995. The government is responsible for the main part of this delinquency. Penalties for evasion and delinquency have increased but are still quite low, given the high inflation rate. Therefore, an increase in the contribution rate, without other reforms, would only make the coercion and delinquency situation worse. The total overdue debt is calculated to be 538 billion bolívares or $3.2 billion (and this is an incomplete estimate), of which 88 percent is owed by the government.

IVSS real average annual investment yield was −13.5 percent in the 1980s, and the yield did not improve significantly in the first years of the 1990s. This was partly because of the persistence of mandatory deposits in the Venezuelan Central Bank and partly because of the concentration of investment in public securities with strong negative yields. Although in 1993 forced investments were lifted, the IVSS did not receive any reimbursement for the accumulated losses it had incurred (some 88 percent in real terms).

Another serious problem is the lack of profitable investment alternatives since the Venezuelan capital is still underdeveloped. This problem is independent of IVSS management in investment flows. It should be addressed before any viable long-term solution can be achieved for the pensions problem.

Expenditures: Total and Benefits

IVSS expenses as a proportion of GDP are among the lowest in the region and show a decreasing trend. This is remarkable, given the relatively high population coverage and the existence of an unemployment program. On the other hand the pension program is quite new and its expenses should therefore be low. However, entitlement conditions for retirement in the IVSS system are relatively generous in the Latin American context. The health care program has entitlement conditions that are close to the regional average, but its contributions are too low. The IVSS has tried to contain costs by letting real pensions drop by around 90 percent, reducing the quality of the health services, and increasing the waiting period before granting benefits.

Administration

The share of total IVSS expenditures going to administrative expenses (excluding health care administration costs) has shown an increasing trend in recent years. International statistics show that such a share (16 percent in 1990) is within the Latin American average but is still too high. Overstaffing is the principal reason of high administrative expenditures: the number of employees increased by 70 percent in 1986–1993 while the insured with health care increased by only 29 percent. The IVSS policy to reduce its personnel included a reduction of 12,500 in 1993–1994; and an additional cutback of 10,000–20,000 in 1995. In order to continue with personnel reduction and their benefits it would be necessary to intervene in the IVSS and suspend the laws and agreements that grant preferential conditions to IVSS employees. Inefficient management is also a result of inadequate systems in accounting, treasury, auditing, and computing. Several projects to deal with improvements in these areas were approved by the FIV in 1995.

In the mid-1980s Venezuela ranked relatively high in the region in terms of resources assigned to health care. However, per capita doctors and beds indicators have become stagnant or have decreased in the last decade. The bed occupancy ratio has had a tendency to increase but is still low according to international standards (73 percent in 1994). Nevertheless, the average length of stay (nine days) is rather high and reducing it would lead to a fall in the bed occupancy ratio. Over two-thirds of the beds offered by IVSS are owned by the institute and the remainder is contracted through private clinics at supposedly very high costs.

Financial and Actuarial Equilibrium

Two of the four IVSS funds (health care and administration) have consistently suffered deficits and required transfers from the pension funds. Lack of historical series and conflicting statistical information complicate the analysis of the IVSS's financial and actuarial balance. The unemployment insurance fund also had losses at the beginning. It is not known whether the 100 percent increase in the contribution rate will be enough to balance it.

The pension fund generated financial surpluses in 1978–1989 but now suffers a serious actuarial deficit. In the early 1990s the financial deficit aggravated the actuarial deficit. In 1991 the fund's actual reserve equaled only 25 percent of the required reserve, and this situation has been deteriorating even further. The real reserve decreased by 54 percent in 1980–1991. Once the pension fund stopped showing a financial surplus it was impossible to balance the other two funds that had survived only with pension fund transfers. This situation has caused the overall IVSS financial deficit. To cope with this situation the Venezuelan government took action through massive transfers to bolster the institute's revenues. Thus, it is obvious that a deep reform of the system is needed. The question is, What type of reform should be implemented, given the specific Venezuelan economic, social, political, and social security issues?

POLITICAL CONTEXT OF THE SOCIAL SECURITY REFORM

Over twelve reform proposals and law projects on social security reform were produced in 1989–1995. It is impossible even to summarize them here. The political context of the reform is very complex, with different and sometimes contradictory approaches used, even among members of the government and within political parties.

The movement for the social security reform started in 1989, in the Carlos Andrés Pérez administration. The Chamber of Commerce and FEDECAMARAS (a major business association) prepared a study on the social security system. In 1990 a technical commission headed by CORDIPLAN prepared a law proposal based on that study. The Labor Ministry also prepared two similar projects, but the workers' unions opposed them and the remission of President Pérez left the debate unresolved. Velázquez was granted extraordinary powers by Congress to solve the "social benefits" problem (double indemnization for dismissal) but not the social security reform, and he was not successful anyway.

In the 1994 presidential campaign, all candidates except Caldera supported the modification of social benefits, but there was no similar debate about social security. In November 1994 President Caldera appointed a commission to study the reform of both social benefits and the more comprehensive social security system. The commission invited all interested parties to submit their points of view concerning the reform and elaborated two separate reports, one for each area.

There were divergent positions within the governing coalition, political parties, and even ministries. For instance, the Finance Ministry, and some Central Bank officials supported a structural reform that privatized social security as a substitute for IVSS. The Labor and Health Ministries did not take such a radical position and were in favor of an intermediate approach. IVSS officials proposed partial or minor reforms of the institute, to improve its management and efficiency without eliminating it but without solving its structural problems either.

Within the political parties there were no unanimous positions either. The Social Democrats (Alianza Democrática, AD) and the Christian Democrats (COPEI) seemed to lean toward the structural reform and privatization of the pension funds. The Moderate Socialists (MAS) were more divided: the majority supported a nonstructural reform with a complementary pension regime while the minority favored privatization as a substitute for IVSS. "Causa R" organized retired workers and pensioners, and this has become a very strong force obstructing the reform. Within Congress there were four groups with different positions about reform of the pension funds and similar voting power. To enact the reform (especially if it is a radical one) the government would require support from AD and COPEI congressmen.

The majority of the workers' unions were opposed to the substitution of the IVSS by private pension funds. However, their power decreased along with their membership (the unionization rate was under 15 percent in 1994–1995) but began to gain momentum thereafter. If we add the fragmentation that exists among labor groups, with different positions toward the reform, we conclude that their influence could be limited. On the other side, businessmen, particularly FEDECAMARAS, favor a structural reform and the full privatization of pensions. They strongly oppose increases in contribution rates and would like to eliminate the IVSS.

In April 1995 the minister of labor intervened in the IVSS, arguing that this intervention was an essential step to introduce the needed reforms. One year later, no measure to reform the present system had been taken. Not even a preliminary draft proposing a reform had been elaborated. Government had failed to design and implement an effective macroeconomic stabilization policy, and economic conditions further deteriorated. The momentum reached in 1995 to pass some type of social security reform disappeared. In 1997 there were government discussions with the World Bank and the Inter-American Development Bank about pension reform, but none had been introduced by the end of that year.

Note

All references to dollars ($) are to U.S. dollars.

References

Banco Nacional de Ahorro y Préstamo (BANAP). 1995. "Programa de administración del fondo de pensiones y demás prestaciones en dinero del IVSS." Caracas.

CEPAL. 1994. *Balance preliminar de la economía de América Latina y del Caribe, 1994.* Santiago.

Clemente H., Antonio. 1995. "Seguridad social en Venezuela." Caracas.

Congreso de la República. 1986, 1991. Legislación sobre el régimen de jubilación y pensiones de los funcionarios y empleados públicos. *Gaceta Oficial.* Caracas.

Escalante, Luis Manuel. 1994. *¿Cómo alcanzar el salario real? Propuesta.* Caracas: Gráficas Evi.

Febres, Carlos Eduardo. 1993. *Los indicadores sociales en Venezuela.* Caracas: Universidad de los Andes.

Gil Yepes, José A. 1994. "Relatoría y opinión pública sobre alternativas de seguridad social." Caracas: Jornadas de Recursos Humanos, Fundamental.

Instituto Venezolano de Seguros Sociales (IVSS). 1993a. *Anuario estadístico, 1990.* Caracas: División de Estadístico, September.

———. 1993b. "Acciones, cambios y reformas sometidos por el consejo directivo del IVSS al ejecutivo nacional para ser implementado en el primer semestre de 1994." Caracas. December.

———. 1994a. *IVSS 50 años de historia.* Caracas. October.

———. 1994b. *Memoria y cuenta.* Caracas.

———. 1994c. "Exposición de motivos: Proyecto de reforma parcial de la ley de seguro social." Caracas.

———. 1995. *Estádisticas del IVSS, entregadas al consultor.* Caracas. January 27.

International Labour Organization (ILO). 1994a. *The Cost of Social Security, 1984–1986.* Geneva.

———. 1994b. "Reforma de la Seguridad Social en Venezuela." Caracas.

International Monetary Fund (IMF). 1994. *International Financial Statistic Yearbook.* Washington, D.C.

La Fuente, Sandra. 1995. "IVSS debe ser intervenido por el Ejecutivo Nacional." Interview to Juan Vicente Vera. *El Globo* (23 January): 33.

López Fajardo, Antonio (Grupo Cisneros). 1994. *Un nuevo sistema de previsión social en Venezuela.* Caracas.

Malagardis, Antonis N. 1994. "La reforma de seguro social (y especialmente el fondo de pensiones) en Venezuela: Evaluaciones y opciones." Caracas: Informe de Consultoría GTZ.

Márquez, Gustavo. 1991. "La reforma del sistema de prestaciones sociales en Venezuela." In *Sistema de pensiones en América Latina: Diagnóstico y alternativas de reforma,* ed. Andrés Uthoff and Raquel Szalachman, 197–253. Santiago: CEPAL.

———. 1993. "El sistema de seguros sociales en Venezuela." Paper presented in the 1993 Conference on Social Security and Pension Fund: Reform in Latin America, 7–9. La Jolla: Institute of the Americas, March.

Méndez, Absalón, et al. 1995. "Dos escenarios posibles" and "Cómo mejorar la situación de inseguridad social en Venezuela?" Caracas.

Mesa-Lago, Carmelo. 1985. *El desarrollo de la seguridad social en América Latina.* Estudios e Informes de la CEPAL, no. 43. Santiago.

———. 1990. *La seguridad social y el sector informal.* Santiago: PREALC.

———. 1991. *Portfolio Performance of Selected Social Security Institutes in Latin America.* World Bank Discussion Papers, no. 139. Washington, D.C.

———. 1992. *Health Care for the Poor in Latin America and the Caribbean.* Washington, D.C.: PAHO-IAF.

———. 1993. *Aspectos económico-financieros de la seguridad social en América Latina y el Caribe: Tendencias, problemas y alternativas para el año 2000.* Santiago: CIEDES.

———. 1994a. *La reforma de la seguridad social y las pensiones en América Latina: Importancia y evaluación de las alternativas de privatización.* 2d edition. Quito: INCAE.

———. 1994b. *Changing Social Security in Latin America: Towards Alleviating Social Costs of Economic Reform.* Boulder, Colo: Lynne Reinner.

———. 1995. Interviews in Caracas. January.

Ministerio de Hacienda. 1994. "Programa de consolidación fiscal y financiera 1995." Caracas.

Ministerio de Sanidad y Asistencia Social (MSAS). 1994. *Memoria y cuenta.* Caracas: Departamento de Publicaciones.

———. N.d. "Políticas de salud" and other reports. Caracas.

Sainz Muñoz, Carlos. 1994. "Las prestaciones sociales y los fondos de pensiones." Caracas: Lito-Jet.

Seijas C., Guillermo, and Guillermo Clemente H. 1994. "Seguridad social: De la reflexión a la acción propuesta." Caracas.

U.S. Social Security Administration (US-SSA). 1994. *Social Security Programs Throughout the World, 1993.* Washington D.C.: GPO.

17 / Conclusion

Conditioning Factors, Cross-Country Comparisons, and Recommendations

María Amparo Cruz-Saco Oyague and Carmelo Mesa-Lago

The development of new technologies to produce social protection is fully endogenous to the political and economic dynamics of any country in question. The external influence of preset paradigms combined with country specific conditions bring about reform processes of various types. None of the reforms in place are the same. Even specific cases within a general paradigm or model are different. Thus, an important conclusion of our study is that reforms are country specific. Countries considering health care and pension reforms should not be led by the false pretense that there is any universal or perfect model of reform. Instead, reformers should study the various types of reforms in existence as well as their performance. Their goal should be to formulate a reform proposal that is functional to their own conditions and needs. In this process fundamental attention should be given to reducing the transition costs as much as possible. The transition costs include not only the more quantifiable fiscal and administrative costs, but more important, a fair judgment of the welfare and equity gains that the reform should attain.

In this chapter, first we formulate a simple model of conditioning factors of reform options and test whether such factors are present or not in all the countries under study. Second, we compare the features of pension and health care reforms in the various countries, noting major similarities and differences among them. Third, we summarize our findings, in answer to the seven crucial questions raised in the introduction to this study, contrasting the structural reform assumptions with reality. And fourth, we offer major policy recommendations for prospective reformers.

Our evaluation of pension reform is much more thorough and deeper than that of health care reforms. This is not surprising because the latter have been historically more difficult to introduce and only partially implemented in a few countries. Assessment of their performance is therefore still incomplete. It is crucial to continue research on the analysis of health care reforms and of their impact on countries that have implemented them already or that are in the process of doing so (Argentina, Brazil, Chile, Colombia, Peru), as well as in those countries that are considering reforms.

A SIMPLE MODEL OF CONDITIONING FACTORS

The integration, into a common framework, of the evidence on structural reforms developed by the contributors of this book makes it possible to identify the following four underlying conditioning factors that affect social security change in each country. These four conditioning factors are: (1) political conditions and institutional restrictions, (2) the state of socioeconomic development, (3) success of economic restructuring and stabilization efforts, and (4) maturity of the social security system.

Political Conditions and Institutional Restrictions

Change, of course, does not take place in a vacuum. The old social security system was fading out, immersed in endogenous excesses and failures as well as exogenous adverse conditions and pressures. Appointments of new ministers and heads of social security agencies, the creation of new programs, attempts to restore financial and actuarial equilibria, and efforts to improve the level of benefits and the quality of services usually failed to correct the fundamental problems of such systems. By its own nature, the social security crisis could not on its own inspire a major change in direction. Its leaders lacked the power to accomplish such a difficult task, facing, as they did, significant resistance and opposition from both inside and outside of the system.

Thus, the political will of the executive branch to change policies, procedures, and ultimately practice for either a pension or a health sector reform is the most salient active conditioning factor initiating the process of reform. The government becomes an arbitrator of the balancing of forces between *pushers* and *resisters*, and in any solution to the deadlock the degree of freedom and power enjoyed by the executive varies greatly. On one extreme extraordinary presidential powers allow a unilateral definition of the reform (as happened in Chile and Peru). On the other extreme the full interaction of political constituencies in the legislative branch results in a strong consensus, which significantly shapes the type and scope of the reform (in Argentina, Colombia, and Uruguay, for example). In between the two extremes there are various degrees of public national discussion, from minimal to partial, because of control of a hegemonic party or a wide majority in congress or similar conditions, which leads to a reform that is largely coined by the executive branch without a solid consensual base (in El Salvador and Mexico, for example).

It is obvious that the radical privatization of the pension system in Chile was possible because an authoritarian government had banned political opposition. Therefore, there was no resistance to the adoption of a new social protection technology that, in pension, rests fully on individual accounts and, in health, rests in the supplementary role of the public and the private sectors. In Peru the decree that created the private pension program was enacted when President Fujimori had closed Congress after the *autogolpe* of April 5, 1992. Fujimori added a fully funded individual (FFI) system that runs parallel to the old traditional public pension system (not reformed until 1995), because he wanted to maintain the political support of *resisters* to any change, namely, the workers and the middle class who opposed full substitution.

Conversely, the strong role of political parties, organized labor, interest groups, and experts have precluded the adoption of substitutive FFI systems. In Argentina, Colombia, and Uruguay organized pressure groups were extremely important in the sanctioning of mixed or selective reforms that include the public sector in the management of supplementary or alternative pension programs. *Resisters* here were powerful enough to successfully oppose attempts to Chileanize their pension systems.

In Mexico, in spite of the power of the hegemonic party, structural pension reform proposals from the executive were opposed, and the approval of the 1992 reform was a compromise. The 1992 reform tried to strengthen the public system while introducing a new supplementary individual savings program, but this failed to solve the public pension crisis and only postponed its reform. After a public acknowledgment of the impending crisis by the Mexican Institute of Social Insurance itself, a reform proposal was jointly presented to the executive by government-controlled confederations of workers and entrepreneurs, and in December 1995 and April 1996 laws were enacted that followed the essentials of the Chilean model albeit with significant differences. Implementation began in July 1997, after more than seven years of executive efforts to overcome resistance and reach a minimum compromise.

In El Salvador, the executive enjoyed an ample majority in Congress and the political opposition was inexperienced and fragmented. The government reform proposal was kept virtually secret, without any significant discussion with the principal actors or the opposition. This proposal was quickly endorsed in late December 1996 by a congressional commission chaired by the president's sister, and Congress subsequently approved it, with minor changes, in less than two days. And yet the loss of the congressional majority by the incumbent party has led to a situation in which the opposition is now demanding a reform of the pension reform.

In other countries the government has not made the social security reform a high priority in their agendas because of the political risks involved in the sanctioning of legislation that is strongly opposed or blocked by organized interest groups or the political opposition. In these countries with absent or insufficient political will, reform proposals are awaiting better timing despite the worsening of the social security crisis. Often, political leaders have deliberately delayed reforms in order to incite the collapse of the old traditional public system, thus eventually facilitating its full substitution (in Ecuador, for example). In Brazil the new constitution mandates the reform of social security, but the pension reform demands the elimination of the costly (heavily state subsidized) and privileged seniority pensions enjoyed by civil servants who strongly oppose such a change. President Cardozo waited for his reelection to be able to tackle this difficult task. In Venezuela, initial government inertia combined with changes in President Caldera's position, strong political opposition, and other more urgent economic issues postponed the social security reform, which will probably have to wait for the new administration elected by the end of 1998. The institutional crisis in Ecuador and the eventual removal of the president from office resulted in a stagnant situation (in spite of the previous fifteen years of study and debate on the social security reform) and no executive action is expected until a new president is elected. The president of Guatemala had pension reform à la Chile high on his agenda, but the Guatemalan Institute of Social Security and two private foundations produced proposals for a mixed system that challenged the government's proposal, which was then considerably delayed. When it was finally released in 1997, an independent actuarial report showed that fiscal costs would be huge, so the official proposal now seems to have been put on the back burner.

The evidence shows that governments are more inclined to implement pension reforms first and then move to health sector reforms, with the exceptions of Brazil (no pension reform yet) and Chile (almost simultaneous pension and health sector reforms). In Colombia the two reforms were jointly approved by Congress but the implementation of the health care program was postponed and was not fully operational by the end of 1997. In Peru social security was reformed by both pension and health care laws in 1991–1992. The pension law was implemented in 1993, but new health care reforms were approved only in 1996 and 1997 and are not expected to begin implementation beginning in 1998 and 1999.

Another important point is that, whereas full privatization of the pension system is advocated by the most radical view, full privatization of health care has not been suggested by any group. In contrast to pensions, then, it seems there is a common belief that health care reform sticks very closely to the principles of solidarity, pluralism, and universality. Solidarity implies that individuals contribute in direct proportion to their income levels (progressive) and that each of them has access to effective service when needed. Pluralism means that individuals are free to choose from various options that include both public and private provision of services. Universality signifies that the entire population is covered by a package of services that is effective and affordable (Frenk 1995).

The evidence suggests that in countries with a very strong presence and participation of political parties, labor unions, and organized pressure groups representing the armed forces, civil servants, oil workers, and even the pensioners (in Uruguay, for example), pension reforms tend to be of the mixed or parallel type, with the public sector constituting an important pillar in the architecture of the reform. Despite the region's democratization trend since the mid-1980s, the armed forces continue to be a solid interest group with extraordinary power to exclude themselves from the reform (even when they have been the *pushers* and *reformers*, as in Chile) and preserve their own separate system with privileged entitlement conditions.

When evaluating the prereform conditions, analysts need to look very carefully at the type of regime, political representation, action of organized pressure groups, and the pull of forces of *pushers* and *resisters*. While technological change is inevitable in the long run, its pace, scope, depth, effectiveness, and modus operandi will vary depending upon previous preparation, tolerance, and ability to adapt to the transition process. If political conditions are not conducive to change and if institutional restrictions abound, reforms will be obstructed until those conditions are altered.

The State of Socioeconomic Development

The size of the rural and the informal sectors, the incidence of poverty, the composition of the labor force, the degree of population coverage by social security, the development of a capital market, and the past role of the state as supporter or abuser of social security (to cite a few factors) are important socioeconomic variables affecting the design of the reform. In countries in which a large segment of the labor force is rural or informal and the incidence of poverty is high, a substitutive model would be a phenomenal barrier to the expansion of coverage, and scarce state resources would be depleted to consolidate the protection of a small minority of the labor force mainly in the middle-income group. In this type of country there is seldom a capital market, or it is incipient and risky; therefore erasing another barrier to the success of an FFI system. A well-targeted public social assistance program (particularly on primary health care) for the poor and destitute should be more adequate in these countries, and all fiscal transfers should be geared to that program and to help in the expansion of coverage of a basic pension program.

Conversely, countries with a very large formal labor force (mostly urban) that is already covered and a relatively low incidence of poverty can rely more strongly on mandatory social security programs (public and private) with smaller well-targeted social assistance programs to help the poor. In these countries there is more probability of an existing capital market and insurance industry, and the state should regulate and consolidate them, in order to promote the creation of profitable financial instruments and portfolio diversification of pension-fund investment. Finally, the previous role of the state could be a cue to its future behavior in the reform: in countries with a record of the government's fulfilling its social security obligations there is a high probability that the state will honor the fiscal costs of the transition, but in countries where the state has pilfered social security resources, chances are it will not honor such commitments.

Success of Economic Restructuring and Stabilization Efforts

A third conditioning factor in the implementation of a reform is that it is an integral part of a more comprehensive restructuring of the economy (along the lines described in the introduction to this study). This means that the government has initiated a series of institutional reforms that will modernize and liberalize markets, strengthen the private sector, raise international competitiveness, and redirect economic growth along a sustained path. The creation of an FFI pension program, for example, implies the acknowledgment of an implicit public pension deficit and payment of current pensions as well as future benefits to affiliates that remain in the old system. Such a deficit needs to be met with revenues generated by tax reforms, debt, privatization of public enterprises, or a combination of the three.

During the initial stages of reform, the government ought to provide clear signals of support. These include (1) a transparent regulatory framework that gives confidence to financial intermediaries, private pension fund administrators, and insurance companies; (2) the emission of recognition bonds that confirm the government's commitment to honor past contributions; and (3) the creation, regulation, and promotion of a capital market with diverse financial instruments either before or at the very start of the new pension system. A successful stabilization program reduces inflation and restores confidence in the domestic financial market in which private or public pension fund administrators, institutions administering personal and occupational programs, insurance companies, and private health providers (both for-profit and not-for-profit) operate. Reduction and control of inflation also facilitate the generation of positive real yields of pension funds.

Maturity of the Social Security System

The maturity of the social security system is the fourth conditioning factor in the design of reform and in the period of transition. For example, *latecomer* countries with young social security systems and populations should begin to introduce regulations and practices that avoid the common mistakes of the generous entitlement conditions and benefits, the high payroll contributions that encourage evasion and payment delays, the inequitable benefits, the escalation of administrative costs, and the mismanagement of financial investments that afflicted the traditional public systems. At the same time these countries should set up a series of fundamental innovations or modifications that create the preconditions for the future development of their social security systems. These fundamentals should include cheap, innovative techniques to extend basic benefits to the population; regulations for personal saving and occupational pension plans and the development of the insurance market; encouragement of the voluntary affiliation to FFI supplementary pension programs; social assistance to the very poor; and encouragement of informal support systems to protect the old and the sick in the household.

In *intermediate* countries with more mature social security systems and populations entering the demographic transition, the public system should be reformed to reduce costs and increase revenues. Measures to reduce costs include separation of funds and management of programs (pensions and health); efficiency gains and drastic cuts in administrative expenses; standardization of entitlement conditions and benefits; elimination of duplication of services (provided by social insurance and the Ministry of Health); modernization of the registry; processing and paying of benefits, and so on. Measures to increase revenues should include the reduction of evasion and the payment of debts to the social security system; the increase in contribution rates, if feasible; the professional financial management of the reserve fund without governmental interference, and so on. Recommendations concerning the fundamentals—transparent regulations for the development of saving plans, insurance companies, investment instruments, and so on—that ought to be put in place for a structural social security reform in the case of the *latecomers* are more urgent for the *intermediates*.

Finally, *pioneer* countries with rapidly aging populations and fully mature social security systems (Brazil and Cuba, for example) should implement drastic structural reforms of both the public pension and the health care systems. In pensions, these countries should design new systems that eliminate privileged schemes, standardize and tighten entitlement conditions, introduce the concept of multipillarity, and develop (Cuba) or strengthen (Brazil) capital markets and the insurance industry. In health, they should seek decentralization, cost reduction, the redefinition of responsibilities and roles (public and private), with increased competition and participation of the private sector, and improvements in efficiency.

Divergent Conditioning Factors

Chile offers to the world first-class wine, delicious fruits, and the new technology of an FFI privately managed pension system. Experts in the design of this model, executives of the private pension funds, and public officers are strong advocates of this technology as if it were of a universal nature and could be adopted by any country regardless of how it differs from Chile. Could this model be replicated in an identical way elsewhere? To answer this question we should look at conditioning factors determining the type of social security reform in Chile and assess if similar conditions actually exist in other countries. Keep in mind that Bolivia, El Salvador, and Mexico—all with conditioning factors that differ from those in Chile—in 1995–1996 approved substitutive models, although with important differences vis-à-vis the Chilean prototype.

We have already discussed briefly some of the important differences among countries concerning the first conditioning factor. In the 1970s and 1980s, Chile had unique political and institutional conditions that were conducive to the introduction of a radical structural pension reform. An authoritarian government controlled the three branches of power (executive, legislative, and judicial) for an uninterrupted period of seventeen years; it suppressed political opposition and public debate, disbanded trade unions, and prevented organized interest groups from blocking the reform.

In Argentina, Colombia, and Uruguay, however, the reform was approved by a pluralistic type of democracy and it was much more moderate, resulting in mixed and parallel models. In Uruguay, nevertheless, even such a moderate approach was rejected by Congress in 1992, and it took three more years to finally pass it. In Argentina the proposal of the mixed model was preceded by several years of study and was substantially changed in Congress. In Colombia the initial proposal of the substitutive model failed because of fierce resistance from Congress, political parties, several public institutions, and experts that voiced publicly their opposition to a model that was perceived as being improper for a country in which coverage was low and poverty high.

In Mexico, where there is a limited democracy, a substitutive model was introduced in 1997. It was preceded by two attempts to solve the crisis of social security in effect since the late 1980s. A nonstructural pension reform was tried in 1991, which implied increasing contributions (from a total of 6 percent in 1990 to 8.5 percent in 1996), more flexibility in investment, and separation of the sickness/maternity and pension programs. In 1992 a new "system for retirement savings" (SAR) was established. Changes were not enough to fund the deficit expected to hit hard beginning the year 2002, and reserves were expected to disappear by 1997. As the government judged it unfeasible to further increase contributions, so it decided to move for a structural reform and was able to build a minimum consensus among workers' and employers' organizations that were largely manipulated by the executive. The government approved the reform in a congress where the hegemonic party still had a wide majority. Such minimum consensus, however, required some important concessions: (1) current insured can choose, at the time of retirement, the best pension according to the rules of the old or the new system; (2) pensions are adjusted to inflation; (3) employers contributions were not eliminated and the state contribution to the system was increased; (4) the disability and survivor insurance was not transferred to private insurance companies but was retained by the social security institute (IMSS); (5) administrators of the new old-age-pension system are not only private with exclusive dedication but could also be banks, public agencies (including the IMSS), and mixed; and (6) the systems for federal employees (ISSSTE), the armed forces, and oil workers (all powerful pressure groups) were excluded from the reform. On the other hand the government tried to reduce the fiscal costs of the transition, not only keeping the employer's contribution but also eliminating certain guarantees that are granted in Chile: the recognition bond, the minimum investment yield, and state responsibility in case of bankruptcy of administrators of pension funds.

With regard to the second conditioning factor, Chile had additional specific socioeconomic characteristics that (combined with its political-institutional conditions) facilitated its radical pension reform. (1) A very large majority of the population was covered by the old public system. (2) A large majority of the labor force was formal (salaried) and it had a relatively small rural sector. (3) The Chilean middle class was one of the largest in Latin America. (4) The incidence of poverty was among the lowest in the region in the 1970s. (5) The average payroll contribution was the highest in the region and benefits had deteriorated in many funds. (6) There was a wide multiplicity of pension funds with different benefits, entitlement conditions, and sources of revenue. (7) A capital market had existed and functioned for some ninety years prior to the reform. (8) For decades reform attempts to improve social security had failed.

Argentina and Uruguay have socioeconomic characteristics that resemble those of Chile, but these countries decided to go for a mixed system. Resistance to the Chilean model was effective (within a context of pluralistic democracy and open discussion of the reform) because of three apparent reasons. First, both countries suffered a more severe social security crisis, and the fiscal cost of the transition to an FFI system would have been higher than in Chile and impossible to honor. Second, the Chilean model lacks solidarity and runs the risk of regressivity because it devotes enormous resources to subsidize the insured at the price of cutting public social programs (in health, education, and to alleviate poverty), adverse effects that were more difficult to accept in an open political system. Third, in Argentina and Uruguay there is a profound distrust of private pension fund managers, pure FFI, and the potential of relatively lower capital returns (a fear apparently justified in Uruguay but not, so far, in Argentina), considering recent high inflation or even hyperinflationary episodes.

Bolivia and El Salvador have certainly quite opposite socioeconomic characteristics to Chile and the other two pioneers, and yet they have adopted an FFI privately administered pension model. These two countries have the following common features: (1) they are among the least developed countries in the region; (2) their population coverages are some of the smallest in the region; (3) they have very large informal and rural populations; (4) their middle-classes are small; (5) their poverty levels are among the highest in the region; and (6) their capital markets are very small and unsophisticated. The reform in Bolivia began to operate in mid-1997 and that in El Salvador was expected to start in 1998. It is too early, therefore, to evaluate the impact of the reform in both countries. And yet the significant socioeconomic differences between them and Chile raise fundamental doubts on whether the substitutive model will be able to (1) expand population coverage (actually high contributions may worsen evasion); (2) promote true competition among administrators of pension funds (only two are legally authorized to operate in Bolivia until the year 2000, and their affiliates have been directly assigned by the government based on their place of residence); (3) generate relatively high real investment yields; and (4) pay better pensions and provide key guarantees by the state (Bolivia does not offer any guarantees, not even a minimum pension; El Salvador provides the minimum pension but neither guarantees a minimum investment yield nor state responsibility in case of bankruptcy of administrators of pension funds or insurance companies).

Let us now consider the third conditioning factor: success of economic restructuring and stabilization. The economic philosophy strongly adhered to by President Pinochet in Chile was neoliberalism: a strengthening of the market, retrenchment of the state from production, services, redistribution, and subsidies, widespread privatization and deregulation, and so forth. No other country in the region has so far implemented a more radical structural adjustment program than that of Chile. After the recession of the early 1980s —which provoked severe social costs and forced temporary governmental intervention to save the liberalization process (and bail the private financial groups out of major trouble)—economic growth was sustained and high, and inflation was reduced and kept under control since the mid-1980s. An influx of foreign capital attracted by investment opportunities in Chile's primary export sectors (the agroindustry, fisheries, and mining) and services (commerce, communications, construction, and finance), debt-swaps, and fast privatization spurred the capital market. Macroeconomic stability and the governmental support gave confidence in both the private and the financial sectors. Within the context of such strong neoliberalism, FFI pension and health care systems privately managed (with a subsidiary role of the government), perfectly matched and became the logical goal of the reformers at the end of the 1970s. Furthermore, the Chilean government had the financial capacity to fund the fiscal cost of the transition.

In Bolivia, El Salvador, and Mexico substitutive pension reforms are also a component of a broader neoliberal reform, although none of the three have advanced as much as Chile and their results are considerably poorer. In Argentina and Uruguay the neoliberal reforms in the 1970s and 1980s were very mild compared with Chile's radical structural adjustment at the time. Actually this program was not introduced in Argentina until the 1990s under President Menem and within a context of pluralistic democracy. Both Argentina and Uruguay endorsed also a less radical pension reform: the mixed model.

Finally, on the fourth conditioning factor, in *pioneer* countries such as Chile, Argentina, and Uruguay the public pension system had matured, the population was aging (thus resulting in a declining ratio of contributing insured to pensioners), payroll contributions were very high and difficult to increase even more, state subsidies to the system were growing and, therefore, a structural reform was required. Chile endured some problems that had been alleviated or solved in Argentina and Uruguay, such as numerous pension funds with significant differences among them in entitlement conditions, benefits, financing and financial-actuarial equilibria, which several attempts at reform failed to correct. This might partly explain the most radical type of reform undertaken in Chile. The other two pioneers had been able (in the 1970s) to unify and standardize entitlement conditions in the large majority of those multiple funds, which could have contributed to a more moderate reform (also transition costs of the FFI model would have been higher in these two countries as has been noted already). Some *intermediate* and the majority of *latecomer* countries do not face the same problems of maturity of the pension system and aging of the population as the *pioneers* do and, hence, are under less pressure for a radical urgent reform, although they need to do some type of reform anyway.

Similarities and Differences in the Reforms and Measures to Reduce Transitional Costs

Pension reforms have been classified into substitutive, mixed, and parallel. Tables 17.1A and 17.1B present, in a systematic fashion, the main characteristics of structural reforms of the substitutive model in Chile, Mexico, Bolivia, and El Salvador. Tables 17.2A and 17.2B do the same for the mixed model (Argentina and Uruguay) and the parallel model (Peru and Colombia). Table 17.3 summarizes basic similarities and differences among the eight reforms. The tables are self-explanatory, but we will rely on them for some comparisons in this section and later in the chapter.

The most appealing advantage of the pension reform in Chile, both for insured and employers, was the reduction in the payroll contribution from an average close to 20 percent (paid by both insured and employers in more than fifty different funds) to an average of 13.5 percent in the new system (paid entirely by the insured, who also received a once-and-for-all increase in salary if transferred to the new system). But the elimination of the employer's contribution raised the fiscal costs of the transition. About half the number of affiliates do not regularly contribute to the new system: temporary and seasonal workers, female workers who have temporarily or permanently left their jobs, and so forth. The multiple old pension funds were closed and unified and their entitlement conditions standardized (with the

Table 17.1A Main Characteristics of Structural Pension Reform in Substitutive Models (Chile, Mexico, Bolivia, and El Salvador)

Main Features	*Chile*	*Mexico*
Date of legislation	November 1980	December 1995
Date of starting operation	May 1981	July–September 1997
Type of legislation	Decree law by president	Congress law
Type of reform	Private substitutive	Private substitutive
Old system	Reformed, shutdown based on pay-as-you-go)	Not reformed (IMSS), old-age program shutdown
% of total insured	5%	None (all must transfer in 4 years)
New system	AFPs; private corporations (fully funded, individual capitalization)	AFORES (fully funded, individual capitalization)
% of total insured	95%	100% in 4 years
Coverage		
Currently insured	Term to stay or move to new system (expired in 1986); no cut by age	All must transfer and start contributing to new system (at time of retirement can choose highest pension between entitlement conditions of old system and accumulated fund in the new)
Self-employed	Voluntary coverage	Voluntary coverage
New entrants in labor force	Mandatory coverage in new system (AFPs)	Mandatory coverage in new system
Groups excluded (retain their own coverage)	Armed forces	Armed forces, federal employees, oil workers
% of labor force covered by both systems	80%	38%
First pillar	Minimum pension within private system; mandatory, defined; social assistance pension paid by state to destitute noninsured	Minimum pension in old and new, mandatory, defined
Second pillar	Pension based on accumulated fund in individual account at AFP; defined contribution but nondefined benefit; public system has defined benefits	Either defined pension (for those insured in old system at end of 1995) or accumulated fund in insured's individual account in new system
Third pillar	Voluntary savings	Voluntary savings
Social assistance pension	Paid by state to the dispossessed	None
General contributions		
Insured	Reduced in new system; unchanged in old	No change

Table 17.1A (cont.)

Main Features	*Chile*	*Mexico*
Employer	Eliminated	No change
State	Covers deficit of old system and transfers to new	No change; covers deficit of old system when reserves are depleted
Recognition of contri– butions in old system	Yes; requires 1 year of contribution, adjusted to inflation, without ceiling; earns 4% real annual interest; state pays at time of retirement (recognition bond in new system)	No; years of contribution to new system are added to those accumulated in old system to meet years required; SAR funds given to insured; AFOREs fund is transferred to IMSS
Distribution of contri- butions by pillars (%)		
Insured	Old: 18.8% to 20.7% New: 10% (OA) + 3.2% (D-S) = 13.2%; all goes to AFP; self-employed the same	New: 1.125% (OA-U) + 1% (D-S) = 2.125%
Employer	None in either system	New: 3.15% (OA-U) + 2.8% (D-S) + 2% (SAR) = 7.95% New: state 0.225% (OA-U) + 0.15% extra (AFOREs) + 2% (D-S) = 2.375%
Total	New: 13.2% (old 18.8% to 20.7%)	New: 12.45%; 8.45% for AFOREs (6.45% OA-U + 2% SAR) and 4% for IMSS (D-S)
Employer's obligation after deducting contribution	Transfers directly to old system or AFPs; multiple forms	Transfers to IMSS, which retains its part (for D-S) and transfers pension part to AFOREs
Voluntary contributions	Up to 10%; deducted automatically from salary by employer	Yes; no limit, deducted automatically from salary by employer
Insured active contributors to affiliates (%)	54%	n.a.
Benefits: Old-age pension	Entitlement conditions are uniform in old and new systems	Entitlement conditions are the same in old and new systems, except for calculation of defined pension in old
Age (female/male)	60/65 in both systems	65 in both systems (OA), 60 (U)
Years of work/ contribution	None in new system (for minimum pension only)	24 in both systems
Base salary for retirement	Old: last 5 years New: not defined	Old: defined New: not defined

Table 17.1A (cont.)

Main Features	*Chile*	*Mexico*
Salary displacement (%)	Old: 50–70% of base salary New: not defined	Old: defined New: not defined
Options for retirement	Old: determined by law New: Annuity with programmed pension with AFP or programmed first and annuity later	New: annuity with insurance company or programmed pension insurance company with AFORE
Minimum pension	Yes; state pays the difference and requires 20 years of contributions	Yes, with 24 years of contribution, equal to minimum wage; state guarantees difference
Benefits: Disability and survivor pensions	AFP contracts with an insurance company and transfers to it the premium collected from the insured	Covered by old system (IMSS)
Benefits: Adjustment of pensions	Constant units (U.F.) based on CPI (not for minimum pensions)	By government, annually, based on CPI
Administration (fully funded system/program)		
No. of administrative units	13	17 (March 1997)
Character of administrator	Private corporations of exclusive dedication, profit-seeking	Multiple corporations of exclusive dedication, but can be private, public (including IMSS), mixed; each AFORE has investment companies (SIEFOREs)
Concentration of insured in 3 major administrative units (%)	69%	n.a.
Required minimum capital	US $650,000 (with more than 10,000 affiliates, which is in all current)	US $3.2 million plus $500,000 for each SIEFORE
Accumulated funds	US $33,000 (September 1997)	US $12,300 (projected December 1997)
Funds as % of GDP	41%	3.6% (projected December 1997)

Investment of fund by instrument (%)	Law (ceiling 96)	Actual (December 96)	Law (95–96; ceilings by CONSAR)	(97, n.a.)
State or public securities	50	42	100 first year	—
Mortgage bonds or banks	50	18	—	—

Table 17.1A (cont.)

Main Features	*Chile*		*Mexico*	
Bank deposits	50	4	20	—
Enterprise stocks	40	25	—	—
Enterprise bonds	40	5	29	—
Other bonds, real estate, etc.	50	2.5	—	—
Lending institution, investment funds	10	3	51 (inflation adusted)	—
Foreign investment, etc.	9	0.5	0	—
Other	5–10	42	—	—
Total	—	100	—	—
Commission for risk ranking	Yes, public (also some private)		Yes, public, can prohibit specific investment and order restructuring of the portfolio (ranks SIEFOREs)	
Regulation of minimum investment yield	Law establishes how the minimum real yield is determined in relation to system averages		Not required by law	
Average annual real yield (%)	12.2% (1981–86)		n.a.	
Commissions charged by administrative units	Fixed or % on contributions; mean is 3.1% in 1996 (2.4% without insurance premium)		Fixed or % on contributions or accumulated fund; mean is 2.75% without D-S (projected)	
Periodic reports to insured	Quarterly		Annually	
Switches of pension managers	No limit (but law is being debated restricting it to two per year)		One per year or when commission or investment policy changes	
Supervision	Superintendency of AFP, autonomous, financed by state		National Commission for System of Retirement Savings (CONASAR)	
Publicity	Initially free; regulated by Superintendency since 1991		Supervised by CONSAR, which can suspend or modify ads	
State guarantees	Minimum yield, responsible for accumulated fund and/or pension annunity if AFP/insurance company go bankrupt		Limited to payment of minimum pension	

Source: Mesa-Lago 1997.

Key: OA = Old Age

D-S = Disability and Survivors

U = Unemployment

SAR = Supplementary Retirement Program

Table 17.1B Main Characteristics of Structural Pension Reform in Substitutive Models (Chile, Mexico, Bolivia, and El Salvador)

Main Features	*Bolivia*	*El Salvador*
Date of legislation	November 1996	December 1996
Date of starting operation	May 1997	1998
Type of legislation	Congress law	Congress law
Type of reform	Private substitutive	Private substitutive
Old system	Shutdown, all their patrimony transferred to the Treasury	Reformed, uniformed (ISSS and INPEP) and shutdown (scaled premium in ISS; pay-as-you-go in INPEP)
% of total insured	None; all must move to new system	n.a.
New system	Same as Chile (AFPs and FFI); also a collective capitalization fund (CCF) was established with proceeds from several public privatized enterprises; fund was changed in 1998	Same as Chile (AFPs)
% of total insured	100%	n.a.
Coverage		
Currently insured	All insured in old system assigned to 2 AFPs (50%/50%); those who have already met retirement conditions may join new system but retain old rights; salaried workers not affiliated to old system must register in the new; beneficiaries of the CCF must register in 5 years in an AFP	Those up to age 35 are transferred to new system; 36–50/55 (f/m) have 6 months to stay or move to new system; older than 50/55 must stay in old system
Self-employed	Voluntary coverage	Voluntary coverage
New entrants in labor force	Mandatory coverage in new system for salaried workers	Mandatory coverage in new system
Groups excluded (retain their own coverage)	Armed forces are included, but may have special conditions	Armed forces; special systems foreseen for domestic servants and agriculture
% of labor force covered by both systems	12%	23%
First pillar	Minimum pension in old system but not in FFI; all citizens age 21 and older in Dec. 97 received from CCF an annual bonus (BONOSOL); the last was suspended in 1998	Minimimum pension within public and private (both defined)

Table 17.1B (cont.)

Main Features	*Bolivia*	*El Salvador*
Second pillar	Pension based on accumulated fund in individual account; defined contribution but nondefined benefit	Pension based on accumulated fund in individual account; defined contribution but nondefined benefit; public system has defined benefit
Third pillar	Voluntary savings	Voluntary savings
Social assistance pension	No; but see BONOSOL	No
General contributions		
Insured	Increased in new system	Increased and fairly standardized in old and new systems
Employer	Eliminated (except OR) but initially must increase employees' wages by same amount of contribution raise	Increased and fairly standardized in old and new systems
State	Finances pensions in old system and transfers to the new; also transfers 50% of shares of privatized enterprises to the CCF	Covers deficit of old system and transfers to the new
Recognition of contributions in old system?	Yes; requires 1 month of contribution, calculated by formula; earns interest, with ceiling; state pays at time of retirement; those insured who had paid less than 5 years of contribution receive a lump sum; those with 5 years or more receive monthly payments for life	Yes; adjusted, no interest, no ceiling; state pays at time of retirement
Distribution of contributions by pillars (%)		
Insured	Old: 2.5% to basic and from 3.5% to 13% to complementary (average is 6%) New: 10% (OA) + 2% (D-S) + 5% commission = 12.5%	Old: 1% (ISSS), 4.5% + 6% (INPEP) increasing to 7% in 6 years New: increasing to 6.75% in 6 years; 3.25% (OA) + 3.5% (D-S)
Employer	Old: 4.5% (OADS) + 1.5% (OR) = 6% New: none (except OR: 2%, also administered by AFP)	Old: 2% (ISSS), 4.5% to 6% (INPEP) increasing to 7% in 6 years New: increasing to 6.75% in 6 years
Total	Old: 16% (includes 1.5% state for OADS) New: 14.5% (includes OR, state contributions eliminated)	Old: 3% (ISSS), 9% + 12% (INPEP) increasing to 14% (ceiling) New: increasing to 13.5%: 10% (OA) + 3.5% (D-S) (ceiling)

Table 17.1B (cont.)

Main Features	*Bolivia*	*El Salvador*
Employer's obligation after deducting contribution	Old: collected by state and assigned to a Treasury account New: collected by AFPs	Transfers to old system and AFPs
Voluntary contributions	Yes, deducted automatically by employer from salary; maximum US $3,000 monthly	Yes, no limit; deducted automatically by employer from salary
Insured active contributors to affiliates (%)	n.a.	n.a.
Benefits: Old-age pension	Entitlement conditions in old system maintained for those who have met them at time the reform began	Entitlement conditions are gradually standardized in old system to match those in new
Age (female/male)	Old: 50/55 New: accumulation in account of no less than 70% of average wage in last 5 years; otherwise age 65 is required to receive reduced pension	Old: 55/60 New: 55/60 or accumulation in account equal to 70% of basic wage or 170% of minimum pension
Years of work/contribution	Old: 15 years New: Not defined	Old: 25 years for those 55/60 or 30 years regardless of age New: Same as old
Base salary for retirement	Old: average of wages in last 2 years New: Average of wages in last 5 years (only to determine right to retirement)	Old: Average of wages in last 10 years, adjusted for inflation New: Not defined
Salary replacement (%)	Old: defined New: not defined	Old: 30–60% of base salary New: not defined
Options for retirement	Annuity either fixed or variable, paid by AFP or insurance company when the latter start operations	Same as for Chile
Minimum pension	Not established by law; an insured person age 65 with a pension of less than 70% of the minimum wage can withdraw that proportion monthly until fund is depleted	Yes, with 25 years of contribution; set by state according to average contributory wage and limited by fiscal resources available
Benefits: Disability and survivor pensions	AFP collects premiums for D-S and OR and covers the insured until insurance companies are allowed to function	Old: by old system New: Same as for Chile

Table 17.1B (cont.)

Main Features	*Bolivia*		*El Salvador*	
Benefits: Adjustment of pensions	Annual adjustment based on Index of Value Maintenance, which is related to the dollar		Old: set by government New: set by government according to average contributory wage	
Administration (fully funded system/program)				
No. of administrative units	2 in first 5 years of operation; selected by the Superintendency in international competition		2–3 (projected for 1998)	
Character of administrator	Private corporations of exclusive dedication, profit-seeking, which manage both the FFI and CCF programs; the last was suspended in 1998		Private corporations of exclusive dedication, profit-seeking	
Concentration of insured in 3 major administrative units (%)	100%		100% (if 2–3 units, as projected	
Required minimum capital	US $1.4 million		US $570,000 to $1.7 million	
Accumulated funds (in $US millions)	1,700 in CCF; 180 for FFI		n.a.	
Funds as % of GDP	25% in CCF		n.a.	
Investment of fund by instrument (%)	Law (ceiling 97)	Actual (97, n.a.)	Law (ceiling 96)	Actual (97, n.a.)
State or public securities	100%, but no more than $180 million, fixed by Superintendency		20–60% (next lines never over 50% total)	
Mortgage bonds or banks	30–50		30–40	
Bank deposits	20–50		30–40	
Enterprise stocks	20–40		—	
Enterprise bonds	30–45		0–20	
Other bonds, real estate, etc.	20–50		30–40	
Lending institution, investment funds	5–15		0–20	
Foreign investment, etc.	10–50		0	
Other	0–5		0–10	
Total	—		—	
Commission for risk ranking	Superintendencies of Pensions and Regulation of Financial System; private ones will be allowed in the future		Yes, public	

Table 17.1B (cont.)

Main Features	*Bolivia*	*El Salvador*
Regulation of minimum investment yield	Similar to Chile's; not mandatory in first 2 years	Similar to Chile's
Average annual real yield	n.a.	n.a.
Commissions charged by administrative units	Charged on contributions, wages, pensions, or accumulated fund (fixed or percentage): mean is 3% in 1997–2000	Percentage (top 3%) on contributory wage, monthly pension, etc.
Periodic reports to insured	Annually	Biannually (can be requested bimonthly)
Switches of pension managers	Not until 2000 (except for residence change); thereafter one per year	Six months or free if less than minimum investment yield
Supervision	Superintendency of Pensions, autonomous, financed by AFPs	Superintendency of Pensions, autonomous, financed by AFPs and state
Publicity	Supervised by Superintendency of pensions	Controlled by Superintendency which can force an AFP to suspend or modify ads
State guarantees	None	Limited to payment of minimum pension

Source: Mesa-Lago 1997.

exception of the armed forces), which reduced costs, but the state became responsible for the deficit of current and future pensions in the closed public system, a deficit generated by a massive transfer of insured to the new system.

The government also finances past contributions to the public system, for those insured who transferred to the new, with a recognition bond that is adjusted to inflation, has no ceiling, and earns a fixed real annual return of 4 percent. In addition the state also guarantees a minimum pension in the FFI system to all the insured (the majority) that will not accumulate enough in their individual accounts to finance such pension. There are questions about the true competitiveness of the new system, as three out of thirteen AFPs concentrate more than two-thirds of the affiliates and this proportion shows an increasing trend: administrative costs of the new system have not declined. The fiscal cost of the transition has been enormous but manageable because of recurrent government surpluses and investment of a good part of the pension funds in public debt instruments (the overwhelming majority until the mid-1980s and still about 39 percent of total investment,

Table 17.2A Main Characteristics of Structural Pension Reform in Mixed Systems (Argentina and Uruguay)

	Mixed Systems	
Main Features	*Argentina*	*Uruguay*
Date of legislation	October 1993	September 1995
Date of starting operation	July 1994	April 1996
Type of legislation	Congress law	Congress law
Type of reform	Mixed: basic and supplementary	Same as Argentina
Old system	Reformed, continues open (based on pay-as-you-go)	Same as Argentina (BPS: pay-as-you-go)
% of total insured	33%	61%
New system	Social insurance (pay-as you-go) and AFJPs (fully funded and individual capitalization)	Social insurance (BPS: pay-as-you-go) and AFAPs (fully funded and individual capitalization)
% of total insured	67%	39%
Coverage		
Currently insured	Term to stay or move (expired in 1994) but always can move from old-reformed to new system (not from new to old); cut by age (applicable to all over 18); those who stay in old-reformed system receive an additional permanent benefit	All those below age 40 must move to new system (BPS does selection if insured doesn't decide); those over 40 cannot stay or move to new system
Self-employed	Mandatory coverage	Same as Argentina
New entrants in labor force	Can choose between old system (public reformed) and new system (mixed)	Must enter the new (mixed) system
Groups excluded (retain their own coverage)	Armed forces, provinces, and municipalities (the latter two can join through agreements)	Armed forces, plus four other groups (the Executive must determine incorporation of those four)
% of labor force covered by both systems	82%	80%
First pillar	Basic pension within social insurance, mandatory, defined; AFJP; social assistance pension paid by the state to destitute noninsured	Basic pension within social insurance, mandatory, defined; not in AFAP; social assistance pension paid by state to destitute noninsured
Second pillar	Supplementary pension in AFJP	Supplementary pension in AFAP

Table 17.2A (cont.)

Main Features	*Mixed Systems* *Argentina*	*Uruguay*
	(as in Chile) for those who select mixed system; additional pension (defined) for those who stay in public reformed system	(as in Chile) for those who select mixed system; defined pension for those who stay in public reformed systems
Third pillar	Voluntary savings in AFJP	Voluntary savings in AFAP
Social assistance pension	Same as Chile (ages 60–70 according to various cases)	Same as Chile (age 70+ or disabled)
General contributions		
Insured	No change	Increased (but salary is raised proportionally)
Employer	No change	Decreased
State	Taxes for new system (social insurance) and coverage of any resulting deficit	Taxes for new system (social insurance) and other aid if needed
Recognition of contributions in old system	Yes, but requires 30 years of contribution, has a ceiling, doesn't pay interest; social insurance pays (compensatory pension added to basic and supplementary pension)	No, because contributions are used to pay basic pension in BPS, but number of years of contribution are acknowledged to fulfill retirement conditions
Distribution of contributions by pillars (%)		
Insured	Old: All goes to old (reformed) system New: 11% to 2nd pillar (includes 3.5% for D-S and Comm.); self-employed: 16% to 1st pillar and 11% to 2nd pillar	Old: all goes to old (reformed system) New: 15% divided by 3 salary brackets: up to 5,000 pesos goes to 1st pillar, 5,000–15,000 to 2nd, and above 15,000 to 3rd; D-S not clear
Employer	Old: all goes to old system New: 16% goes to 1st pillar	Old: all goes to old system New: 12.5% to 1st pillar (up to 15,000 pesos)
Total	Both: 27%	Both: 27.5%
Employer's obligation after deducting contribution	Transfers to state tax collection agency (with one single form), which in turn transfers to AFPs and/or public program	Transfers to BPS that keeps share of 1st pillar and transfers 2nd pillar share to AFAPs
Voluntary contributions	Yes, no limit, deducted automatically by employer from salary	Yes, no limit, paid directly to AFAP by insured
Insured active contributors to affiliates (%)	52%	67%

Table 17.2A (cont.)

Main Features	*Mixed Systems* *Argentina*	*Uruguay*
Benefits: Old-age pension	Entitlement conditions are uniformed in old and new systems	Entitlement conditions are uniformed in old and new systems
Age (female/male)	60/65 in both systems (gradually increased from 55/60)	60 for both sexes, in both systems (female age gradually increased in 5 years)
Years of work/contribution	None for supplementary pension, only for basic pension	35 (increased from 30)
Base salary for retirement	Basic pension equal to 2.5 AMPOS (1 AMPO = total insured's contributions over total number of insured) estimated twice a year; compensatory pension up to 53% of the average salary over last 20 years; 2nd pillar not defined	Basic pension equal to average of last 20 years (indexed) or 20 best years (indexed) plus 5%; 2nd pillar not defined
Salary replacement (%)	—	50% for 35 years of contribution, plus 0.5% for each additional year (up to 2.5%) and 3% for each year above age 60 (up to 30%)
Options for retirement	First 2 similar to Chile and a third for insured with low pensions	Accumulated fund in an AFAP is transferred to an insurance company with similar options as in Chile
Minimum pension	Yes, paid by social insurance (basic pension), requires 30 years of contributions	Same as Argentina
Benefits: Disability and survivor pensions	Similar to Chile in mixed systems, but life-disability and annuity insurance companies are separated; selection is done through bidding; covers occupational hazards	Same as Chile
Benefits: Adjustment of pensions	Annually set by government budget	Constant values of 1995 (adjusted according to Constitution)
Administration (fully funded system/program)		
No. of administrative units	21	6
Character of administrator	Multiple: private (for-profit or not), public, unions, banks, etc.	Multiple: public (first AFAP must be established by BPS) or private (various types)

Table 17.2A (cont.)

Main Features	*Mixed Systems* *Argentina*		*Uruguay*	
Concentration of insured in 3 major administrative units (%)	40%		72%	
Required minimum capital	US $3 million		US $1 million (60,000 constant monetary units in 1995)	
Accumulated funds (in $US millions)	5,031 (Nov. 1996)		51 (Dec. 1996)	
Funds as % of GDP	1.4%		0.4%	
Investment of fund by instrument (%)	Law (ceiling 96)	Actual (June 96)	Law (ceiling 95)	Actual (96, n.a.)
State or public securities	50	49	60–100	—
Mortgage bonds or banks	15	4	30	—
Bank deposits	28	15	30	—
Enterprise stocks	35	18	25	—
Enterprise bonds	42	8	20 (1st year) later 70	—
Other bonds, real estate, etc.	—	—	30	—
Lending institution, investment funds	14	2	15	—
Foreign investment, etc.	10	0.2	0	—
Other	—	3.8	—	—
Total	—	100	—	—
Commission for risk ranking	Yes, but the National Stock Commission and the Central Bank are more important		Central Bank or the Executive will regulate it	
Regulation of minimum investment yield	Same as Chile but in nominal terms		Similar to Chile	
Average annual real yield (%)	16.2% (1994–96)		n.a.	
Commissions charged by administrative units	Fixed or % of contribution or account balance; mean is 3.5% in 1996 (2.9% without premium)		Fixed or % of contribution; mean is 2.93 in 1996 (2.1% without premium)	
Periodic reports to insured	Triannually		Biannually	
Changes of administrative units	Two per year		Two per year	

Table 17.2A (cont.)

Main Features	*Mixed Systems*	
	Argentina	*Uruguay*
Supervision	Superintendency of AFJP, autonomous, financed by AFJPs	Central Bank (the BPS has minimal functions); no financing additional
Publicity	State-regulated (cannot start until AFJP is established)	Veracity controlled (same as in Argentina)
Other state guarantees	Same as Chile except minimum yield guaranteed only in public AFJPs	Same as Argentina, but responsibility for bankruptcy also limited to public AFAP only

Source: Mesa-Lago 1997.

which results in high interest payments). And yet, the annual net effect of the savings in the private pension fund minus the fiscal deficit resulting from the transition was negative in every year of the period 1981–1995, although it is decreasing and should eventually become positive.

The magnitude of the prereform public pension debt in Argentina and Uruguay were much higher than in Chile, which would have implied an overwhelming fiscal cost of the transition if they had followed the substitutive approach. The mixed models of Argentina (there is the option of choosing between the public reformed and the mixed system) and Uruguay (the mixed system is mandatory) integrate the reformed public program (with new stringent eligibility conditions) and an FFI program that offers supplementary pensions. In both countries the fiscal cost of the transition has been lessened because the public program remains open. In Argentina a sort of recognition bond (which does not exist in Uruguay) has a ceiling and does not bear interest. In the two countries there is no minimum pension guaranteed because the public program pays a basic pension. The mixed system thus should reduce fiscal costs of the transition and maintain solidarity within the public program. But the long-run sustainability of the reformed public program—which continues to be based on pay-as-you-go (PAYG), albeit with strengthened finances—is a matter of concern in both countries.

In the parallel models of Peru and Colombia, the insured can choose between public and FFI systems. Colombia's public system is more financially sustainable than Peru's because it has introduced comprehensive, stricter changes in entitlement conditions that have led to substantial increases in reserves. By contrast the Peruvian public system was not reformed until

Table 17.2B Main Characteristics of Structural Pension Reform in Parallel Systems (Peru and Colombia)

	Parallel Systems	
Main Features	*Peru*	*Colombia*
Date of legislation	December 1992	December 1996
Date of starting operation	June 1993	April 1994
Type of legislation	Presidential decree	Congress law
Type of reform	Parallel or selective	Same as Peru
Old system	Not reformed, continues open (IPSS now ONP)	Reformed, continues open (ISS: scaled premium)
% of total insured	42%	62%
New system	Same as Chile (AFPs)	SAFPs (fully funded and individual capitalization)
% of total insured	58%	38%
Coverage		
Currently insured	Can choose between IPSS/ ONP and AFP and move back to the former (the return is not clearly allowable since 1995)	Those age 35/40 and over can maintain their old entitlement conditions (including civil servants), but if they change jobs, may become covered by new system; those younger than 35/40 are covered by new system and can select between public (ISS) and private (SAFP) programs; those age 50/55 cannot join SAFPs unless they contribute for 10 additional years
Self-employed	Voluntary coverage	Voluntary coverage
New entrants in labor force	Legally can join IPSS or AFPs	Covered by new system (including civil servants) and can select between public and private programs
Groups excluded (retain their own coverage)	Armed forces, fishermen, artists, chauffeurs, civil servants are allowed to join AFPs; large majority of labor is not covered by social insurance	Armed forces, public teachers and oil workers; many provincial and municipal funds are excluded; large majority of the labor force is not covered by social insurance
% of labor force covered by both systems	32%	35% (a wage contribution of 1% devoted to extend coverage of ISS)
First pillar	Minimum pension to be established	Minimum pension (with limits); social assistance pension for the destitute
Second pillar	If public program is selected, only one pillar and defined benefit; if private program is selected, same as Chile	Same as Peru

Table 17.2B (cont.)

Main Features	*Parallel Systems* *Peru*	*Colombia*
Third pillar	Voluntary savings in AFP	Voluntary savings in SAFP
Social assistance pension	No	Yes, to be financed by state and municipalities (age 65+)
General contributions		
Insured	Unchanged in old, increased in new; since 1997 old is higher than new	Increased in equally in old and new systems
Employer	Initially unchanged in old (eliminated 1995); eliminated in new	Increased equally in both systems
State	Covers deficit of pensions in old system	Same as Peru
Recognition of contributions in old system	Yes, but requires 4 years of contributions to old system; has ceiling; amount adjusted to inflation, does not earn interest; few bonds have been issued by the state, but a new state fund has been created to help guarantee it	Yes, but requires 3 years of previous contributions, bond adjusted to inflation; ceiling; real interest of 3–4%; if the change is from private to public, the former's individual fund is transferred to the latter
Distribution of contributions by pillars (%)		
Insured	Old: initially 3%, increased to 11% in 1995 and to 13% in 1997 New: 8% (OA) + 3.8% (D-S + Comm.); 1% (solidarity) went to IPSS for welfare but was eliminated in 1995	Equal in both systems as of 1996 2.5% (OA)+ 0.9% (D-A + Adm.) + 1% (solidarity) = 4.4%
Employer	Old: 6% (none since 1995) New: none (only voluntary)	7.5% (OA) + 2.6% (D-S + Adm.) = 10.1%
Total	Old: initially 9%; 13% since 1996 New: 11.8% since 1996 (was 14.5%)	Both: 14.5% (13.5% for insured below certain wage level)
Employer's obligation after deducting contribution	Transfers directly to IPSS or AFPs	Transfers directly to ISS or SAFPs
Voluntary contributions	Yes, up to 20% (with tax deferral); deducted automatically by employer from salary	Yes, no limit; deducted automatically by employer from salary
Insured active contributors to affiliates (%)	45%	50–53%

Table 17.2B (cont.)

Main Features	*Parallel Systems* *Peru*	*Colombia*
Benefits: Old-age pension	Entitlement conditions in old system are basically unchanged (except age) but uniformed in new system	Entitlement conditions are tightened in old system (ISS)
Age (female/male)	Old: 55/60 (65 since 1995) New: 65	Old: 55/60 (gradual increase to 57/62) New: No fixed age; accumulated fund must finance a pension 15% higher than minimum wage
Years of work/ contribution	Old: 13–15 New: 20	Old: 20 (increased from 10) New: Not fixed (see above)
Base salary for retirement	Old: 3–5 best years New: not defined	Old: increase from 10 to 20 years New: not defined
Salary replacement (%)	Old: 50–100% New: not defined, except for early retirement	Old: 65–85% New: not defined
Options for retirement	Similar to Chile in new system	Same as Chile in new system
Minimum pension	Not originally; promise of introduction but not regulated yet	Yes, but with limitations (age 57/62 and 23 years of contribution); administered by ISS (state pays the difference); if not right acquired in new system, the accumulated fund is reimbursed
Benefits: Disability and survivor pensions	New: same as Chile	Old: granted by ISS New: Same as Chile; rules and calculations are the same in both systems
Benefits: Adjustment of pensions	Old: adjusted by law	Annual adjustment by government based on CPI
Administration (fully funded system/program)		
No. of administrative units	5 (initially 8)	9
Character of administrator	Same as Chile	Multiple: private, public, co-ops, unions, mutual-aid societies, family allowances
Concentration of insured in 3 major administrative units (%)	73%	58%
Required minimum capital	US $500,000 (500,000 soles as of 1992)	US $4 million
Accumulated funds (in $US millions)	1,780 (May 1998)	470 (June 1996)

Table 17.2B (cont.)

Main Features	*Parallel Systems* *Peru*		*Colombia*	
Funds as % of GDP	3%		0.6%	
Investment of fund by instrument (%)	Law (ceiling 95)	Actual (Dec. 97)	Law (ceiling 95 not specified in law)	Actual (March 96)
State or public securities	40	2	50	10
Mortgage bonds or banks	40	1	30	4
Bank deposits	30	27	—	26
Enterprise stocks	35	35	30	0.2
Enterprise bonds	3	19	20	—
Other bonds, real estate, etc.	25	4	50	33
Lending institution, investment funds	10	12	—	12.8
Foreign investment, etc.	5	0.2	10	0
Other	—	—	—	14
Total		100		100
Commission for risk ranking	Yes, public-autonomous		Not public, but there are private (regulated by Superintendency of Stocks)	
Regulation of minimum investment yield	Same as Chile		Minimum is determined by the state based on overall investment yield in capital market	
Average annual real yield (%)	6.9% (1993–98)		6.7% (July 95–March 96)	
Commissions charged by administrative units	Same as Chile but no fixed commissions since 1997; mean is 3.8% in 1996 (2.34% without premium)		Similar to Chile, mean is 3.5% (2.6% without premium) n.a.	
Periodic reports to insured	Quarterly		Quarterly	
Changes of administrative units	One per year (in practice)		Two per year	
Supervision	Superintendency of AFPs, autonomous, financed by AFPs		Superintendency of Banks regulates investment	
Publicity	Supervised by Superintendency of AFPs and a consumer protection agency		State-regulated	
Other state guarantees	Neither for minimum yield nor for bankruptcy of AFP or insurance company		Similar to Chile	

Source: Mesa-Lago 1997.

Table 17.3 Similarities and Differences Between Structural Reforms in Pensions in Eight Latin American Countries

Similarities

1. The pension program is separated from health care and other social security programs.

2. Entitlement conditions and benefits are standardized and usually tightened (but special privileged separate programs for some groups persist, e.g., the armed forces in all countries, except possibly in Bolivia).

3. The public program is shut down in half of the countries (Chile, Bolivia, El Salvador, Mexico) and left open in the other half (Argentina, Colombia, Peru, Uruguay), although might be reformed.

4. Introduction of the fully funded individual capitalization method with defined contributions, either exclusively (Chile, Mexico, Bolivia, El Salvador) or supplementary (Argentina and Uruguay) or selective (Colombia and Peru).

5. Government (and fiscal) regulation and supervision of FFI and coverage of deficit of public program.

6. Basic pension or minimum pension guaranteed (except in Bolivia).

7. Years of service or past contributions are acknowledged (recognition bonds) except in Uruguay and Mexico.

8. Several options for payment of the pension at time of retirement.

9. Disability and survivors' insurance is mandatory in all cases.

10. Pension funds and the capital of FFI fund administrators are kept separate.

Differences

1. The multipillarity of the pension program varies according to the four conditioning factors that affect the type of reform.

2. Entitlement conditions for the benefit differ (age of retirement, years of contribution, conditions for early retirement, etc.).

3. Employer contribution is eliminated (Chile, Bolivia, Peru) or continues to exist (state in Argentina, Colombia, El Salvador, Mexico, Uruguay).

4. Presence or absence of a solidarity component in the arrangement differs.

5. The method (FFI, partially funded capitalization or pay-as-you-go) and the sources of finance (contributions, earmarked taxes, general revenues) of each of the pillars varies.

6. Nature of FFI pension fund administrators varies (private with exclusive dedication or multiple).

7. Type of basic pension and guaranteed minimum pension varies.

8. Method used to estimate years of service and characteristics of the recognition bond varies.

9. Movement between systems, and within the FFI system/program between pension fund administrators varies.

10. Freedom to choose between mandatory systems for new entrants differs.

Source: Tables 17.1 and 17.2.

1995 and then only partially. It apparently has improved its financial condition but continues in actuarial imbalance. Thus, it remains to be seen how the Peruvian government will remedy the potential crisis of its public system.

All countries have learned at least ten lessons from Chile's reform (the one with the longest experience) to reduce fiscal costs of the transition and administrative costs in the new system.

1. Introducing restrictions on the recognition bond: the capping of it by a ceiling (Argentina, Bolivia, Colombia, and Peru); the requirement of a minimum number of years of previous contributions (thirty in Argentina, five in Bolivia, four in Peru, three in Colombia); and no paying of interest (Argentina, El Salvador, and Peru). Furthermore, Peru has actually emitted a very small number of recognition bonds. Uruguay chose not to issue such bonds because past and current contributions to the public program are used to pay a basic pension—past years of contribution, however, are acknowledged to fulfill retirement conditions. Mexico does not pay recognition bonds either (although it has a substitutive system), although past years of contribution are counted in the public system to meet retirement conditions.

2. Paying a basic pension in the public program (Argentina and Uruguay) makes it unnecessary for the state to guarantee a minimum pension in the FFI program. Furthermore, years of contribution in order to be entitled to this benefit in the FFI system have been increased over the twenty years required by Chile as follows: thirty in Argentina, twenty-five in El Salvador, four in Mexico, and three in Colombia. Finally, Peru has not yet regulated the minimum pension, and Bolivia does not offer it.

3. Raising the age of retirement in the old system (and often in the new) as follows: plus five years in Argentina and Peru for both sexes, plus five in Uruguay for females, and two in Colombia for both sexes.

4. Increasing the years of contribution required for retirement in the public system (and sometimes in the new too) by fifteen in El Salvador, ten in Colombia, from five to seven in Peru, and five in Uruguay.

5. Expanding the number of years used to calculate the base salary for the pension in the public program to ten years in Colombia and from five to seven in El Salvador.

6. Maintaining the employer's contribution unchanged in Argentina, El Salvador, and Mexico; raised in Colombia; and slightly reduced in Uruguay. Only Chile, Bolivia, and Peru, after 1995, eliminated that contribution.

7. Raising the insured's contribution in Bolivia, Colombia, El Salvador, Peru, and Uruguay, or keeping it unchanged in Argentina and Mexico (con-

versely that contribution was reduced in Chile's new system).

8. Eliminating state guarantees for bankruptcy of administrators of pension funds and insurance companies and for the minimum investment yield in Bolivia, El Salvador, Mexico, and Peru (in Argentina and Uruguay the guarantee against bankruptcy is limited to publicly managed pension funds).

9. Limiting the number of transfers among private pension fund administrators in all seven countries to reduce inefficiencies and costs.

10. Regulating and supervising the operation of salespersons and marketing expenses to reduce administrative costs. Table 17.3 presents a summary of basic similarities and differences for the eight countries in question.

HEALTH SECTOR REFORMS IN COMPARATIVE PERSPECTIVE

Health care reforms in Chile, Brazil, and Colombia possess important common goals. These include decentralization, universalization of coverage, promotion of private participation in the provision of health care under new organizational and financial arrangements, and achievement of greater effectiveness, efficiency, and quality in the public sector. Table 17.4 compares the main characteristics of these three reforms.

One common purpose of health reform in Chile and Colombia was the vertical decentralization of the provision of health care. Municipalities and local governments were given the administration of preventive and primary health care by means of direct servicing (Chile) or subcontracting services (Colombia). This measure gave local levels spending authority and autonomy in the management of health care. In Brazil, whose health sector is structured along a modified Health Maintenance Organization model (it relies on the reimbursement of health expenses), the Reforma Sanitária aimed at the transference of responsibility and authority for health care to the local level and merged social security and public health services. It is expected that by bringing the provision of basic health care closer to the beneficiaries, both quality and actual coverage will increase.

A second goal was the expansion of coverage. In Chile coverage was already very large before the reform was initiated with the 1980 Constitution. However, the ultimate purpose of decentralization or the so-called "munipalization" of public health services was the correction of the past overcentralization and increases in coverage to reach universality. In Brazil the

Table 17.4 Main Characteristics of Structural Health Care Reforms by Type

	Selective Dual Reform	*Selective Multiple Reforms*	
	Chile	*Brazil*	*Colombia*
Date of reform	Constitution 1980; decree-laws 1979, 1981, etc.	Constitution 1988; decree 1987; law 1990, 1993	Constitution 1991; laws 1991, 1993
Date of implementation	May 1981 (private system)	First phase of decentralization began in 1984	December 1994, but not fully until 2000
Type of reform	Public, including social insurance (institutional and free choice) and private (ISAPREs)	Merged federal financing and delivery systems; decentralized service delivery to municipalities; expanded services toward universalization; changed method of payment for public and private providers; offered broad choice to patients	Two regimes: contributive (former social insurances) and subsidized (rest and poor); all can select management agencies (EPS: organized by social insurances, public sector, private firms, family allowance funds, etc.) and providers of services
Public system	Not closed but reformed; the insured (current and future) selects between the public and private systems	Services available to population along with the contrated private sector that is reimbursed by the federal government; state and municipal governments receive some transfers for their public systems	
Private system	ISAPRES: private corporations of exclusive dedication, for or not for profit; insured can shift among them or go back to the public system	Large proportion of ambulatory and hospital services in private sector reimbursed by federal government; private insurance grew rapidly during the reform	
Coverage	Salaried workers and pensioners (mandatory); self-employed (voluntary); includes dependent relatives	All the population under the 1988 Constitution	All the population (law 1993) by year 2000, but little expansion; insured (ISS, public sector, armed forces) continue under that system and the noninsured and the poor under public decentralized program
% of population covered			
Public system	1993: 65% (+ 4% armed forces)	1995: 100%	n.a.

Table 17.4 (cont.)

	Selective Dual Reform	*Selective Multiple Reforms*		
	Chile	*Brazil*	*Colombia*	
Private system	1993: 25%	1995: publicly reimbursed hospitals virtually accessible to all (some tertiary facilities created as "foundations" and charge for services)		
Not covered	5% (commercial insurance, mutual aid, direct service)	25% of population is also covered by private insurance	n.a.	
Contributions (% of salary income)			Contributive	Subsidized
Salaried insured	7% (same for both systems); transferred fully to public or private system. Subsidies according to income (poor exempted);	n.a.	4% plus 1% solidarity for extension to the poor	"Subsidized contribution"
Self-employed insured	Better health package by ISAPREs requires additional 3–4% contribution	n.a.		
Employer	None	n.a.	8%	—
State	Covers deficit in public system	As of 1993, health is financed out of general revenues and special earmarked taxes	None	Taxes and public general revenues
	7% (without fiscal support)		13%	—
Benefits				
Public system	Health promotion, preventive and curative, paid leave for labor disability	Equal across the population; include prevention, treatment, and catastrophic care, subject to authorization ceilings for hospital admission; benefits also restricted by reimbursement levels, especially for outpatient services that reduce provider availability owing to refusal to accept low payments for services	Mandatory Health Plan: preventive, health promotion, catastrophic risks; by 2000, basic benefits will be equal for all; during the transition, only subsidized members get first-level care	

Table 17.4 (cont.)

	Selective Dual Reform	*Selective Multiple Reforms*	
	Chile	*Brazil*	*Colombia*
Private system	Same, except preventive and promotion; additional health package is optional	n.a.	n.a.
Administration			
Public system	FONSA in charge of finances; SNSS provides services through 27 regional units; supervised by the Ministry of Health	Federal services financed under reimbursement administered by the Ministry of Health/INAMPS; state or municipalities administer their services; autonomous hospital directors administer tertiary care foundations	Ministry of Health administers the system through National Council of Social Security Health and a Solidarity and Guarantee Fund (mechanism for compensation between the two regimes)
Private system	Direct or contracted services	Federal Ministry of Health/INAMPS administers reimbursement for private hospitals; states or municipalities administer out-patient reimbursement program for physicians	n.a.
No. of administrators	35 (1993)	n.a.	n.a.
Minimum capital	US $123,500 (1995)	n.a.	n.a.
Shift in affiliation	After one year	Only one system	Free
Supervision	Superintendency of ISAPREs	n.a.	Superintendency of the Ministry of Health

Source: Chapters 10–12 of this volume.

1988 Constitution went even further, it guaranteed unrestricted access by all citizens to publicly provided or financed care. Consequently, an excess demand for services led to severe financial imbalances. The Colombian strategy was slightly more conservative: social security reform legislation (which was preceded by a constitutional reform in 1991) has promised universal coverage by the year 2000 (the reform process is expected to last ten years). Serious reservations exist, however, about Colombia's capacity to achieve this goal. In 1996 the government took half of the social insurance's revenue for fiscal expenditures and, instead of fulfilling its financial obligation to extend coverage, the government wanted family allowances to shift 1 percent (out of 4 percent contribution) to meet this purpose.

The participation of the private sector in the provision of health care is one of the most visible outcomes of structural reforms. In Chile the new health care system implies the subsidiary but regulatory role of the state in the provision of health services, the promotion of the private sector participation through tax incentives, and the contracting of private health services by the public sector. The Colombian model is quite innovative because it reorients how health care delivery is organized (demand-driven) and how providers are paid (capitation). Here, the old social security institute and the Ministry of Health that provided services in the traditional way (supply-driven) are replaced by private corporations that represent and enroll individuals according to shared characteristics (occupation, income level, location) and that demand health care services from privately managed providers. Public funds will subsidize social insurance premiums for low-income groups. This model is based on the belief that demand-side subsidization is preferable to supply-side financing of direct delivery systems that eventually end up with enormous wastage, low-quality services, and no advancements in coverage. The new health care system in Colombia is very complex, with tedious accounting and administrative procedures, and it is advancing very slowly. Brazil relies heavily on privately provided health services. The reform process has increased private sector alternatives to deliver and fund health care, the development of a public insurance system based on prospective payment for all health services, and the universal access to publicly financed services paid for through direct payroll taxes.

Health sector reforms seek the attainment of greater effectiveness and efficiency and improved quality of services in the public sector. While the Colombian reform contains important elements of solidarity, the Chilean model has been criticized for being highly stratified and less solidarian. In Chile a combination of lower public sector revenue (because of the disaffiliation of the upper-level income groups from the public program) and a smaller percentage of government funding led to a decrease in both quantity and quality of public health services at all levels. It also caused greater monetary strain in municipalities to compensate for the decrease in funding, and further, it generated an increase in wage contributions from 3 to 7 percent.

From the point of view of infrastructure, hospitals and clinics have faced serious limitations in the acquisition of modern technology resulting in the deterioration of secondary and tertiary health care. In Colombia the Ministry of Health has had little success in improving the quality and efficiency of health care, and it is unlikely that municipal governments can change this situation with similar organizational structures and incentives, notwithstanding the decentralization process. It is expected, however, that as the reform begins to trickle down, greater efficiency and quality should result from the subcontracting of services in the private sector.

There seems to be, however, an element of inertia that keeps each group under the former institutional provider. One of the major purposes of the social security reform in Colombia is the provision of a standard benefit package to every citizen, which is to be accomplished through the joint collaboration of the contributory and subsidized regimes (in ten years). In Brazil the universalization of coverage has been attained legally, but financial mismanagement and chaos are leading to unfulfilled expectations. Because of the lack of public oversight and supervision, increased access to publicly financed health care has motivated considerable increases in costs, little control on volume and price, and lack of planning, to cite a few problems. Therefore, the quality of publicly financed health care is deteriorating.

FINDINGS OF THE STUDY: ANSWERING THE KEY QUESTIONS OF THE REFORM

This section is mainly confined to pension reform because of the lack of enough implemented reforms in health care. Herein we resume our findings and answer the seven key questions raised in the introduction. We contrast the structural reform assumptions with the evidence generated in this book and elsewhere (see Mesa-Lago 1997).

Question 1: Coverage and Compliance

Coverage of the EAP in the country cases discussed in this book range from 80 percent in Argentina, Chile, and Uruguay to approximately 30 percent in Guatemala, then only 23 percent in El Salvador and 12 percent in Bolivia (two of the lowest in the region). In Argentina, Chile, and Uruguay, postreform coverage is very close to prereform levels. In Guatemala, El Salvador, and Bolivia, the structure of the EAP is an important limitation to the extension of coverage because the majority of the labor force is self-employed, informal, or rural. Only 11 percent of the self-employed in Chile are covered by the FFI pension system where coverage is voluntary and only 4 percent are active contributors. In Argentina and Uruguay coverage is higher both because the percentage of the labor force that is self-employed is small and because coverage is mandatory for this group. In all other countries contribution rates in the FFI system are too high (even higher if employer's contributions have been eliminated) and thus, self-employed, informals, and rural workers do not affiliate.

A few countries with low population coverage and a high proportion of self-employed, informals, and agricultural workers in the labor force have introduced mechanisms to extend coverage, but it is not clear what the results are. In Colombia a solidarity contribution rate of 1 percent was introduced for this purpose. In Peru a similar solidarity contribution was established in 1993 but was eliminated in 1995. In Bolivia a solidarity fund was created, with partial proceeds from the privatization of public enterprises, but it is used to pay annual cash benefits to every affiliate of a certain age regardless of income or social protection.

The presumption that ownership of the FFI account is an incentive for compliance because the insured strive to increase their individual accounts to generate a higher pension at retirement has faced serious constraints in the real world. Thus, about half of the affiliates are not active contributors—ranging from 45 percent in Peru (despite state actions to make the FFI more attractive) to 67 percent in Uruguay (where the administration is multiple)—because of the following reasons. First, when workers withdraw temporarily or permanently from the labor force—which happens more often with women—they stop contributing. Second, low-income workers, generally unskilled laborers who make up a large segment of the labor force, minimize their contributions in order to maximize the state subsidy to guarantee a minimum pension, a behavior that leads to moral hazard. Third, double-counting of the same insured in two or more administrators (because of frequent changes) inflates statistical coverage when effective coverage is actually much less. And fourth, in countries with larger populations of self-employed, informals, and rural workers, income levels are too low for pension savings. Since coverage is voluntary, the rational choice is to feed oneself today and hope for a state subsidy tomorrow.

In summary, ownership of the individual account and the existence of a strict, direct relationship between contributions and pension in the FFI pension system are not really providing incentives for workers to register, pay their contributions punctually, and declare their full salary income in order to increase their individual fund. As a result of all this, about half the affiliates are either not really covered or they, at best, would be entitled only to a minimum pension. The small size of the labor force in some countries and the existence of minimum pension guarantees have become major obstacles to increased coverage.

Question 2: Competition, Efficiency, and Administrative Costs

Reforms have reduced costs because entitlement conditions have been tightened. Temporarily, however, two systems will coexist with divergent conditions: the old public system and the new one. The reform has eliminated all independent special programs with divergent entitlement conditions and contributions, except for the armed forces (in all countries except possibly in Bolivia), federal and provincial employees (Mexico and Argentina), oil workers (Colombia and Mexico), and other special groups of workers (Colombia, Peru, and Uruguay); these excluded groups have been allowed to keep their privileged systems. Often, these systems are facing major crises.

The market, private administration, and freedom to select private pension managers do not necessarily secure competition and reduction in administrative costs as is assumed. There is a very high concentration of insured in the three major administrators: 100 percent in Bolivia and (probably) in El Salvador; 70 percent in Chile, Peru, and Uruguay; 60 percent in Colombia; and 40 percent in Argentina. As in any market activity, the selection of a pension fund manager is strongly influenced by marketing expenses, which take an overwhelming majority of administrative expenditures. The premium paid to insurance companies (to cover disability and survivor pensions) have been declining in most countries with a system in operation, but the commission charged by pension managers has increased, and the combination of the two has either been stagnant or rising. The high costs of operation (ranging from 25 percent in Chile to 32 percent in Peru over the total contribution) attest to the infancy of the industry and the enormous transactional costs that workers have to pay for developing a new technology.

In Chile, where the reformed system has a fairly large number of insured and the longest period of operation, the number of pension managers has remained basically stagnant in the long run (twelve in 1981 and thirteen in 1997) in spite of a relative low starting capital required and because of the high administrative costs of operation. Unlimited freedom to move conveys a high price in turnover, administrative costs, and confusion in individual accounts.

To avoid or reduce these flaws, most countries have established a limit of one or two annual changes between pension administrators. Such limitation reduces the problems noted above but restrains freedom to move as well as competition, which is supposed to be the foundation of the FFI pension system. Bolivia has only two administrators, as noted earlier (the insured were allocated to one or the other by the government, based on their residence) and changes between the two administrators are not allowed until the year 2000. Obviously there is no competition in this system.

Question 3: Capital Markets and National Savings

Contrary to the widespread assumption that the FFI system generates an expansion of the capital market and national savings, the evidence is not conclusive. In Chile there is no proof that this system has been the decisive factor, or even an important component, for the development of financial markets. While pension funds made the financial markets deeper and more liquid and sophisticated, there is no evidence that pension funds enhanced competitiveness and risk allocation. In 1981–1995 the FFI system did not influence net savings and the reform as a whole had a negative impact on savings. The net balance of the Chilean pension reform (subtracting its fiscal costs from the generation of savings in the FFI system) was negative in each year in 1981–1995, although declining, and it averaged –2.6 percent of GDP in the period. This means that a net positive impact on national savings takes decades.

Question 4: Portfolio Diversification and Higher Investment Yields

We have seen that the creation of an FFI pension system does not automatically generate a dynamic and relatively safe capital market and, therefore, it does not assure portfolio diversification and high investment yields. Countries with low insured populations and lack of or incipient nonregulated capital markets and insurance industries face significant barriers to diversify the portfolio and find profitable financial instruments. In the four countries in which the reform has operated for some time (Argentina, Chile, Colombia, and Peru), the average gross real investment yield ranges from 7 to 16 percent. This is quite impressive, but all four countries had relatively large insured populations and regulated capital markets to start with. Those yields are not necessarily going to be achieved by countries with different conditions. Chile is facing difficulties in placing the growing capital flow in an increasingly saturated domestic capital market. The real investment yield was negative in 1995, and positive but very low in 1996. The government now projects that the investment yield would be between one-third and one-half of the 1981–1996 average (and yet investments in foreign-denominated instruments are well below the authorized level). Furthermore, the net investment yield (after deducting the administrative commissions) in Chile was lower than the interest paid by bank deposits during the first fourteen years of operation of the FFI system. Only after that period has the net yield become slightly higher (similar results were found in Peru in the first three years of operation). The state guarantee of an annual minimum investment yield is a laudable safety measure for the insured. But it creates distortions: long-term risks are avoided (including investment abroad), the largest pension managers become trend setters, and the portfolio composition tends to be alike among all pension managers to ensure they do not fall outside the limits.

Question 5: Higher Pensions

Chile is the country with the longest operation of the reform but still the pension system has not matured. So far, however, pensions paid in the new system are considerably higher than in the old pension funds. This outcome has been the result of steady economic growth since the mid-1980s, reduction and control of inflation, and high investment yields (including high interests paid by the state on public securities where 42 percent of the investment is), combined with strict state regulation and financing of the fiscal costs of the transition (including recognition bonds and minimum pensions). But we noted above that the investment yield declined sharply in 1995–1996 and is projected to be considerably lower in the future. Hence, it will have negative effects on the pension level. Furthermore, we also noted that about half of the insured in the FFI system would receive a minimum pension, which will be barely sufficient to cover basic needs. Other countries that do not meet the conditions and success of the Chilean system would have a lower probability to pay high and adequate pensions. This issue, nevertheless, requires more time and research to be tested.

Question 6: Fairness and Equity

In countries with a very low coverage of the labor force, concentrated in middle-income salaried workers, fiscal subsidies to consolidate the system for the minority covered have regressive effects. Mixed systems combine elements of public social security (with solidarity). The fully funded system should have more progressive (or less regressive) effects than the substitutive system, provided they are financially viable in the long run to secure those positive effects.

Public systems are "gender neutral" because they have defined benefits and solidarity and, therefore, set equal replacement rates for female and male insured, assuming those systems are financially viable in the long run. FFI systems are "gender differentiated" because their benefits are nondefined and they lack solidarity. As insured women often retire earlier and live longer than men, and they also have lower salary and density of contributions, their replacement rates are considerably lower. Mixed systems reduce the gender gap in replacement rates because they combine a public component (which provides equal rates) with a fully funded component (which does not), and thus, the outcome is less differences in such rates.

Question 7: Government Behavior

The role of government has been crucial in all types of reform even in the substitutive ones with private administration, because the government has made the system mandatory, financed its transition, established a superintendency that strictly regulates and supervises the system, and provided multiple guarantees to the system and the insured. There is a long tradition of "proper behavior" of the state in Argentina, Chile, Colombia, Mexico, and Uruguay, both before and after the reform. The same is not true for countries such as El Salvador, Guatemala, or Peru. In this second group the government was one main reason why the old traditional public system eroded. It did not pay its contributions as employer and third party thus generating a huge debt, and it forced social security agencies to place their reserves in the central bank or in public securities without indexation of the principal and paying negative interest rates.

The Peruvian government, for example, owes more than $200 million to the fully funded system for nonpaid contributions as employer, has issued recognition bonds to only 1 percent of those insured who moved to this system, and has not met its promise to regulate and guarantee the payment of the minimum pension. There are legitimate concerns that if government does not honor its obligations to fund the deficit of the public system and to pay back its debt to affiliates in the FFI system, current and future pensioners will suffer the consequences. Regardless of the type of pension reform, the government must be committed and professional and must fulfill its obligations as employer and third party in order to secure the success of the reform. This is perhaps the most important lesson learned, not only from the ongoing pension reform but from more than seventy years of social security operations in Latin America.

POLICY RECOMMENDATIONS FOR REFORMERS: HEALTH CARE AND PENSIONS

Current and prospective structural reformers must assess the experiences of ongoing structural reforms and use all available information in the most efficient manner to avoid mistakes and improve the design of their reform models. The comparative analysis of the international evidence is thus an essential undertaking. In addition, we recommend that structural reformers follow five recommendations (as presented in table 17.5), which are that (1) the reform has clear goals, (2) it is politically and technically viable, (3) it is financially sustainable, (4) it redistributes, and (5) it is flexible.

First Policy Recommendation: Clear Goals

There is no universal consensus—but heated debate instead—on which should be the main goal of pension reform. The ILO and the International Social Security Association (ISSA) take the position that the first goal of the pension reform must be the adequate coverage of the old age risk, or the delivery of appropriate benefits for the elderly, and only in second place should there be concern with the capacity of the reform to generate financial effects

Table 17.5 Policy Recommendations

	For Pension Reform	*For Health Care Reform*
Clear goals	Coverage of old-age risk, universal coverage, standardization of benefits, private participation (FFI), greater efficiency, economic accelerator	Effective health care coverage, universal coverage, private participation, decentralization, greater efficiency, increase in quality and generation of virtuous cycle
Viability	Political will and indestructible commitment; long-lived impetus for reform; effective and multi-institutional agents of change; proposed reform goals are technically consistent and simple	
Sustainability	Consistent arrangement of pillars with sustainable financial methods; resources available to fund transition	Separation of administrative roles (public and private) in the organization, financing, and delivery of services
Redistribution	Social assistance, basic pension for the noninsured, minimum pension guaranteed for the insured	Basic health package for every citizen; choice of additional packages to be paid by user
Flexibility	Accommodation to the evolution of the reform and the need to overcome challenges	

(the ISSA questions even whether the financial goal is part of social security). The World Bank argues that pension reform will raise domestic savings, expand the capital market, and ultimately promote economic growth, and that the accomplishment of such goals will result in better and more secure pensions. These two goals, therefore, are mutually reinforcing. Whether the two goals are indeed reinforcing each other needs further research.

This book has shown (see mainly chapter 3) that the financial goals, so far, have not materialized. There is no evidence that the Chilean pension reform (now sixteen years in operation), as a whole, has significantly contributed to any expansion of capital markets or increase in national savings. Actually, there is evidence to the contrary in national savings. Since the assumption that the FFI system fosters national savings has so far been disproved by the evidence, this should not be the principal goal of a pension reform, which should strive instead for other, more urgent goals such as standardization, the elimination of privileges, the expansion of population coverage, adequate pensions, public assistance to the destitute, private participation, and so on.

Each country, nevertheless, must study whether these goals are viable, according to their specific conditions and needs. The public philosophy in which a reform should be conceived is one that optimally combines the attainment of freedom for every individual with the achievement of more welfare for the people. Hopefully, a virtuous cycle might eventually be formed, where increased savings and stronger capital markets lead to more intermediation and economic growth.

Health sectors in most of Latin America are facing tremendous strains and are in critical status. Structural reforms have converged toward decentralization, universalization of coverage, private participation, greater effectiveness and efficiency, and increase in quality. These five goals must be non-negotiable if we expect to raise health indicators and the quality of life and, in general, improve the human capital of the region.

Why are health sector reforms so difficult to implement? There are several reasons: the perception that some of these goals imply trade-offs instead of goals that are mutually reinforcing; the action and politics of an enormous bureaucratic apparatus, that is, the Ministry of Health; an overstaffed, incompetent, traditional social security system; a buoyant private sector comprised of a multitude of providers, insurance companies, nontraditional practitioners, nongovernmental agencies, and so on; very little public funding; very little priority in the agendas for restructuring; and, clearly, the population that most needs a change has no voice in the design of macroeconomics policies. Thus, countries that make the health sector reform a priority must acquire enough impetus for the reform and create strong momentum to implement changes.

Second Policy Recommendation: Political and Technical Viability

In both pensions and health care, the political will begins the process of change and reforms are shaped by the conditioning factors discussed above. The reform proposal that is politically feasible is the only one that is truly viable. Some technocrats have the view that technically adequate reform proposals should be pursued and that politics should not be the concern of an expert. Such an approach ignores the rich and varied institutional scenario in which a reform proposal is approved. Reform proposals should be both technically sound and politically viable (with a minimum national consensus), both comprehensive and at the same time relatively easy to understand and apply. For example, the reform of El Salvador was done with no national discussion and only a minimum consensus, hence, when the incumbent president lost the majority in Congress, he had to confront the danger of either amendment or abolition of the reform. The complexity of the Colombian health reform is a problem because its implementation becomes a difficult process that nobody understands. Similarly, the lack of an initial comprehensive and consistent reform of the pension system in Peru revealed a structural weakness in its design, affected its sustainability, and forced subsequent reforms to correct these problems, some of which still are unresolved.

Countries with a small number of insured should be careful to establish an FFI system because they may not have a market large enough to sustain several pension administrators and competition. An exclusively private administration faces significant barriers, and a multiplicity of pension managers is probably more viable. Opening the market to other financial intermediaries should be considered an adequate option, particularly in smaller countries. In all cases, limitations in the freedom to change administrators are needed (once per year), tougher control of salespersons and publicity should be established, and incentives and penalties should be created (a surrender fee for transfer, a bonus for those who stay more than one year in the same pension manager) to avoid or at least alleviate the problems discussed in previous sections.

A central collection agency (as in Argentina, Uruguay, and possibly Mexico) will reduce paperwork among small administrators and cut down system expenditures. It could also provide a better control of compliance (by cleaning the registry of workers who have abandoned the labor force), eliminate double counting, and reduce the number of freeloaders who do not declare their income. This will also allow a more accurate estimate of the labor force really covered by the system and the elimination of statistical distortions.

There is a serious and urgent need to better inform and help the insured to understand the reasons for the selection of pension administrators. Data on commissions charged by the administrators and their real investment yields should be made homogenous, more simple to understand and compare by the average insured, and widely diffused in order to facilitate a more educated selection. The insured needs information and advice at the time of retirement to select the type of pension that best suits his or her needs.

Countries contemplating a pension reform, that have neither a capital market nor an insurance industry or that lack state control, should enact first the corresponding laws to introduce or strengthen those markets, establish a superintendency of securities and insurance, and allow a reasonable period for their consolidation, before passing the pension reform law. Those countries with a reform in place or about to begin should flexibilize investment regulations. They should empower the superintendency of pension administrators to push for portfolio diversification and provide incentives for investment in long-term instruments. They should extend from one to three years the period of time where the mandatory minimum yield is measured. They should lift the prohibition to invest abroad, support the creation of new financial instruments, and allow some flexibility—within certain safety parameters—to tailor the insured's portfolio according to their needs (for instance, young insured are willing to take more risks whereas those closer to retirement want to reduce volatility).

Third Policy Recommendation: Financial Sustainability

Structural reforms must be correctly designed to be sustainable in the long run. A structural reform that contains major cracks in its architecture is not sustainable. The Chilean substitutive model in pensions is an example of a sustainable structural reform, but at enormous fiscal cost that has required government's commitment, which is something traditional in Chilean history. But how many other countries have these conditions? By contrast, the Peruvian parallel pension reform does not appear to be sustainable, because the public system was not thoroughly reformed initially, and despite legal and financial improvements, it continues to face an actuarial disequilibrium and a potential financial imbalance in the immediate future.

There is an urgent need to carefully evaluate the pension debt and the fiscal costs of the transition, as well as the net balance of the pension reform. In order to reduce transition costs, very serious consideration should be given to the following measures: selection of a mixed or parallel versus a substitutive model; maintenance of the employer contribution; limitations to the recognition bond—not granted in a mixed system and, in the FFI system, submitted to a ceiling, minimum years of previous contributions, reasonable adjustment to the cost of living, but with no interest or at low rate; and conditions to the minimum pension (minimum years of contribution and adequate control to reduce moral hazard). It is better to carefully assess a priori the cost of the reform and the granting of the above benefits, without limitations, than to find after the reform that the transition costs are considerably higher than anticipated, that the state cannot honor some or all of those benefits, and that the reform is not financially viable.

To make health reforms possible, the public and the private roles in the organization and the financing and delivery of services have to be clearly delineated. The public sector should formulate policies and supervise the overall operation of the system. Furthermore, the public sector has the responsibility of funding basic health care services for the poor, designing effective promotion and preventive care, and supplementing the private sector.

Fourth Policy Recommendation: Redistribution

Reforms should standardize entitlement conditions, and also eradicate privileges, in order to eliminate regressiveness and improve equity. The exclusion of the armed forces, civil servants, and other powerful groups from the reform are unjustifiable and create incentives for other included groups to try to get out of the unified-standardized system or get special conditions within it. The Bolivian example (if indeed the armed forces are incorporated without special conditions) should be followed, aiming at the full inclusion of all workers in the new system.

Pension reforms must provide the guarantee of a minimum income level to the elderly (and hopefully protect the needy) by means of a basic pension in the public sector (Argentina and Uruguay) or a minimum pension guaranteed in the FFI system (Chile, Colombia, El Salvador, Mexico), and a public assistance program where feasible. Since the FFI system lacks endogenous solidarity, adverse effects have to be mitigated by introducing exogenous solidarity. The state must guarantee minimum and social assistance pensions, and a reasonable adjustment of pensions (including the minimum or basic) to the cost of living.

The funding method of the solidarity component of pension reforms has to be clearly determined: Colombia has a payroll contribution to expand coverage but it is very small and does not seem to be working. Peru established a solidarity fund with unclear objectives, and it was later abolished. Bolivia's solidarity fund is not targeted to the noninsured or the low-income insured; a better alternative would have been to use this fund to expand coverage for low-income groups within the labor force or help the poor. In other countries, the increase in state payroll contributions (as in Mexico) should be partially assigned to subsidize the incorporation of low-income self-employed. All these groups should be given flexibility to choose coverage of individual risks, including the three types of pensions as well as health care.

Fixed commissions should be eliminated to correct the regressive effect on low-income insured, while commissions on contributions could be changed to commissions based on assets managed. These measures would improve equity among insured with different incomes, eliminate subsidies of active contributors to inactive affiliates, and create incentives to reduce evasion and payment delays.

Countries need to understand that the Chilean substitutive models have regressive effects when institutional restrictions are present such as a large majority of the population uncovered, both informal and rural, combined with the high incidence of poverty. Scarce fiscal resources that are allocated to pay the cost of the transition to an FFI system for a minority of the population (old public system deficit, recognition bond, and guaranteed minimum pension) are needed to expand coverage to the majority of the population and alleviate the miserable situation of the poor. State subsidies in those countries, therefore, should be geared to extend coverage to low-income groups or help the poor who are the majority.

We have documented the existence of gender bias in the FFI system. To reduce the gender gap in substitutive systems, the state should also provide solidarity in order to increase the women insured's replacement rates. For example, fixing the same age of retirement attenuates but does not eliminate the gap.

In the health sector, a basic health package (Colombia) or the universal coverage of preventive and primary care health services through public assistance must be guaranteed. The Brazilian option of universal coverage with publicly funded services could be too costly and lead to financial unbalances. The Chilean health model was easier to implement because most of the population was already covered. However, the transfer of the 7 percent contribution from the highest-income insured from the public to the private system is regressive. Part of this contribution should be kept in the public system for solidarity purposes and to help finance prevention and improve the medical infrastructure (public hospitals for example).

Fifth Policy Recommendation: Flexibility

This is a fundamental condition that reforms must possess: be ready to correct mistakes, accommodate unexpected movements, change direction if the process is ineffective, and, in general, permanent monitoring, supervision, and evaluation. Peru has changed its pension reform twice and its health reform thrice, while Brazil is ready for a third round of reforms in its health sector reform. Flexibility is a crucial element that can transform a bad structural reform into a better one. Chile's numerous public regulations in pensions and health care have played a key role in adapting reforms, allowing them to be sustainable and better. On the other side, however, too many regulations and changes in practices may lead to confusion and instability.

EPILOGUE

Individuals have the right to social protection. This means that, collectively, a society has devised effective and efficient technologies to cover individual risks, such as health care and old age risks. As a public good, governments play an important role in the design of social protection and should intervene in the market to guarantee full satisfaction of needs. Social protection, by the nature of our societies, implies solidarity and redistribution. Absence of a universal basic health care package may threaten those who have good health care coverage (in the case of epidemics), and absence of a minimum or social assistance pension for the needy leads to greater poverty and potential social rupture.

In all the above, education plays a fundamental role. Citizens must be informed about the prospective reform processes in health and pensions and must support them. After reforms are approved, they must be updated continually, to further facilitate their implementation and help improve and adapt to changes and consequences of changes. Political and technical viability in large measure rests on people's participation, understanding, and support. Reformers must explain what are the financial constraints of the reform and how benefits (pensions or high-quality health care) are only feasible if there are resources to pay for them (taxes or wage contributions).

References

Frenk, Julio. 1995. "Comprehensive Policy Analysis for Health Sector Reform." In *Health Sector Reform in Developing Countries: Making Health Development Sustainable*, ed. Peter Berman. Cambridge, Mass.: Harvard University Press.

Mesa-Lago, Carmelo. 1997. "Comparative Analysis of Structural Pension Reform in Eight Latin American Countries: Description, Evaluation and Lessons." In *Capitalization: The Bolivian Model of Social and Economic Reform*, ed. Margaret H. Peirce. La Paz: Ministerio de Capitalización.

Contributors

Mariela Arenas, Licenciada in Economics, Universidad del Pacífico, received an M.A. in international studies from the University of Miami and is a Ph.D. candidate at the Graduate School of International Studies, University of Miami. She has been chief coordinator of *Punto de Equilibrio,* a monthly economic journal of the Universidad del Pacífico, and a member of the Research Center at the Universidad del Pacífico.

Alberto Arenas de Mesa, Ph.D. in economics, University of Pittsburgh, is director of the economic studies division of the Ministry of Finance in Chile. He has published on the economic and gender implications of the privatization of social security in Chile.

Julián F. Bertranou, M.A. in social sciences, Facultad Latinoamericana de Ciencias Sociales in Mexico, is a consultant for the Democratic Governability in Latin America Project, funded by the U.N. Development Program. He has conducted research on social security reform in Mexico and Argentina and published in professional journals in both countries.

Silvia Borzutzky, Ph.D. in political science, University of Pittsburgh, is a lecturer in political science at the University of Pittsburgh and adjunct assistant professor of political science at Carnegie Mellon University. She is the author of several articles on social security issues in professional journals and books.

Miguel Eduardo Cárdenas Rivera, M.A. in economic and political relations, Universidad Nacional de Colombia, is scientific advisor to the Friedrich Ebert Stiftung, FESCOL, in Bogotá.

Brian Cartin, M.A. in economics, University of Pittsburgh, is a consultant on public policy and health care, with particular emphasis on reform of the health sector in Chile.

Ricardo Córdova Macías, M.A. in political science, University of Pittsburgh, is executive director of Fundación Dr. Guillermo Manuel Ungo and professor of political science at the Universidad Tecnológica in San Salvador. He is the author of several chapters in books on political transition and governance in Central America, in particular San Salvador.

María Amparo Cruz-Saco Oyague, Ph.D. in economics, University of Pittsburgh, is the Lenore Tingle Howard Associate Professor of Economics at Connecticut College. She is the author of *La macroeconomía de una economía abierta,* coauthor of *La Naturaliza del Ciclo Económico en el Perú,* and of several research articles in professional journals and books. She has been a consultant for international multilateral organizations, including the Inter-American Development Bank, the World Bank, the Acuerdo de Cartagena, and official agencies such as COFIDE, the Peruvian Banking and Insurance Activities Supervising Office, and the government of Paraguay.

Ernesto Aldo Isuani, Ph.D. in political science, is a faculty member at the Facultad Latinoamericana de Ciencias Sociales (FLACSO), Buenos Aires, and the author of over thirty publications on social security and public policy. He has taught at various universities in Argentina and Brazil and has served as a consultant for international multilateral organizations in Latin America. He has won several prestigious grants and awards in Argentina and the United States.

Cheikh Kane, Ph.D. in economics, Georgetown University, is a senior economist at the World Bank. He has assessed the sustainability of pension systems and reform options in various countries and regions, and in particular the role of the state in developing countries. He is the author of several articles on the reform of pension systems in Brazil, China, Peru, Ukraine, and Uruguay.

Gerard La Forgia, Sc.D. in health services administration, University of Pittsburgh, is a senior health policy officer at the InterAmerican Development Bank. He is the author of over ten publications, including a two-volume report on the economic and institutional features of fifteen health insurance schemes in developing countries. He has authored numerous technical reports and working papers on health reform, health care financing, health insurance, health sector assessments, and private health services in Latin America.

Maureen Lewis, Ph.D. in population economics, John Hopkins University, is a senior economist at the World Bank. She is the author of over twenty publications in major professional journals and books dealing with health economics, population and family planning, and nutrition. She has written working papers and lectured extensively on the organization, delivery, and financing of health care services in Africa, Asia, and Latin America.

Rubén M. Lo Vuolo, M.A. in economics, University of Pittsburgh, is director of the Centro Interdisciplinario para el Estudio de Políticas Públicas (CIEPP) in Buenos Aires. He serves as a consultant for multilateral organizations and official agencies, which include the InterAmerican Development Bank, the U.N. Development Program, the Economic Commission for Latin America and the Caribbean, and the government of Argentina. He is the author of more than ten publications on social policies.

André Medici, M.A. in economics, Campinas State University, Brazil, is a health economist at the InterAmerican Development Bank. He has written extensively on health policies and health economics in Latin America and the United States. His work *Economía e financiamento do setor Saúde no Brasil: Balanços e perspectivas do processo de descentralização* was published by the Universidade de São Paulo in 1994.

Carmelo Mesa-Lago, Ph.D. in labor economics and social security, Cornell University, is Distinguished Service Professor of Economics and Latin American Studies at the University of Pittsburgh. He is the author of 40 books and more than 150 articles and chapters on Latin America's social security and health care and the Cuban economy. He has been a consultant for the World Bank, the ILO, the IADB, the Inter-American Foundation, USAID, UNCTAD, UNDP, OAS, and PAHO. He has received awards and grants from the Ford, Tinker, Rockefeller, Mellon, Kellogg, and Heinz Foundations, the SSRC, the NSF, Fulbright Program, and Japan Foundations, as well as the Arthur Whitaker Prize (for best book, 1982), the Hoover Institution Prize (for best article, 1986), the Alexander von Humboldt Senior Prize (for outstanding research on social security), the University of Pittsburgh President's Senior Research Award (for work on Cuba), and *Choice* award for outstanding book (on social security, 1995).

Jorge Papadópulos, M.A. in political science, University of Pittsburgh, is the coordinator of the Facultad de Administración y Ciencias Sociales, Universidad ORT.

Jorge Antonio San Martino, M.S. in public administration, Universidad de Buenos Aires, is professor of sociology at the Universidad de Buenos Aires. He was a technical consultant in the reform of the social security in Argentina during the early 1990s and has conducted research in social security and public policy.

Index